Microsoft®

OFFICE EXCEL 2003

Complete Course

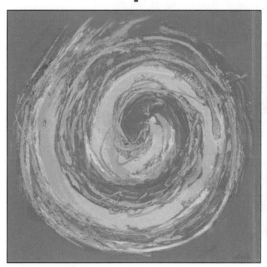

by Pasewark and Pasewark*, Cable

William R. Pasewark, Sr., Ph.D.
Professor Emeritus, Business Education, Texas Tech University

Scott G. Pasewark, B.S.
Occupational Education, Computer Technologist

William R. Pasewark, Jr., Ph.D., CPA
Professor, Accounting, Texas Tech University

Carolyn Denny Pasewark, M.Ed.
National Computer Consultant, reading and Math
Certified Elementary Teacher, K-12 Certified Counselor

Jan Pasewark Stogner, MBA
Financial Planner

Beth Pasewark Wadsworth, B.A.
Graphic Designer

*Pasewark and Pasewark is a trademark of the Pasewark LTD.

Sandra Cable, Ph.D.
Texas A&M University

THOMSON
COURSE TECHNOLOGY

Australia • Canada • Mexico • Singapore • Spain • United Kingdom • United States

THOMSON
COURSE TECHNOLOGY

Microsoft® Office Excel 2003 Complete Course
by Pasewark and Pasewark*

Authors

William R. Pasewark, Sr., Ph.D.
Professor Emeritus, Texas Tech University

William R. Pasewark, Jr., Ph.D., CPA
Professor of Accounting, Texas Tech University

Scott G. Pasewark, B.S.
Occupational Education, Computer Technologist

Jan Pasewark Stogner, MBA
Financial Planner

Beth Pasewark Wadsworth, B.A.
Graphic Designer

Carolyn Pasewark Denny, M.Ed.
National Computer Consultant, Reading and Math Certified Elementary Teacher, Certified Counselor, K-12

Publishers

Cheryl Costantini
Executive Director

Kim Ryttel
Senior Marketing Manager

Alexandra Arnold
Senior Editor

Robert Gaggin
Product Manager

Meagan Putney
Associate Marketing Manager

Justine Brennan
Editorial Assistant

GEX Publishing Services
Production Services

CEP Inc.
Developmental Editor
Production Editor

Experience Office for the Future!

This series offers a flexible, accessible program for a wide range of students. All of the books are written at a basic reading level and provide a variety of instructional hours to best meet your course needs.

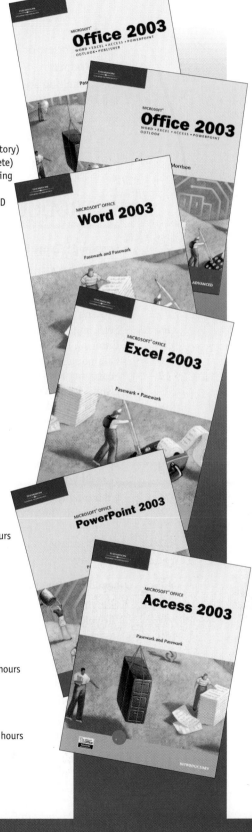

Users Love This Series Because It:
- Teaches students with a variety of abilities and previous computer experience
- Contains numerous step-by-step exercises, review exercises, and case projects to enhance students' learning experiences
- Includes strong end-of-lesson material, including Commands, Skills, Concepts Review, and On-the-Job simulations
- Incorporates a Capstone Simulation at the end of the book that provides students with the opportunity to apply the skills they've learned, either individually or in a team setting

NEW! for Microsoft Office 2003 Introductory and Advanced Courses:
- Instructor notes rate the level of difficulty for activities and projects (Introductory)
- New Careers marginal learning boxes encourage students to explore future careers (Introductory)
- Time Savers provide Office tips, tricks, and shortcuts for completing tasks (Advanced and Complete)
- Integration Tips offer explanations on how features in a lesson can be useful when integrating applications in the Office 2003 suite (Advanced and Complete)
- Grading Rubrics, Annotated Solutions, and a Spanish Glossary on the Instructor Resources CD
- Durable, hardcover and hardcover, spiral-bound editions available

NEW! Microsoft Office 2003 Introductory Course by Pasewark and Pasewark
75+ hours of instruction for beginning features on Word, Excel, PowerPoint, and Access.
0-619-18339-X	Textbook, hardcover
0-619-18387-X	Textbook, hardcover, spiral-bound
0-619-18340-3	Textbook, softcover
0-619-18342-X	Activities Workbook
0-619-18341-1	Annotated Instructor Edition (AIE)
0-619-18343-8	Instructor Resources (IR) CD, includes testing software
0-619-18344-6	Review Pack (Data CD)

NEW! Microsoft Office 2003 Advanced Course by Cable, CEP, Inc., Morrison
75+ hours of instruction for intermediate through advanced features on Word, Excel, PowerPoint, and Access.
0-619-18345-4	Textbook, hardcover
0-619-18388-8	Textbook, hardcover, spiral-bound
0-619-18346-2	Textbook, softcover
0-619-18348-9	Activities Workbook
0-619-18347-0	Annotated Instructor Edition (AIE)
0-619-18349-7	Instructor Resources (IR) CD, includes testing software
0-619-18350-0	Review Pack (Data CD)

NEW! Microsoft Office Word 2003 by Pasewark and Pasewark, Morrison
0-619-18352-7	Complete, hardcover, Expert Microsoft Office Specialist Certification, 75+ hours
0-619-18351-9	Introductory, softcover, spiral-bound, Specialist Microsoft Office Specialist Certification, 35+ hours

NEW! Microsoft Office Excel 2003 by Pasewark and Pasewark, Cable
0-619-18354-3	Complete, hardcover, Expert Microsoft Office Specialist Certification, 75+ hours
0-619-18353-5	Introductory, softcover spiral-bound, Specialist Microsoft Office Specialist Certification, 35+ hours

NEW! Microsoft Office PowerPoint 2003 by Pasewark and Pasewark, CEP, Inc.
0-619-18358-6	Complete, hardcover, Specialist Microsoft Office Specialist Certification, 75+ hours
0-619-18357-8	Introductory, softcover, spiral-bound, Specialist Microsoft Office Specialist Certification, 35+ hours

NEW! Microsoft Office Access 2003 by Pasewark and Pasewark, Cable
0-619-18355-1	Complete, hardcover, Specialist Microsoft Office Specialist Certification, 75+ hours
0-619-18356-X	Introductory, softcover, spiral-bound, Specialist Microsoft Office Specialist Certification, 35+ hours

TABLE OF CONTENTS

INTRODUCTORY MICROSOFT EXCEL UNIT

ADVANCED MICROSOFT EXCEL UNIT

Overview of This Book

What makes a good computer instructional text? Sound pedagogy and the most current, complete materials. That is what you will find in *Microsoft® Office Excel 2003: Complete*. Not only will you find an inviting layout, but also many features to enhance learning.

Objectives—Objectives are listed at the beginning of each lesson, along with a suggested time for completion of the lesson. This allows you to look ahead to what you will be learning and to pace your work.

SCANS—(Secretary's Commission on Achieving Necessary Skills)—The U.S. Department of Labor has identified the school-to-careers competencies. The eight workplace competencies and foundation skills are identified in exercises where they apply. More information on SCANS can be found on the *Instructor Resources* CD.

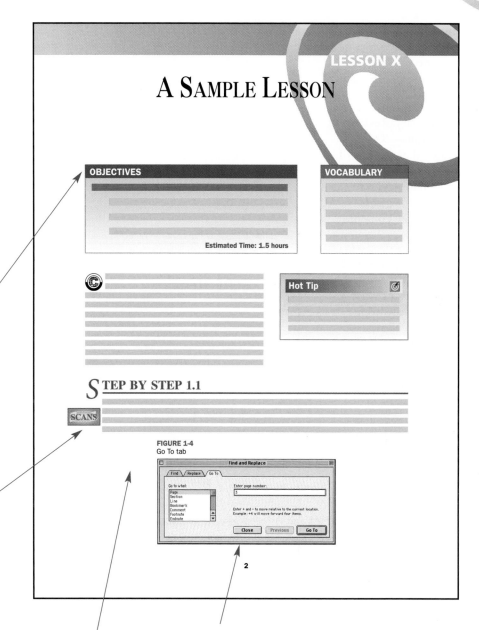

LESSON X

A SAMPLE LESSON

OBJECTIVES

VOCABULARY

Estimated Time: 1.5 hours

Hot Tip

STEP BY STEP 1.1

SCANS

FIGURE 1-4
Go To tab

Find and Replace

Find | Replace | Go To

Go to what:
Page
Section
Line
Bookmark
Comment
Footnote
Endnote

Enter page number:
5

Enter + and – to move relative to the current location.
Example: +4 will move forward four items.

Close | Previous | Go To

2

Learning Boxes—These boxes expand and enrich learning with additional information or activities: Hot Tips, Did You Know?, Computer Concepts, Internet, Extra Challenge, Teamwork, and Careers.

Enhanced Screen Shots—Screen shots come to life on each page with color and depth.

Overview of This Book

Summaries—At the end of each lesson, prepare you to complete the end-of-lesson activities.

Vocabulary/Review Questions—Review material at the end of each lesson and each unit enables you to prepare for assessment of the content presented.

Lesson Projects—End-of-lesson hands-on application of what has been learned in the lesson allows you to actually apply the techniques covered.

Critical Thinking Activities—Each lesson gives you an opportunity to apply creative analysis and use the Help system to solve problems.

Command Summary—At the end of each unit, a command summary is provided for quick reference.

End-of-Unit Projects—End-of-unit hands-on application of concepts learned in the unit provides opportunity for a comprehensive review.

Unit Simulation—A realistic simulation runs throughout the text at the end of each unit, reinforcing the material covered in the unit.

Lesson X   Unit Sample

Intro Excel   **3**

SUMMARY

VOCABULARY*Review*

REVIEW*Questions*

PROJECTS

CRITICAL*Thinking*

COMMAND SUMMARY

REVIEW*Questions*

CROSS-CURRICULAR*Projects*

Capstone Simulation—There is a comprehensive simulation at the end of the text, to be completed after all the lessons have been covered, to give you an opportunity to apply all of the skills you have learned and see them come together in one application.

Appendices—Appendices cover Windows Basics, Computer Concepts, Concepts for Microsoft Office Programs, The Microsoft Office Specialist Program, and Keyboarding Touch System Improvement. The Models for

Formatted Documents, E-Mail Writing Guide, Letter Writing Guide, Proofreader's Marks, Speech Recognition Basics lesson, and Spanish Glossary are located on the *Instructor Resources CD*.

PREFACE

Why This Is an Ideal Book for Everyone

Because computers are such an important subject for all learners, instructors need a well-designed, educationally sound textbook that is supported by strong ancillary instructional materials. *Microsoft® Office Excel 2003: Complete Course* is just such a book.

The textbook includes features that make learning easy and enjoyable—yet challenging—for learners. It is also designed with many features that make teaching easy and enjoyable for you.

This book is ideal for computer courses with learners who have varying abilities and previous computer experiences. It includes a wide range of learning experiences from activities with one or two commands to simulations and projects that challenge and sharpen learners' problem-solving skills.

The lessons in this course contain the following features designed to promote learning:

- Objectives that specify goals students should achieve by the end of each lesson.
- Concept text that explores in detail each new feature.
- Screen captures that help to illustrate the concept text.
- Step-by-Step exercises that allow students to practice the features just introduced.
- Summaries that review the concepts in the lesson.
- Review Questions that test students on the concepts covered in the lesson.
- Projects that provide an opportunity for students to apply concepts they have learned in the lesson.
- Critical Thinking Activities that encourage students to use knowledge gained in the lesson or from the application's Help system to solve specific problems.

Each unit also contains a Unit Review with the following features:

- A Command Summary that reviews menu commands and toolbar shortcuts introduced in the unit.
- Review Questions covering material from all lessons in the unit.
- Projects that give students a chance to apply many of the skills learned in the unit.

Teaching and Learning Resources for this Book

Instructor Resources CD

The *Instructor Resources CD* contains a wealth of instructional material you can use to prepare for teaching Office 2003. The CD stores the following information:

- Both the data and solution files for this course.

- ExamView® tests for each lesson. ExamView is a powerful testing software package that allows instructors to create and administer printed, computer (LAN-based), and Internet exams. ExamView includes hundreds of questions that correspond to the topics covered in this text, enabling learners to generate detailed study guides that include page references for further review. The computer-based and Internet testing components allow learners to take exams at their computers, and also save the instructor time by grading each exam automatically.

- Instructor's Manual that includes lecture notes for each lesson, answers to the lesson and unit review questions, and references to the solutions for Step-by-Step exercises, end-of-lesson activities, and Unit Review projects.

- Instructor lesson plans that can help to guide students through the lesson text and exercises.

- Copies of the figures that appear in the student text, which can be used to prepare transparencies.

- Grids that show skills required for Microsoft Office Specialist certification, SCANS workplace competencies and skills, and activities that apply to cross-curricular topics.

- Suggested schedules for teaching the lessons in this course.

- Additional instructional information about individual learning strategies, portfolios and career planning, and a sample Internet contract.

- Answers to the Activities Workbook exercises.

- PowerPoint presentations showing Office 2003 features for each unit.

- Speech Recognition Basics lesson

- Spanish Glossary

- Models for Formatted Documents, such as a business letter, resume, research paper, etc.

- E-Mail Writing Guide and Letter Writing Guide

- Proofreader's Marks

Annotated Instructor Edition

The Annotated Instructor Edition helps you to prepare for and to teach Office 2003.

Activities Workbook

An *Activities Workbook* is available to supply additional paper-and-pencil exercises and hands-on computer applications for each unit of this book.

SCANS

The Secretary's Commission on Achieving Necessary Skills (SCANS) from the U.S. Department of Labor was asked to examine the demands of the workplace and whether new learners are capable of meeting those demands. Specifically, the Commission was directed to advise the Secretary of Labor on the level of skills required to enter employment.

SCANS workplace competencies and foundation skills have been integrated into Microsoft® Office 2003: Introductory Course. The workplace competencies are identified as 1) ability to use resources, 2) interpersonal skills, 3) ability to work with information, 4) understanding of systems, and 5) knowledge and understanding of technology. The foundation skills are identified as 1) basic communication skills, 2) thinking skills, and 3) personal qualities.

Exercises in which learners must use a number of these SCANS competencies and foundation skills are marked in the text with the SCANS icon.

The Microsoft Office Specialist Program

What Does This Logo Mean?

It means this courseware has been approved by the Microsoft® Office Specialist Program to be among the finest available for learning Microsoft Office 2003, Microsoft Office Word 2003, Microsoft Office Excel 2003, Microsoft Office PowerPoint® 2003, and Microsoft Office Access 2003. It also means that upon completion of this courseware, you may be prepared to become a Microsoft Office Specialist.

What is a Microsoft Office Specialist?

A Microsoft Office Specialist is an individual who has certified his or her skills in one or more of the Microsoft Office desktop applications of Microsoft Office Word, Microsoft Office Excel, Microsoft Office PowerPoint®, Microsoft Office Outlook®, or Microsoft Access. The Microsoft Office Specialist Program typically offers certification exams at the "Specialist" and "Expert" skill levels.* The Microsoft Office Specialist Program is the only Microsoft approved program in the world for certifying proficiency in Microsoft Office desktop applications. This certification can be a valuable asset in any job search or career advancement.

More Information

To learn more about becoming a Microsoft Office Specialist, visit *www.microsoft.com/learning/mcp/officespecialist*. To purchase a Microsoft Office Specialist certification exam, visit *www.DesktopIQ.com*.

*The availability of Microsoft Office Specialist certification exams varies by application, application version, and language.

Assessment Instruments

SAM 2003 Assessment & Training

SAM 2003 helps you energize your class exams and training assignments by allowing students to learn and test important computer skills in an active, hands-on environment.

With SAM 2003 Assessment, you create powerful interactive exams on critical applications such as Word, Outlook, PowerPoint, Windows, the Internet, and much more. The exams simulate the application environment, allowing your students to demonstrate their knowledge and think through the skill by performing real-world tasks.

- Build hands-on exams that allow the student to work in the simulated application environment

- Add more muscle to your lesson plan with SAM 2003 Training. Using highly interactive text, graphics, and sound, SAM 2003 Training gives your students the flexibility to learn computer applications by choosing the training method that fits them the best.

- Create customized training units that employ various approaches to teach computer skills

- Designed to be used with the Microsoft Office 2003 series, SAM 2003 Assessment & Training includes built-in page references so students can create study guides that match the Microsoft Office 2003 textbooks you use in class. Powerful administrative options allow you to schedule exams and assignments, secure your tests, and run reports with almost limitless flexibility.

- Deliver exams and training units that best fit the way you teach

- Choose from more than one dozen reports to track testing and learning progress

ExamView®

ExamView is a powerful objective-based test generator that enables you to create paper, LAN, or Web-based tests from test banks designed specifically for your Course Technology text. Utilize the ultra-efficient QuickTest Wizard to create tests in less than five minutes by taking advantage of Course Technology's question banks, or customize your own exams from scratch.

MESSAGE FROM THE AUTHORS

Acknowledgments

The authors gratefully thank Rhonda Davis for coordinating the preparation of manuscript and for using her business experiences to write several segments of Office 2003.

All of our books are a coordinated effort by the authors and scores of professionals working with the publisher. The authors appreciate the dedicated work of all these publishing personnel and particularly those with whom we have had direct contact:

- Course Technology: Robert Gaggin, Cheryl Costantini, and Meagan Putney
- Custom Editorial Productions, Inc.: Rose Marie Kuebbing and Jean Findley
- Many professional Course Technology sales representatives make educationally sound presentations to instructors about our books. We appreciate their valuable work as "bridges" between the authors and instructors.

About the Authors

Pasewark LTD is a family-owned business. We use Microsoft® Office in our business, career, personal, and family lives. Writing this book, therefore, was a natural project for six members of our family who are identified on the title page of this book.

The authors have written more than 100 books about computers, accounting, and office technology.

Pasewark LTD authors are members of several professional associations that help authors write better books.

The authors have been recognized with numerous awards for classroom teaching. Effective classroom teaching is a major ingredient for writing effective textbooks.

Our Mission Statement

The authors have more than 90 years of combined experience authoring award-winning textbooks. During that time, they developed their mission statement:

To help our students live better lives.

When students learn how computers can help them in their personal, school, career, and family activities, they can live better lives — now and in the future.

Our Commitment

In writing this series, the authors have dedicated themselves to creating a comprehensive and appealing instructional package to make teaching and learning an interesting, challenging, and rewarding experience.

With these instructional materials, instructors can create realistic learning experience so learners can successfully master concepts, knowledge, and skills that will help them live better lives—now and in the future.

Award-Winning Books by the Pasewarks

The predecessors to this book, *Microsoft® Office 2000: Introductory* and *Microsoft Office XP: Introductory*, by the Pasewarks, won the Text and Academic Authors Association *Texty Award* for the best el-hi computer book for the years 2000 and 2002.

In 1994, the Pasewarks also won a *Texty* for their Microsoft Works computer book. Their book, *The Office: Procedures and Technology*, won the first William McGuffey Award for Textbook Excellence and Longevity. The Pasewarks' book *Microsoft® Works 2000 BASICS* won the Texty Award for the best computer book for the year 2001.

GETTING STARTED

Start-Up Checklist

HARDWARE

Minimum Configuration
- ✓ PC with Pentium 233 MHz or higher processor. Pentium III recommended.

- ✓ RAM requirements:
  - ✓ Windows XP - 128 MB of RAM
  - ✓ Windows 2000 Professional – 128 MB of RAM

- ✓ Hard disk with 400 MB free for typical installation

- ✓ CD-ROM drive

- ✓ Super VGA monitor with video adapter. (800 × 600) or higher-resolution.

- ✓ Microsoft Mouse, IntelliMouse, or compatible pointing device

- ✓ For e-mail, Microsoft Mail, Internet SMTP/POP3, or other MAPI-compliant messaging software

- ✓ Printer

GUIDE FOR USING THIS BOOK

Please read this Guide before starting work. The time you spend now will save you much more time later and will make your learning faster, easier, and more pleasant.

Terminology

This text uses the term keying to mean entering text into a computer using the keyboard. Keying is the same as "keyboarding" or "typing."

Text means words, numbers, and symbols that are printed.

Conventions

The different type styles used in this book have special meanings. They will save you time because you will soon automatically recognize from the type style the nature of the text you are reading and what you will do.

WHAT YOU WILL DO	TYPE STYLE	EXAMPLE
Text you will key	**Bold**	Key **Don't litter** rapidly.
Individual keys you will press	**Bold**	Press **Enter** to insert a blank line.

WHAT YOU WILL SEE	TYPE STYLE	EXAMPLE
Filenames in book	**Bold upper and lowercase**	Open **IW Step2-1** from the data files.
Glossary terms in book	***Bold and italics***	The ***menu bar*** contains menu titles.
Words on screen	*Italics*	Highlight the word *pencil* on the screen.
Menus and commands	**Bold**	Open the **File** menu and choose **Open**.
Options/features with long names	*Italics*	Select **Normal** from the *Style for following paragraph* text box.
Names of sections/boxes	*Italics*	Click **Monthly Style** in the *Print Style* box.

Review Pack CD

All data files necessary for the Step-by-Step exercises, end-of-lesson Projects, end-of-unit Projects and Jobs, and Capstone Simulation exercises in this book are located on the *Review Pack* CD. Data files for the *Activities Workbook* are also stored on the *Review Pack* CD.

Data files are named according to the first exercise in which they are used and the unit of this textbook in which they are used. A data file for a Step-by-Step exercise in the Introductory Microsoft Word unit would have a filename such as **IW Step1-1**. This particular filename identifies a data file used in the first Step-by-Step exercise in Lesson 1. Other data files have the following formats:

- End-of-lesson projects: **IW Project1-1**
- End-of-unit projects: **IW Project2**
- Simulation jobs: **IW Job3**

INTRODUCTION

Unit

Lesson 1   1.5 hrs
Microsoft® Office 2003 Basics and the Internet

🕐 **Estimated Time for Unit: 1.5 hours**

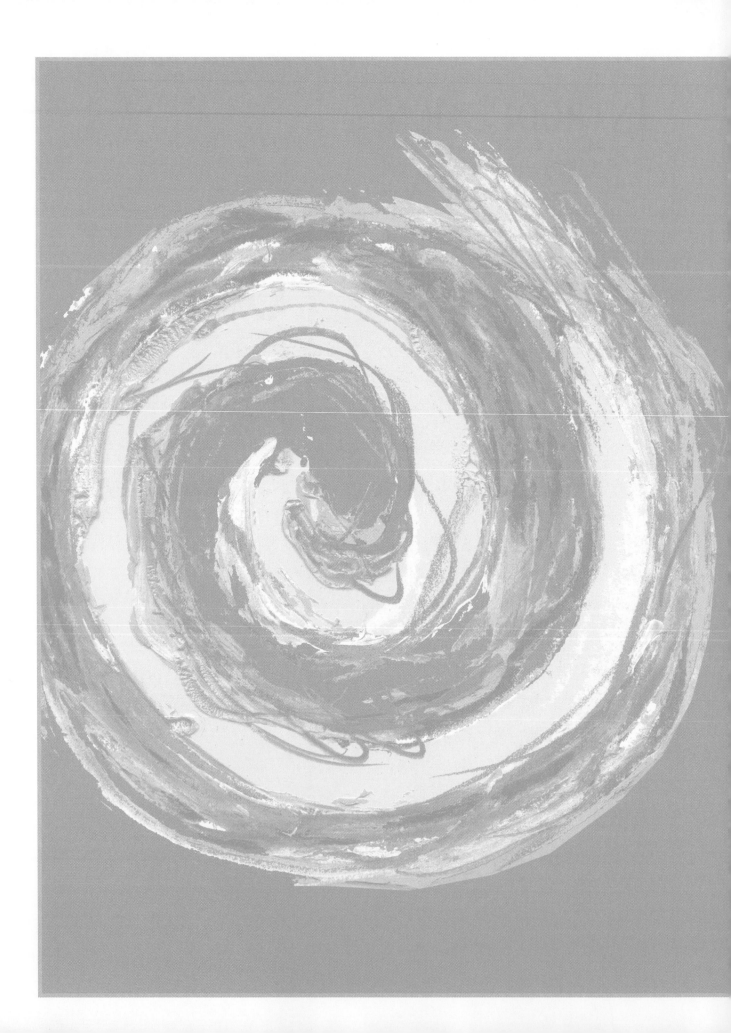

MICROSOFT® OFFICE 2003 BASICS AND THE INTERNET

VOCABULARY

Close

Default

Drop-down menu

Home page

Icon

Integrated software package

Internet

Internet Explorer

Intranet

Link

Menu

Open

Save

Task pane

Toolbar

Uniform Resource Locators (URLs)

World Wide Web

Web browser

Introduction to Microsoft Office 2003

Office 2003 is an integrated software package. An *integrated software package* is a program that combines several computer applications into one program. Office consists of a word processor application, a spreadsheet application, a database application, a presentation application, a schedule/organization application, and a desktop publishing application.

Internet

For more information on Microsoft Word and other Microsoft products, visit Microsoft's Web site at *http://www.microsoft.com.*

The word processor application (Word) enables you to create documents such as letters and reports. The spreadsheet application (Excel) lets you work with numbers to prepare items such as budgets or to determine loan payments. The database application (Access) organizes information such as addresses or inventory items. The presentation application (PowerPoint) can be used to create slides, outlines, speaker's notes, and audience handouts. The schedule/organization application (Outlook) increases your efficiency by keeping track of e-mail, appointments, tasks, contacts, events, and to-do lists. The desktop publishing application (Publisher) helps you design professional-looking documents.

Because Office is an integrated program, the applications can be used together. For example, numbers from a spreadsheet can be included in a letter created in the word processor or in a presentation.

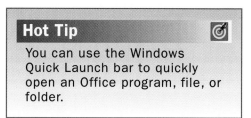

Hot Tip

You can use the Windows Quick Launch bar to quickly open an Office program, file, or folder.

Computer Concepts

You can open a new file from within an application by opening the **File** menu and choosing **New**. You can also click the **New** button in the standard toolbar to create a new file. In the Word program, the button is titled, **New Blank Document**.

Starting an Office Application

To open an Office application, click the Start button, point to All Programs, point to Microsoft Office, and then click the name of the application you want to open.

STEP-BY-STEP 1.1

1. Click the **Start** button to open the Start menu.

2. Point to **All Programs**, point to **Microsoft Office**, and then click **Microsoft Office PowerPoint 2003.** PowerPoint starts and a blank presentation appears, as shown in Figure 1-1.

FIGURE 1-1
A blank presentation in the PowerPoint program

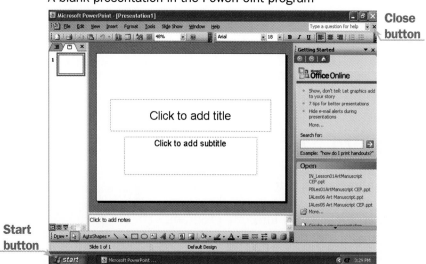

3. Click the **Close** button on the right side of the menu bar to close the blank presentation. The PowerPoint program will remain open.

STEP-BY-STEP 1.1 Continued

4. Click the **Start** button again.

5. Point to **All Programs**, point to **Microsoft Office**, and then click **Microsoft Office Word 2003.** Word starts and a blank document appears, as shown in Figure 1-2. Leave Word and PowerPoint open for use in the following Step-by-Steps.

FIGURE 1-2
Word opening screen

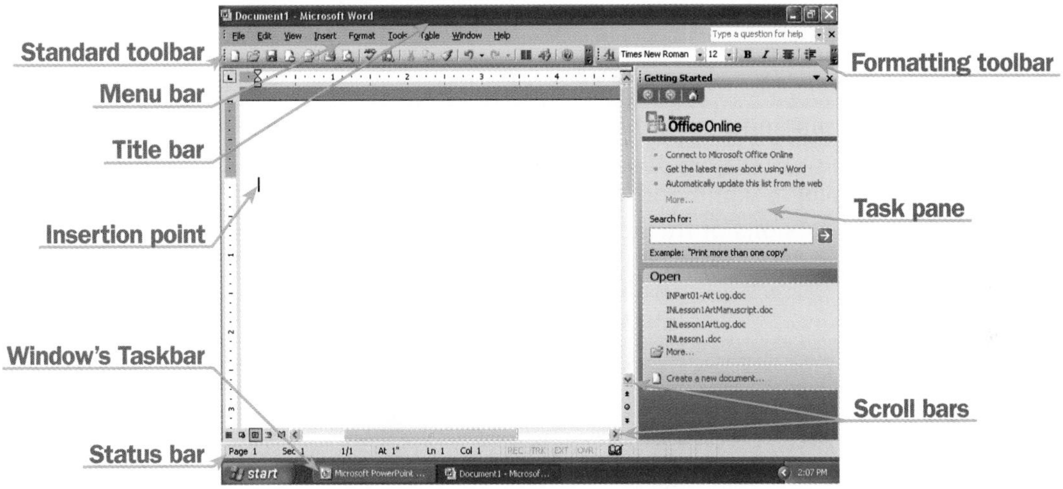

Understanding the Opening Screen

Most of the features you will use to complete tasks in an Office application can be found within the opening screen of each application. Look carefully at the parts of the opening screen for the Word program labeled in Figure 1-2. These basic parts of the screen are similar in all of the Office programs and are discussed below in Table 1-1.

TABLE 1-1
Understanding the opening screen

ITEM	FUNCTION
Title bar	Displays the name of the Office program and the current file.
Menu bar	Contains the menu titles from which you can choose a variety of commands. All features of an application can be accessed from within the menus.
Standard toolbar	Contains buttons you can use to perform common tasks.
Formatting toolbar	Contains buttons for changing formatting, such as alignment and type styles.
Insertion point	Shows where text will appear when you begin keying.
Scroll bars	Allow you to move quickly to other areas of an Office application.
Status bar	Tells you the status of what is shown on the screen.
Taskbar	Shows the Start button, the Quick Launch toolbar, and all open programs.
Task pane	Opens automatically when you start an Office application. Contains commonly used commands that pertain to each application.

The *task pane* is a separate window on the right-hand side of the opening screen, as shown in Figure 1-1 and Figure 1-2. It opens automatically when you start an Office application and contains commonly used commands that can help you work more efficiently. To close the task pane, simply click the Close button in the upper right corner of the task pane. To view the task pane, open the View menu and choose Task Pane.

Using Menus and Toolbars

A *menu* in an Office application is like a menu in a restaurant. You look at the menus to see what the program has to offer. Each title in the menu bar represents a separate *drop-down menu*. By choosing a command from a drop-down menu, you give the program instructions about what you want to do.

When you first use a program, each menu displays only basic commands. To see an expanded menu with all the commands, click the arrows at the bottom of the menu. As you work, the program adjusts the menus to display the commands used most frequently, adding a command when you use it and dropping a command when it hasn't been used recently. Figure 1-3 compares the short and expanded versions of the Edit menu.

FIGURE 1-3
Short menu vs. expanded menu

Arrows

Toolbars provide another quick way to choose commands. The toolbars use *icons*, or small pictures, to remind you of each button's function. Toolbars can also contain drop-down menus. Unless you specify otherwise, only the Standard and Formatting toolbars are displayed, but many more are available. To see a list of the toolbars you can use, right-click anywhere on a toolbar; or you can open the View menu and select Toolbars.

Computer Concepts

If you do not know the function of a toolbar button, move the mouse pointer to the button, but do not click. The name of the function will appear below the button.

As with the menus, toolbars initially display buttons only for basic commands. To see additional buttons, click Toolbar Options (the button at the far right on each toolbar) on the toolbar and choose from the list that appears, as shown in Figure 1-4. When you use a button from the list, it is added to the toolbar. If you haven't used a button recently, it is returned to the Toolbar Options list.

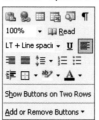

FIGURE 1-4
Toolbar Options list

Opening, Saving, and Closing Office Documents

In all Office applications, you *open*, *save*, and *close* files in the same way. Opening a file means loading a file from a disk onto your screen. Saving a file stores it on a disk. Closing a file removes it from the screen.

Opening an Existing Document

To open an existing document, you can choose Open in an application's File menu, select the Open button from the Standard toolbar, or choose the option to open an existing document from the task pane. In all Office applications, you would choose the More option in the Open section of the task pane. No matter which option is selected, the Open dialog box appears (see Figure 1-5).

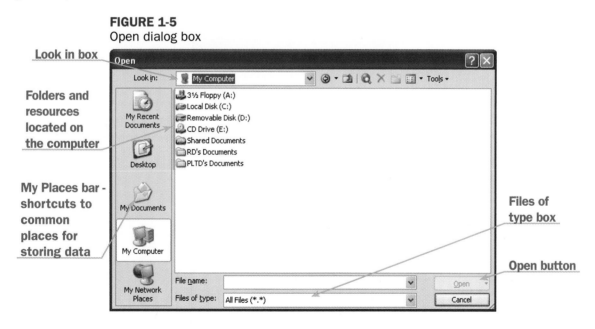

FIGURE 1-5
Open dialog box

Look in box

Folders and resources located on the computer

My Places bar - shortcuts to common places for storing data

Files of type box

Open button

The Open dialog box enables you to open a file from any available disk or folder. The *Look in* box, near the top of the dialog box, is where you locate the disk drive that contains the file you want to open. Below that is a list that shows you the folders or resources that are on the disk. Double-click a folder to see what files and folders are contained within. To see all the files or office documents in the folder instead of just those created with a particular application, choose All Files from the *Files of type* drop-down list box located near the bottom of the dialog box. The My Places bar on the left side of the dialog box provides a shortcut for accessing some of the common places to store documents.

When you have located and selected the file you want to open, click the Open button. If you click the down arrow next to the Open button, a menu is displayed, as shown in Figure 1-6. Among other choices, you can choose to open a copy of the document or open the document in your browser if it is saved in Web page format.

FIGURE 1-6
Open menu

STEP-BY-STEP 1.2

1. With Word on the screen, choose **More** in the Open section of the task pane. The Open dialog box appears, as shown in Figure 1-5. (If the task pane is not displayed, open the **View** menu and choose **Task Pane**.)

2. Click the down arrow to the right of the *Look in* box to display the available disk drives.

3. Click the drive that contains your data files and locate the **Employees** folder, as shown in Figure 1-7.

FIGURE 1-7
Employees folder

4. Double-click the **Employees** folder. The folders within the Employees folder appear (see Figure 1-8).

FIGURE 1-8
Contents of the Employees folder

5. Double-click the **Perez** folder. The names of all the files in the Perez folder display. (If necessary, click the down arrow at the right of the *Files of type* box and select **All Files** to display all the files.)

6. Click **Schedule Memo** to select it and then click **Open** to open the file. Leave the file open for the next Step-by-Step.

You can see how folders help organize and identify documents. The Perez folder also contains a spreadsheet with the work schedule for the first two weeks in April. In the next Step-by-Step, you will start Excel, the Office spreadsheet application, and open the spreadsheet that goes with the memo.

STEP-BY-STEP 1.3

1. Open another Office document by clicking the **Start** button.

2. Point to **All Programs**, point to **Microsoft Office**, and then click **Microsoft Office Excel 2003.** Excel starts and a blank spreadsheet appears.

3. Open the **File** menu and choose **Open**. The Open dialog box appears.

4. Click the down arrow at the right of the *Look in* box. If necessary, click the drive that contains your data files and locate the Employees folder.

5. Double-click the **Employees** folder; then double-click the **Perez** folder.

6. Double-click **April Schedule** to open the file. The April Schedule spreadsheet appears on the screen, as shown in Figure 1-9. Leave the file open for the next Step-by-Step.

FIGURE 1-9
April Schedule file

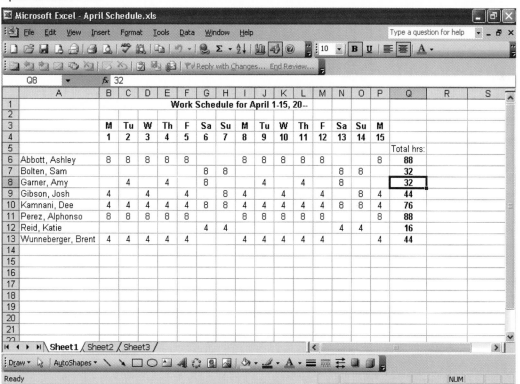

	M	Tu	W	Th	F	Sa	Su	M	Tu	W	Th	F	Sa	Su	M	Total hrs:
	1	2	3	4	5	6	7	8	9	10	11	12	13	14	15	
Abbott, Ashley	8	8	8	8	8			8	8	8	8	8			8	88
Bolten, Sam						8	8						8	8		32
Garner, Amy		4		4		8			4		4		8			32
Gibson, Josh	4		4		4		8	4		4		4		8	4	44
Kamnani, Dee	4	4	4	4	4	8	8	4	4	4	4	4	8	8	4	76
Perez, Alphonso	8	8	8	8	8			8	8	8	8	8			8	88
Reid, Katie						4	4						4	4		16
Wunneberger, Brent	4	4	4	4	4			4	4	4	4	4			4	44

Work Schedule for April 1-15, 20--

Saving a File

Saving is done two ways. The Save command saves a file on a disk using the current name. The Save As command saves a file on a disk using a new name. The Save As command can also be used to save a file to a new location.

FILENAMES

Unlike in programs designed for the early versions of Windows and DOS, filenames are not limited to eight characters. With Windows, a filename may contain up to 255 characters and may include spaces. However, you will rarely need this many characters to name a file. Name a file with a descriptive name that will remind you of what the file contains, such as Cover Letter or Quarter 1 Sales. The filename can include most characters found on the keyboard, with the exception of those shown in Table 1-2.

TABLE 1-2
Characters that cannot be used in filenames

CHARACTER	NAME	CHARACTER	NAME
*	asterisk	<	less than sign
\	backslash	;	semicolon
[ ]	brackets	/	slash
:	colon	"	quotation mark
=	equal sign	?	question mark
>	greater than sign	|	vertical bar

STEP-BY-STEP 1.4

1. *April Schedule* should be on the screen from the last Step-by-Step. Open the **File** menu and choose **Save As**. The Save As dialog box appears, as shown in Figure 1-10.

FIGURE 1-10
Save As dialog box

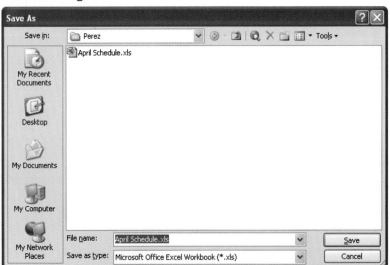

STEP-BY-STEP 1.4 Continued

2. In the *File name* box, key **April Work Sched**, followed by your initials.

3. Click the down arrow to the right of the *Save in* box and choose the **Employees** folder.

4. Double-click the **Garner** folder.

5. Click **Save** to save the file with the new name in the Garner folder. Leave the document open for the next Step-by-Step.

Closing an Office Document

You can close an Office document either by opening the File menu and choosing Close or by clicking the Close button on the right side of the menu bar. If you close a file, the application will still be open and ready for you to open or create another file.

Hot Tip

All of the programs in Office 2003 allow you to open new documents while you are working in other documents. You can even work in documents created in another Office program, such as Excel, while working in Word. To move back and forth between documents just click the taskbar button for the document you want to display.

STEP-BY-STEP 1.5

1. Open the **File** menu and choose **Close**. *April Work Sched* closes.

2. Click the **Microsoft Word** button on the taskbar to make it active. *Schedule Memo* should be displayed.

3. Click the **Close** button in the right corner of the menu bar to close *Schedule Memo*.

4. Leave Word open for the next Step-by-Step.

Shortcuts for Loading Recently Used Files

Office offers you two shortcuts for opening recently used files. The first shortcut is to choose My Recent Documents from the Start menu. A menu will open listing the fifteen most recently used documents, similar to that shown in Figure 1-11. To open one of the recently used files, click the file you wish to open.

FIGURE 1-11
Most recently used files

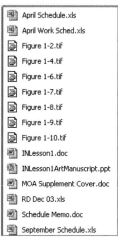

The second and third shortcuts can be found on each Office application's File menu and task pane. The bottom part of the File menu and the Open section of the task pane show the filenames of the four most recently opened documents, with the most recently opened first, as shown in Figure 1-12. When a new file is opened, each filename moves down to make room for the new most recently opened file. To open one of the files, you simply choose it as if it were a menu selection. If the document you are looking for is not on the File menu, use Open to locate and select the file.

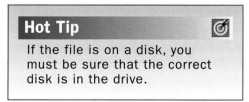

Hot Tip

If the file is on a disk, you must be sure that the correct disk is in the drive.

FIGURE 1-12
Most recently used files on the File menu and task pane

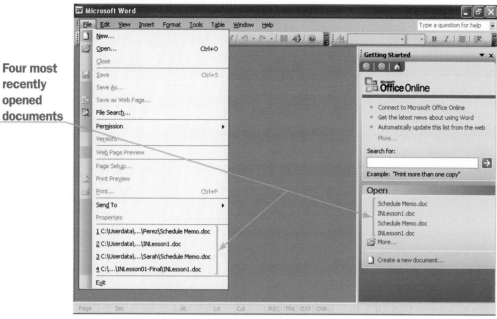

Four most recently opened documents

Office Help

This lesson has covered only a few of the many features of Office applications. For additional information, use the Office Help system as a quick reference when you are unsure about a function. To get specific help about topics relating to the application you are using, access help from the Help menu on the application's menu bar. Or, key a question in the *Type a question for help* box on the menu bar. Then, from the Help task pane, shown in Figure 1-13, you can choose to see a Table of Contents displaying general topics and subtopics or search the Help system using a keyword. You can also access the Microsoft Office Online Help system to find more information on various topics.

FIGURE 1-13
Word Help task pane

Many topics in the Help program are linked. A *link* is represented by colored, underlined text. By clicking a link, the user "jumps" to a linked document that contains additional information about that topic.

STEP-BY-STEP 1.6

1. Display the Word Help task pane, shown in Figure 1-13, by opening the **Help** menu and choosing **Microsoft Office Word Help**.

2. Click the **Table of Contents** link to display a list of topics. If you have Internet access, this information is downloaded from the Microsoft Online Help system. If you do not have Internet access, the information is accessed from the Offline Table of Contents.

3. Click the topic, **Working with Text**, click **Copy and Paste**, and then click **Move or copy text and graphics**. A list of topics displays in a separate window.

4. Click the **Move or copy a single item** topic in the Microsoft Office Word Help window.

5. Read the contents of the Help window and leave it open for the next Step-by-Step.

When you want to search for help on a particular topic, use the *Search for* box and key in a word. Windows will search alphabetically through the list of help topics to try to find an appropriate match. Click a topic to see it explained in the Help window, as shown in Figure 1-14.

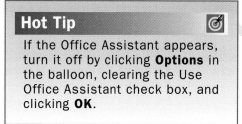

Hot Tip

If the Office Assistant appears, turn it off by clicking **Options** in the balloon, clearing the Use Office Assistant check box, and clicking **OK**.

FIGURE 1-14
Help topic explained in the Help window

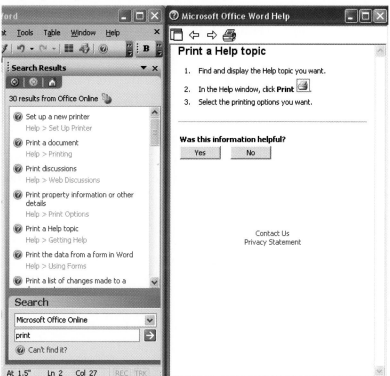

STEP-BY-STEP 1.7

1. Double-click the green back arrow at the top of the Word Help task pane to display the *Search for* box. (*Note:* You may need to drag the Microsoft Office Word Help window out of the way to see the task pane.)

2. Click in the *Search for* box to place the insertion point within it, key **print**, and click the green *Start searching* arrow.

3. Search through the list of results until you find **Print a Help topic**. Click it to display information in the Microsoft Office Word Help window, as shown in Figure 1-14.

4. Read the information, then print the information by following the instructions you read.

5. Close the Help program by clicking the **Close** button in the Help window as well as in the task pane.

Office Assistant

The Office Assistant is a feature found in all the Office programs that offers a variety of ways to get help. The Assistant, shown in Figure 1-15, is an animated character that offers tips, solutions, instructions, and examples to help you work more efficiently. The default Office Assistant character is a paper clip, named Clippit. A *default* setting is the one used unless another option is chosen.

FIGURE 1-15
Default Office Assistant

The Office Assistant monitors the work you are doing and anticipates when you might need help. It appears on the screen with tips on how to save time or use the program's features more effectively. For example, if you start writing a letter in Word, the Assistant pops up to ask if you want help, as shown in Figure 1-16.

FIGURE 1-16
Office Assistant automatically volunteering assistance

Dear Zack,

It looks like you're writing a letter.

Would you like help?

- Get help with writing the letter
- Just type the letter without help
- ☐ Don't show me this tip again

If you have a specific question, you can use the Office Assistant to search for help. To display the Office Assistant if it is not on the screen, choose Show the Office Assistant from the Help menu. Key your question and click Search. The Assistant suggests a list of help topics in response.

STEP-BY-STEP 1.8

1. If necessary, open the **Help** menu and choose **Show the Office Assistant**. The Office Assistant appears, as shown in Figure 1-15. Click the **Office Assistant** to display the text box.

2. Key **How do I use the Office Assistant?** in the text box.

3. Click **Search**. A list of help topics is displayed in the Search Results task pane.

STEP-BY-STEP 1.8 Continued

4. Choose one of the topics listed and click it to display information in the Microsoft Office Help window.

5. Read and print the information.

6. Click the **Close** boxes in the Help window and the task pane to remove the Help window from the screen.

7. Click the **New Blank Document** button in the standard toolbar to open a new Word document.

8. Key **Dear Zack,** and press **Enter**. A message from the Office Assistant appears, asking if you want help writing your letter, as shown in Figure 1-16. (*Note:* If the message does not appear, you may not have keyed the comma after Zack. Add the comma and press Enter again. The message should display.)

9. Click **Just type the letter without help**.

10. Close the Word document without saving. Leave Word open for the next Step-by-Step.

Quitting an Office Application

The Exit command on the File menu provides the option to quit Word or any other Office application. You can also click the Close button on the right side of the title bar. Exiting an Office application takes you to another open application or back to the Windows desktop.

STEP-BY-STEP 1.9

1. Open the **File** menu. Notice the files listed toward the bottom of the menu. These are the four most recently used files mentioned previously in this lesson.

2. Choose **Exit**. Word closes and Excel is displayed on the screen.

3. Click the **Close** button in the right corner of the title bar. Excel closes and the desktop appears on the screen. The taskbar shows an application is still open.

4. Click the **PowerPoint** button on the taskbar to display it on the screen. Exit PowerPoint. The desktop appears on the screen again.

Accessing the Internet

The *Internet* is a vast network of computers linked to one another. The Internet allows people around the world to share information and ideas through Web pages, newsgroups, mailing lists, chat rooms, e-mail, and electronic files.

Connecting to the Internet requires special hardware and software and an Internet Service Provider. Before you can use the Internet, your computer needs to be connected, and you should know how to access the Internet.

The **World Wide Web** is a system of computers that share information by means of hypertext links on "pages." The Internet is its carrier. To identify hypertext documents, the Web uses addresses called **Uniform Resource Locators (URLs)**. Here are some examples of URLs:

http://www.senate.gov

http://www.microsoft.com

http://www.course.com

The Web toolbar, shown in Figure 1-17, is available in all Office programs. It contains buttons for opening and searching documents. You can use the Web toolbar to access documents on the Internet, on an **Intranet** (a company's private Web), or on your computer. To display the Web toolbar in an application, choose View, Toolbars, Web.

FIGURE 1-17
Web toolbar

Back
Forward
Stop
Search the Web
Start Page
Refresh
Show Only Web Toolbar
Address

The Back button takes you to the previous page and the Forward button takes you to the next page. Click the Stop button to stop loading the current page. The Refresh button reloads the current page. Click the Start Page button to load your **home page**, the first page that appears when you start your browser. The Search the Web button opens a page in which you can type keywords and search the Web. The Favorites button shows a list to which you can add your favorite sites so that you can return to them easily. From the Go button's menu, you can choose to go to different sites or key in an address using the Open Hyperlink command. Click Show Only Web Toolbar when you want to hide all the toolbars except the Web toolbar. When you know the specific address you want to jump to, key it in the Address box.

To view hypertext documents on the Web, you need special software. A **Web browser** is software used to display Web pages on your computer monitor. Microsoft's **Internet Explorer** is a browser for navigating the Web that is packaged with the Office software. When you click the Start Page button or the Search the Web button, or key an URL in the Address box of the Web toolbar, Office automatically launches your Web browser. Depending on your type of Internet connection, you may have to connect to your Internet Service Provider first. Figure 1-18 shows a Web page using Word as a browser.

Computer Concepts

There are two basic types of Internet connections, dial-up and direct. Dial-up access uses a modem and a telephone line to communicate between your computer and the Internet. Most individual users have dial-up access. Direct access uses a special high-speed connection, such as a DSL cable, between your computer and the Internet. This access is faster but more expensive than dial-up access. Most businesses and institutions, and some individuals, have direct access.

Hot Tip

Toolbars display buttons for basic commands only. To see additional buttons, click **Toolbar Options** on the toolbar and choose from the list that appears. When you use a button from the list, it is added to the toolbar. If you haven't used a button recently, it is added to the Toolbar Options list.

FIGURE 1-18
Web browser

STEP-BY-STEP 1.10

1. Connect to your Internet Service Provider if you are not connected already.

2. Open **Word**. Open the **View** menu, choose **Toolbars**, and then choose **Web** from the submenu if the Web toolbar isn't displayed already.

3. Click the **Start Page** button on the Web toolbar. The Start Page begins loading, as shown in Figure 1-18. Wait a few moments for the page to load. (Your start page may be different from the one shown.)

4. Close Internet Explorer by clicking its **Close** button, and return to Microsoft Word.

5. Click the **Search the Web** button. The Internet Explorer program opens and displays the MSN Search screen.

Hot Tip

You can display the Web toolbar in any Office application and use it to access the World Wide Web.

Hot Tip

Since this page is updated every day, your page may not look exactly like the one shown even if you enter the same URL.

STEP-BY-STEP 1.10 Continued

6. Key **pets** in the *Search* box.

7. Click **Search** and a list of pet-related Web sites appears.

8. Click on one of the Web sites to display more information on pets.

9. Click the **Back** button to return to the previous page. Click another Web site to display.

10. Click the **Home** button to return to the Start Page for Internet Explorer.

11. Close Internet Explorer. Close Word. If a message appears asking you if you want to save changes, click **No**.

12. If necessary, disconnect from your Internet Service Provider.

SUMMARY

In this lesson, you learned:

- Microsoft Office 2003 is an integrated software package that consists of a word processor application, a spreadsheet application, a database application, a presentation application, a schedule/organizer application, and a desktop publishing application. The documents of an integrated software package can be used together.

- Office applications can be started by clicking the Start button, pointing to All Programs, pointing to Microsoft Office, and then clicking the name of the application.

- Most Office tasks can be completed from the opening screen of each application. The basic parts of the opening screen are similar in all of the Office programs except Outlook. The task pane is a separate window on the right-hand side of the opening screen. The task pane contains commonly used commands that can help you work more efficiently.

 Careers

Find out about careers in business by going to www.careers-in-business.com.

- Each title in the menu bar represents a separate drop-down menu. When you first use a program, each menu displays only basic commands. As you work, the program adjusts the menus to display the commands used most frequently, adding a command when you choose it and dropping a command when it hasn't been used recently.

- Toolbars provide another quick way to choose commands. The toolbars use icons, or small pictures, to remind you of each button's function. Toolbars can also contain drop-down menus.

- You can open an existing document from the File menu or from the task pane. You can also click the Open button on the Standard toolbar. The Open dialog box will be displayed, enabling you to open a file from any available disk or directory.

- No matter which Office application you are using, files are opened, saved, and closed the same way. Filenames may contain up to 255 characters and may include spaces.

- Recently used files can be opened quickly by choosing the filename from the bottom of the File menu or from the task pane. You can also click the Start button and select My Recent Documents to list the fifteen most recently used files. To exit an Office application, open the File menu and choose Exit or click the Close button on the title bar.

- The Office Help program provides additional information about the many features of the Office applications. You can access the Help program from the menu bar and use the Table of Contents or the *Search* box to get information. You can also access the Microsoft Office Online Help system to find more information on various topics.

- The Office Assistant is a help feature found in all Office applications. It offers tips, advice, and hints on how to work more effectively. You can also use it to search for help on any given topic.

VOCABULARY *Review*

Define the following terms:

Close	Internet Explorer	Task pane
Default	Intranet	Toolbar
Drop-down menu	Link	Uniform Resource Locators
Home page	Menu	(URLs)
Icon	Open	World Wide Web
Integrated software package	Save	Web browser
Internet		

REVIEW *Questions*

WRITTEN QUESTIONS

Write a brief answer to the following questions.

1. List four of the applications that are included in Office 2003.

2. How do you start an Office application?

3. What is the difference between the Save and Save As commands?

4. If the Web toolbar is not on the screen, how do you display it?

5. What is the location and the function of the title bar, menu bar, status bar and taskbar?

TRUE/FALSE

Circle T if the statement is true or F if the statement is false.

T   F   1. In all Office applications, you open, save, and close files in the same way.

T   F   2. A filename may include up to 356 characters and may include spaces.

T   F   3. The Office Assistant is available in all Office programs.

T   F   4. The Web uses addresses called URLs to identify hypertext links.

T   F   5. As you work in Office, the menus are adjusted to display the commands used most frequently.

PROJECTS

PROJECT 1-1

You need to save a copy of April's work schedule into each of the employee's folders.

1. Open Word and a blank document appears.

2. Open Excel. Use the **File** menu to locate the **Employees** folder in the data files. Open the **April Schedule** file from the **Perez** folder.

3. Use the **Save As** command to save the file as **April Work Sched**, followed by your initials, in the Abbott folder.

4. Repeat the process to save the file in the **Bolten, Gibson, Kamnani, Reid,** and **Wunneberger** folders.

5. Close April Work Sched and exit Excel. The blank Word document should be displayed.

6. Use the task pane to open the **Schedule Memo** Word file from the **Perez** folder.

7. Save the file with the same name in the **Garner** folder.

8. Close **Schedule Memo.** Close the Word document without saving and exit Word.

PROJECT 1-2

1. Open Word and access the Help system.

2. Search on the word **tip.**

3. Choose from the list of topics to find out how to show the tip of the day when Word starts.

4. Print the information displayed in the Microsoft Office Help window.

5. Search on the question **What should I do if the Office Assistant is distracting?**

6. Choose from the list of topics to find out how to troubleshoot Help.

7. In the Microsoft Office Help window, choose the option to find out what to do if the Office Assistant is distracting.

8. Print the information displayed in the Microsoft Office Help window.

9. Close the Help system and exit Word.

 Careers

For help in choosing a career or college major, go to *www.careerkey.org*. You can take a test that measures your skills, abilities, talents, values, interest, and personality. Based upon your answers, a list of promising careers and jobs is identified.

PROJECT 1-3

1. If necessary, connect to your Internet Service Provider.

2. Open your Web browser.

3. Search for information on the Internet about Microsoft products.

4. Search for information about another topic in which you are interested.

5. Return to your home page.

6. Close your Web browser and disconnect from the Internet, if necessary.

CRITICAL*Thinking*

SCANS **ACTIVITY 1-1**

Describe how you would use each of the Office applications in your personal life. Imagine that you are a business owner and describe how each of the Office applications would help you increase productivity.

SCANS **ACTIVITY 1-2**

Use the Office Help system to find out how to change the Office Assistant from a paper clip to another animated character. Write down the steps and then change your Office Assistant to another character.

SCANS **ACTIVITY 1-3**

Open your Web browser. Compare the toolbar of your browser with the Web toolbar shown in Figure 1-17. Use the Help system if necessary and describe the function of any buttons that are different. Then describe the steps you would take to print a Web page.

SCANS **ACTIVITY 1-4**

You work for a small advertising agency whose employees depend heavily on reliable and speedy access to the Internet to do their jobs. Recently, some of the employees have complained about sluggish downloads and problems connecting to the Internet. You have decided to evaluate your current Internet service provider and research other ISPs in the area.

Search the Internet for information on at least three ISPs. Use the table below as a guide for gathering information that would be helpful in your evaluation. Which ISP would you recommend? Why?

INTERNET SERVICE PROVIDER	SETUP COSTS/ EQUIPMENT REQUIREMENTS	COST PER MONTH	SPEED	CUSTOMER SERVICE	SYSTEM MAINTENANCE DOWNTIME

INTRODUCTORY MICROSOFT EXCEL

Unit

 Estimated Time for Unit: 16.5 hours

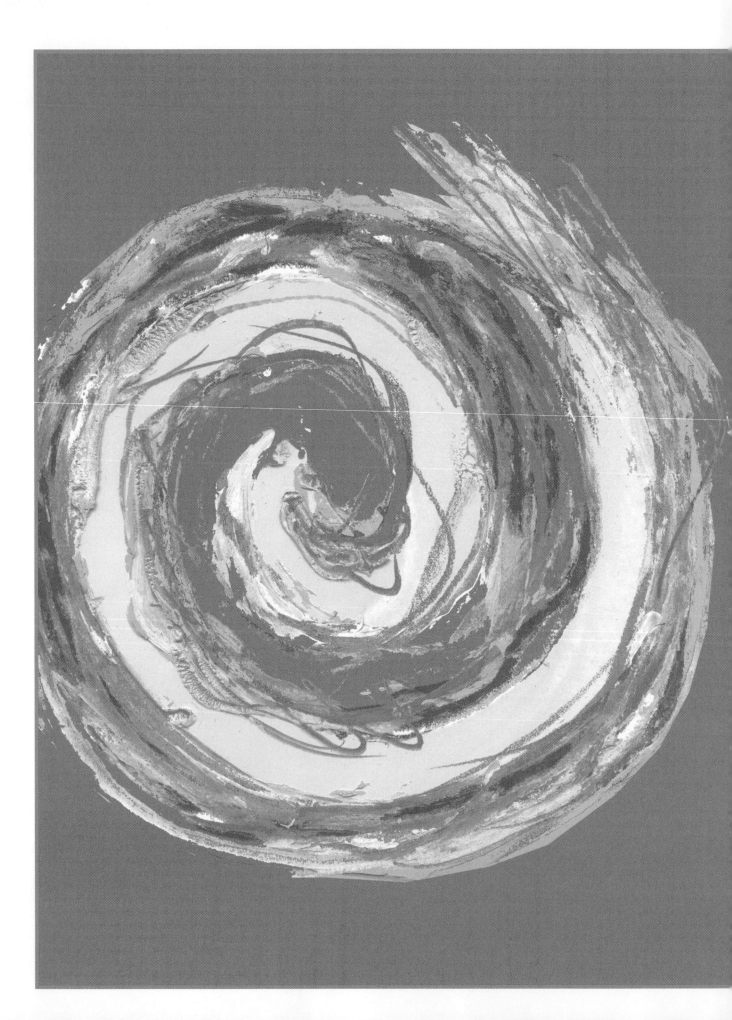

EXCEL BASICS

What Is Excel?

Excel is the spreadsheet application in the Microsoft Office 2003 suite of programs. A *spreadsheet* is a grid of rows and columns containing numbers, text, and formulas. The purpose of a spreadsheet is to solve problems that involve numbers. Without a computer, you might try to solve this type of problem by creating rows and columns on ruled paper and using a calculator to determine results (see Figure 1-1). Computer spreadsheets also contain rows and columns, but they perform calculations much faster and more accurately than spreadsheets created with pencil, paper, and calculator.

FIGURE 1-1
Spreadsheet prepared on paper

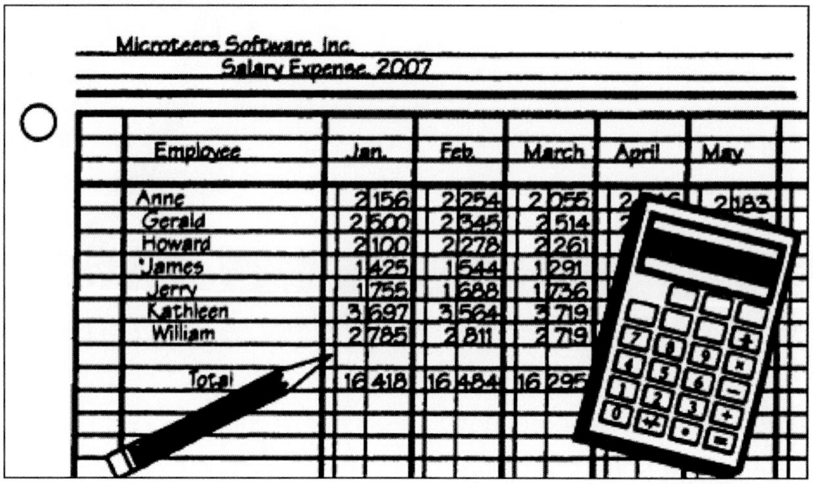

Spreadsheets are used in many ways. For example, a spreadsheet can be used to calculate a grade in a class, to prepare a budget for the next few months, or to determine payments to be made on a loan. The primary advantage of spreadsheets is the ability to complete complex and repetitious calculations accurately, quickly, and easily. For example, you might use a spreadsheet to calculate your monthly income and expenses.

Besides calculating rapidly and accurately, spreadsheets are flexible. Making changes to an existing spreadsheet is usually as easy as pointing and clicking with the mouse. Suppose, for example, you have prepared a budget on a spreadsheet and have overestimated the amount of money you will need to spend on gas, electric, and other utilities. You may change a single entry in your spreadsheet and watch the entire spreadsheet recalculate the new budgeted amount. You can imagine the work this change would require if you were calculating the budget with pencil and paper.

Excel uses the term *worksheet* to refer to computerized spreadsheets. Sometimes you may want to use several worksheets that relate to each other. A collection of related worksheets is referred to as a *workbook*.

Starting Excel

You start Excel from the desktop screen in Windows. One way to start Excel is to click the Start button, point to All Programs, point to Microsoft Office, and then choose Microsoft Office Excel 2003. When Excel starts, a blank worksheet titled *Book1* appears on the screen. You will see some of the basic parts of the screen that you learned about in the Introduction: the title bar, the menu bar, the Standard toolbar, and the task pane. However, as shown in Figure 1-2, Excel has its own unique buttons and screen parts.

FIGURE 1-2
Excel opening screen

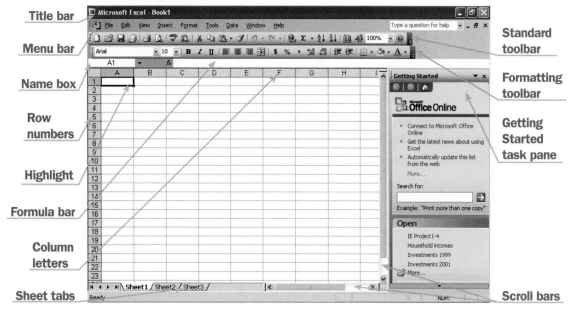

STEP-BY-STEP 1.1

1. With Windows running, click the **Start** button, point to *All Programs,* point to *Microsoft Office,* and then click **Microsoft Office Excel 2003.**

2. Excel starts and a blank worksheet titled *Book1* appears, as shown in Figure 1-2. Maximize the window, if necessary.

3. Leave the blank worksheet on the screen for use in the next Step-by-Step.

Parts of the Worksheet

Columns of the worksheet appear vertically and are identified by letters at the top of the worksheet window. *Rows* appear horizontally and are identified by numbers on the left side of the worksheet window. A *cell* is the intersection of a row and column and is identified by a cell reference, the column letter and row number (for example, C4, A1, B2).

The mouse pointer is indicated by a thick plus sign when it is in the worksheet. If you move the pointer up to the toolbars and menus, the pointer turns into an arrow. In Word, the insertion point indicates the point at which a character is keyed. In the worksheet, the entry point is indicated by a *highlight,* which appears on the screen as a dark border around a cell.

The cell that contains the highlight is the *active cell,* which is distinguished by a dark border. Your screen currently shows a border around cell A1, the active cell.

> **Did You Know?**
>
> Excel comes with several template files that you may use to build commonly used spreadsheets, such as invoices, expense statements, and purchase orders. To open these files, open the **File** menu and choose **New**. In the *Templates* section of the New Workbook task pane, click **On my computer**. In the Templates dialog box, click the **Spreadsheet Solutions** tab, and double-click the template file you want to open.

You may change the active cell by moving the highlight from one cell to another. The *formula bar* appears directly below the Formatting toolbar in the worksheet and displays a formula when the cell of a worksheet contains a calculated value. On the far left side of the formula bar is the *Name box*, or cell reference area, that identifies the active cell.

Opening an Existing Workbook

To open an existing worksheet, open the File menu and choose Open, or click the Open button on the toolbar. In the Open dialog box, specify the file you want to open. When you start Excel, the program displays a new worksheet temporarily titled *Book1*. This worksheet is eliminated if you open another file.

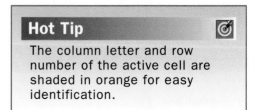

Hot Tip

The column letter and row number of the active cell are shaded in orange for easy identification.

STEP-BY-STEP 1.2

Suppose that you have volunteered to help a local environmental awareness group by conducting a census of bird species. For the remainder of this lesson, you will complete a worksheet that accounts for each species of bird.

1. Click **More** in the *Open* section of the Getting Started task pane. (You might have to point to the down arrow at the bottom of the task pane to bring all of the *Open* section into view.) The Open dialog box appears.

2. Click the down arrow on the *Look in* box, and select the drive and/or folder containing the data files for this course. The files appear in the display window.

3. Double-click the filename **IE Step1-2**. The worksheet appears on the screen similar to Figure 1-3. Leave the worksheet on the screen for the next Step-by-Step.

FIGURE 1-3
Opening a workbook

	A	B	C	D	E	F	G	H	I	J
1	BIRD CENSUS									
2										
3	Species	Period 1	Period 2	Period 3	Period 4	Monthly Total				
4										
5	Boat-Tailed Grackles	9	12	6		27				
6	Goldfinches	6	10	7		23				
7	Black-Capped Chickadees	12	8	17		37				
8	Red-Headed Woodpeckers	2	5	8		15				
9	Eastern Bluebirds	1	3	2		6				
10	English Sparrows	21	15	1		37				
11						0				
12										
13	Total Birds Sighted	51	53	41	0	145				

Moving the Highlight in a Worksheet

The easiest way to move the highlight to a cell on the screen is to move the mouse pointer to the cell and click. When working with a large worksheet, you might not be able to view the entire worksheet on the screen. You can scroll through the worksheet using the mouse by dragging the scroll box in the scroll bar to the desired position. You can also move the highlight to different parts of the worksheet using the keyboard or the Go To command on the Edit menu.

Using Keys to Move the Highlight

You can move the highlight by pressing certain keys or key combinations, as shown in Table 1-1. Many of these key combinations may be familiar to you if you use Microsoft Word. As in Word, when you hold down an arrow key, the highlight will move repeatedly and quickly.

TABLE 1-1
Key combinations for moving the highlight in a worksheet

TO MOVE	PRESS
Left one column	Left arrow
Right one column	Right arrow
Up one row	Up arrow
Down one row	Down arrow
To the first cell of a row	Home
To cell A1	Ctrl+Home
To the last cell containing data	Ctrl+End
Up one window	Page Up
Down one window	Page Down
To the previous worksheet in a workbook	Ctrl+Page Up
To the next worksheet in a workbook	Ctrl+Page Down

Using the Go To Command to Move in the Worksheet

You might want to move the highlight to a cell that does not appear on the screen. The fastest way to move to the cell is by choosing Go To on the Edit menu or by pressing the shortcut key, F5. The Go To dialog box appears, as shown in Figure 1-4. Key the cell reference in the *Reference* box and click OK. The highlight moves to the cell.

Did You Know?

You can also go to specific text or numbers in the worksheet by choosing the Find command on the Edit menu. The Find dialog box opens. In the *Find what* text box, key the data you would like to locate in the worksheet and then click **Find Next.** The highlight moves to the next cell that contains the data.

FIGURE 1-4
Go To dialog box

STEP-BY-STEP 1.3

1. The highlight should be in cell A1. Move to the last cell in the worksheet that contains data by pressing **Ctrl+End**. The highlight moves to cell F13 in the lower-right side of the worksheet.

2. Move to the first cell of row 13 by pressing **Home**. The highlight appears in cell A13, which contains the words *Total Birds Sighted*.

3. Move up three rows by pressing the up arrow key three times. The highlight appears in cell A10, which contains the words *English Sparrows*.

4. Open the Edit menu and choose **Go To.** The Go To dialog box appears, as shown in Figure 1-4.

5. Key **B3** in the *Reference* box.

6. Click **OK.** The highlight moves to cell B3. Leave the worksheet on the screen for the next Step-by-Step.

Selecting a Group of Cells

Often, you will perform operations on more than one cell at a time. A selected group of cells is called a *range*. In a range, all cells touch each other and form a rectangle. The range is identified by the cell in the upper-left corner and the cell in the lower-right corner, separated by a colon (for example, A3:C5). To select a range of cells, place the highlight in the cell that is at one corner of the range and drag the highlight to the cell in the opposite corner. As you drag the highlight, the range of selected cells becomes shaded (except for the cell you originally selected). The column letters and row numbers of the range you select are highlighted in orange.

Teamwork

Have a classmate call out cell references so you can practice moving the highlight to the correct cell using the methods you have learned.

STEP-BY-STEP 1.4

1. With the highlight in B3, hold down the left mouse button and drag to the right until **F3** is highlighted.

2. Release the mouse button. The range B3:F3 is selected. Notice that the column letters B through F and the row number 3 are shaded.

3. Move the highlight to **B5**.

4. Hold down the mouse button and drag down and to the right until **F13** is highlighted.

5. Release the mouse button. The range B5:F13 is selected. Leave the worksheet open for the next Step-by-Step.

Entering Data in a Cell

Worksheet cells can contain text, numbers, formulas, or functions. Text consists of alphabetical characters such as headings, labels, or explanatory notes. Numbers can be values, dates, or times. Formulas are equations that calculate a value. Functions are special formulas that place either values or characters in cells. (Formulas and functions are discussed in later lessons.)

Enter data by keying the text or numbers in a cell, and then either click the Enter button on the formula bar or press the Enter key on the keyboard. If you choose not to enter the data you have keyed, you can simply click the Cancel button on the formula bar or press **Esc** and the keyed data will be deleted.

If you make a mistake, open the Edit menu and choose Undo or click the Undo button on the Standard toolbar to reverse your most recent change. To undo multiple actions, click the down arrow on the Undo button. A list of your previous actions is displayed, and you can choose the number of actions you want to undo.

STEP-BY-STEP 1.5

1. Move the highlight to E5 and key **15**. As you key, the numbers appear in the cell and in the formula bar.

2. Press **Enter**. The highlight moves to E6.

3. Key **4**.

4. Click the **Enter** button on the formula bar. Notice that the totals in F6, E13, and F13 change as you enter the data.

5. Undo the action by clicking the down arrow on the **Undo** button on the Standard toolbar. A menu appears listing the actions you have just performed.

STEP-BY-STEP 1.5 Continued

6. Choose **Typing '4' in E6** on the menu, as shown in Figure 1-5. The data is removed from E6 and the data in F6 and E13 change back to the previous totals.

FIGURE 1-5
Undo multiple actions by clicking the arrow on the Undo button

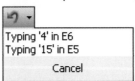

7. Enter the following data in the remaining cells in column E:

Cell	Data
E6	5
E7	20
E8	4
E9	10
E10	16

8. In addition to the species above, you sighted a blue heron. Click cell **A11** and key **Heron.**

9. Click cell **E11** and key **1.** Leave the worksheet open for the next Step-by-Step.

Changing Data in a Cell

As you enter data in the worksheet, you might change your mind about it or make a mistake. If so, you can edit, replace, or clear the data.

Editing Data

Editing is performed when only minor changes to cell data are necessary. Data in a cell can be edited in the formula bar by using the F2 Edit key on your keyboard. To edit data in a cell, select the cell by placing the highlight in the cell and pressing F2. A blinking insertion point appears in the cell and you can make changes to the data. Press Enter when you are done.

You might prefer to use the mouse pointer to edit a cell. First, click the cell you want to edit; then click in the formula bar at the place you want to change the data. After you have made the changes you need, click the Enter button.

Hot Tip

If you need help while working with any of Excel's features, use the Office Assistant. The Assistant is an animated character that offers tips, solutions, instructions, and examples to help you work more efficiently. It appears on the screen with tips on how to manage spreadsheet data and workbook files. If you have a specific question, you can use the Office Assistant to search for help. To display the Office Assistant if it is not on the screen, open the Help menu and choose **Show the Office Assistant**. Then, click the Assistant and key your question and click **Search.** The Assistant displays a list of help topics in response.

Replacing Data

Cell contents are usually replaced when you must make significant changes to cell data. To replace cell contents, select the cell, key the new data, and enter the data by clicking the Enter button on the formula bar or by pressing the Enter key.

Clearing Data

Clearing a cell empties the cell of its contents. To clear an active cell, press the Delete key or Backspace key, or open the Edit menu and choose Clear. When you choose the Clear command, a submenu opens, providing you with options to delete the format of the cell, the contents of the cell, a comment in the cell, or all of the above.

> **Did You Know?**
>
> A worksheet is usually part of a collection of worksheets called a workbook. A tab near the bottom of the screen identifies a particular worksheet. You can move, copy, or delete a worksheet by right-clicking the worksheet tab and then selecting the operation you desire on the shortcut menu.

S TEP-BY-STEP 1.6

1. Move the highlight to **D10.**

2. Press **F2.** An insertion point appears in the cell.

3. Make sure the insertion point is positioned after the 1 and key **8.**

4. Press **Enter.** The number *18* appears in the cell.

5. Move the highlight to **A11.**

6. Key **Blue Heron** and click the **Enter** button on the formula bar. The words *Blue Heron* replace the word *Heron* in the cell.

7. Move the highlight to **A3.**

STEP-BY-STEP 1.6 Continued

8. Press the **Delete** key. The contents are cleared from the cell. Your screen should appear similar to Figure 1-6. Leave the worksheet open for the next Step-by-Step.

FIGURE 1-6
Changing data in a cell

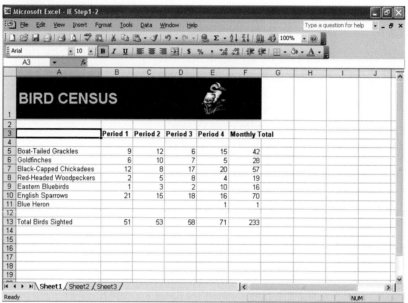

Searching for Data

The Find command enables you to locate specific words or numbers in a worksheet. If you like, you can use the Replace command to change data you have found.

Finding Data

The Find command locates data in a worksheet. It is particularly useful when the worksheet is large. When you choose *Find* (or *Replace*) on the Edit menu, the Find and Replace dialog box opens. You can perform more specific searches by clicking the Options button within the dialog box. The Replace tab in the expanded Find and Replace dialog box is shown in Figure 1-7. Table 1-2 lists the actions you can specify in the Find and Replace dialog box.

FIGURE 1-7
Find and Replace dialog box

TABLE 1-2
Find and Replace options

SEARCH OPTION	SPECIFIES
Find what	the data you are looking for
Replace with	the data that will be inserted in the cell
Format	the format of the data you are looking for, or the format of the replacement data
Within	whether you will search the worksheet or the entire workbook
Search	whether the search will look across rows or down columns
Look in	whether the search will examine cell contents or formulas
Match case	whether the search must match the data's capitalization
Match entire cell contents	whether the search must match all contents of the cell

The Find command locates words or parts of words. For example, searching for *emp* will find the words *employee* and *temporary*. In addition, searching for *85* will find *85, 850,* and *385*.

Replacing Data

The Replace command is an extension of the Find command. Replacing data substitutes new data for the data found. Replace data by choosing the Replace command on the Edit menu or by clicking the Replace tab in the Find and Replace dialog box.

STEP-BY-STEP 1.7

1. Move the highlight to **A1**.

2. Open the **Edit** menu and choose **Find.**

3. Key **Period** in the *Find what* box.

4. Click the **Find Next** button. The highlight moves to **B3**.

5. Click the **Replace** tab in the Find and Replace dialog box.

6. Key **Week** in the *Replace with* box.

7. Click **Replace.** The word *Period* is replaced by *Week* in B3 and the highlight moves to **C3**.

8. Click **Replace All.** A message appears indicating that Excel has completed the search and replaced all instances of the word *Period* with the word *Week* (in this case, three replacements).

9. Click **OK.**

10. Click **Close** in the Find and Replace dialog box. Leave the worksheet open for the next Step-by-Step.

Using Zoom View

You can magnify or reduce the view of your worksheet by using the Zoom button on the Standard toolbar (or by using the Zoom command on the View menu). The default magnification is 100%. If you want a closer view of your worksheet, select a larger percentage. Reduce the view by selecting a smaller percentage. If you want a different magnification from those available on the Zoom drop-down list, you can key your desired percentage directly in the *Zoom* box.

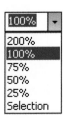

Saving a Workbook

Save a workbook using the same steps that you learned in the Introduction. The first time you save a workbook, the Save As dialog box appears in which you name the workbook file. Once you've saved the workbook, you use the Save command on the File menu, or the Save button on the Standard toolbar to periodically save the latest version of the workbook.

> **Did You Know?**
>
> You can save a file in a new folder by clicking the **Create New Folder** button in the Save As dialog box. In the New Folder dialog box, key a name for the new folder and click **OK**.

STEP-BY-STEP 1.8

1. Click the down arrow on the **Zoom** button on the Standard toolbar.

2. Click **200%**. The view of the worksheet is expanded.

3. Click the **Zoom** button's down arrow again, and then click **50%**. The view of the worksheet is reduced to half of its default size.

4. Click the **Zoom** button's down arrow once more, and then click **100%**. The worksheet returns to its original size.

5. Open the **File** menu and choose **Save As**. The Save As dialog box appears.

6. Key **Bird Survey**, followed by your initials, in the *File name* text box.

7. Click **Save**. Leave the worksheet open for the next Step-by-Step.

Printing a Worksheet

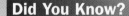

You can print a worksheet by clicking the Print button on the Standard toolbar or by accessing the Print dialog box (see Figure 1-8). Use the Print dialog box to print part of a worksheet or change the way your printed worksheet looks. You will learn more about these options in Lesson 3. For now, you will print the entire worksheet using the default settings.

FIGURE 1-8
Printing a file

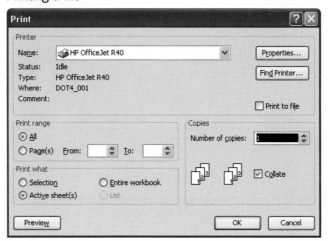

STEP-BY-STEP 1.9

1. Open the **File** menu and choose **Print.** The Print dialog box appears.

2. Click **OK.**

3. Open the **File** menu and choose **Close.** If you are asked to save changes, click **Yes.** The worksheet closes.

SUMMARY

In this lesson, you learned:

■ The purpose of a spreadsheet is to solve problems involving numbers. The advantage of using a spreadsheet is that you can complete complex and repetitious calculations quickly and easily.

■ A worksheet consists of columns and rows intersecting to form cells. Each cell is identified by a cell reference, which is the letter of the column and number of the row.

■ You can move to different cells of the worksheet by clicking the cell with the mouse pointer, using a series of keystrokes, or by scrolling with the mouse.

■ Both text and numerical data can be entered in the worksheet. You can alter data by editing, replacing, or deleting it.

■ You can search for specific characters in a worksheet. You can also replace data you have searched for with specific characters.

■ The Zoom feature enables you to enlarge or reduce the view of the worksheet on the screen.

■ You save changes to a worksheet by using the Save command on the File menu or the Save button on the Standard toolbar.

■ You can print a worksheet to provide a hard copy.

VOCABULARY *Review*

Define the following terms:

Active cell	Highlight	Spreadsheet
Cell	Name box	Workbook
Column	Range	Worksheet
Formula bar	Row	

REVIEW *Questions*

TRUE/FALSE

Circle T if the statement is true or F if the statement is false.

T   F   1. The primary advantage of the worksheet is to summarize text documents.

T   F   2. A cell is the intersection of a row and column.

T   F   3. The Go To command lets you save a file and exit Excel.

T   F   4. You can print a file by using the *Print* command on the File menu or by clicking the Print button on the Standard toolbar.

T   F   5. Once a worksheet has been saved with a new name, you can save further changes to it by clicking the Save button on the Standard toolbar.

WRITTEN QUESTIONS

Write a brief answer to the following questions.

1. What term describes a cell that is ready for data entry?

2. How are columns identified in a worksheet?

3. What term describes a group of cells?

4. What key(s) do you press to move the highlight to the last cell of the worksheet that contains data?

5. What key(s) do you press to remove data from an active cell?

PROJECTS

PROJECT 1-1

In the blank space, write the letter of the keystroke from Column 2 that matches the highlight movement in Column 1.

Column 1	Column 2
___ 1. Left one column	A. Ctrl+Home
___ 2. Right one column	B. Page Up
___ 3. Up one row	C. Right arrow
___ 4. Down one row	D. Home
___ 5. To the first cell of a row	E. Ctrl+Page Up
___ 6. To cell A1	F. Left arrow
___ 7. To the last cell containing data	G. Ctrl+End
___ 8. Up one window	H. Up arrow
___ 9. Down one window	I. Ctrl+Page Down
___10. To the previous worksheet in a workbook	J. Down arrow
___11. To the next worksheet in a workbook	K. Page Down

 **PROJECT 1-2**

The file *IE Project1-2* contains information concerning the percentage of home ownership in the 50 states. Make the following corrections and additions to the worksheet.

1. Open **IE Project1-2** from the data files.

2. Save the file as **Home Owner,** followed by your initials.

3. Enter **GA** in **A15.**

4. Enter **69.8%** in **B15.**

5. Enter **64.9%** in **C15.**

6. Edit the data in **A16** to be **HA.**

7. Edit the data in **B16** to be **55.2%.**

8. Delete the data in **A3.**

9. Save, print, and close the file.

PROJECT 1-3

Residential Developers, Inc., has developed a worksheet to help prospective home buyers estimate the cost of homes in four different neighborhoods. The cost of homes within neighborhoods tends to fluctuate based on the square footage of the home. Each of the four neighborhoods tends to have a different cost per square foot.

1. Open **IE Project1-3** from the data files.

2. Save the file as **Developments,** followed by your initials.

3. Enter the square footages in the following cells to estimate the home costs. The estimated home cost in each neighborhood will change as you enter the data.

Cell	Enter
C7	1250
C8	1500
C9	2200
C10	2500

4. After selling several houses in the Lake View neighborhood, Residential Developers, Inc., has figured that the cost per square foot is $67.00, rather than $65.00. Edit **B7** to show **$67.00.**

5. Save, print, and close the file.

 PROJECT 1-4

1. Open **IE Project1-4** from the data files.

2. Save the file as **Surname,** followed by your initials.

3. Using the Find command, locate the name **Chavez.** Your highlight should appear in A198.

4. Click outside the dialog box and press **Ctrl+Home** to return to A1.

5. Using the Find command, locate the name **Chang.** Your highlight should appear in A691. (*Hint*: The Find and Replace dialog box will remain on screen. You can simply enter the new search in the Find what text box.)

6. Click outside the dialog box and press **Ctrl+Home** to return to A1.

7. Using the Find command, locate the name **Forbes.** Your highlight should appear in A987.

8. Save and close the file.

> **Extra Challenge**
>
> See if you can find your last name, or the names of your friends, in the *Surnames* file you just worked on.

CRITICAL *Thinking*

 ACTIVITY 1-1

The purpose of a spreadsheet is to solve problems that involve numbers. Identify two or three numerical problems in each of the following categories that might be solved by using a spreadsheet.

1. Business

2. Career

3. Personal

4. School

SCANS ACTIVITY 1-2

You have selected a range of cells that is so large it extends several screens. You realize that you incorrectly included one column of cells you do not want within the selected range.

To reselect the range of cells, you must page up to the active cell (the first cell of the range) and drag through several screens to the last cell in the range. You are wondering if there is a better way to reduce the selected range without having to page up to the original screen.

Use the Microsoft Excel Help command on the Help menu to learn how to select fewer cells without canceling your original selection. In your word processor, write a brief explanation of the steps you would take to change the selected range. (*Hint*: The answer appears under a topic that relates to "selecting data or cells.")

CHANGING THE APPEARANCE OF A WORKSHEET

OBJECTIVES

Upon completion of this lesson, you should be able to:

■ Change column width and row height.

■ Position text within a cell by wrapping, rotating, indenting, and aligning.

■ Change the appearance of cells using fonts, styles, colors, and borders.

■ Designate the format of a cell to accommodate different kinds of text and numerical data.

■ Apply and paint formats.

■ Create and use styles.

■ Find and replace cell formats.

Estimated Time: 1.5 hours

VOCABULARY

AutoFormat

Indented text

Rotated text

Style

Wrapped text

Changing the Size of a Cell

Worksheets are useful only when they are understandable to the user. It is important that data in a worksheet is accurate, but it is also important that it is presented in a way that is visually appealing.

Changing Column Width

Sometimes the data you key will not fit in the column. When you enter information that is wider than the column, one of the following will happen:

■ A series of number signs (######) appears in the cell.

■ The numbers or letters that do not fit in the cell are not displayed.

- The numbers or letters extend into the next cell if that cell is empty.

- Numbers are converted to a different numerical form (for example, changing long numbers to exponential form).

You can widen the column by placing the mouse pointer on the right edge of the column heading (the column letter). The pointer then changes into a double-headed arrow. To widen the column, drag to the right until the column is the desired size. When you drag to change the width of a column, a ScreenTip appears near the pointer displaying the new measurement.

Another way to change column width is to use the Column Width dialog box, shown in Figure 2-1. Place the highlight in the column you want to change. Then, open the Format menu, choose Column, and click Width on the submenu. In the Column Width dialog box, key the desired width and click OK.

FIGURE 2-1
Column Width dialog box

Changing Row Height

Change the row height by placing the mouse pointer below the row heading (the row number). The pointer then changes into a double-headed arrow. Drag downward until the row is the desired size. Also, you can use the Row Height dialog box to designate a specific row height. Place the highlight in the row you want to change. Then, open the Format menu, choose Row, and click Height on the submenu. In the Row Height dialog box, key the desired height and click OK.

> **Hot Tip**
>
> You can change the width of several columns at a time by selecting the columns and then dragging the right edge of one of the column headings. You can also change the height of several rows by selecting the rows and then dragging the boundary below a selected row heading.

STEP-BY-STEP 2.1

1. Open **IE Step2-1** from the data files. Notice that the data in D3 extends into column E.

2. Save the workbook as **3Q Budget**, followed by your initials.

3. Place the mouse pointer on the right edge of the column D heading. The pointer turns into a double-headed arrow.

4. Drag the double-headed arrow to the right until the ScreenTip reads *Width: 10.00 (75 pixels)*, as shown in Figure 2-2, and release the mouse button. The entire word *September* now fits within column D.

STEP-BY-STEP 2.1 Continued

FIGURE 2-2
Column width measurement ScreenTip

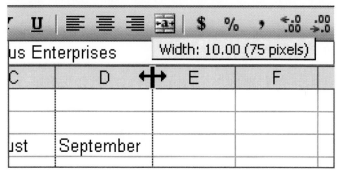

5. Select columns **B** through **D**.

6. Open the **Format** menu, choose **Column**, and then choose **Width** on the submenu. The Column Width dialog box appears (see Figure 2-1).

7. Key **10** in the *Column width* box.

8. Click **OK**. The widths of the selected columns are changed to 10.

9. Scroll down if necessary and place the mouse pointer on the bottom edge of the row 18 heading. The pointer turns into a double-headed arrow.

10. Drag the double-headed arrow down until the ScreenTip reads *Height 18.00 (24 pixels)*.

11. Save the file and leave the worksheet open for the next Step-by-Step.

Letting Excel Find the Best Fit

Suppose you have a column full of data of varying widths. You want the column to be wide enough to display the longest entry, but no wider than necessary. Excel can determine the best width of a column or the best height of a row. To determine the best fit for a column, place the highlight in the cell, open the Format menu, choose Column, and then choose AutoFit Selection on the submenu. To determine the best fit for a row, place the highlight in the cell, open the Format menu, choose Row, and then choose AutoFit on the submenu.

Hot Tip

Another way to find the best fit is to place the mouse pointer on the right edge of the column heading and double-click when the double-headed arrow appears.

STEP-BY-STEP 2.2

1. Place the highlight in **A20**. Notice that the words *Cumulative Surplus* are cut off.

2. Open the **Format** menu, choose **Column**, and then choose **AutoFit Selection** on the submenu. Column A widens to show all the data in A20.

3. Save your work and leave the worksheet open for the next Step-by-Step.

Positioning Text Within a Cell

Unless you specify otherwise, Excel enters text as left justified without wrapping. However, you can change the position of text within a cell in several ways, as described in Table 2-1.

TABLE 2-1
Positioning text within a cell

TEXT POSITION	FUNCTION	EXAMPLE OF USE
Wrapped	Begins a new line within the cell	Moves text to a new line when it is longer than the width of the cell
Rotated	Displays text at an angle	Turns the text so that it might be displayed in a narrower column
Indented	Moves the text several spaces to the right	Subheadings below primary headings
Left	Begins the text on the left side of the cell	Default justification for text data
Centered	Places the text in the middle of the cell	Column headings
Right	Begins the text on the right side of the cell	Default justification for numerical data
Merge and Center	Merges multiple cells into one cell and places the text in the middle of the merged cell	Title across the top of a worksheet

Text Wrap

Text that is too long for a cell spills over into the next cell if the next cell is empty. If the next cell is not empty, the text that does not fit in the cell will not display. You can choose to have text wrap within a cell in the same way that text wraps within a word-processing document using the text wrap option. The row height will automatically adjust to show all of the lines of text. This is referred to as *wrapped text*.

> **Hot Tip**
>
> You can access the Format Cells dialog box by right-clicking an active cell or range and choosing **Format Cells** on the shortcut menu.

To turn on the text wrap option, select the cells in which you intend to wrap text. Then, open the Format menu and choose Cells. In the Format Cells dialog box, click the Alignment tab, as shown in Figure 2-3. In the *Text control* section, click Wrap text.

FIGURE 2-3
The Wrap text option on the Alignment tab in the Format Cells dialog box

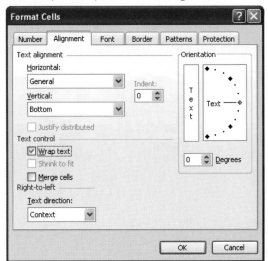

STEP-BY-STEP 2.3

1. Move the highlight to **A22**.

2. Open the **Format** menu and choose **Cells**. The Format Cells dialog box appears.

3. Click the **Alignment** tab, if necessary.

4. Click the **Wrap text** box in the *Text control* section to insert a check mark.

5. Click **OK**. The text wraps in the cell and the cell height adjusts automatically.

6. Save your work and leave the worksheet open for the next Step-by-Step.

Rotate Text

Sometimes column headings are longer than the data in the columns. Excel allows you to save space by rotating the text to any angle. Using *rotated text* can also help give your worksheet a more professional look.

To rotate text, select the cells containing the text you want to rotate, open the Format menu, and choose

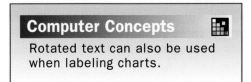

Computer Concepts

Rotated text can also be used when labeling charts.

Cells. In the Format Cells dialog box, choose the Alignment tab (see Figure 2-3). In the *Orientation* box, click a degree point, drag the angle indicator, or type the angle you want in the *Degrees* text box.

STEP-BY-STEP 2.4

1. Select **B3:D3**.

2. Open the **Format** menu and choose **Cells**. The Format Cells dialog box appears.

3. Click the **Alignment** tab, if it is not already selected.

4. In the *Orientation* section, key **45** in the *Degrees* text box. The Text indicator moves to a 45-degree angle, as shown in Figure 2-4.

FIGURE 2-4
Orientation section of Alignment tab in the Format Cells dialog box

5. Click **OK**. The text in B3 through D3 is now displayed at a 45-degree angle.

6. Change the width of columns **B** through **D** to **8**.

7. Save your work and leave the worksheet open for the next Step-by-Step.

Indenting Text

Indented text within cells can help distinguish categories or set apart text. Instead of trying to indent text by keying spaces, you can click the Increase Indent button on the toolbar to accomplish this task easily. To move the indent in the other direction, click the Decrease Indent button.

Decrease Indent   Increase Indent

Aligning Text

You can align the contents of a cell several ways: left, centered, right, and centered across several columns (refer to Table 2-1). Excel automatically left-aligns all text entries. All numbers are right-aligned unless you specify a different alignment.

Computer Concepts

You can indent text in a cell up to 16 levels.

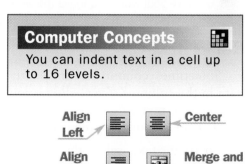

Align Left   Center

Align Right   Merge and Center

To change the alignment of a cell, place the highlight in the cell and click one of the four alignment buttons on the toolbar.

For other alignment options, open the Format menu, choose Cells, and then click the Alignment tab. Click the alignment you want from the *Horizontal* or *Vertical* list boxes, and click OK.

> **Hot Tip**
>
> When you highlight cells in a row and choose the **Merge and Center** button, the cells are merged and the contents are centered.

S TEP-BY-STEP 2.5

1. Move the highlight to **A5.**

2. Click the **Increase Indent** button on the Formatting toolbar.

3. Select **A6** and click the **Increase Indent** button.

4. Select **A10:A16** and click the **Increase Indent** button.

5. Select **B3:D3.**

6. Click the **Center** button on the Formatting toolbar. The headings are centered.

7. Select **A7.**

8. Click the **Align Right** button. *Total Income* is aligned at the right of the cell.

9. Right-align **A17**, **A19**, and **A20.**

10. Select **A1:D1.**

11. Click the **Merge and Center** button. *Asparagus Enterprises* is centered across cells A1 through D1.

12. Merge and center the *Third Quarter Budget* subheading across **A2:D2.**

13. Save and leave the worksheet open for the next Step-by-Step.

Changing Cell Appearance

You can change the appearance of a cell's contents to make it easier to read. You can alter the appearance of cell contents by changing the font, size, style, color, alignment, format, and borders.

Fonts and Font Sizes

The font and font size you choose may significantly affect the readability of the worksheet. The number, types, and sizes of fonts available depend largely on what fonts are installed on your computer. You can choose different fonts for different parts of a worksheet.

Changing fonts and sizes in a worksheet is similar to changing the fonts and sizes in a word-processing document. Highlight the cells you want to change, click the arrow on the Font button on the Formatting toolbar, and choose a font from the list. To change the font size, click the arrow on the Font Size button on the Formatting toolbar, and choose a size from the list. You can also open the Format menu and choose Cells. In the Format Cells dialog box, click the Font tab. As shown in Figure 2-5, the Format Cells dialog box has options for changing the font, font style, font size, and color.

FIGURE 2-5
Font tab in the Format Cells dialog box

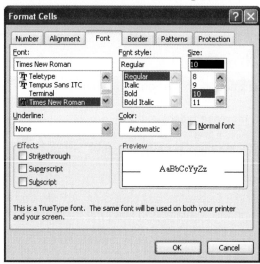

Font Style

Bolding, italicizing, or underlining can add emphasis to the contents of a cell. These features are referred to as *font styles*. To apply a font style, highlight the cell or cells you want to change and click the appropriate style button on the toolbar. To return the contents of the cell to a regular style, simply click the button again.

STEP-BY-STEP 2.6

1. Select **B3:D3**.

2. Click the arrow on the **Font** button on the Formatting toolbar. Scroll down and choose **Times New Roman** (or a similar font).

Careers

CAREERS IN SALES

Excel worksheets are helpful in the sales business. Salespeople use worksheets to find out what items are available in inventories. Worksheets are also used to keep track of customer orders.

STEP-BY-STEP 2.6 Continued

3. Click the arrow on the **Font Size** button on the Formatting toolbar and choose **8.**

4. Move the highlight to **A1.**

5. Open the **Format** menu and choose **Cells.** The Format Cells dialog box appears.

6. Click the **Font** tab, if necessary.

7. In the *Font list* box, scroll down and click **Times New Roman.**

8. In the *Font style* list box, click **Bold.**

9. In the *Size* list box, scroll down and click **14,** and then click **OK.**

10. Highlight **A2** and click the **Bold** button on the Formatting toolbar.

11. Bold the following cells using the same procedure: **A4, A7, A9, A17, A19,** and **A20.**

12. Widen column **A** to **18.**

13. Select the range **B6:D6,** and click the **Underline** button on the Formatting toolbar.

14. Underline **B16:D16.**

15. Select **A5:A6,** and click the **Italic** button on the Formatting toolbar.

16. Italicize **A10:A16.**

17. Save your work and leave the worksheet open for the next Step-by-Step.

Extra Challenge

Experiment by changing the font, size, and style of text in the worksheet. Use the **Undo** button to undo changes you make.

Color

Changing the color of cells or cell text is another way to add emphasis. To change the color of a cell using the toolbar, move the highlight to the cell and click the down arrow on the Fill Color button on the Formatting toolbar. A menu of colors appears, as shown in Figure 2-6. Click the color you want, and the cell is filled with that color.

FIGURE 2-6
Fill Color button color palette

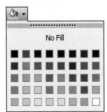

To change the color of text using the toolbar, move the highlight to the cell you want to change and click the down arrow on the Font Color button. A menu of colors appears as shown in Figure 2-7. Click the color you want, and the text is changed to your color choice.

FIGURE 2-7
Font Color button color palette

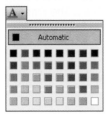

You can also change the color of cells and text using the Format Cells dialog box. Open the Format menu and choose Cells, and then click the Patterns tab. Click a color in the *Cell shading* section. You can also click the down arrow on the *Pattern* box and choose a pattern from the menu.

STEP-BY-STEP 2.7

1. Select **A1:D1** (which is now merged into one cell).

2. Click the arrow on the **Font Color** button. A menu of colors appears.

3. Click the **Green** square in the second row of the color menu. (As you point to each square, a ScreenTip displays the name of the color.) The title changes to green text.

4. With A1:D1 still selected, click the arrow on the **Fill Color** button. A menu of colors appears.

5. Click the **Gray-25%** square in the fourth row. The cell becomes light gray.

6. Save your work and leave the worksheet open for the next Step-by-Step.

> **Extra Challenge**
> Change the text and cell color of all the headings.

Borders

You can add emphasis to a cell by placing a border around its edges. You can place the border around the entire cell or only on certain sides of the cell. You can add borders in two ways. Highlight the cell and choose the Cells command on the Format menu. In the Format Cells dialog box, click the Border tab. Choose the border placement, style, and color (see Figure 2-8), and then click OK. In addition, you can insert a border quickly by clicking the down arrow on the Borders button on the Formatting toolbar. A box of border choices appears, as shown in Figure 2-9. Click one of the options to add the border you want.

> **Computer Concepts**
> Selecting cells and clicking the Borders button (instead of the down arrow) applies the border that was chosen using the toolbar.

FIGURE 2-8
Border tab in the Format Cells dialog box

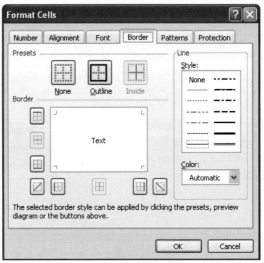

FIGURE 2-9
Borders button

STEP-BY-STEP 2.8

1. Select **A4**.

2. Open the **Format** menu and choose **Cells.** The Format Cells dialog box appears.

3. Click the **Border** tab.

4. In the *Style* box, click the thin, solid line (last choice in the first column).

5. In the *Presets* section, click the **Outline** button.

6. Click **OK.** When the highlight is moved, a border outlines the cell.

7. Highlight **A9.**

8. Click the arrow on the **Borders** button. From the menu that appears, choose **Outside Borders** (third choice on the last row).

9. Save your work and leave the worksheet open for the next Step-by-Step.

Cell Formats

Format affects the way data is shown in a cell. The default format is called *General*, which accommodates both text and numerical data. However, you can use several other formats described in Table 2-2. You can format a cell by highlighting the cell or range and choosing Cells on the Format menu. In the Format Cells dialog box, click the Number tab, select a format (see Figure 2-10) from the *Category* list, and then click OK. You can also apply formats for currency, percentage, commas, and the number of decimals by clicking the appropriate button on the toolbar.

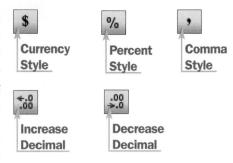

TABLE 2-2
Cell formats

FORMAT NAME	EXAMPLE	DISPLAY DESCRIPTION
General	1000	The default format; displays either text or numerical data as keyed
Number	1000.00	Displays numerical data with a fixed number of places to the right of the decimal point
Currency	$1,000.00	Displays numerical data preceded by a dollar sign
Accounting	$1,000.00 $ 9.00	Displays numerical data in a currency format that lines up the dollar sign and the decimal point vertically within a column
Date	6/8/02	Displays text and numerical data as dates
Time	7:38 PM	Displays text and numerical data as times
Percentage	35.2%	Displays numerical data followed by a percent sign
Fraction	35 7/8	Displays numerical data as fractional values
Scientific	1.00E+03	Displays numerical data in exponential notation
Text	45-875-33	Displays numerical data that will not be used for calculation, such as serial numbers containing hyphens
Special	79410	Displays numerical data that requires a specific format, such as ZIP codes or phone numbers
Custom	000.00.0	Displays formats designed by the user, including formats with commas or leading zeros

FIGURE 2-10
Number tab in the Format Cells dialog box

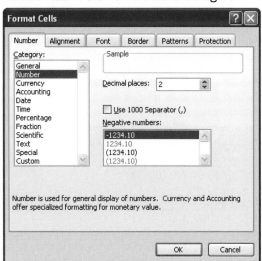

Using the Style Command

A *style* is a combination of formatting characteristics such as alignment, font, border, or pattern. When you apply a style to a cell or range, you apply all the formatting characteristics simultaneously, saving you the time of applying the formats individually. Excel has several styles that are predefined. You also can define custom styles of your own. To define a style, select a cell that has the combination of formats you want. Open the Format menu and choose Style. In the Style dialog box, enter a name for the style, click Add, and then click Close.

To apply a style, select the cells to be formatted. Open the Format menu, choose Style, and select the style you want from the *Style name* box. Click OK. To remove a style that has been applied, simply open the Format menu, choose Style, and choose Normal in the *Style name* box.

Painting Formats

Format painting allows you to copy the format of a worksheet cell without copying the contents of the cell. For example, after formatting one cell for a percentage, you may format other cells for a percentage by painting the format.

To paint a format, select a cell that has the format you want to copy. Click the Format Painter button on the Standard toolbar, and then select the cell or range of cells that you would like to format in the same manner.

> **Did You Know?**
>
> If you want to paint the same format to nonadjacent cells or ranges, double-click the Format Painter button on the toolbar and then select the desired cells or ranges.

S TEP-BY-STEP 2.9

1. Change the width of columns **B** through **D** using AutoFit Selection.

2. Select **B5:D5.**

STEP-BY-STEP 2.9 Continued

3. Open the **Format** menu and choose **Cells**. The Format Cells dialog box appears.

4. Click the **Number** tab.

5. Click **Currency** in the *Category* list box.

6. Click **OK.**

7. Highlight **B5.**

8. Click the **Format Painter** button on the toolbar.

9. Drag from **B20** to **D20**. The format of B20:D20 changes to currency format.

10. Select the range **B6:D19.**

11. Open the Format Cells dialog box and click the **Number** tab, if necessary.

12. Click **Number** in the *Category* list box.

13. Click the **Use 1000 Separator (,)** box so that it is checked.

14. Click **OK.** Deselect the range. Your screen should look similar to Figure 2-11.

15. Save, print, and close the file.

FIGURE 2-11
By changing the appearance of a worksheet, you can make it easier to use

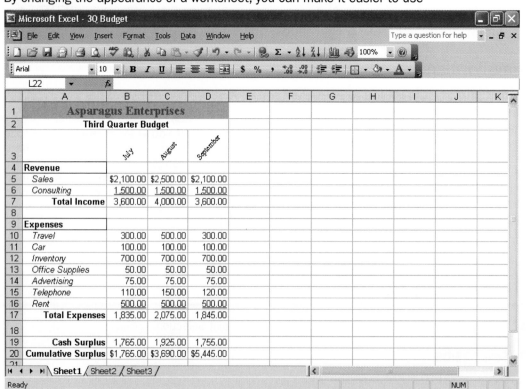

Clearing Cell Formats

You have learned how to change the appearance of a worksheet by bolding, italicizing, and underlining. You have also learned to add color and borders. You can remove the formats you apply to a cell or range of cells by selecting the cell or range, choosing Clear on the Edit menu, and then clicking Formats on the submenu. This removes the formatting *only*.

Applying an AutoFormat

An AutoFormat is a collection of font, patterns, and alignments that can be applied to a range of data. AutoFormats are applied by choosing the AutoFormat command on the Format menu.

STEP-BY-STEP 2.10

1. Open **IE Step2-10** from the data files.

2. Save the workbook as **4Q Budget**, followed by your initials.

3. Select **A3:D20.**

4. Open the **Format** menu and choose **AutoFormat.**

5. Click **Accounting 2** in the AutoFormat dialog box.

6. Click **OK.**

7. Click **A1.**

8. Open the **Edit** menu and choose **Clear,** and then click **Formats** on the submenu. Notice that applied formats have now been removed.

9. Click the arrow on the **Font Color** button and choose **Violet.**

10. Click the **Bold** button.

11. Click the arrow on the **Font Size** button and click **16.**

12. Select **A1:D1.**

13. Click the **Merge and Center** button.

14. Save, print, and close the file.

Finding and Replacing Cell Formats

In Lesson 1, you learned to find and replace data in a workbook. You can also find specific formats in a workbook and replace the format with another format. For example, you might want to replace all italicized text with bolded text, or you might want to replace a cell filled with one color with another color.

STEP-BY-STEP 2.11

1. Open **IE Step2-11** from the data files.

2. Save the workbook as **Basketball Standings,** followed by your initials.

3. Open the **Edit** menu and choose **Replace.**

4. If necessary, click the **Options** button to expand the Find and Replace dialog box. If there are any entries in the *Find what* or *Replace with* boxes, delete them now.

5. Click the arrow on the top **Format** button, and select **Choose Format From Cell.** The Find and Replace dialog box disappears and a pointer with a dropper appears.

6. Click **E5.** The Find and Replace dialog box reappears.

7. Click the lower **Format** button. The Replace Format dialog box appears.

8. Click the **Number** tab, if necessary.

9. Click **Number** in the *Category* box.

10. Key **3** in the *Decimal places* box.

11. Click **OK.**

12. Click **Replace All.** A message appears stating that 24 replacements have been made.

13. Click **OK.**

14. Click **Close** in the Find and Replace dialog box. Your screen should appear similar to Figure 2-12.

15. Save, print, and close the file.

FIGURE 2-12
Changing formats using the Find and Replace command

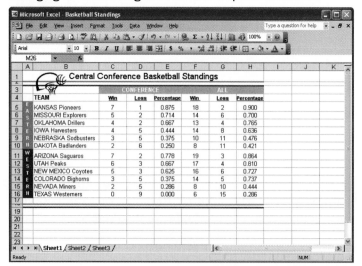

SUMMARY

In this lesson, you learned:

■ Worksheet columns can be widened to accommodate data that is too large to fit in the cell.

■ You can use wrap, rotate, indent, or align features to change the position of text within the cells of a worksheet.

■ The appearance of cell data can be changed to make the worksheet easier to read. Font, font size, and style (bolding, italicizing, and underlining) can be changed. Color and borders can also be added.

■ The appearance of the cell can be changed to accommodate data in a variety of numerical formats.

■ A combination of formatting characteristics such as alignment, font, border, or pattern can be applied by using the Styles command.

■ Format painting is used to copy the format of a worksheet cell without copying the contents of the cell.

■ Various collections of fonts, patterns, and alignments can be applied to a range of data by using the AutoFormat command.

■ The Find and Replace commands can be used to change cell formats.

VOCABULARY*Review*

Define the following terms:

AutoFormat	Rotated text	Wrapped text
Indented text	Style	

REVIEW *Questions*

TRUE/FALSE

Circle T if the statement is true or F if the statement is false.

T   F   1. A series of number signs (######) appearing in a cell indicates that the data is wider than the column.

T   F   2. Wrapped text will begin a new line within the cell of a worksheet when the data exceeds the width of a column.

T   F   3. The **Merge and Center** button will combine several cells into one cell and place the text in the middle of the merged cell.

T   F   4. You can place a border around the entire cell or only on certain sides of the cell.

T   F   5. The default format for data in a cell is *Text*.

WRITTEN QUESTIONS

Write a brief answer to the following questions.

1. What cell format(s) displays numerical data preceded by a dollar sign?

2. What is one way to let Excel determine the best width of a column?

3. What is one reason for rotating text?

4. What is the difference between the Fill Color and Font Color buttons?

5. What four cell alignment buttons are available on the Formatting toolbar?

PROJECTS

PROJECT 2-1

Write the letter of the cell format option in Column 2 that matches the worksheet format described in Column 1.

Column 1   **Column 2**

____ 1. Displays both text and numerical data as keyed

____ 2. Displays numerical data with a fixed amount of places to the right of the decimal point

____ 3. Displays numerical data preceded by a dollar sign; however, dollar signs and decimal points do not necessarily line up vertically within the column

____ 4. Displays numerical data with dollar signs and decimal points that line up vertically within a column

____ 5. Displays text and numerical data as dates

____ 6. Displays text and numerical data as times

____ 7. Displays numerical data followed by a percent sign

____ 8. Displays the value of 0.5 as 1/2

____ 9. Displays numerical data in exponential notation

____10. Displays numerical data that will not be used for calculation such as serial numbers containing hyphens

____11. Displays formats designed by the user

____12. Displays text in numerical format such as ZIP codes

A. Accounting

B. Time

C. Scientific

D. Fraction

E. Text

F. General

G. Date

H. Number

I. Percentage

J. Custom

K. Currency

L. Special

PROJECT 2-2

In this project, you improve the appearance of a worksheet to better present your results.

1. Open **IE Project2-2** from the data files.

2. Save the file as **Bird Census**, followed by your initials.

3. Bold cell **A1**.

4. Bold the range **B3:F3**.

5. Rotate the text in **B3:F3** by 45 degrees.

6. Change the width of columns **B** through **E** to **6**.

7. Bold the range **A13:F13**.

8. Italicize the range **A5:A11**.

9. Right-align **A13**.

10. Center-align the data in cells **B3** through **F3**.

11. Change the font size in **A1** to **14**.

12. Merge and center cells **A1:F1**.

13. Place a single, thin line border around the heading *Bird Census*.

14. Save, print, and close the file.

 PROJECT 2-3

The file *IE Project2-3* is a workbook containing the inventory of The Pager Shop. The headings and numerical data have already been keyed in the worksheet. You are to make the spreadsheet easier to read and more attractive.

1. Open **IE Project2-3** from the data files.

2. Save the file as **Pager Shop**, followed by your initials.

3. Center the text in cells **B4:D5**.

4. Indent the text in **A7:A10**.

5. Change the width of columns **B, C,** and **D** to **10**.

6. Bold **B12** and **D12**.

7. Change the size of text in **A1** to **12**. Merge and center **A1:D1**.

8. Change the size of text in **A2** to **11**. Merge and center **A2:D2**.

9. Change the color of cells **A1:D1** to green using the **Fill Color** button (use the Green in the second row).

10. Change the color of cells **A2:D2** to yellow (use the Light Yellow in the last row).

11. Format **C7:D10** and **D12** for **Currency** with two decimal places.

12. Change the color of text in **B12** and **D12** to the same green used to color the cells in **A1:D1**.

13. Save, print, and close the worksheet.

 PROJECT 2-4

A college student would like to estimate her mobile phone bill. Each time she makes a phone call, she notes the time of day and the number of minutes she spoke. She has prepared a worksheet to calculate the cost of the phone calls she has made. She must now format and print the worksheet.

1. Open **IE Project2-4** from the data files.

2. Save the file as **Phone Bill**, followed by your initials.

3. Key **Estimate of Mobile Phone Bill** in **A1**.

4. Bold **A1**.

5. Change the font size of the text in **A1** to **12**.

6. Merge and center **A1:D1**.

7. Change the cell color of the range **A1:D1** to blue.

8. Change the color of the text in **A1** to white.

9. Underline the contents of **B3:C3**.

10. Center the contents of **B3:C3**.

11. Format **C4:D7** for **Currency** with two decimal places.

12. Underline the contents of **D6**.

13. Widen column **A** to **17**.

14. Save, print, and close the file.

 PROJECT 2-5

A balance sheet is a corporate financial statement that lists the assets (resources available), liabilities (amounts owed), and equity (ownership in the company). *IE Project2-5* contains the balance sheet of Microsoft Corporation, which needs to be formatted so that it is easier to read.

1. Open **IE Project2-5** from the data files.

2. Save the file as **Microsoft**, followed by your initials.

3. Change the column width of column **C** to **5**.

4. Change the font size of **A1** to **12**.

5. Change the font size of **A2:A3** to **10**.

6. Bold **A1**.

7. Merge and center **A1:E1**, **A2:E2**, and **A3:E3**.

8. Bold **A5**, **A6**, **A20**, **D5**, **D6**, **D17**, and **D21**.

9. Underline **B8**, **B13**, **B19**, **E11**, **E19**, and **E20**.

10. Format **B7, E7, B20,** and **E21** for Accounting with a dollar ($) symbol and no decimal places.

11. Format **B8:B19, E8:E15,** and **E18:E20** for Accounting with no decimal places and no symbol.

12. Save, print, and close the file.

 PROJECT 2-6

The file *IE Project2-6* is a mileage chart between major cities in the United States. In this project you will make the data easier to read.

1. Open **IE Project2-6** from the data files.

2. Save the file as **Mileage,** followed by your initials.

3. Format **B2:O15** for **Number** with no decimal places and a comma separator.

4. Bold **B1:O1** and **A2:A15.**

5. Change the width of column **A** to **10.**

6. Rotate **B1:O1** to -75 degrees.

7. Change the width of columns **B** through **O** to **5.**

8. Save, print, and close the file.

CRITICAL*Thinking*

 ACTIVITY 2-1

To be useful, worksheets must be easy to view, both on screen and on the printed page. Identify ways to accomplish the following:

1. Emphasize certain portions of the worksheet.

2. Make text in the worksheet easier to read.

3. Distinguish one part of the worksheet from another.

4. Keep printed worksheet data from spilling onto another page.

 ACTIVITY 2-2

You have been spending a lot of time formatting the bottom rows of worksheets when you enter new data. Your friend tells you that you could save some time by "extending" the formats that you have already created. She did not have time to explain how extending works and so you are left curious.

Use the Help function in Excel to determine (1) how extended formatting works and (2) how to turn the extended formatting on or off.

ORGANIZING THE WORKSHEET

Data is not always useful in its orginal format. Data in a worksheet should be arranged so that it is easy to access and read. You can reorganize data by moving it to another part of the worksheet. You can also reduce data entry time by copying data to another part of the worksheet. If you decide that certain data is not needed you can delete entire rows or columns. If you would like to include additional information in a worksheet, you can insert another row or column.

Copying Data

When creating or enlarging a worksheet, you might want to use the same text or numbers in another part of the worksheet. Rather than key the same data over again, you can copy the data. There are several ways to copy data in a worksheet. In this lesson, you will learn to copy and paste, use the drag-and-drop method, and fill cells.

Hot Tip

Data copied to a cell replaces data already in that cell. Check your destination cells for existing data before copying.

Copy and Paste

To copy the contents of a cell or cells to the Clipboard, choose the Copy command on the Edit menu or click the Copy button on the Standard toolbar. A border appears around the selection, as shown in Figure 3-1. The Copy command does not affect the data in the original cell(s).

FIGURE 3-1
Copying data to another part of the worksheet

Next, place the highlight in the cell where you want the data to be copied. Then, open the Edit menu and choose Paste or click the Paste button on the toolbar. The copied data is pasted from the Clipboard to the cell or cells.

The data stored on the Clipboard remains there until it is replaced with new data. If you want to make multiple copies of that data, choose the Paste command again as many times as needed.

STEP-BY-STEP 3.1

1. Start Excel, if necessary, and open **IE Step3-1** from the data files.

2. Save the file as **Utility,** followed by your initials.

3. Select the range **A3:D6.**

4. Open the **Edit** menu and choose **Copy.** A border surrounds the range.

5. Highlight **A8.**

Hot Tip

If you are pasting a range of cells, it is not necessary to select the entire range; you need only highlight the upper-left corner of the range into which data will be pasted.

Computer Concepts

You might want to choose Paste Special instead of Paste if you want to paste only certain qualities of the data from the Clipboard. For example, you can choose to paste just formats or you can choose to paste the formula results rather than formulas.

STEP-BY-STEP 3.1 Continued

6. Open the **Edit** menu and choose **Paste.** The range of cells is copied from A3:D6 to A8:D11. (The border around A3:D6 continues to revolve until you start the next step.)

7. Key **Natural Gas** in **A7.**

8. Key **100 cf** in **B7** to indicate the amount of cubic feet in hundreds.

9. Key **Cost / 100 cf** in **C7** to indicate the cost per hundred cubic feet.

10. Copy cell **D2** and paste it to **D7.**

11. Save the worksheet and leave it open for the next Step-by-Step.

Using the Drag-and-Drop Method

You can quickly copy data using the drag-and-drop method. First highlight the cells you want to copy. Then, move the pointer to the top border of the highlighted cells. It changes shape from a cross to a four-headed arrow. While holding down the Ctrl key, drag the cells to a new location and release the mouse button. As you drag, a small plus sign (+) appears above the mouse pointer and a ScreenTip appears showing where the highlighted cells will be positioned when you release the mouse button.

STEP-BY-STEP 3.2

1. Select the range **A8:D11.**

2. Move the pointer to the top edge of cell A8 until it turns into an arrow pointer.

3. Press and hold down the **Ctrl** key. The plus sign appears.

4. Click and drag down until the pointer is in cell **A13** and the ScreenTip reads *A13:D16.*

5. Release the mouse button, and then the **Ctrl** key. The data is copied from A8:D11 to A13:D16.

6. Key **Water** in **A12.**

7. Key **1000 gallons** in **B12.**

8. Key **Cost / 1000 gal** in **C12** to indicate the cost per 1,000 gallons of water.

9. Use the drag-and-drop method to copy **D7** to **D12.**

STEP-BY-STEP 3.2 Continued

10. Bold the contents of cells **A7:C7** and **A12:C12**. Your screen should look similar to Figure 3-2.

FIGURE 3-2
Copying and pasting using the drag-and-drop method

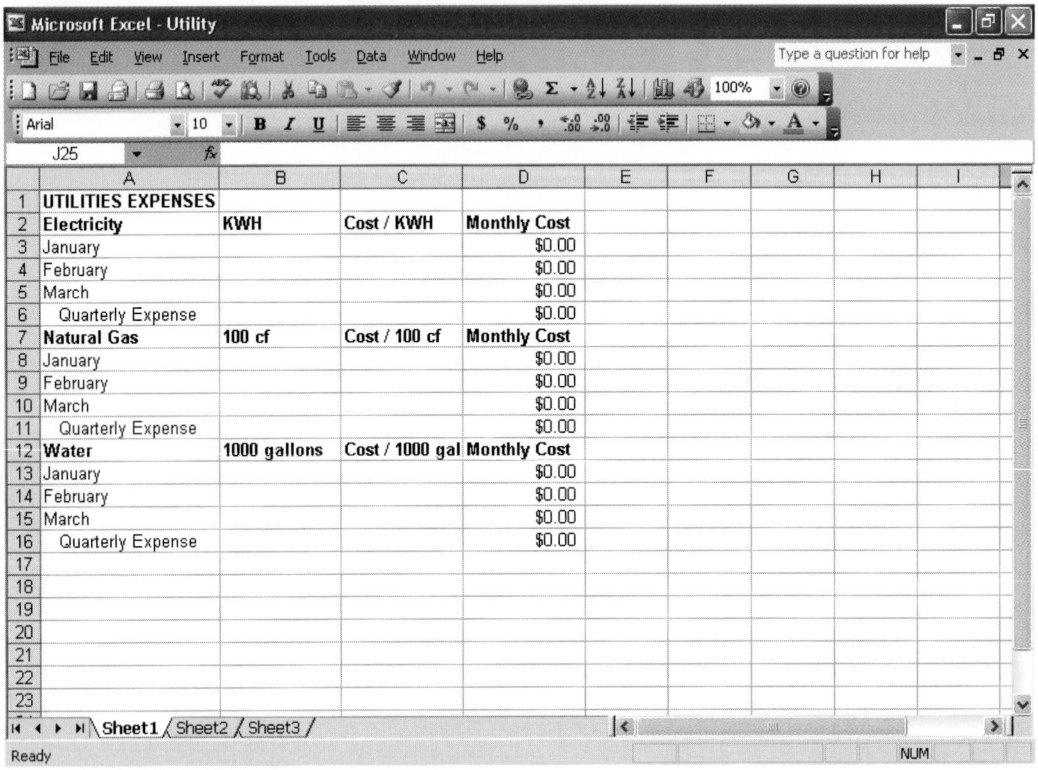

11. Save and leave the worksheet open for the next Step-by-Step.

Using the Fill Command

Filling copies data to adjacent cells. The Fill command on the Edit menu has several options on its submenu, including Down, Right, Up, and Left. Choose Down to copy data to the cell(s) directly below the original cell, as shown in Figure 3-3. Fill Up copies data into the cell(s) directly above the original cell.

Hot Tip

Sometimes you may want to fill in a series of numbers or dates. For example, you might want a column to contain months such as January, February, March, and so on. To fill cells with a series of data, begin by entering data in at least two cells. Then select the starting cells and drag the fill handle over the range of cells you want to fill.

FIGURE 3-3
Fill Down copies data to adjacent cells below the original cell

	A	B	C	D	E	F	G	H	I
1	UTILITIES EXPENSES								
2	Electricity	KWH	Cost / KWH	Monthly Cost					
3	January		$0.086	$0.00					
4	February		$0.086	$0.00					
5	March		$0.086	$0.00					
6	Quarterly Expense			$0.00					
7	Natural Gas	100 cf	Cost / 100 cf	Monthly Cost					
8	January			$0.00					
9	February			$0.00					
10	March			$0.00					
11	Quarterly Expense			$0.00					
12	Water	1000 gallons	Cost / 1000 gal	Monthly Cost					
13	January			$0.00					
14	February			$0.00					
15	March			$0.00					
16	Quarterly Expense			$0.00					
17									
18									
19									
20									
21									
22									
23									

When you fill to the right or to the left, the data is copied to the cell(s) to the right or left of the original cell. All options make multiple copies if more than one destination cell is selected. For example, the Down option can copy data to the next several cells below the original cell. Filling data is somewhat faster than copying and pasting because filling requires choosing only one command. However, filling can be used only when the destination cells are adjacent to the original cell.

STEP-BY-STEP 3.3

1. The cost of electricity for all three months is $0.086 per kilowatt hour. Enter **.086** in **C3**.

2. Drag from **C3** to **C5** to select the range to be filled.

3. Open the **Edit** menu, choose **Fill**, and then choose **Down** on the submenu. The contents of C3 are copied to cells C4 and C5.

4. Enter **.512** in **C8** to record the cost per 100 cubic feet of natural gas.

5. Use the **Fill Down** command to copy the data from **C8** to **C9** and **C10**.

6. Enter **.69** in **C13** to record the cost per 1000 gallons of water.

STEP-BY-STEP 3.3 Continued

7. Use the **Fill Down** command to copy the data from **C13** to **C14** and **C15**.

8. Enter the following utility usage data in the worksheet:

Electricity	**KWH**
January	**548**
February	**522**
March	**508**
Natural Gas	**100 cf**
January	**94**
February	**56**
March	**50**
Water	**1000 gallons**
January	**9**
February	**10**
March	**12**

9. After completing the worksheet, notice that the monthly costs have been calculated based on the data you entered. Your screen should look similar to Figure 3-4.

10. Save and leave the worksheet open for the next Step-by-Step.

FIGURE 3-4
Using the Fill Down command

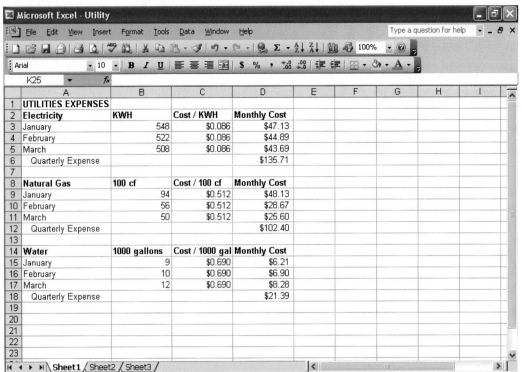

Moving Data

There may be times when you want to move data to a new location in a worksheet. You can move data two ways. The first method, cutting and pasting, is most appropriate when you want to move data to an area of the worksheet that is not currently in view on the screen. You've learned that the Copy command places a copy of the data on the Clipboard that can then be pasted to another area of the worksheet. The Cut

> **Computer Concepts**
>
> The drag-and-drop method is the easiest way to move data in a worksheet because you can do it without touching a key or using a menu.

command also places selected data on the Clipboard; however, the Cut command removes the data from its original position in the worksheet. After cutting data, place the highlight in the cell where you want the data to appear and open the Edit menu and choose Paste or click the Paste button on the toolbar.

You can also use the drag-and-drop method to move data in the worksheet. Simply select the cell or range you want to move and drag it to the new location. You do not need to hold down the Ctrl key as you do when you are copying data.

*S*TEP-BY-STEP 3.4

1. Select the range **A12:D16**.

2. Click the **Cut** button on the toolbar. A revolving border surrounds the data in the range.

3. Highlight **A14.**

4. Click the **Paste** button on the toolbar. The data moves to the range A14:D18.

5. Select the range **A7:D11.**

6. Move the pointer to the top edge of A7 until it turns into an arrow.

7. Click and drag down to **A8** until the ScreenTip reads *A8:D12*.

STEP-BY-STEP 3.4 Continued

8. Release the mouse button. The data moves to the range A8:D12. Your screen should look similar to Figure 3-5.

9. Save and leave the worksheet open for the next Step-by-Step.

FIGURE 3-5
The Cut command moves data to another part of the worksheet

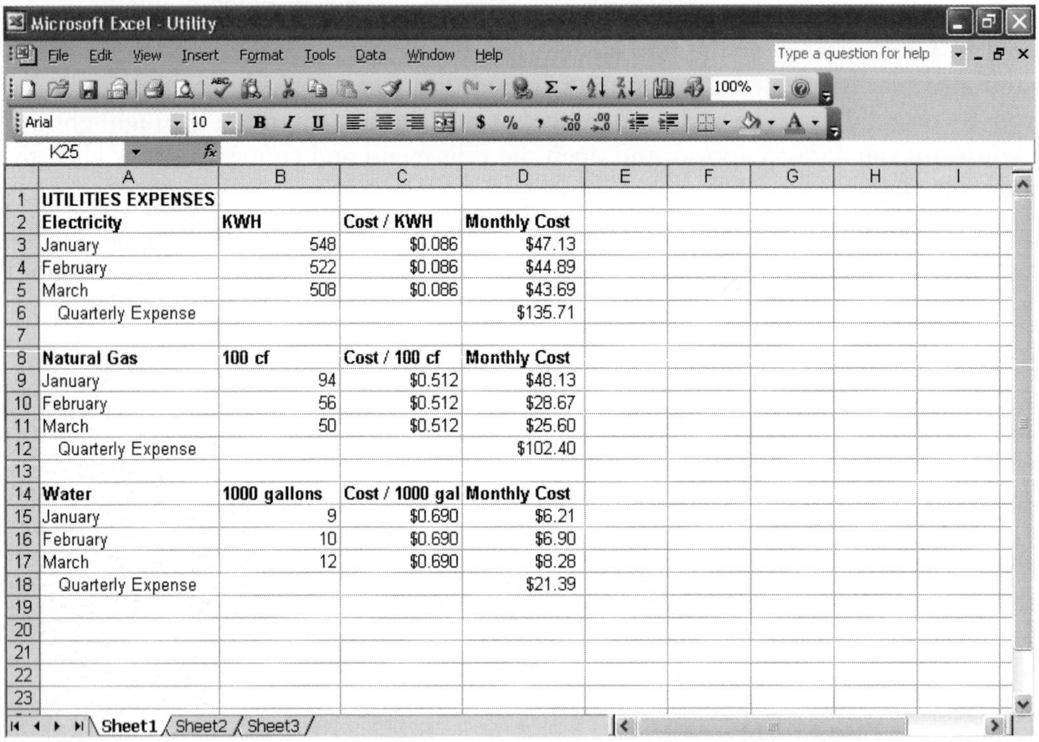

	A	B	C	D
1	**UTILITIES EXPENSES**			
2	**Electricity**	**KWH**	**Cost / KWH**	**Monthly Cost**
3	January	548	$0.086	$47.13
4	February	522	$0.086	$44.89
5	March	508	$0.086	$43.69
6	Quarterly Expense			$135.71
7				
8	**Natural Gas**	**100 cf**	**Cost / 100 cf**	**Monthly Cost**
9	January	94	$0.512	$48.13
10	February	56	$0.512	$28.67
11	March	50	$0.512	$25.60
12	Quarterly Expense			$102.40
13				
14	**Water**	**1000 gallons**	**Cost / 1000 gal**	**Monthly Cost**
15	January	9	$0.690	$6.21
16	February	10	$0.690	$6.90
17	March	12	$0.690	$8.28
18	Quarterly Expense			$21.39

Inserting and Deleting Rows and Columns

You can also change the appearance of a worksheet by adding and removing rows and/or columns. In the previous Step-by-Step, you could have inserted rows between the types of utilities rather than move existing data.

To insert a row, open the Insert menu and choose Rows. A row is added above the highlight. To insert a column, open the Insert menu and choose Columns. A column is added to the left of the highlight.

When entering a long column of data, you might discover that you omitted a number at or near the top of the worksheet column. Rather than move the data to make room for the omitted data, it might be easier to insert a cell. Open the Insert menu and choose Cells. The Insert dialog box opens. Designate whether you want existing cells to be shifted to the right or down.

When you want to delete a row or column, place the highlight in the row or column you want to delete. Then, open the Edit menu and choose Delete. The Delete dialog box appears, as shown in Figure 3-6. Choose Entire row to delete the row, or choose Entire column to delete the column.

FIGURE 3-6
Delete dialog box

The easiest way to delete a row is to click the row number to highlight the entire row. Then, open the Edit menu and choose Delete. This process skips the Delete dialog box. You can easily delete a column the same way. Simply click the column letter to highlight the entire column, and then choose the Delete command. The Delete command erases all the data contained in the row or column. If you accidentally delete the wrong column or row, you can choose Undo to restore the data. Use Redo to cancel the Undo action.

You can also delete an individual cell by using the Delete command on the Edit menu. Suppose that you accidentally entered a number twice while entering a long column of numbers. To eliminate the duplicate data, highlight the cell, open the Edit menu, and choose Delete. In the Delete dialog box (see Figure 3-6), click Shift cells up and then click OK. The cell is removed and the data in the cell below it is moved up one cell.

S TEP-BY-STEP 3.5

1. Highlight any cell in row **2**.

2. Open the **Insert** menu and choose **Rows**. Excel inserts a new, blank row 2. The original row 2 becomes row 3.

3. Highlight any cell in column **B**.

4. Open the **Insert** menu and choose **Columns.** A blank column appears as column B. The original column B becomes column C.

 Careers in Management

Business managers use Excel worksheets in a variety of ways. For example, human resource managers use spreadsheets to conduct performance reviews and keep track of employee records. Production managers use spreadsheets to track machine production efficiency and to keep machine maintenance records.

STEP-BY-STEP 3.5 Continued

5. Enter **Date Paid** in **B3**. Notice that it is automatically formatted like the other headings in that row.

6. Highlight any cell in column **B.**

7. Open the **Edit** menu and choose **Delete**. The Delete dialog box appears as shown in Figure 3-6.

8. Click **Entire column** and click **OK.**

9. Click the row **3** number (left of *Electricity*). The entire row is selected.

10. Open the **Edit** menu and choose **Delete.** Row 3 is deleted.

11. Click the **Undo** button on the toolbar. The row is restored.

12. Highlight **B17.**

13. Open the **Insert** menu and choose **Cells.**

14. Click **Shift cells down** and click **OK.** The data in B17:B18 is shifted to B18:B19.

15. Highlight **B17** if it is not currrently selected, open the **Edit** menu, and choose **Delete.**

16. Click **Shift cells up** and click **OK.** The data in B18:B19 is shifted back to B17:B18.

17. Save and leave the worksheet open for the next Step-by-Step.

Freezing Titles

Often a worksheet can become so large that it is difficult to view the entire worksheet on the screen. As you scroll to other parts of the worksheet, titles at the top or side of the worksheet might disappear from the screen, making it difficult to identify the contents of particular columns. For example, the worksheet title *Utilities Expenses* in previous Step-by-Steps might have scrolled off the screen when you were working in the lower part of the worksheet.

Freezing keeps row or column titles on the screen no matter where you scroll in the worksheet. As shown in Figure 3-7, rows 1 and 2 are frozen so that when you scroll down, rows 3 through 13 are hidden. To freeze titles, place the highlight below the row you want to freeze or to the right of the column you want to freeze. Then, select Freeze Panes on the Window menu. All rows above the highlight and columns to the left of the highlight are frozen. Frozen titles are indicated by a darkened gridline that separates the frozen portion of the worksheet from the unfrozen portion. To unfreeze a row or column title, open the Window menu and choose Unfreeze Panes; the darkened gridline disappears and the titles are unfrozen.

FIGURE 3-7
Freezing titles

	A	B	C	D	E	F	G	H	I
1	UTILITIES EXPENSES								
2		Units Used	Unit Cost	Billed Amount					
14									
15	Water	1000 gallons	Cost / 1000 gal	Monthly Cost					
16	January	9	$0.690	$6.21					
17	February	10	$0.690	$6.90					
18	March	12	$0.690	$8.28					
19	Quarterly Expense			$21.39					

Microsoft Excel - Utility — A14

Sheet1 / Sheet2 / Sheet3

Splitting Workbook Screens

You might want to view different parts of a large worksheet at the same time. *Splitting* divides the screen into two or four parts. Splitting is particularly useful when you want to copy data from one area to another in a large worksheet. You can click and move within one part and continue to view the other part or parts. You can split the screen two ways:

■ To split the screen horizontally, select a *row*, open the Window menu, and choose Split.

■ To split the screen vertically, select a *column*, open the Window menu, and choose Split.

STEP-BY-STEP 3.6

1. Enter the following column titles into the designated cells:

Cell	Column Title
B2	**Units Used**
C2	**Unit Cost**
D2	**Billed Amount**

2. Underline and bold the contents of **B2**, **C2**, and **D2**.

3. Highlight **A3**.

STEP-BY-STEP 3.6 Continued

4. Open the **Window** menu and choose **Freeze Panes.** The title and column headings in rows 1 and 2 are now frozen. A darkened gridline appears between rows 2 and 3.

5. Scroll to the lower part of the worksheet to highlight cell **D19.** You will notice that the column headings remain at the top of the screen no matter where you move.

6. Open the **Window** menu and choose **Unfreeze Panes.** The title and column headings are no longer frozen.

7. Select row **15** by clicking to the right of the row number.

8. Open the **Window** menu and choose **Split.** A split bar appears.

9. Click in the lower screen and scroll up as high as possible. Notice that the same part of the workbook appears in both the top and bottom half of the screen.

10. Double-click the split bar. The split is removed.

11. Save and leave the worksheet open for the next Step-by-Step.

Printing Options

In Lessons 1 and 2, you printed a worksheet using the default settings. There are, however, other options for printing parts of a worksheet or changing the way a worksheet prints.

Printing Options in the Print Dialog Box

You can print part of a worksheet using the Print command. To define the part of the worksheet you want to print, select the range to be printed, open the File menu, and choose Print. In the Print dialog box (see Figure 3-8), click Selection in the *Print what* section.

FIGURE 3-8
Print dialog box

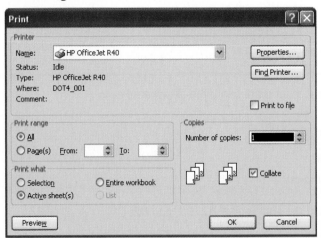

You can also choose to print the active sheet(s) or the entire workbook. In addition, the Print dialog box lets you choose the number of copies to print. The Page range options let you specify whether you want to print all pages of the worksheet or certain pages.

Setting Page Breaks

If awkward breaks occur in a worksheet that prints on more than one page, you can manually set where the page breaks occur. To force a page break above a selected cell, open the Insert menu and choose Page Break. To remove a page break, select a cell below the page break and then choose Remove Page Break on the Insert menu.

Designing the Printed Page

The Page Setup command on the File menu allows you to set page margins and page lengths and widths, designate page numbers, and determine whether column letters, row numbers, and gridlines should be printed. The Page Setup dialog box contains four tabbed sections, shown in Figure 3-9. These sections are discussed below.

FIGURE 3-9
Page Setup dialog box

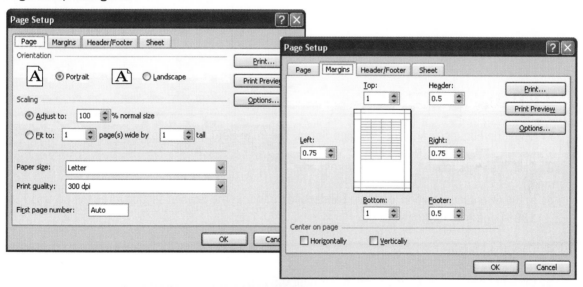

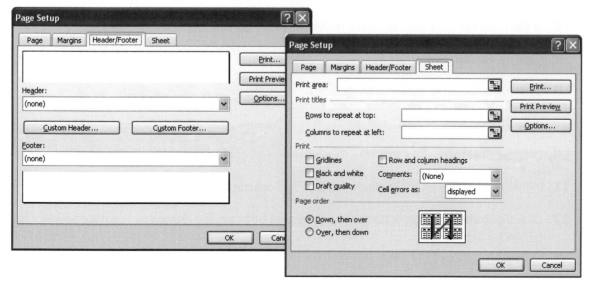

■ **Page.** Page orientation (portrait or landscape), scaling, paper size, and print quality are designated under the **Page** tab. In addition, you can designate the page number of the first page of the worksheet.

■ **Margins.** The Margins tab lets you change the margins of the printed page by keying the margin size in the appropriate box. You can also choose to center the worksheet horizontally and/or vertically on the page.

■ **Header/Footer.** On the Header/Footer tab, you can key text to be printed at the top and bottom of each page.

■ **Sheet.** On the Sheet tab, you can set the print area and title of the worksheet. You can also choose whether gridlines, row headings, and column headings are printed.

> **Did You Know?**
>
> Sometimes you might want to print the same worksheet for different people with different information needs. A custom view will save print settings so that you can convert the spreadsheet to the view desired. To create a custom view, specify the page setup and print settings. Then, select **Custom Views** on the **View** menu. Click **Add** in the Custom Views dialog box, and then key the name for the custom view. Click **OK** to save the view format and settings. You can apply the customized view at any time by opening the Custom Views dialog box, selecting the view you want, and then clicking **Show**.

S TEP-BY-STEP 3.7

1. Open the **File** menu and choose **Page Setup.** The Page Setup dialog box appears.

2. Click the **Page** tab if it is not chosen already.

3. In the *Orientation* section, click the **Landscape** button. In the *Scaling* section, click the up arrow until **130** appears in the **Adjust to** box.

4. Click the **Margins** tab.

5. Click the down arrow on the **Bottom** box until **0.5** appears.

6. In the *Center on page* section, check **Horizontally** and **Vertically.**

7. Click the **Header/Footer** tab.

8. Click the down arrow in the **Header** text box.

9. Click **Utilityxxx.xls, Page 1** (in which xxx is your initials)**.**

10. Click the **Sheet** tab.

11. In the *Print* section, check **Gridlines** and **Row and column headings.**

12. Click the **Collapse Dialog** button on the **Print area** text box. The dialog box is collapsed and the worksheet is active.

STEP-BY-STEP 3.7 Continued

13. Select **A1:D19**.

14. Click the **Expand Dialog** button at the right side of the **Page Setup - Print area** dialog box. The Page Setup dialog box expands and *$A$1:$D$19* appears in the *Print area* text box.

15. Click **OK**.

16. Save and leave the worksheet open for the next Step-by-Step.

Previewing a Worksheet before Printing

The Print Preview command shows how your printed pages will appear before you actually print them. To access the Print Preview screen (see Figure 3-10), open the File menu and choose Print Preview or click the Print Preview button on the toolbar.

FIGURE 3-10
Print Preview screen

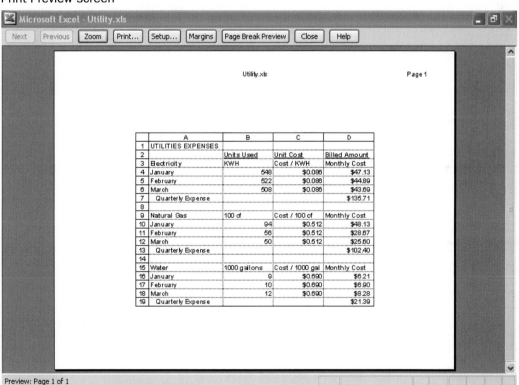

The buttons across the top of the screen provide options for viewing your worksheet. Choose Next and Previous to see other pages of your worksheet. Use the Zoom button or click the mouse pointer (which automatically turns into a magnifying glass in Print Preview) anywhere on the page to get a magnified view. Click the Margins button to change the margins of the worksheet, or click the Setup button to go to the Page Setup dialog box discussed earlier. Click Page Break Preview to adjust the page breaks and control what appears on each page when the worksheet is printed. When you have finished previewing the printed pages, you can return to the worksheet by choosing Close, or print the worksheet by choosing the Print button.

STEP-BY-STEP 3.8

1. Click the **Print Preview** button on the toolbar. The Print Preview screen appears, as shown in Figure 3-10.

2. Click the **Zoom** button. A portion of the previewed page becomes larger so that it can be examined in more detail.

3. Click **Setup**.

4. Click the **Sheet** tab, if it is not open already.

5. In the *Print* box, click the **Gridlines** box and the **Row and column headings** box to remove the check marks.

6. Click **OK**.

7. Click the **Print** button. The Print dialog box appears.

8. Print the active sheet by clicking **OK**.

9. Save and close the file.

> **Extra Challenge**
>
> Use the formatting commands you learned in Lesson 2 to make the spreadsheet more attractive.

Checking Spelling on a Worksheet

Excel has a dictionary tool that checks the spelling of words on a worksheet. Excel uses the same dictionary that is available in Microsoft Word. To spell-check a worksheet, select the Spelling command on the Tools menu, or click the Spelling button on the Formatting toolbar.

STEP-BY-STEP 3.9

1. Open **IE Step3-9** from the data files, and save it as **Currency Conversion,** followed by your initials.

2. Click the **Spelling** button on the Standard toolbar. The Spelling dialog box appears. The Spelling tool has correctly identified *Agentina* as a misspelled word and has offered several suggestions for change.

3. Click **Argentina** in the *Suggestions* box. Then, click **Change**. The Spelling tool corrects the spelling and moves to the next word that is misspelled (*Koria*).

4. Click **Korea**, and then click **Change.**

5. Next, the Spelling tool identifies *Krona* as a misspelled word. However, Krona is the correct spelling of the Swedish currency. (The term is identified as "Not in dictionary" because it is not a commonly used English word.)

> **Internet**
>
> The *Currency Conversion* file contains conversion rates for several countries. Currency exchange rates change on a daily basis. Search the Internet for current rates and replace the rates that are currently in the file.

STEP-BY-STEP 3.9 Continued

6. Click **Ignore All.** A dialog box indicating that the spelling check is complete appears. Click **OK.** Your screen appears similar to Figure 3-11.

7. Save, print, and close the file.

FIGURE 3-11
Using the spell check tool

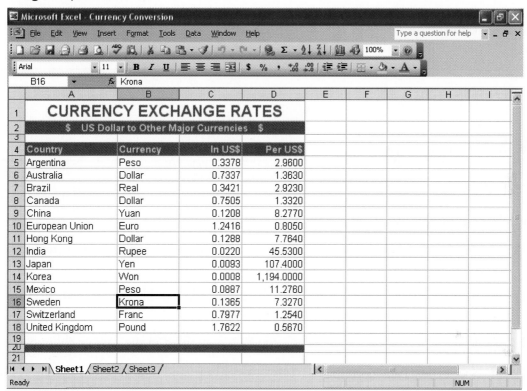

SUMMARY

In this lesson, you learned:

■ The data in a worksheet can be moved or copied to another location by using the Cut, Copy, Paste, and Fill commands on the Edit menu. These commands save time by eliminating the need to rekey large quantities of data. The drag-and-drop method can also be used to copy and move data in worksheets.

■ Inserting or deleting rows and columns can change the appearance of the worksheet. When a worksheet becomes large, the column or row titles will disappear from the screen as you scroll to other parts of the worksheet. You can keep the titles on the screen at all times by freezing them.

■ You can designate a portion of the worksheet to print using the Selection option in the Print dialog box. The Page Setup command controls the page size and the margins that will be used when printing. To view the worksheet as it will appear before actually printing it, use the Print Preview command.

■ You can check the spelling of words in a worksheet by using the Spelling command on the Tools menu.

VOCABULARY *Review*

Define the following terms:

| Filling | Freezing | Splitting |

REVIEW *Questions*

TRUE/FALSE

Circle T if the statement is true or F if the statement is false.

T F 1. If you copy data to cells already containing data, the existing data is replaced by the copied data.

T F 2. The Fill commands are available only if you are copying data to cells that are adjacent to the original cell.

T F 3. Deleting a row or column erases the data contained in the row or column.

T F 4. The Freeze Panes command freezes rows above and columns to the right of the highlight.

T F 5. You can preview a worksheet before printing by clicking the Print Preview button on the toolbar, or by choosing the Print Preview command on the File menu.

WRITTEN QUESTIONS

Write a brief answer to the following questions.

1. What key do you press to copy data using the drag-and-drop method?

2. How do you make multiple copies of data that has been copied to the Clipboard?

3. What should you do if you accidentally delete a column or row?

4. What command keeps the titles of a worksheet on the screen no matter where the highlight is moved?

5. Which menu contains the Spelling command?

PROJECTS

PROJECT 3-1

Match the correct command in Column 2 you would use to execute the action in Column 1.

Column 1

_____ 1. You are tired of keying repetitive data

_____ 2. A portion of the worksheet would be more useful in another area of the worksheet.

_____ 3. You forgot to key a row of data in the middle of the worksheet.

_____ 4. You no longer need a certain column in the worksheet.

_____ 5. Column headings cannot be viewed on the screen when you are working in the lower part of the worksheet.

_____ 6. You want to be sure that all words are spelled correctly in the worksheet.

_____ 7. Your boss would rather not view your worksheet on the screen and has requested a copy on paper.

_____ 8. You would like to print only the selected area of a worksheet.

Column 2

A. Print command or Print button

B. Fill command or Copy command

C. Rows or Columns command

D. Spelling command

E. Cut command, Paste command

F. Selection option in the Print dialog box

G. Delete command

H. Freeze Panes command

PROJECT 3-2

IE Project3-2 contains a list of assets of Pelican Retail Stores. Perform the following operations to make the worksheet more useful to the reader.

1. Open **IE Project3-2** from the data files.

2. Save the file as **Pelican Stores**, followed by your initials.

3. Insert a column to the left of column **B**.

4. Change the width of column **A** to **45**.

5. Move the contents of **D4:D17** to **B4:B17**.

6. Change the width of columns **B** and **C** to **10**.

7. Insert a row above row **4**.

8. Indent the contents of **A11**, **A15**, and **A18**.

9. Underline the contents of **B5:C5**.

10. Save, print, and close the file.

PROJECT 3-3

IE Project3-3 is a list of countries that trade with the United States. Because the spelling of some countries is complicated, you would like to check the spelling of the words in the worksheet.

1. Open **IE Project3-3** from the data files.

2. Save the file as **Import**, followed by your initials.

3. Freeze the column headings in rows 1 through 5. (*Hint*: Place the highlight in **A6** before choosing the Freeze Panes command.)

4. Check the spelling of the countries listed in the worksheet.

5. Change the printed page so that the worksheet prints in portrait orientation.

6. Adjust the scaling of the printed page so that it is 80% of its original size.

7. Change the printed page so that the top and bottom margins are 0.5 inch.

8. Save, print, and close the file.

PROJECT 3-4

The file *IE Project3-4* accounts for the inventory purchases of a small office supply store. The worksheet is not currently organized by suppliers of the inventory.

1. Open **IE Project3-4** from the data files.

2. Save the file as **Supply Inventory**, followed by your initials.

3. Organize the worksheet so that it looks like the following table. The new worksheet should have inventory items organized by supplier, with proper headings inserted. Some of the data is out of order and needs to be moved. Remember to bold appropriate data.

Item	Ordering Code	Quantity
Mega Computer Manufacturers		
Mega X-39 Computers	X-39-25879	20
Mega X-40 Computers	X-40-25880	24
Mega X-41 Computers	X-41-25881	28
Xenon Paper Source		
Xenon Letter Size White Paper	LT-W-45822	70
Xenon Letter Size Color Paper	LT-C-45823	10
Xenon Legal Size White Paper	LG-W-45824	40
Xenon Legal Size Color Paper	LG-C-45825	5
MarkMaker Pen Co.		
MarkMaker Blue Ball Point Pens	MM-Bl-43677	120
MarkMaker Black Ball Point Pens	MM-Bk-43678	100
MarkMaker Red Ball Point Pens	MM-R-43679	30

4. The following inventory item has been accidentally excluded from the worksheet. Add the item by using the Fill Down command and then editing the copied data.

Item	Ordering Code	Quantity
MarkMaker Green Ball Point Pens	MM-G-43680	30

5. Delete the following items.

Item	Ordering Code	Quantity
Mega X-39 Computers	X-39-25879	20

6. Change the page orientation to landscape.

7. Save, print, and close the file.

 PROJECT 3-5

1. Open **IE Project3-5** from the data files.

2. Save the file as **Time Record,** followed by your initials.

3. Delete rows **4** and **5.**

4. Insert the following information on the time record. (*Note:* The AutoComplete function might automatically enter some of the work descriptions for you as you begin to enter the data. To accept the data as it appears, press **Enter.**)

Date	From	To	Admin.	Meetings	Phone	Work Description
9-Dec	8:15 AM	12:00 PM		1.00	2.75	Staff meeting and call clients
10-Dec	7:45 AM	11:30 AM	2.00		1.75	Paperwork and call clients
11-Dec	7:45 AM	11:30 AM			3.75	Call clients
13-Dec	8:00 AM	12:00 PM		2.00	2.00	Mail flyers and meet w/KF

5. Freeze headings above row **8.**

6. Insert a blank row above row 16. Insert the following information:

Date	From	To	Admin. Meetings	Phone	Work Description
12-Dec	7:45 AM	11:30 AM	2.00	1.75	Paperwork and call clients

7. Copy **D15** to **D16.**

8. Preview the worksheet and zoom in to see the total hours worked.

9. Change the orientation of the worksheet to landscape. Center horizontally and vertically on the page.

10. Save, print, and close the worksheet.

 PROJECT 3-6

The file *IE Project3-6* contains the grades of several students taking Biology 101 during the spring semester. The instructor has asked that you, the student assistant, help maintain the grade records of the class.

1. Open **IE Project3-6** from the data files.

2. Save the file as **Class Grades,** followed by your initials.

3. Merge and center **A1:H1.** Merge and center **A2:H2.**

4. Column A contains the last names of students in the class.
   A. Add a column between the current columns **A** and **B** to hold the first names of the students.
   B. Enter **First Name** in **B3** of the new column.
   C. Enter the following names in the new column you created:

Row	Entry
4	Ashley
5	Kevin
6	Cindy
7	Raul
8	Haley
9	Cameron

5. Preview the worksheet.

6. Change the worksheet to landscape orientation and center it both vertically and horizontally on the page.

7. Remove the header.

8. Change the footer to read **Page 1.**

9. Save, print, and close the file.

 PROJECT 3-7

You are a member of the Booster Club, an organization that raises money to purchase sports equipment for the local high school. You have been allocated $1,210 to purchase sports equipment for the school. You prepare a worksheet to help calculate the cost of various purchases. (*Note:* The AutoComplete function might enter some of the data for you as you begin to key. To accept the data as it appears, press Enter.)

1. Open the file **IE Project3-7** from the data files.

2. Save the file as **Booster Club**, followed by your initials.

3. Bold and center the column headings in row **2**.

4. Insert a row above row **3**.

5. Freeze the column headings in row **2**.

6. Insert a row above row 8 and key **Bats** in cell **A8** (the new row).

7. Use the Fill Down command to copy the formula in **E4** to **E5:E11**. Do not copy the formula to E12.

8. Format the *Cost* (**D4:D11**) and *Total* (**E4:E12**) columns for currency with two decimal places.

9. Key the data for *Sport* and *Cost*, as given in the following table. Use the Fill Down command as needed to copy repetitive data. Widen the columns if necessary.

Item	Sport	Cost
Basketballs	Basketball	28
Hoops	Basketball	40
Backboards	Basketball	115
Softballs	Softball	5
Bats	Softball	30
Masks	Softball	35
Volleyballs	Volleyball	25
Nets	Volleyball	125

10. You have $1,210 to spend on equipment. The organization has requested you to purchase the following items. Any remaining cash should be used to purchase as many basketballs as possible.

Basketballs	5
Hoops	2
Backboards	2
Softballs	20
Bats	5
Masks	1
Volleyballs	7
Nets	1

11. Increase the number of basketballs and watch the dollar amount in the total. You should use $1,203.00 and have $7.00 left over.

12. Save, print, and close the file.

PROJECT 3-8

IE Project3-8 contains attendance data for a neighborhood swimming pool. Format the worksheet in a way that you find appealing. You can move data in the worksheet. You can also change the column width, color, alignment, borders, format, and font of the data. When you have finished, name and save the file as **Swimming Pool**, followed by your initials. Then print and close the file.

CRITICAL *Thinking*

 ACTIVITY 3-1

As a zoo employee, you have been asked to observe the behavior of a predatory cat during a three-day period. You are to record the number of minutes the animal displays certain behaviors during the time that the zoo is open to visitors. Set up a worksheet that can be used to record the number of minutes that the cat participates in these behaviors during each of the three days.

- Sleeping
- Eating
- Walking
- Sitting
- Playing

Make your worksheet easy to read by using bolded fonts, italicized fonts, varied alignment, and color.

WORKSHEET FORMULAS

OBJECTIVES

Upon completion of this lesson, you should be able to:

■ Enter and edit formulas.

■ Distinguish between relative, absolute, and mixed cell references.

■ Use the AutoSum button and the point-and-click method to enter formulas.

■ Preview a calculation.

■ Display formulas in the worksheet.

■ Perform immediate and delayed calculations.

Estimated Time: 2.5 hours

VOCABULARY

Absolute cell reference

Formulas

Mixed cell reference

Operand

Operator

Order of evaluation

Point-and-click method

Relative cell reference

What Are Formulas?

Worksheets can use numbers entered in certain cells to calculate values in other cells. The equations used to calculate values in a cell are known as *formulas*. Excel recognizes the contents of a cell as a formula when an equal sign (=) is the first character in the cell. For example, if the formula =8+6 is entered in cell B3, the value of 14 is displayed in B3. The formula bar displays the formula =8+6, as shown in Figure 4-1.

FIGURE 4-1
Formula appears in the formula bar and the result displays in the cell

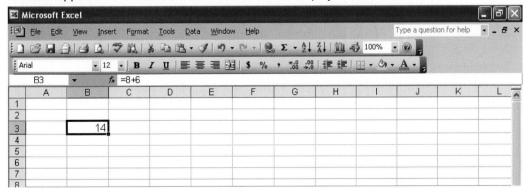

Structure of a Formula

A worksheet formula consists of two components: operands and operators. An *operand* is a number or cell reference used in formulas. You can key cell references in uppercase (A1) or lowercase (a1). An *operator* tells Excel what to do with the operands. For example, in the formula =B3+5, *B3* and *5* are operands. The plus sign (+) is an operator that tells Excel to add the value contained in cell B3 to the number 5. The operators used in formulas are shown in Table 4-1. After you have keyed the formula, enter it by pressing the Enter key or by clicking the Enter button on the formula bar.

> **Computer Concepts**
>
> As you enter cell references in the formula bar, the reference appears in a specific color. The cell referenced in the formula will be outlined in the same color. You can adjust the color-coded reference in the formula by moving or dragging the outlined cell in the worksheet.

TABLE 4-1
Formula operators

OPERATOR	OPERATION	EXAMPLE	MEANING
+	Addition	B5+C5	Adds the values in B5 and C5
–	Subtraction	C8–232	Subtracts 232 from the value in C8
*	Multiplication	D4*D5	Multiplies the value in D4 by the value in D5
/	Division	E6/4	Divides the value in E6 by 4
^	Exponentiation	B3^3	Raises the value in B3 to the third power

STEP-BY-STEP 4.1

1. Open **IE Step4-1** from the data files.

2. Save the worksheet as **Calculate,** followed by your initials.

3. Highlight **C3**.

4. Key **=A3+B3** and press **Enter.** The formula result *380* appears in the cell.

5. In **C4**, key **=A4–B4** and press **Enter.**

6. In **C5**, key **=A5*B5** and press **Enter.**

7. In **C6**, key **=A6/B6** and press **Enter.**

8. Check your results by comparing them to Figure 4-2. Save the worksheet and leave the file open for the next Step-by-Step.

FIGURE 4-2
Entering formulas

	A	B	C	D	E	F	G	H	I	J	K	L
1												
2												
3	141	239	380									
4	263	509	-246									
5	58	325	18850									
6	800	400	2									
7												
8												

Order of Evaluation

Formulas containing more than one operator are called complex formulas. For example, the formula =C3*C4+5 will perform both multiplication and addition to calculate the value in the cell. The sequence used to calculate the value of a formula is called the *order of evaluation*.

Formulas are evaluated in the following order:

1. Contents within parentheses are evaluated first. You can use as many pairs of parentheses as you want. The innermost set of parentheses is evaluated first.

2. Mathematical operators are evaluated in order of priority, as shown in Table 4-2.

3. Equations are evaluated from left to right if two or more operators have the same order of evaluation. For example, in the formula =20–15–2, the number 15 would be subtracted from 20; then 2 would be subtracted from the difference (5).

TABLE 4-2
Order of evaluation priority

ORDER OF EVALUATION	OPERATOR	SYMBOL
First	Exponentiation	^
Second	Positive or negative	+ or –
Third	Multiplication or division	* or /
Fourth	Addition or subtraction	+ or –

STEP-BY-STEP 4.2

1. In **D3**, key **=(A3+B3)*20**. The values in A3 and B3 will be added, and then the result will be multiplied by 20.

2. Press **Enter**. The resulting value is 7600.

STEP-BY-STEP 4.2 Continued

3. You can see the importance of the parentheses in the order of evaluation by creating an identical formula without the parentheses. In **E3**, key **=A3+B3*20**, the same formula as in D3 but without the parentheses.

4. Press **Enter.** The resulting value is 4921. This value differs from the value in D3 because Excel multiplied the value in B3 by 20 before adding the value in A3. In D3, the values in A3 and B3 were added together and the sum multiplied by 20.

5. Save the worksheet and leave it open for the next Step-by-Step.

Editing Formulas

Excel will not let you enter a formula with an incorrect structure. If you attempt to do so, a dialog box explaining the error appears. For example, if you enter a formula with an opening parenthesis but no closing parenthesis, a message box describing the error and how to correct the error appears. You can then correct the formula by editing it in the formula bar. You can also edit formulas directly in the worksheet cell. Highlight the cell and then press the Edit key (F2), or double-click the cell and move the insertion point as needed to edit the entry.

STEP-BY-STEP 4.3

1. Move the highlight to **E3.** The formula is shown in the formula bar.

2. Place the insertion point after the **=** in the formula bar and click.

3. Key **(.**

4. Press **Enter.**

5. Choose **No** so that you can correct the error yourself. A dialog box describing the error appears.

6. Click **OK.**

7. Move the insertion point in the formula bar between the 3 and the *.

8. Key **).**

9. Press **Enter.** The value changes to 7600.

10. Save the file and leave it open for the next Step-by-Step.

Relative, Absolute, and Mixed Cell References

Three types of cell references are used to create formulas: relative, absolute, and mixed. A *relative cell reference* adjusts to its new location when copied or moved. For example, in Figure 4-3, the formula =A3+A4 is copied from A5 to B5 and the formula changes to =B3+B4. In other words, this formula is instructing Excel to add the two cells directly above. When the formula is copied or moved, the cell references change; but the operators remain the same.

FIGURE 4-3
Copying a formula with relative cell references

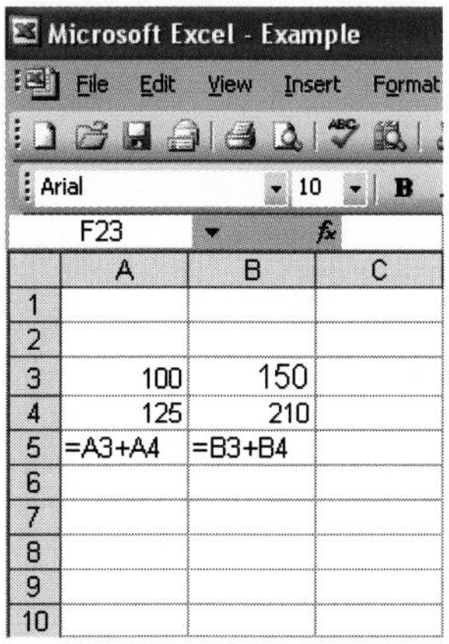

Absolute cell references do not change when moved or copied to a new cell. To create an absolute reference, you insert a dollar sign ($) before the column letter and/or the row number of the cell reference that you want to stay the same. For example, in Figure 4-4, the formula =$A$3+$A$4 is copied from A5 to B7 and the formula remains the same in the new location.

FIGURE 4-4
Copying a formula with absolute cell references

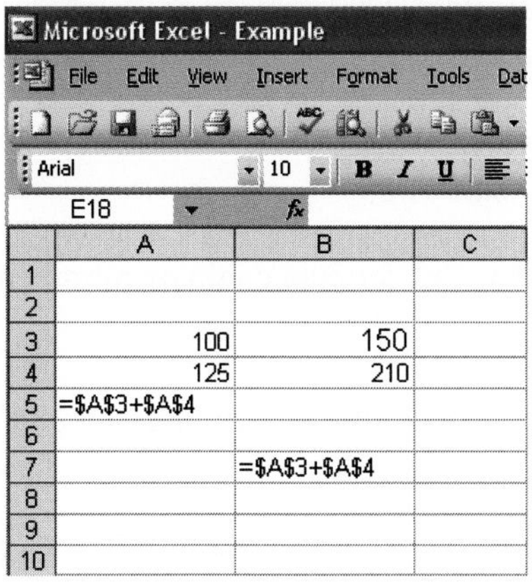

Cell references containing both relative and absolute references are called *mixed cell references*. When formulas with mixed cell references are copied or moved, the row or column references preceded by a dollar sign will not change; the row or column references not preceded by a dollar sign will adjust relative to the cell to which they are moved. As shown in Figure 4-5, when the formula =A$3+A$4 is copied from A5 to B7, the formula changes to =B$3+B$4.

FIGURE 4-5
Copying a formula with mixed cell references

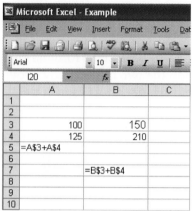

STEP-BY-STEP 4.4

1. Place the highlight in **D3.** The formula =(A3+B3)*20 (shown in the formula bar) contains only relative cell references.

2. Use **Fill Down** to copy the formula in **D3** to **D4.**

3. Place the highlight in **D4.** The value in D4 is 15440 and the formula in the formula bar is =(A4+B4)*20. The operators in the formula remain the same, but the relative cell references changed to reflect a change in the location of the formula.

4. Click **D5** and enter **=$A$3*($B$3-200).** The value in D5 is 5499. The formula contains absolute cell references, which are indicated by the dollar signs that precede row and column references.

5. Copy the formula in **D5** to **D6.** The value in D6 is 5499, the same as in D5.

6. Move the highlight to **D5** and look at the formula in the formula bar. Now move the highlight to **D6** and look at the formula. Because the formula in D5 contains absolute cell references, the formula is exactly the same as the formula in D6.

7. Click **E4** and enter **=$A$4+B4.** This formula contains mixed cell references (relative and absolute). The value in E4 is 772.

8. Copy the formula in **E4** to **E5.** Notice the relative reference B4 changed to B5, but the absolute reference to A4 stayed the same. The value in E5 is 588.

9. Copy the formula in **E5** to **F5.** Again, notice the relative reference changed from B5 to C5. The absolute reference to A4 stayed the same. The value in F5 is 19113.

10. Save, print, and close the file.

Creating Formulas Quickly

You have already learned how to create formulas by keying the formula or editing existing formulas. In this section, you learn to create formulas quickly by using the point-and-click method and the AutoSum feature.

Point-and-Click Method

Earlier, you constructed formulas by keying the entire formula in the cell of the worksheet. You can include cell references in a formula more quickly by clicking on the cell rather than keying the reference. This is known as the *point-and-click method*. The point-and-click method is particularly helpful when you have to enter long formulas that contain several cell references.

To use the point-and-click method, simply click the cell instead of keying the cell reference. For example, to enter the formula =A3+B3, highlight the cell that will contain the formula. Next, press =, click A3, press +, click B3, and press Enter.

STEP-BY-STEP 4.5

The manager of the Fruit and Fizz Shop would like to determine the total sales of juice and soda during the month, as well as to calculate the percentage of the total items sold for each type of juice and soda. Prices of individual servings are as follows:

	Large	Small
Juice	$1.50	$0.90
Soda	$0.80	$0.50

1. Open **IE Step4-5** from the data files.

2. Save the file as **Drinks**, followed by your initials.

3. Click **D6** and key **=(1.5***. (The price for a large juice is $1.50.)

4. Click **B6.** (You see a moving colored border around the cell, and the cell reference in the same color appears in the formula.)

5. Key **)+(.9***. (The price for a small juice is 90 cents.)

6. Click **C6.**

7. Key **)**.

8. Press **Enter.** The amount $567.00 appears in the cell.

9. Use **Fill Down** to copy the formula in **D6** to **D7** and **D8.** The value in D7 is $393.90. The value in D8 is $142.50.

10. Click **D9** and key **=(.8***. (The price for a large soda is 80 cents.)

11. Click **B9.**

STEP-BY-STEP 4.5 Continued

12. Key **)+(.5*.** (The price for a small soda is 50 cents.)

13. Click **C9.**

14. Key **)** and press **Enter.** The value in D9 is $282.20.

15. Use **Fill Down** to copy the formula in **D9** to **D10** and **D11.** Your screen should look similar to Figure 4-6.

16. Save and leave the worksheet open for the next Step-by-Step.

FIGURE 4-6
Inserting formulas using the point-and-click method

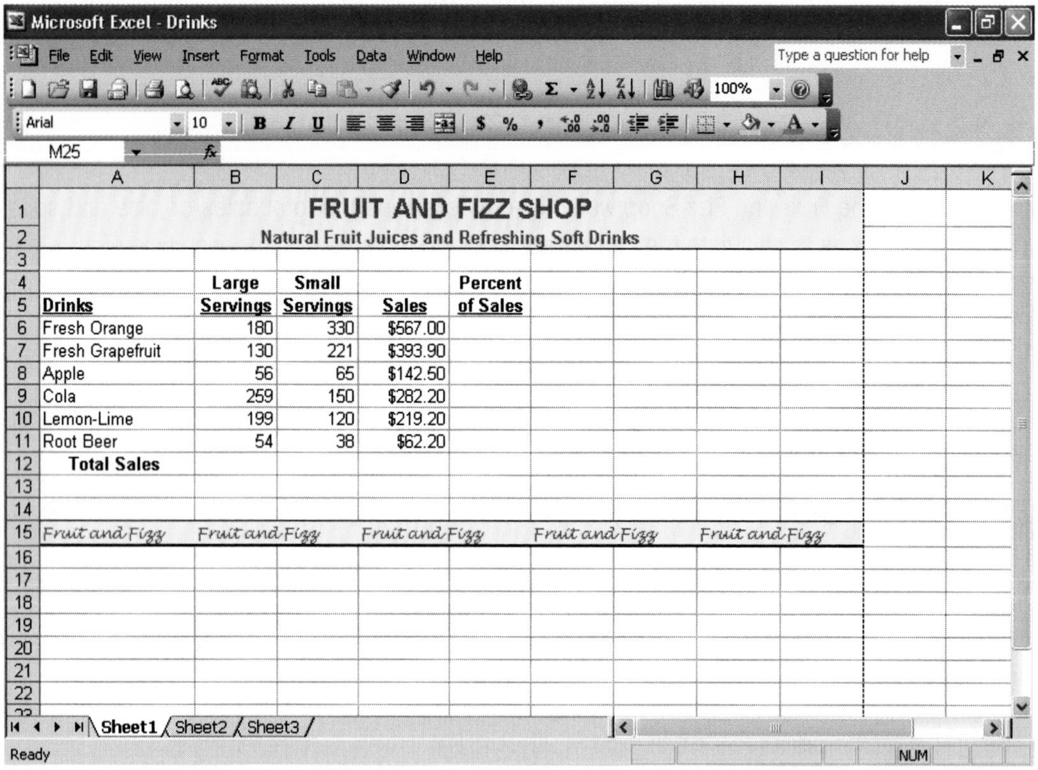

Using the AutoSum Feature

Worksheet users frequently need to sum long columns or rows of numbers. The AutoSum button on the Standard toolbar makes this operation simple. The AutoSum button is identified by the Greek letter *sigma* ($\sum$). To use AutoSum, place the highlight in the cell where you want the total to appear. Click the AutoSum button, and Excel scans the worksheet to determine the most logical column or row of adjacent cells containing numbers to sum. Excel then displays an outline around the range it has selected. This range is identified in the highlighted cell. If you prefer a range other than the one Excel selects, drag to select those cells. Press Enter to display the sum in the cell.

The sum of a range is indicated by a special formula in the formula bar called a *function* formula. For example, if the sum of the range D5:D17 is entered in a cell, the function formula will be =SUM(D5:D17). The SUM function is the most frequently used function formula. Function formulas are discussed in greater detail in the next lesson.

S TEP-BY-STEP 4.6

1. Highlight **D12**.

2. Click the **AutoSum** button. The range D6:D11 is outlined. Excel has correctly selected the range of cells you would like to sum. The formula =SUM(D6:D11) appears in the formula bar.

   Σ

3. Press **Enter.** D12 displays $1,667.00, the sum of the numbers in column D.

4. Highlight **E6**.

5. Press **=**.

6. Click **D6**.

7. Press **/**.

8. Key **$D$12** and press **Enter.**

9. Copy the formula in **E6** to **E7:E12**. Your screen should look similar to Figure 4-7.

10. Save and leave the worksheet open for the next Step-by-Step.

FIGURE 4-7
Using the AutoSum button

	Drinks	Large Servings	Small Servings	Sales	Percent of Sales
6	Fresh Orange	180	330	$567.00	34.0%
7	Fresh Grapefruit	130	221	$393.90	23.6%
8	Apple	56	65	$142.50	8.5%
9	Cola	259	150	$282.20	16.9%
10	Lemon-Lime	199	120	$219.20	13.1%
11	Root Beer	54	38	$62.20	3.7%
12	Total Sales			$1,667.00	100.0%

FRUIT AND FIZZ SHOP
Natural Fruit Juices and Refreshing Soft Drinks

Previewing a Calculation

You might want to determine a calculated amount from worksheet data before entering a formula. By using a feature called Auto Calculation, you can determine, for example, the number of entries within a range or the average of amounts in a range. To use Auto Calculation to determine the sum of data contained in a range, select the range and then right-click the status bar at the bottom of the screen. A menu appears. Click Sum, and the summation of data in the range appears in the status bar.

Hot Tip

Auto Calculation can also be used to determine the minimum or maximum value that lies within a range.

STEP-BY-STEP 4.7

1. Select the range **B6:C6**.

2. Right-click anywhere in the status bar. A menu appears.

3. If it is not already checked, click **Sum** so that a check mark appears. The number of large and small orange juices served, 510, appears in the status bar.

4. Select the range **B6:C11**. The total number of large and small drinks, 1,802, appears in the status bar. Click outside the range to deselect it and remain in this screen for the next Step-by-Step.

| None |
| Average |
| Count |
| Count Nums |
| Max |
| Min |
| ✓ Sum |

Formula Helpers

The Options dialog box, which you display by choosing Options on the Tools menu, contains several tabbed sections that define features in the worksheet. Two of the calculation features are described in the following sections.

Extra Challenge

Auto Calculation can be used to check the formula results. D12 contains a function formula that determines the sum of D6:D11. To check the results of the formula, right-click the status bar and click **Sum**. Then select **D6:D11**. The sum in the status bar should equal the value in D12.

Showing Formulas on the Worksheet

In previous Step-by-Steps, you viewed formulas in the formula bar or in the cell as you were keying the formula. Cells of the worksheet contain the values determined by formulas rather than the formulas themselves. When creating a worksheet containing many formulas, you might find it easier to organize formulas and detect formula errors when you can view all formulas at once. To do this, check the *Formulas* box in the *Window options* section on the View tab (see Figure 4-8). The formula results are replaced with the actual formulas. If a cell does not contain a formula, Excel displays the data entered in the cell. To redisplay formula results, click to remove the check mark from the *Formulas* box.

FIGURE 4-8
View tab in the Options dialog box

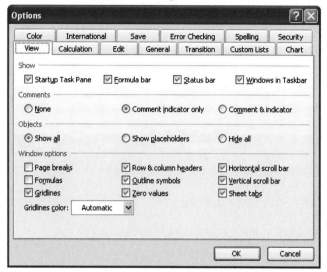

Delayed Calculations

Values in the worksheet are usually calculated as a new formula is entered, but you can also calculate the formula at a specified moment. Delayed calculation (also called manual calculation) can be useful when you are working with a large worksheet that will take longer than usual to calculate. You might also want to view the difference in a particular cell after you have made changes throughout the worksheet.

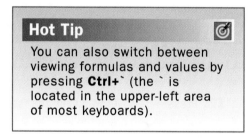

Hot Tip

You can also switch between viewing formulas and values by pressing **Ctrl+`** (the ` is located in the upper-left area of most keyboards).

To delay calculation, click the Manual button on the Calculation tab of the Options dialog box (see Figure 4-9) and then press F9 to start calculation. To return to automatic calculation, click the Automatic button in the *Calculation* section of the tab.

FIGURE 4-9
Calculation tab in the Options dialog box

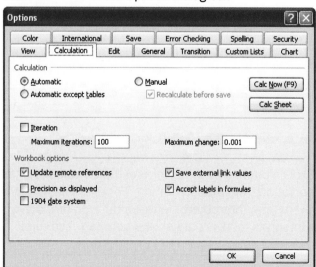

STEP-BY-STEP 4.8

1. Open the **Tools** menu and choose **Options**. The Options dialog box appears, as shown in Figure 4-8.

2. Click the **View** tab, if necessary.

3. In the *Window options* section, click the **Formulas** box so that a check mark appears.

4. Click **OK**. If the **Formula Auditing** toolbar appears, you may move or close it.

5. Scroll to the right so that columns D and E appear on the screen. All formulas are now visible.

6. Press **Ctrl+`**. Cells with formulas now show values again.

7. Open the **Tools** menu and choose **Options**.

8. Click the **Calculation** tab in the Options dialog box (see Figure 4-9).

9. Click the **Manual** button in the *Calculation* section.

10. Click **OK**. Calculation is now delayed.

11. Change the following values in the worksheet.
    a. In **B6**, key **182**.
    b. In **C7**, key **220**.
    c. In **C10**, key **125**.

12. Press **F9** while watching the screen. Calculations occur as you press the key. The total sales in cell D12 should be $1,671.60.

13. Access the Options dialog box and the **Calculation** tab.

14. Click the **Automatic** button in the *Calculation* section and click **OK**.

15. Change the page orientation to landscape.

16. Save, print, and close the file.

> **Extra Challenge**
>
> Open the **Drinks** workbook. The current number of large orange juices sold is 182. Determine how many large orange juices must be sold in order to achieve over $1,700 in sales by entering larger amounts in cell B6. When you have determined the amount, close the file.

Careers

Engineers use Excel worksheets to perform complex calculations in areas such as construction, transportation, and manufacturing. For example, Excel worksheets are used to fit equations to data, interpolate between data points, solve simultaneous equations, evaluate integrals, convert units, and compare economic alternatives.

SUMMARY

In this lesson, you learned:

■ Worksheet formulas perform calculations on values referenced in other cells of the worksheet.

■ Relative cell references adjust to a different location when copied or moved. Absolute cell references describe the same cell location in the worksheet regardless of where they are copied or moved. Mixed cell references contain both relative and absolute cell references.

■ Formulas can be created quickly by using the point-and-click method. With this method, you insert a cell reference by clicking the cell rather than keying its column letter and row number.

■ You can sum a group of cells quickly by using the AutoSum button on the Standard toolbar. This feature inserts the SUM function and determines the most likely range to be summed.

■ You can view the formulas instead of the formula results in a worksheet by making selections in the Options dialog box.

■ Calculation in a worksheet usually occurs as values or formulas are entered. You can delay calculation, however, until a time you specify by using the delayed (or manual) calculation feature available through the Options dialog box.

VOCABULARY *Review*

Define the following terms:

Absolute cell reference	Operand	Point-and-click method
Formulas	Operator	Relative cell reference
Mixed cell reference	Order of evaluation	

REVIEW *Questions*

TRUE/FALSE

Circle T if the statement is true or F if the statement is false.

T F 1. An operator is a number or cell reference used in formulas.

T F 2. In a complex formula, subtraction is performed before multiplication.

T F 3. Operations within parentheses are performed before operations outside parentheses in a formula.

T F 4. An absolute cell reference changes if the formula is copied or moved.

T F 5. Manual calculation is performed by pressing the F2 key.

WRITTEN QUESTIONS

Write a brief answer to the following questions.

1. Which operator has the highest priority in the order of evaluation in a worksheet formula?

2. What type of cell reference adjusts to its new location when it is copied or moved?

3. Write an example of a formula with a mixed cell reference.

4. Explain how to enter the formula =C4+B5+D2 using the point-and-click method.

5. Which keystroke combination do you use to display formulas in the worksheet?

PROJECTS

PROJECT 4-1

Match the letter of the worksheet formula in Column 2 to the description of the worksheet operation performed by the formula in Column 1.

Column 1	**Column 2**
___ 1. Adds the values in A3 and A4	A. =A3/(27+A4)
___ 2. Subtracts the value in A4 from the value in A3	B. =A3^27
___ 3. Multiplies the value in A3 times 27	C. =A3^27/A4
___ 4. Divides the value in A3 by 27	D. =A3+A4
___ 5. Raises the value in A3 to the 27th power	E. =A3/27
___ 6. Divides the value in A3 by 27, and then adds the value in A4	F. =A3/27+A4
___ 7. Divides the value in A3 by the result of 27 plus the value in A4	G. =(A3*27)/A4
___ 8. Multiplies the value in A3 times 27, and then divides the product by the value in A4	H. =A3–A4
___ 9. Divides 27 by the value in A4, and then multiplies the result by the value in A3	I. =A3*(27/A4)
	J. =A3*27
___ 10. Raises the value in A3 to the 27th power, and then divides the result by the value in A4	

 PROJECT 4-2

1. Open **IE Project4-2** from the data files.

2. Save the file as **Formulas,** followed by your initials.

3. Enter formulas in the specified cells that perform the operations listed below. After you enter each formula, write the resulting value in the space provided.

Resulting Value	Cell	Operation
_____ a.	C3	Add the values in A3 and B3.
_____ b.	C4	Subtract the value in B4 from the value in A4.
_____ c.	C5	Multiply the value in A5 by the value in B5.
_____ d.	C6	Divide the value in A6 by the value in B6.
_____ e.	B7	Sum the values in the range B3:B6.
_____ f.	D3	Add the values in A3 and A4, then multiply the sum by 3.
_____ g.	D4	Add the values in A3 and A4, then multiply the sum by B3.
_____ h.	D5	Copy the formula in D4 to D5.
_____ i.	D6	Subtract the value in B6 from the value in A6, then divide by 2.
_____ j.	D7	Divide the value in A6 by 2, then subtract the value in B6.

4. Save, print, and close the file.

PROJECT 4-3

You are a fundraiser for Zoo America. Because winter is typically a slow time for the zoo, you decided to have a special fundraiser during the holidays. Zoo employees will set up booths at holiday events to sell T-shirts, sweatshirts, and coffee mugs. You have been asked to create a worksheet that calculates the bills of individuals who purchase these items. You are required to charge a sales tax of 7% on each sale. The file *IE Project4-3* is a worksheet in which you need to enter formulas required to calculate the bills. Complete the worksheet following these steps:

1. Open **IE Project4-3** from the data files.

2. Save the file as **Zoo,** followed by your initials.

3. Enter formulas in **D6, D7, D8,** and **D9** that multiply values in column B times the values in column C.

4. Enter a formula in **D10** to sum the totals in **D6:D9.**

5. Enter a formula in **D11** to calculate a sales tax of 7% of the subtotal in **D10.**

6. Enter a formula in **D12** to add the subtotal and sales tax.

 7. Change the worksheet for manual calculation.

8. Format **D6:D12** for currency with two places to the right of the decimal point.

9. Underline the contents of **D9** and **D11.** The worksheet is now ready to accept data unique to the individual customer.

10. A customer purchases two tiger T-shirts, three dolphin T-shirts, one sweatshirt, and four coffee mugs. Enter the quantities in column **C** and press **F9** to calculate.

11. Make sure that you have entered the formulas correctly. If any of the formulas are incorrect, edit them and recalculate the worksheet.

12. When you are confident that the worksheet is calculating as you intended, save the file.

13. Print the customer's bill and close the file.

PROJECT 4-4

Part 1

Alice Grant has been saving and investing part of her salary for several years. She decides to keep track of her investments on a worksheet. The file *IE Project4-4* contains a list of her investments:

■ **Money Market Account**—a bank savings account that does not require notification before money is withdrawn

■ **Stocks**—shares of ownership in a corporation

■ **Mutual Fund**—a collection of several stocks and/or bonds (borrowings) of corporations that are combined to form a single investment

Alice's stock and mutual fund shares are sold on a major exchange and she may look up the value of the shares in the newspaper after any business day.

1. Open **IE Project4-4** from the data files.

2. Save the file as **Investments**, followed by your initials.

3. In column D, calculate the values of the stocks by entering formulas in **D6** through **D8**. The formulas should multiply the number of shares in column B times the price of the shares in column C.

4. Also in column D, calculate the values of the mutual funds by entering formulas in **D10** and **D11**. Similar to the stocks, the formulas should multiply the number of shares in column B by the price of the shares in column C.

5. Enter a formula in **D12** that sums the values in **D4** through **D11**.

6. Alice wants to determine the percentage of each investment with respect to her total investments. Enter the formula **=D4/$D$12** in **E4**.

7. You might have noticed that the formula you entered in E4 contains an absolute cell reference. If this formula is copied to other cells, the absolute reference to D12 will remain the same. Copy the formula in E4 to cells **E6** through **E8**, and cells **E10** through **E12**.

8. Save the file.

Part 2

After reading the financial section of her newspaper, Alice realizes that the values of her investments have changed significantly. She decides to update the worksheet containing her investment records.

9. Change the worksheet to manual calculation.

10. Enter the following updated share price amounts:

Investment	Price
MicroCrunch Corp.	$16.00
Ocean Electronics, Inc.	$20.25
Photex, Inc.	$14.50
Prosperity Growth Fund	$ 5.50
Lucrative Mutual Fund	$13.00

11. Perform manual calculation by pressing **F9**.

12. Save, print, and close the file.

PROJECT 4-5

Abundant Prairie Development is a real estate development company that builds residential homes. One of the employees at the company has determined that housing prices in the Prairie Home neighborhood are primarily a function of the amount of square footage in the home, the number of bathrooms, and the number of car garages. Buyers are also willing to pay more for a house if it is on a cul-de-sac or if it has a swimming pool. You will use this information to develop a worksheet that estimates new home prices based on the variables that affect the home value.

1. Open **IE Project4-5** from the data files.

2. Save the file as **Home Price**, followed by your initials.

3. Before considering other factors, the cost of a home is approximately $55 per square foot. Enter a formula in **D5** that multiplies the amount of square footage in **B5** times the value per square foot in **C5**.

4. The cost of a home is increased by $3,000 for each bathroom in the house. Enter a formula in **D6** that multiplies the number of bathrooms in **B6** by the value per bathroom in **C6**.

5. The cost of a home is increased by $2,500 for each car garage. Enter a formula in **D7** that multiplies the number of car garages in **B7** by the value per car garage in **C7**.

6. The cost of a home is increased by $2,000 if the house is located on a cul-de-sac. Enter a formula in **D8** that enters the increase in value in **C8** if a 1 is entered in **B8**.

7. The cost of a home is increased by $5,000 if the house has a swimming pool. Enter a formula in **D9** that enters the increase in value in **C9** if a **1** is entered in **B9**.

8. Using AutoSum, enter the sum in cell **D10** to sum the numbers contained in **D5:D9**.

9. A potential buyer inquires about the price of a home with the following qualities:
   Square feet: **2,000 square feet**
   Number of bathrooms: 3
   Number of car garages: 2
   On a cul-de-sac?   **No**
   With a swimming pool?   **Yes**

   Enter this data in **B5:B9** to determine the estimated price of the house.

10. Save, print, and close the file.

CRITICAL*Thinking*

 ACTIVITY 4-1

 You have been offered three jobs, each paying a different salary. You have been told the gross pay (the amount before taxes), but have not been told your net pay (the amount after tax has been taken out).

Assume that you will have to pay 10% income tax and 7% Social Security tax. Develop a spreadsheet with formulas that will determine the amount of net pay. The format should be similar to that shown in Figure 4-10.

FIGURE 4-10

	A	B	C	D	E
1	DETERMINATION OF MONTHLY NET PAY				
2	Job Offer	Gross Pay	Income Tax	Social Security Tax	Net Pay
3	Job 1	$24,500			
4	Job 2	$26,600			
5	Job 3	$27,100			

Your worksheet should include the following:

■ Formulas in **C3:C5** that multiply the gross pay in column B times .10.

■ Formulas in **D3:D5** that multiply the gross pay in column B times .07.

■ Formulas in **E3:E5** that subtract the amounts in columns C and D from the amount in column **B**.

When you finish, save the file as **Job Offer**, followed by your initials. Then, print and close the file.

 ACTIVITY 4-2

 One of the most difficult aspects of working with formulas in a worksheet is getting them to produce the proper value after they are copied or moved. This requires an understanding of the differences between absolute and relative cell references.

If you experience difficulty after moving or copying formulas, you might not always have a text available to help you correct the problem. Use the Help system to locate an explanation of the differences between absolute and relative cell references. Print the explanation.

FUNCTION FORMULAS

VOCABULARY

Argument

Financial function

Function formula

Logical function

Mathematical function

Statistical function

Trigonometric function

Function Formulas

F*unction formulas* are special formulas that do not use operators to calculate a result. They perform complex calculations in specialized areas of mathematics — statistics, logic, trigonometry, accounting, and finance. Function formulas are also used to convert worksheet values to dates and times. In this section, you learn

> **Did You Know?**
>
> Excel has more than 300 function formulas.

about some of Excel's frequently used function formulas. A more comprehensive explanation of many Excel functions appears in the *Excel Function Reference* at the end of this unit.

Parts of Function Formulas

A function formula contains three components: the equal sign, a function name, and an argument. The equal sign, as you have learned, identifies the data to be entered in the cell as a

Equal sign ⟶ **=SUM(D5:D10)**
Function name ⟶   ⟵ Argument

formula. The function name identifies the operation to be performed. The *argument* is a value, cell reference, range, or text that acts as an operand in a function formula. The argument is enclosed in parentheses after the function name. If a function formula contains more than one argument, commas separate the arguments. A colon separates the range of cells that make up the argument.

In the previous lesson, you created a function formula by using the AutoSum button. When you click the AutoSum button, an equal sign followed by the word *SUM* is automatically entered. The range of cells to be summed is designated within parentheses; for example, =SUM(D5:D10). In this function formula, the word *SUM* is the function name that identifies the operation. The argument is the range of cells that will be summed.

Function formulas can be entered in the worksheet in two ways. First, you can enter a function formula directly in the cell by keying an equal sign, the function name, and the argument. Or, you can enter a function formula using the Insert Function and Function Arguments dialog boxes, which are shown in Figure 5-1.

FIGURE 5-1
Insert Function and Function Arguments dialog boxes

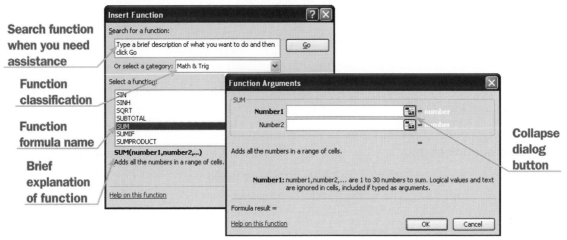

The Insert Function dialog box makes it easy to browse through all of the available functions to select the one you want. The dialog box also provides a brief explanation of any function you choose. You can choose a function classification by clicking it in the *Or select a category* box. Then, choose the function you want from the *Select a function* box. A description of the selected function formula appears near the bottom of the dialog box. Click OK to proceed to the Function Arguments dialog box.

> **Hot Tip**
>
> The Insert Function dialog box also contains a text box titled *Search for a function*. Enter a brief description of what you want to do and click **Go.** Excel will suggest the functions best suited for the task you want to perform.

In the Function Arguments dialog box, you can select a cell or range to appear 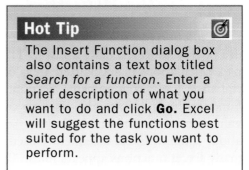 in the argument. You can enter arguments in two ways. First, you can key the argument in the Function Arguments dialog box. Alternatively, you can click the Collapse Dialog button at the end of the *Number* text boxes, and then select the cell or range directly in the worksheet. When you have finished specifying the argument, click the Expand Dialog button to restore the Function Arguments dialog box. When you have entered the desired argument, click OK, and your choices will be inserted as a function in the highlighted cell.

Entering a Range in a Formula by Dragging

Ranges are often included in function formulas. You can enter a range in a formula quickly by dragging on the worksheet. For example, suppose you want to enter the function formula =SUM(E5:E17). You would first enter =SUM(. Then drag from E5 to E17. Complete the formula by keying the closing parenthesis and pressing Enter. Dragging can also be used when you are using the Function Arguments dialog box and collapse the dialog box. In this case, you simply select your range and then expand the dialog box—the function as well as the opening and closing parentheses are entered automatically.

Types of Functions

Mathematical and Trigonometric Functions

Mathematical functions and *trigonometric functions* manipulate quantitative data in the worksheet. Some mathematical operations, such as addition, subtraction, multiplication, and division, do not require function formulas. However, mathematical and trigonometric functions are particularly useful when you need to determine values such as logarithms, factorials, sines, cosines, tangents, and absolute values.

You have already learned to use one of the mathematical and trigonometric functions when you used the AutoSum button to create SUM functions. One trigonometric function, the natural logarithm, and two other mathematical functions, the square root and rounding functions, are described in Table 5-1. Notice that two arguments are required to perform the rounding operation.

TABLE 5-1
Mathematical and trigonometric functions

FUNCTION	OPERATION
SQRT(number)	Displays the square root of the number identified in the argument. For example, =SQRT(C4) will display the square root of the value in C4.
ROUND(number,num_digits)	Displays the rounded value of a number to the number of places designated by the second argument. For example, =ROUND(14.23433,2) will display 14.23. If the second argument is a negative number, the first argument will be rounded to the left of the decimal point. For example =ROUND(142.3433,-2) will display 100.
LN(number)	Displays the natural logarithm of a number. For example, =LN(50) will display 1.69897.

S TEP-BY-STEP 5.1

1. Open **IE Step5-1** from the data files.

2. Save the file as **Functions**, followed by your initials.

3. Enter **=SUM(B3:B7)** in **B8.** (The same operation could be performed using the AutoSum button on the toolbar or by dragging to select the range.)

4. Highlight **B9,** open the **Insert** menu, and choose **Function.** The Insert Function dialog box appears, similar to Figure 5-1.

5. Click the arrow on the *Or select a category* box, and click **Math & Trig.**

6. Scroll down and click **SQRT** in the *Select a function* box, and then click **OK.** The Function Arguments dialog box appears.

7. Enter **B8** in the *Number* text box. You will notice the value in B8, 2466, appears to the right of the *Number* box. The value that will appear in B9, 49.65883607, appears under the function as well as at the bottom of the dialog box next to *Formula result =*.

8. Click **OK.** The function formula in B9 is =SQRT(B8).

9. Highlight **B10** and click the **Insert Function** button on the formula bar. The Insert Function dialog box opens.

10. Click **Math & Trig** in the *Or select a category* box if it is not selected already.

11. Click **ROUND** in the *Select a function* box, and click **OK.** The Function Arguments dialog box appears.

12. Enter **B9** in the *Number* box.

13. Enter **2** in the *Num_digits* box.

14. Click **OK.** The function formula in B10 is =ROUND(B9,2). Your screen should appear similar to Figure 5-2.

15. Save and leave the worksheet open for the next Step-by-Step.

FIGURE 5-2
Entering mathematical functions

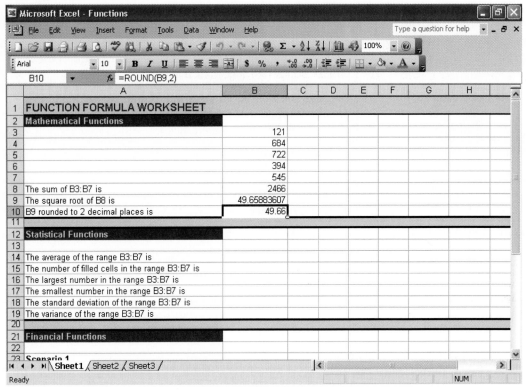

Statistical Functions

Statistical functions are used to describe large quantities of data. For example, function formulas can be used to determine the average, standard deviation, or variance of a range of data. Statistical functions can also be used to determine the number of values in a range, the largest value in a range, and the smallest value in a range. Table 5-2 shows some of the statistical functions available in Excel. Notice that all the statistical functions contain a range for the argument. The range is the body of numbers the statistics will describe.

TABLE 5-2
Statistical functions

FUNCTION	OPERATION
AVERAGE(number1,number2...)	Displays the average of the range identified in the argument. For example, =AVERAGE(E4:E9) displays the average of the numbers contained in the range E4:E9.
COUNT(value1,value2...)	Displays the number of cells with numerical values in the argument range. For example, =COUNT(D6:D21) displays 16 if all the cells in the range are filled.
MAX(number1,number2...)	Displays the largest number contained in the range identified in the argument.
MIN(number1,number2...)	Displays the smallest number contained in the range identified in the argument.
STDEV(number1,number2...)	Displays the standard deviation of the numbers contained in the range of the argument.
VAR(number1,number2...)	Displays the variance for the numbers contained in the range of the argument.

STEP-BY-STEP 5.2

1. To find the average of values in B3:B7, place the highlight in **B14.**

2. Click the **Insert Function** button on the formula bar. The Insert Function dialog box appears.

3. Click the arrow on the *Or select a category* box, and click **Statistical.**

4. Click **AVERAGE** in the *Select a function* box, and click **OK.** The Function Arguments dialog box appears.

5. Click the **Collapse Dialog** button at the right side of the *Number1* text box.

6. Select **B3:B7** by dragging directly on the worksheet.

7. Click the **Expand Dialog** button on the right side of the dialog box to expand the Function Arguments dialog box, and then click **OK.**

  Careers

Scientists use Excel worksheets to help them in conducting research. Worksheets are used to record collected data. Statistical function formulas are used to analyze experimental results.

STEP-BY-STEP 5.2 Continued

8. To find the number of filled cells in B3:B7, highlight **B15.**

9. Open the Insert Function dialog box.

10. Click **Statistical** in the *Or select a category* box if it is not already selected, click **COUNT** in the *Select a function* box, and then click **OK.**

11. Enter **B3:B7** in the *Value1* box, and click **OK.**

12. To find the largest number in B3:B7, highlight **B16** and enter **=MAX(B3:B7).**

13. To find the smallest number in B3:B7, highlight **B17** and enter **=MIN(B3:B7).**

14. To find the standard deviation of B3:B7, highlight **B18** and enter **=STDEV(B3:B7).**

15. To find the variance of B3:B7, highlight **B19** and enter **=VAR(B3:B7).** Your screen should look similar to Figure 5-3.

16. Save the worksheet and leave it open for the next Step-by-Step.

FIGURE 5-3
Entering statistical functions

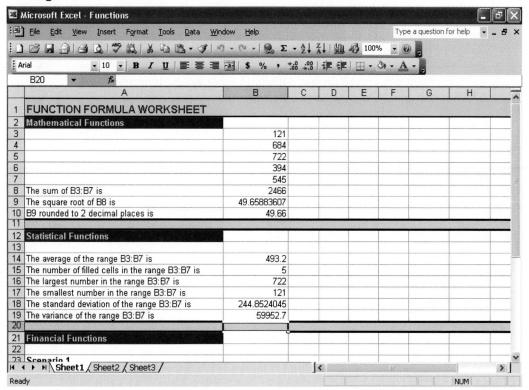

Financial Functions

Financial functions are used to analyze loans and investments. The primary financial functions are future value, present value, and payment, which are described in Table 5-3.

TABLE 5-3
Financial functions

FUNCTION	OPERATION
FV(rate,nper,pmt,pv,type)	Displays the future value of a series of equal payments (third argument), at a fixed rate (first argument), for a specified number of periods (second argument). (The fourth and fifth arguments are optional.) For example, =FV(.08,5,100) determines the future value of five $100 payments at the end of five years if you can earn a rate of 8%.
PV(rate,nper,pmt,fv,type)	Displays the present value of a series of equal payments (third argument), at a fixed rate (first argument), for a specified number of payments (second argument). (The fourth and fifth arguments are optional.) For example, =PV(.1,5,500) displays the current value of five payments of $500 at a 10% rate.
PMT(rate,nper,pv,fv,type)	Displays the payment per period needed to repay a loan (third argument), at a specified interest rate (first argument), for a specified number of periods (second argument). (The fourth and fifth arguments are optional.) For example, =PMT(.01,36,10000) displays the monthly payment needed to repay a $10,000 loan at a 1% monthly rate (a 12% yearly rate divided by 12 months), for 36 months (three years divided by 12).*

*The rate and term functions should be compatible. In other words, if payments are monthly rather than annual, divide the annual rate by 12 to determine the monthly rate.

S TEP-BY-STEP 5.3

Scenario 1: You plan to make six yearly payments of $150 into a savings account that earns 3.5% annually. Use the FV function to determine the value of the account at the end of six years.

1. Enter **.035** in **B24.** The value 3.5% appears in the cell.

2. Enter **6** in **B25.**

STEP-BY-STEP 5.3 Continued

3. Enter **-150** in **B26.** The value $(150.00) appears in the cell. (A negative number is entered when you pay cash; positive numbers indicate that you receive cash. In this case, you are paying cash to the bank.)

4. Click **B27** and access the Insert Function dialog box.

5. Click **Financial** in the *Or select a category* box, click **FV** in the *Select a function* box, and then click **OK.**

6. Key **B24** in the *Rate* box, key **B25** in the *Nper* box, key **B26** in the *Pmt* box, and then click **OK.** The savings account will have grown to the amount shown in B27 after six years.

7. Save the file.

Scenario 2: You have a choice of receiving $1,200 now or eight annual payments of $210 that will be invested at your bank at 3% interest for the entire eight years. Use the PV function to determine the most profitable alternative.

1. Enter **.03** in **B29.**

2. Enter **8** in **B30.**

3. Enter **-210** in **B31**. (A negative number is entered when you pay cash. In this case, you are paying cash to the bank.)

4. Enter **=PV(B29,B30,B31)** in B32. The best decision is to take the delayed payments because the present value, $1,474.14, is greater than $1,200.

5. Save the file.

Scenario 3: You need to borrow $5,000. Your banker has offered you an annual rate of 12% interest for a five-year loan. Use the PMT function to determine what your monthly payments on the loan would be and how much interest you will pay over the life of the loan.

1. Enter **.01** in **B34.** (A 1% monthly rate [12% divided by 12 months] is used because the problem requests monthly, rather than annual, payments.)

2. Enter **60** in **B35.** (A period of 60 months—or 5 years times 12 months—is used because the problem requests monthly, rather than annual, payments.)

3. Enter **5000** in **B36.**

STEP-BY-STEP 5.3 Continued

4. Enter **=PMT(B34,B35,B36)** in **B37**. The value ($111.22) will be red in the cell. The number is negative because you must make a payment. Under the conditions of this loan, you will pay a total of $1,673.20 ([$111.22 * 60 months] – $5,000 principal) in interest over the life of the loan. Your screen should look similar to Figure 5-4.

5. Save, print, and close the file.

FIGURE 5-4
Entering financial functions

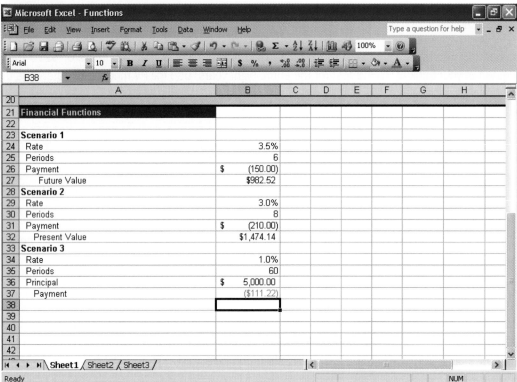

Date, Time, and Text Functions

Functions can also be used to insert dates and certain kinds of text in a worksheet. For example, date and time functions can be used to convert serial numbers to a month, a day, or a year. A date function can also be used to insert the current date or current time.

A text function can be used to convert text in a cell to all uppercase or lowercase letters. Text functions can also be used to repeat data contained in another cell. These functions are described in Table 5-4.

Did You Know?

Lookup (LOOKUP, VLOOKUP, HLOOKUP) and reference (ADDRESS, COLUMN, ROW) functions can be used to find cell contents or cell locations and use them as data in another part of the worksheet. For example, you might use the LOOKUP function to display the name of a person you have located in a worksheet by entering a Social Security number.

TABLE 5-4
Date, time, and text functions

FUNCTION	OPERATION
DATE(year,month,day)	Displays the date in a variety of formats such as *12/17/07* or *December 17, 2007*.
NOW()	Displays the current date or time based on the computer's clock. For example, =NOW() in a cell will display the current date and time, such as 5/23/07 *10:05*.
REPT(text,number_times)	Displays the text (first argument) a specified number of times (second argument). For example, REPT(B6,3) will repeat the text in cell B6 three times.

S TEP-BY-STEP 5.4

1. Open **IE Step5-4** from the data files.

2. Replace the words *NEXT YEAR* in **A1** with next year's date (such as 2006).

3. Highlight **B13** and click the **Insert Function** button.

4. Click **Date & Time** in the *Or select a category* box, click **NOW** in the *Select a function* box, and click **OK.** The Function Arguments dialog box appears.

5. Click **OK.** The function formula =*NOW()* appears in the formula bar. The current date and time appear in B13.

6. To format the date, open the **Format** menu and choose **Cells.**

7. Click the **Number** tab if it is not selected already, click **Date** in the *Category* box if it is not selected already, and then choose the format that displays the day in numerical form, the month in abbreviated form, followed by the last two digits of the year, such as 14-Mar-01. Click **OK.**

8. Copy the contents of **B13** to **C13.**

9. With the highlight in **C13,** open the **Format** menu and choose **Cells** to insert the current time.

10. Click the **Number** tab if it is not selected already. Click **Time** in the *Category* box, and then choose the format that displays the time in numerical form followed by either AM or PM, such as 1:30 PM. Click **OK**. The time appears in C13.

11. To repeat the text in A1 in B14, place the highlight in **B14** and access the Insert Function dialog box.

12. Click **Text** in the *Or select a category* box, click **REPT** in the *Select a function* box, and click **OK.**

13. Enter **A1** in the *Text* box, and enter **1** in the *Number_times* box.

14. Click **OK.** The title will be repeated in B14. If the title of the worksheet is changed, the text in B14 will instruct the user to rename the file.

STEP-BY-STEP 5.4 Continued

15. Save the file under the name appearing in B14. Your screen should look similar to Figure 5-5.

16. Print and close the file.

FIGURE 5-5
Using function formulas to insert dates

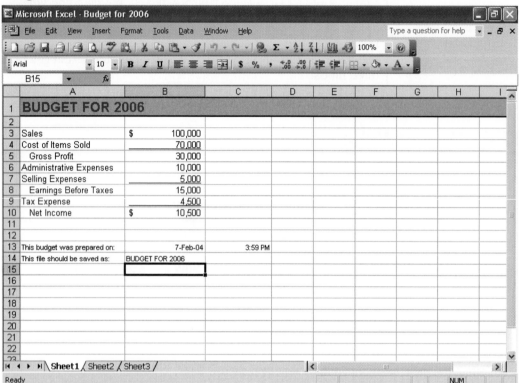

Logical Functions

Logical functions, such as the IF function, can be used to display text or values if certain conditions exist. In the IF function, the first argument sets a condition for comparison called a logical test. The second argument determines the value that displays if the logical test is true. The third argument determines the value that displays if the logical test is false.

For example, a teacher might use the IF function to determine whether a student has passed or failed a course. The function formula IF(C4>60,"PASS","FAIL") will display "PASS" if the value in C4 is greater than 60. The formula will display "FAIL" if the value in C4 is not greater than 60.

STEP-BY-STEP 5.5

Occidental Optical has noticed that its shipping costs have increased because retailers are asking for smaller amounts of optical solutions on a more frequent basis. To offset these costs, Occidental has decided to charge a $25 shipping fee for orders of quantities less than five cartons. The company decides to use an IF function to determine whether the fee is applied to an order.

1. Open **IE Step5-5** from the data files.

2. Save the file as **Optics**, followed by your initials.

3. In **D6**, enter **=IF(B6<5,25,0).**

4. Copy the function formula in **D6** to **D7:D15.** Your screen should appear similar to Figure 5-6.

5. Save, print, and close the file.

FIGURE 5-6
Using an IF function

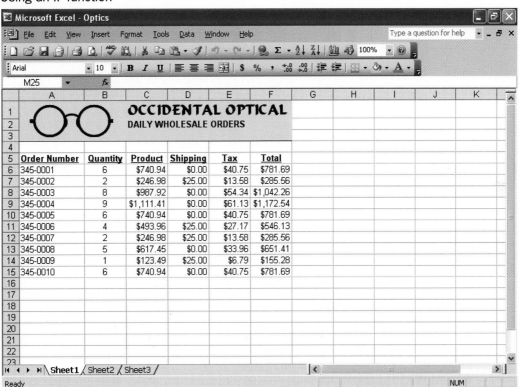

SUMMARY

In this lesson, you learned:

■ Function formulas are special formulas that do not require operators.

■ Excel has more than 300 function formulas.

■ Function formulas can be used to perform mathematical, statistical, financial, and logical operations.

■ Function formulas can also be used to format text and insert dates and times.

VOCABULARY *Review*

Define the following terms:

Argument	Logical function	Trigonometric function
Financial function	Mathematical function	
Function formula	Statistical function	

REVIEW *Questions*

TRUE/FALSE

Circle T if the statement is true or F if the statement is false.

T F 1. Function formulas do not have operators.

T F 2. The AutoSum button creates the function formula =SUM in the highlighted cell.

T F 3. The SMALL function formula displays the smallest number contained in the range identified in the argument.

T F 4. It is necessary to use the Function Arguments dialog box to insert a function formula in a worksheet.

T F 5. The NOW() function will insert either the current date or current time in a worksheet cell.

FILL IN THE BLANK

Complete the following sentences by writing the correct word or words in the blanks provided.

1. The _____ is enclosed in parentheses in a function formula.

2. The _____ function formula is inserted in a cell when you click the AutoSum button.

3. The _____ dialog box specifies elements to be included in the function formula.

4. _____ functions perform various operations, such as finding present and future values.

5. _____ functions describe large quantities of data, such as the average, standard deviation, or variance of a range of data.

PROJECTS

PROJECT 5-1

Write the appropriate function formula to perform each of the described operations. You may refer to Tables 5-1 through 5-3 to help you prepare the function formulas.

_____ 1. Determine the smallest value in A4:A90.

_____ 2. Determine the standard deviation of the values in K6:K35.

_____ 3. Determine the average of the values in B9:B45.

_____ 4. Determine the yearly payments on a $5,000 loan at 8% for 10 years.

_____ 5. Determine the value of a savings account at the end of 5 years after making $400 yearly payments; the account earns 8%.

_____ 6. Round the value in C3 to the tenths place.

_____ 7. Determine the present value of a pension plan that will pay you 20 yearly payments of $4,000; the current rate of return is 7.5%.

_____ 8. Determine the square root of 225.

_____ 9. Determine the variance of the values in F9:F35.

_____ 10. Add all the values in D4:D19.

_____ 11. Determine how many cells in H7:H21 are filled with data.

_____ 12. Determine the largest value in E45:E92.

PROJECT 5-2

The file *IE Project5-2* contains a worksheet of student grades for one examination.

1. Open **IE Project5-2** from the data files.

2. Save the file as **Course Grades,** followed by your initials.

3. Determine the number of students taking the examination by entering a function formula in **B26.**

4. Determine the average exam grade by entering a function formula in **B27.**

5. Determine the highest exam grade by entering a function formula in **B28.**

6. Determine the lowest exam grade by entering a function formula in **B29.**

7. Determine the standard deviation of the exam grades by entering a function formula in **B30.**

8. Format cells **B27** and **B30** for numbers with one digit to the right of the decimal.

9. Save, print, and close the file.

PROJECT 5-3

Generic National Bank makes a profit by taking money deposited by customers and lending it to others at a higher rate. In order to encourage depositing and borrowing, you have developed a worksheet that informs depositors about the future value of their investments. Another portion of the worksheet determines the yearly payments that must be made on their loans. The incomplete worksheet is in the file *IE Project5-3*. Complete the worksheet by following the steps below.

1. Open **IE Project5-3** from the data files.

2. Save the file as **Bank,** followed by your initials.

3. Enter a PMT function formula in **B11** that will inform borrowers of the yearly payment. Assume that the loan principal (or present value) will be entered in B5, the lending rate will be entered in B7, and the term of the loan will be entered in B9. (*#DIV/0!,* indicating an error due to division by zero, will appear in the cell because no data is in the argument's cell references yet.)

4. A potential borrower inquires about the payments on a $5,500 loan for four years. The current lending rate is 11%. Determine the yearly payment on the loan. (The number in B11 will appear as a negative because it is an amount that must be paid.)

5. Print the portion of the worksheet that pertains to the loan (**A1:C14**) so that it can be given to the potential borrower.

6. Enter an FV function formula in **B24** informing depositors of the future value of periodic payments. Assume the yearly payments will be entered in **B18,** the term of the payments will be entered in **B20,** and the interest rate will be entered in **B22.** (*$0.00* will appear because no data is in the argument's cell references yet.)

7. A potential depositor is starting a college fund for her son. She inquires about the value of yearly deposits of $450 at the end of 15 years. The current interest rate is 7.5%. Determine the future value of the deposits. (Remember to enter the deposit as a negative because it is an amount that must be paid.)

8. Print the portion of the worksheet that applies to the deposits (**A14:C26**) so that it can be given to the potential depositor.

9. Save and close the file.

  PROJECT 5-4

The Tucson Coyotes have just completed seven preseason professional basketball games. Coach Patterson will soon be entering a press conference in which he is expected to talk about the team's performance for the upcoming season.

Part 1

Coach Patterson would like to be well-informed concerning player performance before entering the press conference. The file *IE Project5-4* contains scoring and rebound data for games against seven opponents. Complete the following worksheet so that Coach Patterson can form opinions on player performance.

1. Open **IE Project5-4** from the data files.

2. Save the file as **Game Stats,** followed by your initials.

3. Enter a formula in **J5** that sums the values in **B5:I5.**

4. Copy the formula in **J5** to **J6:J11.**

5. Enter a formula in **J18** that sums the values in **B18:I18.**

6. Copy the formula in **J18** to **J19:J24.**

7. Enter a function formula in **B12** that averages the game points in **B5:B11.**

8. Enter a function formula in **B13** that determines the standard deviation of the game points in **B5:B11.**

9. Enter a function formula in **B14** that counts the number of entries in **B5:B11.**

10. Copy the formulas in **B12:B14** to **C12:I14.**

11. Enter a function formula in **B25** that averages the rebounds in **B18:B24.**

12. Enter a function formula in **B26** that determines the standard deviation of the rebounds in **B18:B24.**

13. Enter a function formula in **B27** that counts the number of entries made in **B18:B24.**

14. Copy the formulas in **B25:B27** to **C25:I27.**

15. Save and print the file.

Part 2

Based on the worksheet you prepared, indicate in the blanks that follow the names of the players who are likely to be mentioned in the following interview:

Reporter: You have had a very successful preseason. Three players seem to be providing the leadership needed for a winning record.

Patterson: Basketball teams win by scoring points. It's no secret that we rely on (1), (2), and (3) to get those points. All three average at least 10 points per game.

Reporter: One player seems to have a problem with consistency.

Patterson: (4) has his good games and his bad games. He is a young player and we have been working with him. As the season progresses, I think you will find him to be a more reliable offensive talent.

(*Hint:* One indication of consistent scoring is the standard deviation. A high standard deviation might indicate high fluctuation of points from game to game. A low standard deviation might indicate that the scoring level is relatively consistent.)

Reporter: What explains the fact that (5) is both an effective scorer and your leading rebounder?

Patterson: He is a perceptive player. When playing defense, he is constantly planning how to get the ball back to the other side of the court.

Reporter: Preseason injuries can be heartbreaking. How has this affected the team?

Patterson: (6) has not played since being injured in the game against Kansas City. He is an asset to the team. We are still waiting to hear from the doctors on whether he will be back soon.

Reporter: It is the end of the preseason. That is usually a time when teams make cuts. Of your healthy players, (7) is the lowest scorer. Will you let him go before the beginning of the regular season?

Patterson: I don't like to speculate on cuts or trades before they are made. We'll just have to wait and see.

1. _____

2. _____

3. _____

4. _____

5. _____

6. _____

7. _____

When you have finished filling in the blanks, close the file.

PROJECT 5-5

A golf coach has decided that a player must average a score of less than 76 to qualify for the team. In this project, you will indicate those who made the team by using an IF function.

1. Open **IE Project5-5** from the data files.

2. Save the file as **Golf Tryouts**, followed by your initials.

3. Enter a function formula in **I5** that displays *Made* if the average score in H5 is less than 76 and *Cut* if the score is not less than 76. (*Hint*: The IF function has three arguments. The first argument is the logical test that determines whether the value in H5 is less than 76. The second argument is the text that appears if the statement is true. The third argument is the text that appears if the statement is false. Because the items to be displayed are words rather than numbers, they should be entered inside quotation marks.)

4. Copy the function formula from **I5** to **I6:I16**.

5. Enter a function formula in **B21** that displays today's date.

6. Choose the format that displays the month followed by the day and year, such as March 14, 2001.

7. Save and print the file.

 PROJECT 5-6

You have worked for Xanthan Gum Corp. for several years and have been informed that you are now eligible for promotion. Promotions at Xanthan are determined by supervisor ratings and a written examination. To be promoted, you must score an average of 80 or above in four categories:

- Supervisor rating of leadership potential
- Supervisor rating of understanding of duties
- Supervisor rating of willingness to work hard
- Written test score

After receiving your supervisor ratings, you decide to prepare a worksheet to determine the minimum written test score needed for promotion.

1. Open **IE Project5-6** from the data files.

2. Save the file as **Xanthan**, followed by your initials.

3. In cell **B6**, enter **70** as the supervisor rating; in B7, enter 85; and in B8, enter 80.

4. Enter a formula in **B11** that determines the average of the values in B6:B9.

5. Format **B11** for a number with zero places to the right of the decimal.

6. Enter an IF function formula in **B12** that displays **PROMOTION** if the average score in B11 is greater than 80 and **NO PROMOTION** if the average score is less than 80.

7. Bold the contents of **B12**.

8. Enter the following possible test scores in **B9**: 75, 80, 85, 90, and 95. Which ones will result in a promotion?

9. Save, print, and close the file.

CRITICAL*Thinking*

ACTIVITY 5-1

You are considering the purchase of a car and would like to compare prices offered by several dealerships. Some dealerships have a car that includes the accessories you desire; others will need to add the accessories for an additional price. Prepare a worksheet similar to that shown in Figure 5-7.

FIGURE 5-7

	A	B	C	D
1	A COMPARISON OF PRICES BY DEALERSHIP			
2				
3	Dealer	Base Price	Accessories	Total
4	Bernalillo New and Used	$16,300	$500	
5	Los Alamos Auto	$15,800	$400	
6	Mountain Auto Sales	$16,000	$400	
7	Sandia Car Sales	$17,100	$120	
8	Truchas Truck and Auto	$16,500	$550	
9				
10	Highest Price			
11	Lowest Price			
12	Average Price			

Perform the following operations to provide information that will be useful to making the car purchase decision.

■ Enter formulas in **D4:D8** that add the values in column **B** to the values in column **C**.

■ Enter a function formula in **D10** that determines the highest price in **D4:D8**.

■ Enter a function formula in **D11** that determines the lowest price in **D4:D8**.

■ Enter a function formula in **D12** that determines the average price in **D4:D8**.

When you have finished, save the file as **Car Purchase,** followed by your initials, and print your results.

ACTIVITY 5-2

The Insert Function dialog box contains a text box titled *Search for a function.* By entering a brief description of what you want to do and clicking Go, Excel will suggest functions best suited for the task you want to perform.

Suppose you are preparing a large worksheet in which all cells within a range should contain data. You would like to enter a function formula near the end of a range that displays the number of cells in the range that are blank. If a number other than zero appears as the function result, you will know that you must search for the cell or cells that are empty and enter the appropriate data.

In a blank worksheet, open the Insert menu and choose Function. Then enter a description in the *Search for a function* text box that will find a function to count the number of empty cells in a range. If more than one function is suggested, choose each function in the *Select a function* box and read the descriptions of the functions that appear below the text box. Then, identify the function that is most appropriate to complete this task.

 ACTIVITY 5-3

A manufacturing company prepares a budget each month. At the end of the month a report similar to the one shown in Figure 5-8 compares the actual amount spent to the budgeted amount is prepared.

FIGURE 5-8

	A	B	C	D
1	**Manufacturing Expense Report**			
2		Budgeted	Actual Amount	Budget
3	Labor Expense	$54,000	$55,500	-$1,500
4	Raw Material A	$45,000	$44,000	$1,000
5	Raw Material B	$31,000	$32,000	-$1,000
6	Overhead	$100,000	$95,000	$5,000

How could an IF function formula be used to draw attention to a budget that has been exceeded?

MAKING THE WORKSHEET USEFUL

OBJECTIVES

Upon completion of this lesson, you should be able to:

- Sort data in a worksheet.
- Use AutoFilter to extract specified data from the worksheet.
- Hide worksheet columns or rows.
- Use the Drawing toolbar.
- Insert a picture in a worksheet.
- Use Excel templates to format a worksheet.
- Insert a hyperlink in a worksheet.
- Save a workbook in a different file format.
- Add and edit comments.
- Create and respond to discussion comments.
- Use the Research tool.

Estimated Time: 2.5 hours

VOCABULARY

AutoFilter

AutoFilter arrows

Comment

Discussion server

Hiding

Hyperlink

Research tool

Sorting

Template

Web discussion

Sorting Data

Sorting organizes data in an order that is more meaningful. In an ascending sort, data with letters is sorted in alphabetic order (A to Z) and data with numbers is sorted from lowest to highest. You can also sort in descending order in which data with letters is sorted from Z to A and data with numbers is sorted from highest to lowest.

If you have column headings for data, you most likely will not want those to be sorted along with the data contained in the columns. To prevent Excel from including the headings in the sort, select the Header row option in the Sort dialog box, which is shown in Figure 6-1.

FIGURE 6-1
Sort dialog box

STEP-BY-STEP 6.1

1. Open **IE Step6-1** from the data files, and save it as **NCAA,** followed by your initials.

2. Click **B4** to indicate that you want to sort by the data contained in column B.

3. Open the **Data** menu and choose **Sort.** The Sort dialog box appears, similar to Figure 6-1. *Football Average* should appear in the *Sort by* box.

4. Click **Descending**.

5. Click **OK**. The data is sorted from higher to lower attendance. Your screen should appear similar to Figure 6-2.

STEP-BY-STEP 6.1 Continued

FIGURE 6-2
Sorting data in a worksheet

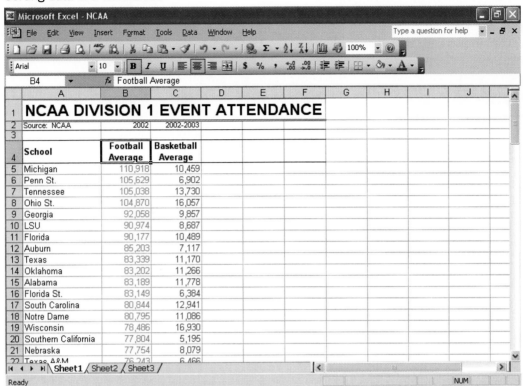

6. Click **A4** to make *School* the new sort criterion.

7. Click the **Sort Ascending** button on the Standard toolbar. The data is sorted alphabetically by school name.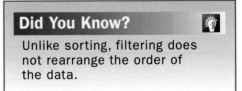

8. Save the file and leave the worksheet open for the next Step-by-Step.

AutoFilter

AutoFilter displays a subset of the data that meets certain criteria. Filtering temporarily hides rows that do not meet the specified criteria.

Start AutoFilter by choosing Filter on the Data menu and then choosing AutoFilter on the submenu. *AutoFilter arrows* appear in the lower right corner of

> **Did You Know?**
>
> Unlike sorting, filtering does not rearrange the order of the data.

the column heading cells, as shown in Figure 6-3. Clicking the AutoFilter arrow displays a list of all the values that appear in that column, plus additional filtering options (All, Top 10, and Custom). Select one of the values to display only those rows in which that value is entered. Or, you can select one of the filtering options.

FIGURE 6-3
AutoFilter arrows and list

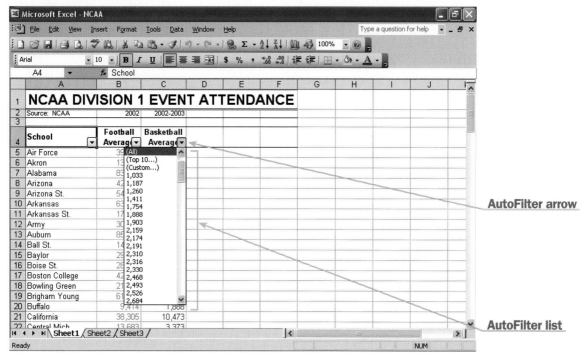

If you select the Top 10 option, the Top 10 AutoFilter dialog box appears, as shown in Figure 6-4. In the Top 10 AutoFilter dialog box, you can specify the highest and lowest values in the column. For example, you might display rows with the 10 largest values in that column of the worksheet. However, you can also change the specifications in the dialog box to display rows with other criteria. For example, you can display the highest tenth percentile or the lowest 50 items.

Hot Tip

When the AutoFilter of a particular column is in use, the AutoFilter arrow turns blue. To redisplay all the rows, click the AutoFilter arrow and choose **(All)** on the AutoFilter list.

FIGURE 6-4
Top 10 AutoFilter dialog box

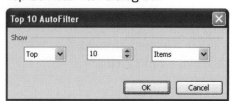

S TEP-BY-STEP 6.2

1. Highlight **C4.**

2. Open the **Data** menu, choose **Filter,** and then choose **AutoFilter** on the submenu. AutoFilter arrows appear in A4 through C4.

3. Click the AutoFilter arrow in **C4.** Your screen should appear similar to Figure 6-3.

4. Click **(Top 10...).** The Top 10 AutoFilter dialog box appears.

5. Click **OK.** The 10 teams with the highest average basketball attendance appear.

6. Click the AutoFilter arrow in **C4** again.

7. Scroll up and click **(All).** All of the data in the worksheet is restored.

8. Click the AutoFilter arrow in **B4.**

9. Click **(Top 10...).** The Top 10 AutoFilter dialog box appears.

10. Increase the number in the middle text box to **15.**

11. Click the arrow on the right box and choose **Percent.**

12. Click **OK.** The teams with football attendance in the top 15th percentile appear.

13. Save, print, and close the file.

Hiding Columns and Rows

H*iding* temporarily removes a row or column from the screen. To hide a selected row or column, select either Row or Column on the Format menu, and then click Hide on the submenu. To redisplay a hidden row, select the rows on each side of the hidden rows you want to display. Then open the Format menu, select Row, and click Unhide on the submenu. To display a hidden column, select columns on both sides, open the Format menu, select Column, and then click Unhide on the submenu.

S TEP-BY-STEP 6.3

The file *IE Step6-3* is a record of oil production for several wells over a six-month period. A manager has asked that you prepare two reports. The first report should show the six-month production for each well in the field. The second report should summarize the production of the entire field for each of the six months.

1. Open **IE Step6-3** from the data files, and save it as **Combustion,** followed by your initials.

2. Select columns **B** through **G.**

STEP 6.3 Continued

ne **Format** menu, choose **Column,** and then choose **Hide** on the submenu. Columns B through
...ʋ hidden.

4. Print the file.

5. Select columns **A** and **H.**

6. Open the **Format** menu, choose **Column,** and then choose **Unhide** on the submenu. Columns B through G reappear.

7. Select rows **6** through **14.**

8. Open the **Format** menu, choose **Row,** and then choose **Hide** on the submenu. Rows 6 through 14 are hidden.

9. Print the file.

10. Select rows **5** and **15.**

11. Open the **Format** menu, choose **Row,** and then choose **Unhide** on the submenu. Rows 6 through 14 reappear.

12. Save the file and leave the worksheet open for the next Step-by-Step.

Using the Drawing Tools

Drawing tools can be used to insert lines and objects that help make a worksheet more informative. For example, you might use a text box to explain a value in the worksheet. Or you might use an object, such as a rectangle or circle, to create a corporate logo.

Creating Objects

Display the Drawing toolbar by clicking the Drawing button on the Standard toolbar. The Drawing toolbar normally appears near the bottom of the screen.

STEP-BY-STEP 6.4

1. Click the **Drawing** button on the Standard toolbar. The Drawing toolbar appears near the bottom of the screen.

2. Click the **Text Box** button on the Drawing toolbar. The pointer changes shape to a crosshair.

3. Drag from **E18** to **G20.** A text box appears.

4. Key **Bad weather caused February production to be low.**

STEP-BY-STEP 6.4 Continued

5. Click the **3-D Style** button on the Drawing toolbar. A menu appears.

6. Click the top left box, **3-D Style 1.**

7. Click the **Arrow** button on the Drawing toolbar. The pointer changes shape to a crosshair.

8. Drag from the left side of the text box to the contents of **C15.** Your screen should appear similar to Figure 6-5.

9. Save the file and leave it open for the next Step-by-Step.

FIGURE 6-5
Using the drawing tools

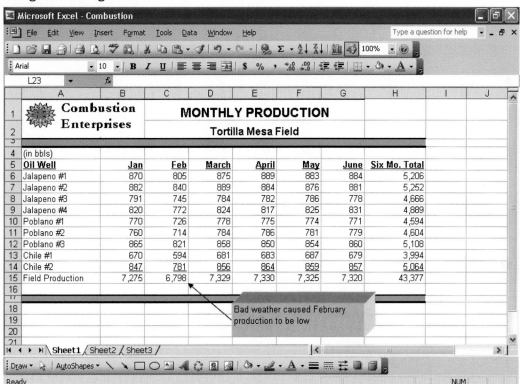

Editing Drawn Objects

Once you have created objects using the drawing tools, you can easily make modifications to them. In most cases, you can make changes by clicking the object and then using a button on the Formatting or Drawing toolbars.

Did You Know?

You can modify or delete lines and 3-D objects you have created in a worksheet. To delete a line or object, click it, and then press **Delete.** To change or modify a line or object, click it, and then modify your line or select a new 3-D object by clicking the line, arrow, or 3-D button on the Drawing toolbar.

STEP-BY-STEP 6.5

1. Click the arrow that points to C15. Handles (small white circles) appear at the ends of the arrow.

2. Click the **Line Style** button on the Drawing toolbar. A submenu with different line thicknesses appears, as shown in Figure 6-6.

FIGURE 6-6
Line Style button options

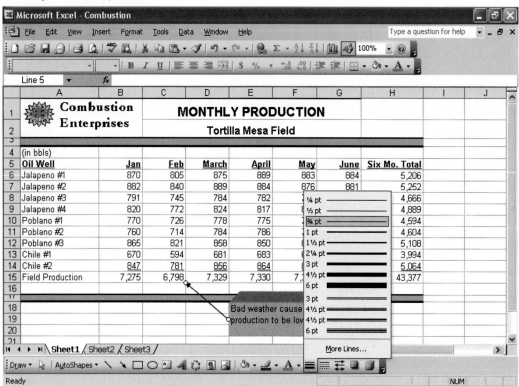

3. Click the **1½ pt** line. The line thickness of the arrow becomes thicker.

4. Click inside the 3-D box you created earlier. Handles appear at each corner and side.

STEP-BY-STEP 6.5 Continued

5. Click the **Shadow Style** button on the Drawing toolbar. A menu similar to the one in Figure 6-7 appears.

FIGURE 6-7
Shadow options

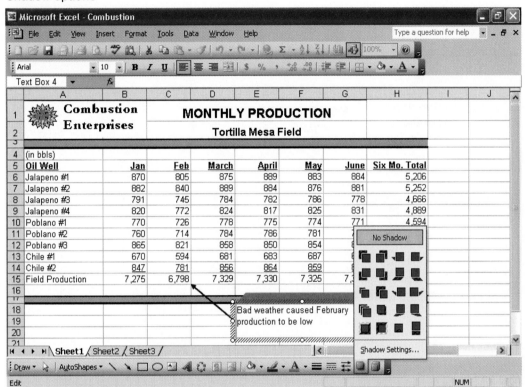

6. Click **Shadow Style 6** on the menu (second column, second row). The box changes from a 3-D box to a rectangle with a shadow along the lower right sides.

7. Select the text within the shadowed box.

8. Click the **Bold** button on the Formatting toolbar.

STEP-BY-STEP 6.5 Continued

9. Click the arrow on the **Font Color** button on the Drawing toolbar, and then click the **Light Orange** box. When you have finished, your screen should appear similar to Figure 6-8.

FIGURE 6-8
Editing drawing objects

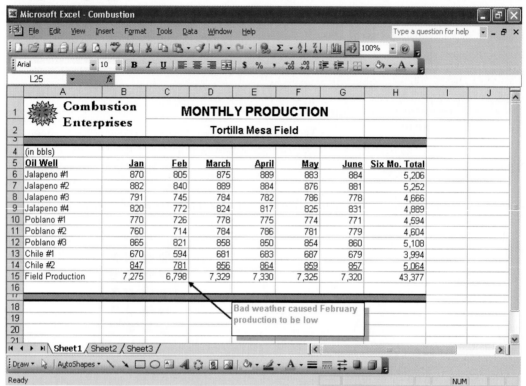

10. Click the **Drawing** button on the Standard toolbar to hide the Drawing toolbar.

11. Save, print, and then close the file.

Adding a Picture to a Worksheet

Y ou might want to change the appearance of a worksheet by adding a picture. For example, some corporations like to include their corporate logo on their worksheets. In addition, pictures are sometimes added to illustrate data contained in a worksheet. For instance, you might want to insert a smile in a worksheet that indicates good financial results (see Figure 6-9).

FIGURE 6-9
Pictures improve worksheet appearance

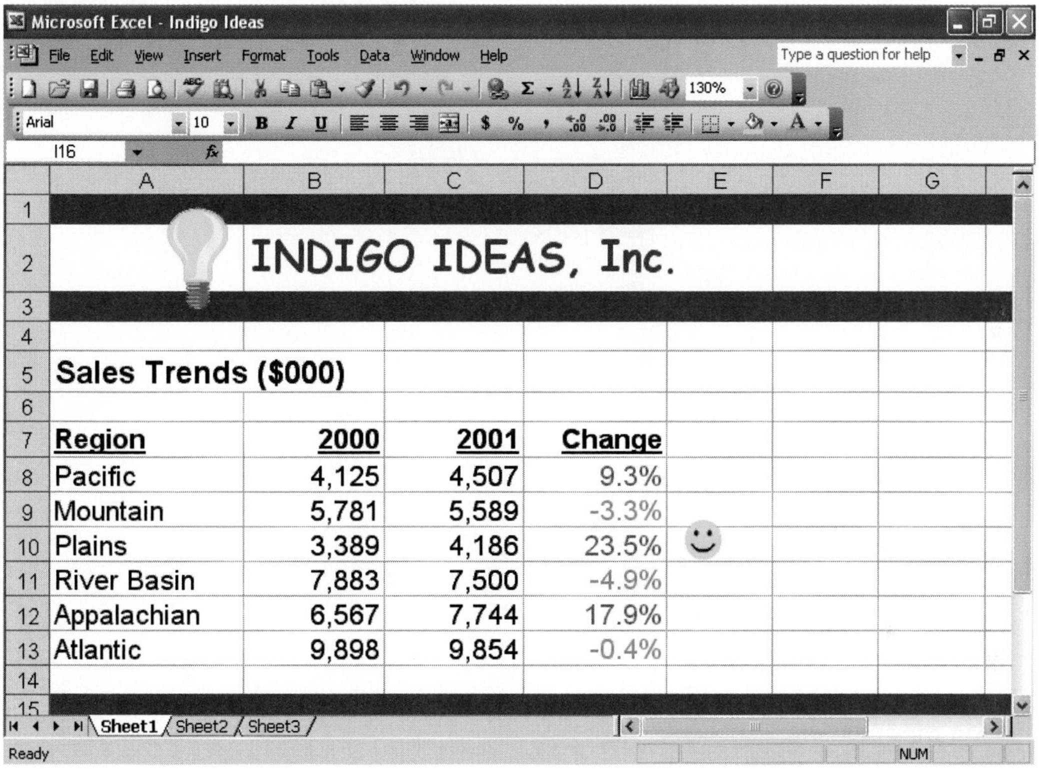

Inserting a Picture in a Worksheet

You can insert a picture from Office Online or from a file that contains a picture. Office Online is a collection of art that can be accessed via the Internet. To insert a picture from Office Online, select Picture on the Insert menu, and then select Clip Art on the submenu. The Clip Art task pane, similar to that shown in Figure 6-10, appears on the right of the screen. Enter the type of picture you want in the *Search for* text box and click Go. Excel will search for pictures that fit the search word.

FIGURE 6-10
Clip Art task pane

You insert a picture from a file by selecting Picture on the Insert menu, and then selecting From File on the submenu.

S TEP-BY-STEP 6.6

1. Open **IE Step6-6** from the data files and save it as **Botany**, followed by your initials.

2. Open the **Insert** menu, choose **Picture**, and then select **From File** on the submenu. The Insert Picture dialog box appears.

3. Choose **Rose** from the data files.

STEP-BY-STEP 6.6 Continued

4. Click the **Insert** button. Your screen should appear similar to Figure 6-11.

FIGURE 6-11
Inserting a picture

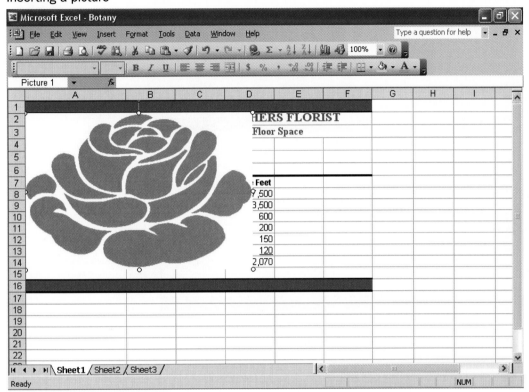

5. Drag the middle lower sizing handle upward until the dark line at the bottom of row 6 is visible.

STEP-BY-STEP 6.6 Continued

6. Drag the middle right sizing handle to the left until the edge of the picture is at the right side of column A. Your screen should appear similar to Figure 6-12.

FIGURE 6-12
Picture size is changed by dragging the sizing handles

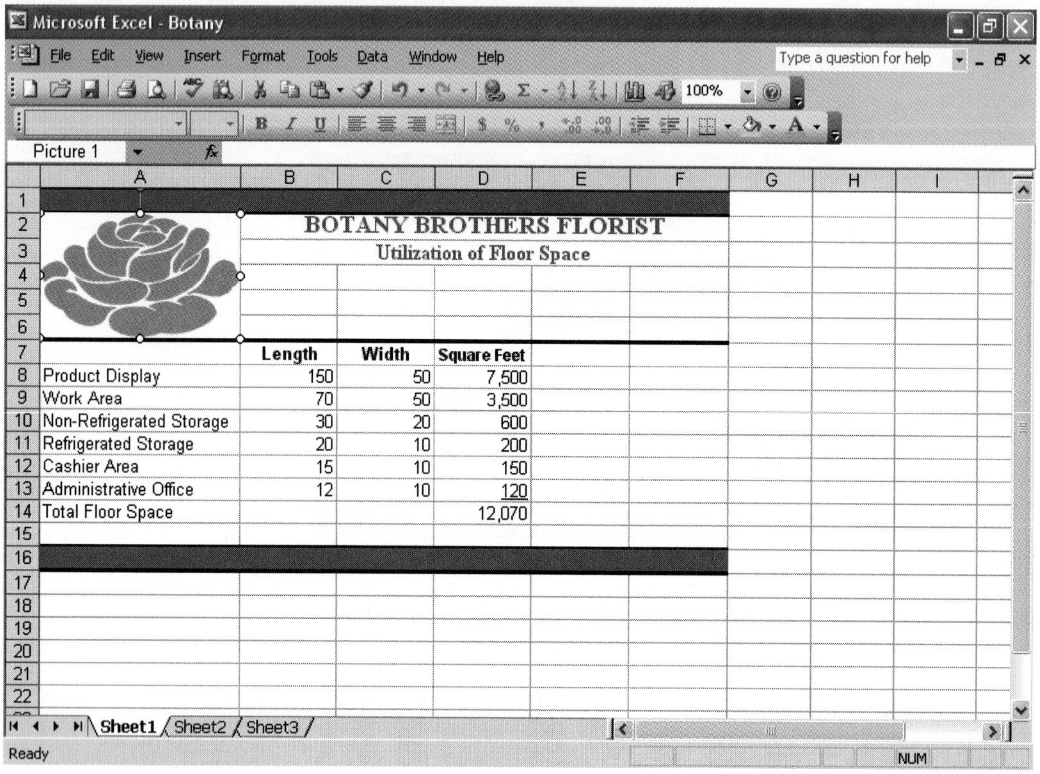

7. Save the file and leave it open for the next Step-by-Step.

Editing a Picture

Once a picture has been inserted in a worksheet, you can move it or edit it to fit your needs. Many of the edit functions are contained on the Picture toolbar (see Figure 6-13), which you can display by right-clicking any toolbar and selecting Picture on the shortcut menu. Table 6-1 explains methods for editing pictures.

FIGURE 6-13
Picture toolbar

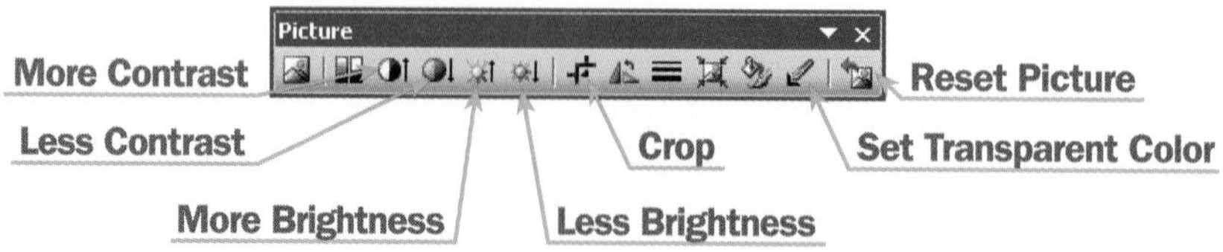

TABLE 6-1
Editing pictures

ACTION	SELECT THE PICTURE AND THEN:
Move the picture	Drag it to the desired position.
Restore the picture to the original format	Click the Reset Picture button on the Picture toolbar.
Resize the picture	Drag the sizing handles on the sides of the picture.
Crop the picture (trim the edges)	Click the Crop button on the toolbar and then drag the sizing handles.
Change the brightness of the picture	Click the More Brightness or Less Brightness buttons on the Picture toolbar.
Change the contrast of the picture	Click the More Contrast or Less Contrast buttons on the Picture toolbar.
Make a color in the picture transparent	Click the Set Transparent Color button on the Picture toolbar, and then click a color in the picture.

S TEP-BY-STEP 6.7

1. If the Picture toolbar is not already displayed, right-click a toolbar and click **Picture** on the shortcut menu.

2. Make sure the picture is selected and click the **Set Transparent Color** button on the Picture toolbar. The pointer changes to the Set Transparent Color icon.

3. Click on a white part of the picture. You are now able to see the gridlines of the worksheet behind the picture.

4. Click the **More Brightness** button on the Picture toolbar five times. The rose in the picture changes color from red to pink. (*Hint*: If you don't notice a change in color, click the **More Brightness** button a few more times.)

STEP-BY-STEP 6.7 Continued

5. Close the Picture toolbar by clicking its **Close** button. Your screen should appear similar to Figure 6-14.

6. Save, print, and close the file.

FIGURE 6-14
Editing a picture using the Picture toolbar

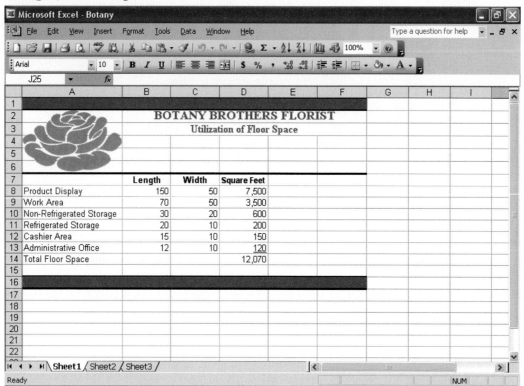

Using Templates

Templates are predesigned workbook files that you can use as the basis or model for new workbooks. You can use a template over and over, and customize it each time to suit your needs. For example, suppose you are required by your employer to submit a time record of your work each week. Each week you use the same worksheet format, but the number of hours that you enter in the worksheet changes from week to week. You can use a template file to save the portion of the worksheet that is the same every week. Then, each week you need only to add the data that is pertinent to that week.

Excel comes with a number of templates, which you access from the New Workbook task pane (see Figure 6-15). In the Templates section of the task pane, click On my computer. The Templates dialog box appears, as shown in Figure 6-16. Click the Spreadsheet Solutions tab to display the templates installed on your computer. The icons for template files have an orange strip across the top to differentiate them from regular Excel workbook files. After you open the template file, you should save it as a regular workbook file.

FIGURE 6-15
Template files can be accessed from the New Workbook task pane

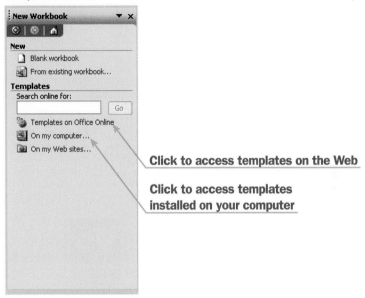

FIGURE 6-16
Spreadsheet Solutions tab in the Templates dialog box

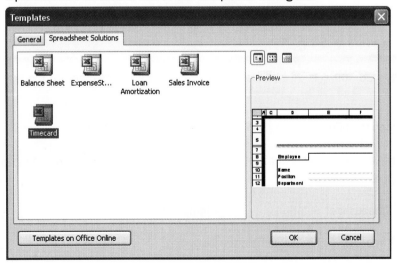

You can download additional templates from Office Online. Click the Templates on Office Online option in the New Workbook task pane to access templates available on Microsoft's Web site (see Figure 6-17). The Web site offers a variety of Excel templates organized by categories, such as Finance and Accounting, Orders and Inventory, and Healthcare and Wellness.

FIGURE 6-17
Office Online provides templates that can be downloaded

S TEP-BY-STEP 6.8

In this step-by-step, you access an Excel template to create a timesheet for the work performed in the last week.

1. Click **New** on the **File** menu. The New Workbook task pane appears.

2. Click **On my computer** in the *Templates* section of the New Workbook task pane. The Templates dialog box appears.

3. Click the **Spreadsheet Solutions** tab in the Templates dialog box.

4. Click the **Timecard** icon in the Templates dialog box.

5. Click **OK.** A template file titled *Timecard1* appears.

6. Open the **File** menu and choose **Save as.**

7. Be sure the proper drive has been selected and save the file as an Excel Workbook file (with the *.xls extension) named **Timecard1,** followed by your initials.

STEP-BY-STEP 6.8 Continued

8. Click the arrow on the **Zoom** button and select **75%** so that column R appears at the right side of the screen.

9. Enter the following data in the designated cells. When you are finished, your screen should look similar to that shown in Figure 6-18.

CELL	DATA
E10	**Andrew Gaston**
E11	**Floor Salesperson**
E12	**Luggage**
E16	**9/1/2006**
G16	**9/5/2006**
I10	**0591**
I11	**555-55-5555**
I12	**Switzer**
D19	**Customer Contact**
I19	**01-0111**
J19	**8**
K19	**12**
L19	**10**
M19	**8**
N19	**5**

FIGURE 6-18
Creating a worksheet from a template

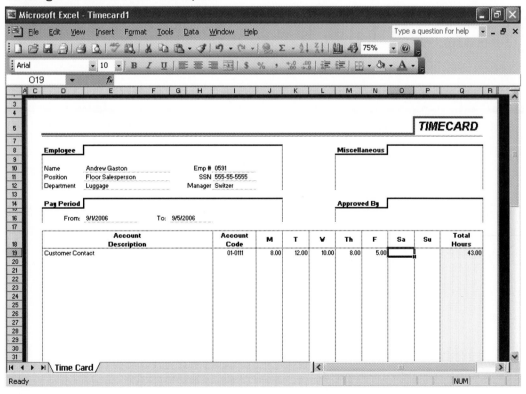

10. Save, print, and close the file.

Inserting Hyperlinks

You can insert *hyperlinks* in a worksheet that "jump" to other files or Web pages on the Internet. For example, you might want to create a link to another Excel file that contains the source data for information used in your current worksheet. You might also want to create a link to a Web page that contains information that relates to items contained in the worksheet.

To create a hyperlink, first select text or a graphic. Then, click the Insert Hyperlink button on the toolbar (or right-click the item and select Hyperlink on the shortcut menu). In the Insert Hyperlink dialog box, key the filename or Web page address in the *Address* text box and click OK. You are returned to the worksheet and the pointer appears as a pointed finger when you point to the linked item.

If you create a hyperlink to a file, that file opens when you click the hyperlink. If you create a hyperlink to a Web page, that page is opened in your Web browser when you click the hyperlink.

STEP-BY-STEP 6.9

1. Open **IE Step6-9** from the data files, and save it as **Tax Estimate,** followed by your initials.

2. Click **A15.**

3. Click the **Insert Hyperlink** button on the Standard toolbar. The Insert Hyperlink dialog box appears.

4. Key **www.irs.gov** in the *Address* box.

5. Click **OK.** The contents of A15 become a hyperlink and appear blue and underlined (as shown in Figure 6-19).

STEP-BY-STEP 6.9 Continued

FIGURE 6-19
Hyperlinks give access to other files or to the Internet

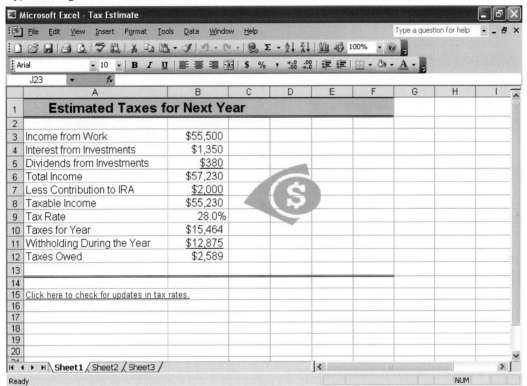

6. If you currently have Internet access, click the hyperlink in A15. The Internet site of the Internal Revenue Service should display.

7. Exit your browser and return to the worksheet.

8. Save, print, and close the file.

Saving Workbooks in a Different Format

Excel workbooks can be saved in a different format so that they can be opened in a different program. For example, if you want to share data with a co-worker or friend who uses Lotus 1-2-3 or Quattro Pro spreadsheet programs, you can save your Excel file in a format that is readable by these programs. You can also save the file in a format that can be viewed as a Web page on the Internet. You can save files in the formats listed in Table 6-2.

TABLE 6-2
Excel can save files in several formats

FILE TYPE	FILE CHARACTERISTIC
CSV	Data separated by commas
Formatted Text	Data separated by spaces
Microsoft Excel 97-2003 & 5.0/95 Workbook	Spreadsheet data created in an earlier version of Excel
Template file	Excel file used to create other similar files
Text	Data separated by tabs
Web Page	File to be displayed on the Internet
WK*	Spreadsheet data usable in LOTUS 1-2-3
WQ1	Spreadsheet data usable in Quattro Pro
XML	Data in Extensible Markup Language

S TEP-BY-STEP 6.10

The file *IE Step6-10* contains a worksheet used to report the expenses of a traveling salesperson. The company has several persons who use other spreadsheet programs. You have been asked to convert the Excel version of the file to one that is readable in Lotus 1-2-3. You have also been asked to save the Excel version of the file as a Web file so that it can be published and observed on the Internet.

1. Open **IE Step6-10** from the data files, and save it as **Excel Expense Report,** followed by your initials.

2. Open the **File** menu and choose **Save As.** The Save As dialog box appears.

3. Click the arrow on the *Save as type* box and select **WK4 (1-2-3).**

4. Key **1-2-3 Expense Report,** followed by your initials, in the *File name* box.

5. Click **Save.** A dialog box appears telling you that all of the features of the worksheet might not be compatible with Lotus 1-2-3.

6. Click **Yes.** The file is saved as a file that can be opened in Lotus 1-2-3.

7. Close the file.

8. Open **Excel Expense Report** (saved with your initials).

STEP-BY-STEP 6.10 Continued

9. Open the **File** menu and choose **Save as Web Page.** The Save As dialog box appears.

10. Click **Publish.**

11. Click the arrow on the *Choose* box and select **Items on Expenses** if it is not selected already.

12. Click the **Add interactivity with** check box, and then click the arrow on its list box.

13. Select **Spreadsheet functionality** in the list box if it is not selected already.

14. In the *File name* box, key **Web Expense Report,** followed by your initials, followed by the file extension **.htm**. The filename should be preceded by the drive in which you store your files.

15. Make sure the *Open published web page in browser* check box is checked, and click **Publish.** Your browser opens the file. The worksheet appears as it would if it were published on the Web. If you use Internet Explorer as your Web browser, your screen should look similar to that shown in Figure 6-20. Notice that the workbook in the browser has full spreadsheet functionality, even though it is displayed in a Web browser.

FIGURE 6-20
Excel file saved as a Web file that can be viewed in a Web browser

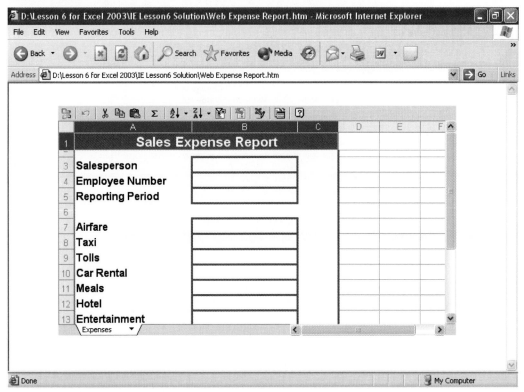

16. Print the file from your browser.

17. Close your browser and all open files.

Viewing and Editing Comments

Inserting a Cell Comment

A cell *comment* is a message that explains or identifies information contained in the cell. For example, when abbreviations have been entered in cells, a cell comment can be used to spell out the words. In addition, comments can be used to explain the calculations in cells that contain formulas.

Most importantly, cell comments are used when one worksheet user wants to provide input to other users without altering the structure of the worksheet. For example, a supervisor might want to provide comments to an employee on how to improve the worksheet format.

Cell comments are inserted by choosing Comment on the Insert menu. A comment box appears with the user name followed by a colon. Key the comment and then click outside the comment box to close it. A red triangle appears in the corner of the cell to indicate that it contains a comment. To read a cell comment, point to the cell that contains it. The comment is displayed, as shown in Figure 6-21.

FIGURE 6-21
Comments inserted in a worksheet cell

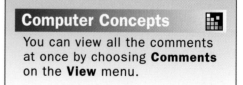

To edit a comment, select the cell that contains the comment, open the Insert menu, and choose Edit Comment. To delete a comment, open the Edit menu, choose Clear, and then choose Comments on the submenu.

> **Computer Concepts**
>
> You can view all the comments at once by choosing **Comments** on the **View** menu.

Using Discussion Comments

Web discussions permit several worksheet users to view and comment on a worksheet that has been posted on the Web. Discussions of Excel spreadsheets can take place either in Excel or in Microsoft Internet Explorer. In either application, Web discussions are started by accessing the Web Discussion toolbar. In Excel, choose Online Collaboration on the Tools menu and then click Web Discussions on the submenu. In Microsoft Internet Explorer, click the Discuss button.

A worksheet must be posted on a *discussion server* before it can be discussed on the Web. Both the file and the comments from worksheet users will be processed on the discussion server.

If you have access to a discussion server, you begin a Web discussion by choosing Online Collaboration on the Tools menu and then choosing Web Discussions on the submenu. The Discussions toolbar appears. Click Discussions and then click the *Insert about the Workbook* option. You can then add discussion subjects and discussion text to which others can respond.

STEP-BY-STEP 6.11

1. Open **IE Step6-11** from the data files and save it as **On-Line Investments,** followed by your initials.

2. Highlight **A6.**

3. Open the **Insert** menu and choose **Comment.** The cell comment box appears.

4. Key **Formerly Beta Disks, Co.** in the cell comment box, as shown in Figure 6-21.

5. Click outside the cell comment box. A small red triangle appears in the upper right corner of the cell, indicating that the cell contains a comment.

6. Point to **A6.** The cell comment appears.

7. Enter the following comments in the designated cells:

Cell	Comment
E9	**Purchased on February 2, 2006.**
A7	**Sell if price reaches $13.00 per share.**
A11	**Analyst recommends buy.**

8. Save, print, and close the file.

Using the Research Tool

The *Research tool* gives you access to information typically found in a dictionary, thesaurus, or encyclopedia. In Excel, the Research tool can provide numerical data typically used in a worksheet, such as statistics or corporate financial data.

To access the Research tool, click the Research button on the Standard toolbar. The Research task pane opens. In the task pane, select a research book, and then search for a subject within that book. The books are available via the Internet, so you must have Internet access in order to utilize this tool.

STEP-BY-STEP 6.12

In this step-by-step you will use the research tool to find the the price of corporate stocks in a stock portfolio. As you enter the stock prices, the worksheet will calcuatate the revised value based on the most recent prices.

1. Open **IE Step6-12** from the data files, and save it as **Stock Quotes,** followed by your initials.

2. Click **C5.**

3. Click the **Research** button on the Standard toolbar. The Research task pane appears.

4. Key **AMZN** in the *Search for* box.

5. Click the arrow on the list box and select **MSN Money Stock Quotes.** Then, click the **Start searching** button.

6. In the search results, note the amount that appears for *Last* and enter it in **C5.** The total value, calculated by multiplying the value in C5 by the value in D5, appears in E5.

7. Repeat the process for the ticker symbols HD, INTC, JNJ, and MSFT. When you finish, your worksheet should appear similar to that shown in Figure 6-22; however, the values in column C should contain the most recent stock prices and E10 should contain the value of the portfolio based on those prices.

8. Save, print, and close the file.

FIGURE 6-22
Updating information using the Research tool

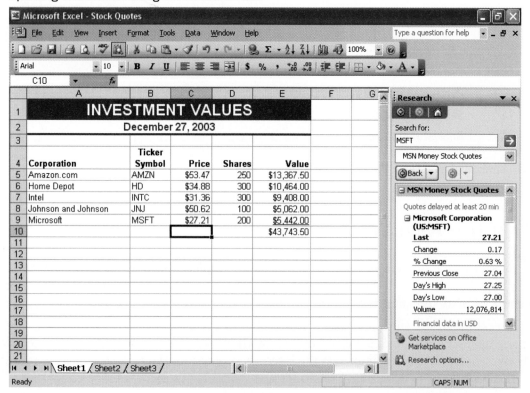

SUMMARY

In this lesson, you learned:

■ Data in a worksheet can be sorted in alphabetic or numeric order.

■ With AutoFilter, you can display a subset of data in the worksheet that meets specific criteria.

■ Rows and columns of a worksheet that are not needed can be hidden temporarily.

■ Drawing tools can be used to insert objects in a worksheet.

■ Pictures can be inserted to make a worksheet's appearance more attractive.

■ Templates are predesigned files that can be used to create new workbooks.

■ Hyperlinks in a worksheet enable the user to move to another file or a Web page on the Internet.

■ Excel worksheets can be saved in formats that can be read by other software programs.

■ Comments are messages that can be added to cells to provide additional information.

■ The Research tool can be used to obtain information that can be used in a worksheet.

VOCABULARY *Review*

Define the following terms:

AutoFilter	Hiding	Template
AutoFilter arrows	Hyperlink	Web discussion
Comment	Research tool	
Discussion server	Sorting	

REVIEW *Questions*

TRUE/FALSE

Circle T if the statement is true or F if the statement is false.

T F 1. When sorting, the worksheet is always ordered with the smallest values listed first.

T F 2. AutoFilter reorganizes data to place it in a different order.

T F 3. Hiding temporarily removes a row or column from a worksheet.

T F 4. Inserting comments in a cell can affect the results of a formula contained in that cell.

T F 5. Excel files can be saved in formats that are readable by other software programs.

MATCHING

Match the correct term in Column 2 to its description in Column 1.

<table>
<tr><td align="center">**Column 1**</td><td align="center">**Column 2**</td></tr>
</table>

___1. Worksheet used to create other worksheets

      A. AutoFilter

___2. Accesses resources, such as a dictionary, on the Web

      B. Template

___3. Organizes data in an order that is more meaningful

      C. Drawing toolbar

___4. Text or graphic that directs you to a file or Web page when clicked

      D. Comment

___5. Displays a subset of data that meet a certain criteria

      E. Hyperlink

___6. A message that explains or identifies information in a cell

      F. Sorting

      G. Research tool

PROJECTS

 PROJECT 6-1

The file *IE Project6-1* contains the salaries and annual ratings of Level 10 employees for Impact Corporation. Level 10 employees are currently paid between $30,000 and $35,000 per year. However, the management is concerned that salaries within that range do not relate to the level of performance of the individuals.

Part 1

In this part of the project, you sort the data by the employee's annual rating. Then, you indicate one of two salary categories using the IF function formula. The salary categories are:

Salary Range	Salary Category
$30,000 to $32,500	Low
$32,501 to $35,000	High

1. Open **IE Project6-1** from the data files, and save it as **Impact,** followed by your initials.

2. Sort the data in **A6:E20** by the Annual Rating in descending numerical order.

3. Enter **=IF(D6<32500,"Low","High")** in **F6.**

4. Copy the formula in **F6** to **F7:F20.**

5. Save the file.

Part 2

If salaries are allocated based on annual ratings, those with higher ratings should appear near the top of the worksheet and have *High* in column F. Those with lower ratings should appear near the bottom of the worksheet and have *Low* in column F. When a salary does not reflect the employee's annual rating, the word in column F might appear to be out of place.

Based on the worksheet you have prepared, determine which employees you believe are currently underpaid. Save, print, and close the file when you have completed the project.

PROJECT 6-2

The file *IE Project6-2* contains the top 100 grossing American films. The films are currently in alphabetical order by film name.

Part 1

Column D of *IE Project6-2* contains the number of dollars that the film grossed. Column C shows the amounts in column B in today's dollars (adjusted for inflation). Determine the most successful film in history by sorting the data.

1. Open **IE Project6-2** from the data files and save it as **Movies**, followed by your initials.

2. Sort the data in descending order by the Gross Adjusted for Inflation data.

3. Save and print the file.

To ascending / desending Sort - Click on title - + go to tool Bar - A↓/Z↓ Z↓/A↓

Part 2

Suppose you would like to rent videotapes of successful movies that have been released in the last few years. Re-sort the data to show the most recently released movies at the top of the worksheet.

1. Sort the data by **Year Released** in descending order.

2. Save, print, and close the file.

PROJECT 6-3

The file *IE Project6-3* contains the facts on the largest cities in the United States. Use AutoFilter to answer the questions at the end of this project.

1. Open **IE Project6-3** from the data files, and save it as **Large Cities**, followed by your initials.

2. Click **B3** and turn on AutoFilter. *under data*

3. Run the following AutoFilters to answer the following questions. Remember to restore the records after each filter by choosing **All** on the AutoFilter list in the column with the blue AutoFilter arrow.

Column	AutoFilter	AutoFilter Criterion
B	Top 10	Top 4 items
C	Top 10	Bottom 4 items
D	Top 10	Top 10 percent
G	0	Not needed

A. What are the four largest cities in the United States?

_____ _____ _____ _____

B. What are the four coldest cities in the United States during January?

_____ _____ _____ _____

C. What cities are in the top 10 percentile of average July temperatures?

_____ _____ _____

D. How many of the 30 largest cities are at sea level (have altitudes of 0)?

_____

4. Save and close the file.

 PROJECT 6-4

An employee of Paper Container Products would like to view the spreadsheet of the company's quarterly sales without the detail of each geographic region and each quarter.

1. Open **IE Project6-4** from the data files and save it as **Paper,** followed by your initials.

2. Remove the quarterly data from view by hiding columns **B** through **E.**

3. Restore the quarterly data by unhiding columns **B** through **E.**

4. Remove the regional data by hiding rows 7 through **14.**

5. Print the summarized worksheet.

6. Restore the regional data by unhiding rows 7 through **14.**

7. Save and close the file.

 **PROJECT 6-5**

1. Display the templates on your computer and open the **Sales Invoice** template file.

2. Save the file as **Sales Invoice1,** followed by your initials.

3. Use the Zoom button to adjust the file so that column **N** is near the right side of the screen.

4. Enter the following data in the worksheet.

CELL	CONTENT
C3	Cloth Crafts
M3	10001
D13	Anita Roberts
D14	4509 Lumpton Road
D15	New Orleans
D16	504-555-8796
F15	LA
H15	70135
M13	10/8/06
M14	100018
M15	013
M16	Dest
C19	5
D19	Fabric #515 per yard
L19	7.50
C20	10
D20	Fabric #440 per yard
L20	8.00
M37	5.00
L38	.05

5. Save, print, and close the file.

 PROJECT 6-6

1. Open **IE Project6-6** from the data files, and save it as **School Bus Activity,** followed by your initials.

2. Open the **Insert** menu, choose **Picture,** and then select **From File** on the submenu. The Insert Picture dialog box appears.

3. Choose **School Bus** from the data files.

4. Click the **Insert** button.

5. Double-click the picture so that the Format Picture dialog box appears.

6. Click the **Size** tab.

7. In the *Scale* section, change the Height and Width to **41%.** Click **OK.**

8. Drag the picture so that it fits within **E1:E3.**

9. Save, print, and close the file.

PROJECT 6-7

1. Open **IE Project6-7** from the data files and save it as **Compact Cubicle,** followed by your initials.

2. In **C8,** insert the comment **Shut down for two hours for maintenance.**

3. In **C9,** insert the comment **Production time increased two hours to make up for maintenance on Machine 102.**

4. In **G9,** insert the comment **Shut down for major repairs.**

5. Save, print, and close the file.

CRITICAL *Thinking*

ACTIVITY 6-1

 Several template files are saved to your computer when you perform a typical installation of Excel. These template files are accessed by clicking **On my computer** in the *Templates* section of the New Workbook task pane. These template files include Balance Sheet, Expense Statement, and Loan Amortization. Open these files and give a brief description of their purpose. You might want to enter data in the worksheet to investigate the formulas contained in the template.

ACTIVITY 6-2

Clip art from the Internet can be accessed by clicking **Clip art on Office Online** in the Clip Art task pane. If you have Internet access, use Office Online to locate the following clip art items:

- Lion
- Valentine heart
- Plumber
- Cactus

WORKING WITH MULTIPLE WORKSHEETS

Worksheets in a Workbook

A workbook is a collection of worksheets. The worksheets within the workbook are identified by *sheet tabs* that appear at the bottom of the workbook window. The name of the sheet appears on the tab. Until the sheet is named, sheets are identified as Sheet1, Sheet2, and so on, as shown in Figure 7-1.

FIGURE 7-1
Sheet tabs in a workbook

Active sheet

To work on a specific sheet, click the tab of the worksheet. The sheet that appears on the screen is referred to as the *active sheet*. The sheet tab of the active sheet is white.

Identifying Worksheets

Worksheets may be identified by naming them and by changing the color of their tabs.

Naming Worksheets

If you choose, you can change the default name (Sheet1, Sheet2,...) of a worksheet to a name that helps you identify the contents. To change the name, double-click the sheet tab, and then key the new name for the worksheet. (Alternatively, you can open the Format menu, choose Sheet, and then choose Rename on the submenu.)

Tab colors

You can also identify a worksheet by changing the color of its sheet tab. To change the tab color of the active sheet, open the Format menu, choose Sheet, and then choose Tab Color on the submenu. In the Format Tab Color dialog box, click the color you want for the tab.

S TEP-BY-STEP 7.1

Continental Corporation currently consists of three divisions. A workbook has been prepared to summarize the sales of each division.

1. Open **IE Step7-1** from the data files, and save it as **Corporate Sales**, followed by your initials.

2. Double-click the **Sheet3** tab. This worksheet will summarize the sales that appear on other worksheets.

3. Key **Corporate**, and then press **Enter**. The word *Corporate* appears on the third tab.

4. Change the name of **Sheet1** to **Western**.

5. Change the name of **Sheet2** to **Eastern**.

6. Change the name of **Sheet4** to **Northern**.

7. Click the **Corporate** sheet tab.

8. Open the **Format** menu, choose **Sheet**, and then choose **Tab Color** on the submenu. The Format Tab Color dialog box appears.

9. Click **black** in the upper left corner of the Format Tab Color dialog box.

10. Click **OK**. A black line appears at the bottom of the **Corporate** sheet tab.

11. Click the **Northern** sheet tab. The **Corporate** sheet tab turns black.

12. Change the color of the **Northern, Western,** and **Eastern** sheet tabs to yellow.

STEP-BY-STEP 7.1 Continued

13. Click the **Corporate** sheet tab. Your screen should appear similar to Figure 7-2.

14. Save the file and leave the worksheet open for the next Step-by-Step.

FIGURE 7-2
Sheet tabs can be renamed and colored

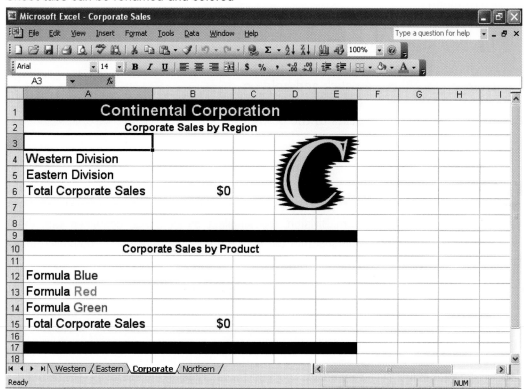

Positioning Worksheets in a Workbook

Hiding and Unhiding Worksheets

Some workbooks have many worksheets. It might be easier to access the worksheets you need by hiding the worksheets you do not need. Choose the worksheet you want to hide, open the Format menu, choose Sheet, and then click Hide on the submenu.

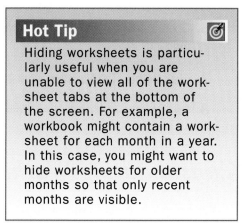

Hot Tip

Hiding worksheets is particularly useful when you are unable to view all of the worksheet tabs at the bottom of the screen. For example, a workbook might contain a worksheet for each month in a year. In this case, you might want to hide worksheets for older months so that only recent months are visible.

Inserting and Deleting Worksheets

Worksheets can be added to or deleted from a workbook. To insert a worksheet, click the tab of the worksheet that will *follow* the new sheet. Then, click Worksheet on the Insert menu. A new worksheet will be inserted before the sheet you selected.

To delete a worksheet, select the worksheet and then click Delete Sheet on the Edit menu. Click OK to confirm the deletion. You can also right-click a sheet tab and select Insert or Delete on the shortcut menu.

Modifying Worksheet Positions

You can change the position of a worksheet by dragging its sheet tab. When you click and hold on a tab, an arrow appears at the left side of the tab. Drag the tab until the arrow appears in the desired position.

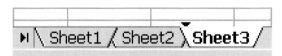

STEP-BY-STEP 7.2

During the last year, the Northern Division, the smallest division, was combined with the Eastern Division. You are to delete the worksheet for the Northern Division. In addition, you move the Corporate worksheet so that it is the first worksheet.

1. Drag the tab of the **Corporate** sheet to the left until the arrow on the tab appears to the left of the Western tab and then release. The tab for the Corporate worksheet should now be first.

2. Select the **Northern** division worksheet.

3. Open the **Format** menu, choose **Sheet**, and then choose **Hide** on the submenu. The Northern division worksheet and its tab disappear from the screen.

4. Open the **Format** menu, choose **Sheet**, and then choose **Unhide** on the submenu. The Unhide dialog box opens, listing the sheets that are currently hidden.

5. Click **Northern** in the list box and then click **OK.** The Northern division worksheet and its tab are restored.

6. Open the **Edit** menu and choose **Delete Sheet**. A message appears warning that data may be permanently deleted.

7. Click **Delete.** The **Northern** worksheet tab should no longer appear at the bottom of the worksheet.

8. Save the file and leave the worksheet open for the next Step-by-Step.

Consolidating Workbook Data

In some cases, you might need several worksheets to solve one numerical problem. For example, in a business that has several divisions, you might want to keep the financial results of each division on a separate worksheet. Then, on a separate worksheet, you might want to combine the results of each division to show summary results for all divisions.

Creating Links between Worksheets

A *link* transfers data from one worksheet to another. To use data from one worksheet in another worksheet of a workbook, select the destination cell and then enter an **=**. Click the sheet tab that contains the source data you would like to link, select the cell or range of cells, and press Enter. The data is linked to the destination sheet. Any changes to the source data also changes the value in the destination cell.

Three-Dimensional References

Three-dimensional references are formula references that incorporate data from other worksheets in the active worksheet. For example, in the active worksheet, you might want to add several numbers contained on other worksheets.

In a three-dimensional reference, the first part of the reference is the name of the worksheet, followed by an exclamation mark. The remaining part of the reference is the cell reference within the worksheet. For example, the reference *Sheet2!B3* refers to the value contained in cell B3 on Sheet 2. Table 7-1 gives other examples of how three-dimensional references might be used.

> **Computer Concepts**
>
> You should be cautious when moving or copying worksheets in a workbook. Moving a worksheet might affect 3-D formula references in the workbook.

TABLE 7-1
Three-dimensional references

FORMULA	DISPLAYS
=Sheet4!D9	Inserts the value contained in D9 from the worksheet named Sheet4.
=DivisionA!D10+DivisionB!D11	Adds the values in D10 of the worksheet named DivisionA and D11 of the worksheet named DivisionB.
=SUM(Sheet2:Sheet4!D12)	Adds the values in D12 on Sheet2, Sheet3, and Sheet4.
=SUM(Sheet2!D10:D11)	Adds the values in D10 and D11 of Sheet2.

S TEP-BY-STEP 7.3

In this Step-by-Step, you summarize values in the Eastern and Western Divisions in the Corporate worksheet.

1. Click the **Corporate** tab.

2. Select **B4** and key **=**.

3. Click the **Western** tab.

STEP-BY-STEP 7.3 Continued

4. Select **B6**. The cell address preceded by the sheet name, =*Western!B6*, appears in the formula bar.

5. Press **Enter.** You are returned to the Corporate sheet, and $543,367 appears in B4.

6. Select cell **B5**, if necessary, and key **=**.

7. Click the **Eastern** tab and select **B6**. The cell address =*Eastern!B6* appears in the formula bar.

8. Press **Enter**.

9. Select **B12**, and enter **=**.

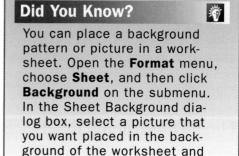

Did You Know?

You can place a background pattern or picture in a worksheet. Open the **Format** menu, choose **Sheet**, and then click **Background** on the submenu. In the Sheet Background dialog box, select a picture that you want placed in the background of the worksheet and then click **OK**.

10. Click the **Western** tab and select **B3**. =*Western!B3* appears in the formula bar.

11. Key **+,** click the **Eastern** tab, and select **B3**. =*Western!B3+Eastern!B3* appears in the formula bar.

12. Press **Enter.** You are returned to the **Corporate** sheet, and $306,744 appears in B12.

13. Copy the formula in **B12** to **B13:B14**. When you are finished, the value in B15 should be the same as the value in B6 and your screen should appear similar to Figure 7-3.

14. Save the file and leave the worksheet open for the next Step-by-Step.

FIGURE 7-3
Summarizing data on one worksheet

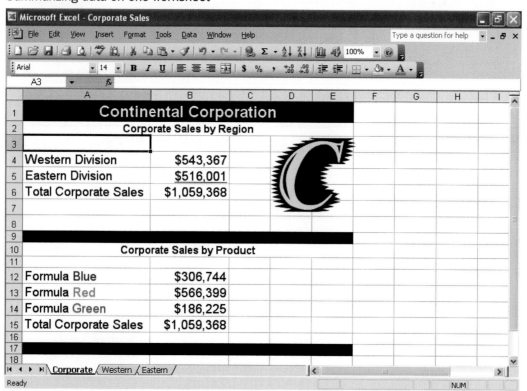

Printing a Workbook

In previous lessons, you learned to print selected areas of an active worksheet. You can also print an entire workbook, selected worksheets, or selected areas of a workbook. You designate the portion of the workbook to be printed in the *Print what* section of the Print dialog box (see Figure 7-4). The print options are described in Table 7-2.

FIGURE 7-4
Print dialog box

TABLE 7-2
Print alternatives

PRINT WHAT SELECTION	PRINT RESULT
Selection	Prints range(s) selected within a single worksheet.
Active sheet(s)	Prints the worksheet that appears on screen, or will print additional worksheets that you have selected by pressing Ctrl+the worksheet tab.
Entire workbook	Prints all worksheets in a workbook.

Printing Nonadjacent Selections of a Worksheet

To designate a print area in a worksheet, you typically select the range you want to print, open the File menu, choose Print Area, and then choose Set Print Area on the submenu. However, there might be times when you want to print selections in more than one part of a worksheet. For example, you want to print the top and bottom part of a worksheet, but not the middle portion.

To select more than one portion of a worksheet, select the first range, hold down the Ctrl key, and select additional ranges. In the Print dialog box, click Selection in the *Print what* section and then click OK.

Printing More than One Worksheet

If you want to print sheets in addition to the active worksheet, you can choose to print the entire workbook or selected worksheets. To print an entire workbook, simply click Entire workbook in the *Print what* section of the Print dialog box (see Figure 7-4).

To print certain worksheets in a workbook, you must first select the worksheets to make them active. To select additional worksheets, hold down the Ctrl key while clicking the worksheet tabs. In the Print dialog box, select Active sheet(s) in the *Print what* section.

S TEP-BY-STEP 7.4

1. On the Corporate worksheet, select **A4:B6.**

2. Hold down the **Ctrl** key and select **A12:B15.**

3. Open the **File** menu and choose **Print.** The Print dialog box appears.

4. Click **Selection** in the *Print what* section.

5. Click **Preview.** Your screen should appear similar to Figure 7-5. The range A4:B6 will print on page 1 and A12:B15 will print on page 2.

FIGURE 7-5
Printing selected ranges in a worksheet

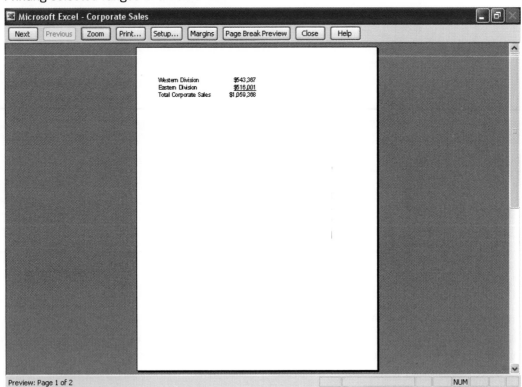

6. Click **Print.** The selected areas will print.

7. Click the **Western** tab.

8. Hold down the **Ctrl** key and click the **Eastern** tab.

STEP-BY-STEP 7.4 Continued

9. Open the **File** menu and choose **Print.**

10. Make sure that **Active sheet(s)** is selected in the *Print what* section of the Print dialog box.

11. Click **Print.** The worksheets of the divisions will print, each on its own page.

12. Save and close the file.

Working with Multiple Workbooks

So far in this lesson you have worked with worksheets that are in the same workbook. Sometimes you might want to use data from worksheets that are in more than one workbook. You can view these worksheets on the screen by *arranging* the workbooks. If you want to use the data from a worksheet in one workbook in another workbook, you can move or copy the worksheet to the new workbook.

Arranging Workbooks

Arranging lets you view more than one workbook on the screen at the same time. To arrange two open workbooks, open the Window menu and choose Arrange. In the Arrange Windows dialog box, choose whether you want to view the workbooks tiled, horizontally, vertically, or in a cascade.

Moving and Copying Worksheets

When you need to use a worksheet from one workbook in another, you can copy or move the worksheet. To move or copy, right click the tab of the worksheet and select Move or Copy on the shortcut menu. The Move or Copy dialog box appears. Click the arrow on the *To book* box and select the workbook you want the sheet to appear in. After you make your selection, the existing sheets in the workbook appear in the *Before sheet* list box. Click the sheet that you want the new sheet to appear before. If you want to move the worksheet, click OK. If you want to copy the worksheet, check the *Create a copy* box before clicking OK.

STEP-BY-STEP 7.5

1. Open **IE Step7-5A** and **IE Step7-5B** from the data files.

2. Save IE Step7-5A as **Income Statement for Year**, followed by your initials; save IE Step7-5B as **Income Statement for February**, followed by your initials.

3. In the Income Statement for Year workbook, open the **Window** menu and choose **Arrange.** The Arrange Windows dialog box appears.

STEP-BY-STEP 7.5 Continued

4. Click the **Horizontal** button and then click **OK.** Both workbooks appear on the screen, similar to Figure 7-6.

FIGURE 7-6
Arranging workbook windows horizontally

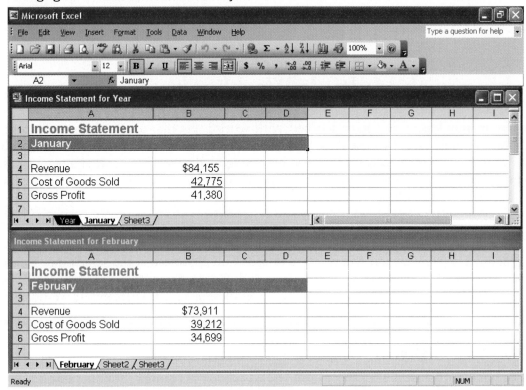

5. Right-click the **February** tab in the Income Statement for February workbook, and click **Move or Copy** on the shortcut menu. The Move or Copy dialog box appears.

6. Click the arrow on the *To book* box and select **Income Statement for Year.xls**.

7. Click **Sheet3** in the *Before sheet* list box so that the February sheet follows the January sheet.

8. Click the **Create a copy** check box. The dialog box settings should appear similar to Figure 7-7.

9. Click **OK.** The February sheet appears in the Income Statement for Year workbook.

Careers

Excel worksheets are extremely useful in areas of business that have a quantitative orientation, such as accounting and finance. In accounting, formulas are used to build financial statements. Financial officers in corporations use spreadsheets to project sales and control costs.

STEP-BY-STEP 7.5 Continued

FIGURE 7-7
Move or Copy dialog box

10. Click in the **Income Statement for February** window and then close the window by clicking the **Close** button.

11. Click the **Maximize** button on the Income Statement for Year workbook. The workbook expands to fill the screen.

12. Print the **January** and **February** sheets. Save and close the file.

SUMMARY

In this lesson, you learned:

■ Worksheets are identified by assigning a name to their sheet tabs and by changing the color of the sheet tabs.

■ Worksheets can be hidden from view and then unhidden when needed.

■ Worksheets can be inserted and deleted.

■ The position of a worksheet can be changed by dragging the worksheet tab.

■ Data in one worksheet can be linked to another worksheet.

■ Three-dimensional references permit data from multiple worksheets to be used in formulas.

■ Entire workbooks, selected worksheets, or selected areas of a workbook can be printed.

■ Several workbooks can be arranged on the screen so that they can be viewed at the same time.

■ Worksheets can be moved or copied from one workbook to another.

VOCABULARY *Review*

Define the following terms:

Active sheet	Link	Three-dimensional cell
Arranging	Sheet tabs	reference

REVIEW *Questions*

MATCHING

Match the correct formula result in Column 2 to its formula in Column 1.

Column 1	**Column 2**
___1. =Sheet2!D10	A. Adds the values in cell D10 on Sheet2 Sheet3, and Sheet4
___2. =Sheet2!D10+Sheet3!D11	B. Adds the values in D10 and D11 of Sheet3
___3. =SUM(Sheet2:Sheet4!D10)	C. Inserts the value in D10 of Sheet2
___4. =SUM(Sheet2!D10:D11)	D. Adds the values in D10 of Sheet2 and D11 of Sheet3
___5. =Sheet3!D10+Sheet3!D11	E. Adds the values in D10 and D11 of Sheet2

FILL IN THE BLANK

Complete the following sentences by writing the correct word or words in the blanks provided.

1. _____ references are formula references that incorporate data from worksheets in an active worksheet.

2. A(n) _____ is a collection of worksheets.

3. _____ identify worksheets within a workbook at the bottom of a workbook window.

4. The sheet of a workbook that appears on the screen is the _____.

5. A(n) _____ transfers data from one worksheet to another.

PROJECTS

PROJECT 7-1

1. Open **IE Project7-1** from the data files, and save it as **Rainfall,** followed by your initials.

2. Rename the sheets of the workbook and change the worksheet tab colors in the following manner:

Existing Sheet Name	New Sheet Name	Tab Color
Sheet1	Annual	Dark Blue
Sheet2	January	Blue
Sheet3	February	Light Blue
Sheet4	March	Pale Blue

3. Link the total rainfall recorded in **B34** of the **January** worksheet to **B3** of the **Annual** worksheet.

4. Link the total rainfall recorded in **B31** of the **February** worksheet to **B4** of the **Annual** worksheet.

5. Link the total rainfall recorded in **B34** of the **March** worksheet to **B5** of the **Annual** worksheet.

6. Save and print the **Annual** worksheet. Close the file.

PROJECT 7-2

1. Open **IE Project7-2** from the data files, and save it as **Voting**, followed by your initials.

2. Rename the sheets of the workbook and change the worksheet tab colors in the following manner:

Existing Sheet Name	New Sheet Name	Tab Color
Sheet1	District 5	Red
Sheet2	P105	Orange
Sheet3	P106	Purple
Sheet4	P107	Green

3. Enter a formula in **D7** of the **District 5** worksheet that adds the values in **C5** of each of the precinct worksheets.

4. Enter a formula in **D9** of the **District 5** worksheet that adds the values in **C7** of each of the precinct worksheets.

5. Enter a formula in **D11** of the **District 5** worksheet that adds the values in **C9** of each of the precinct worksheets.

6. Enter a formula in **D13** of the **District 5** worksheet that adds the values in **C11** of each of the precinct worksheets.

7. Save and print the **District 5** worksheet. Close the file.

PROJECT 7-3

1. Open **IE Project7-3** from the data files, and save it as **Alamo Amalgamated**, followed by your initials.

2. Change the worksheet tab colors in the following manner:

Existing Sheet Name	Tab Color
Consolidated	Green
Alamogordo	Sea Green
Artesia	Light Green

3. Enter a formula in **C6** of the **Consolidated** worksheet that adds the values in **B6** of the **Alamogordo** and **Artesia** worksheets.

4. Enter a formula in **C7** of the **Consolidated** worksheet that adds the values in **B7** of the **Alamogordo** and **Artesia** worksheets.

5. Enter a formula in **C9** of the **Consolidated** worksheet that adds the values in **B9** of the **Alamogordo** and **Artesia** worksheets.

6. Enter a formula in **C10** of the **Consolidated** worksheet that adds the values in **B10** of the **Alamogordo** and **Artesia** worksheets.

7. Save and print all the worksheets in the workbook. Close the file.

 PROJECT 7-4

1. Open **IE Project7-4** from the data files, and save it as **United Circuitry**, followed by your initials.

2. Change the worksheet tab colors in the following manner:

Existing Sheet Name	Tab Color
Year	Red
January	Light Orange
February	Gold
March	Tan

3. Link the total month production of Circuits 370, 380, and 390 recorded in **F4:F6** of the **January** worksheet to **B5:B7** of the **Year** worksheet.

4. Link the total month production of Circuits 370, 380, and 390 recorded in **F4:F6** of the **February** worksheet to **C5:C7** of the **Year** worksheet.

5. Link the total month production of Circuits 370, 380, and 390 recorded in **F4:F6** of the **March** worksheet to **D5:D7** of the **Year** worksheet.

6. Save and print the **Year** worksheet. Close the file.

CRITICAL *Thinking*

SCANS ACTIVITY 7-1

You have learned how to link data in one worksheet to another worksheet within a workbook. Suppose that you want to link data from a worksheet in one workbook to a worksheet in another workbook. Use Excel's Help system to determine how links might be established with other Excel files.

WORKSHEET CHARTS

OBJECTIVES

Upon completion of this lesson, you should be able to:

- Identify the purpose of charting worksheet data.
- Identify the types of worksheet charts.
- Create a chart sheet and save a chart.
- Switch between charts and worksheets, zoom, and rename a chart.
- Preview and print a chart.
- Create an embedded chart.
- Edit a chart and change the type of chart.

Estimated Time: 2.5 hours

VOCABULARY

Axis

Chart

Chart sheet

Chart Wizard

Column chart

Data labels

Data series

Embedded chart

Image handles

Line chart

Pie chart

Scatter chart

What Is a Worksheet Chart?

A *chart* is a graphical representation of data contained in a worksheet. Charts make the data of a worksheet easier to understand. For example, the worksheet in Figure 8-1 shows the populations of three major American cities for three years. You might be able to detect the changes in the populations by carefully examining the worksheet. However, the increases and decreases in the population of each city are easier to see when the data is illustrated in a chart, such as the one shown in Figure 8-2.

FIGURE 8-1
Worksheet data

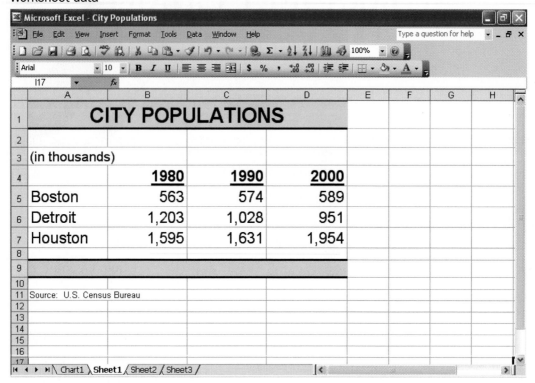

FIGURE 8-2
Charting the worksheet data

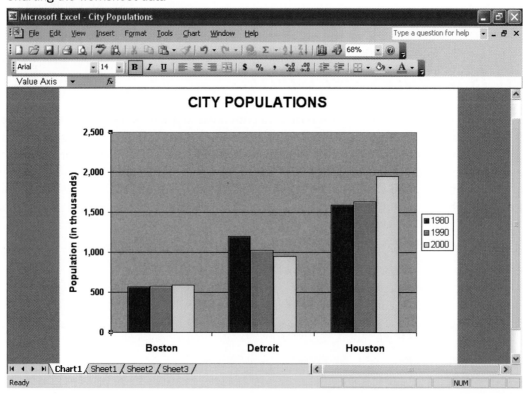

Types of Worksheet Charts

In this lesson, you create four of the most commonly used worksheet charts: column chart, line chart, pie chart, and scatter chart. These charts, and several other types of charts, are illustrated in Figure 8-3.

FIGURE 8-3
Charts available in Excel

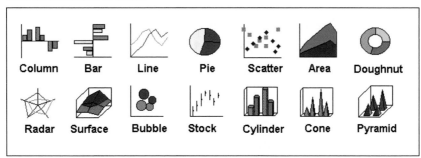

Column Chart

A *column chart* uses bars of varying heights to illustrate values in a worksheet. It is useful for showing relationships among categories of data. For example, the column chart in Figure 8-2 has one vertical column to show the population of a city for each of three years and shows how the population of one city compares to populations of other cities.

Line Chart

A *line chart* is similar to the column chart except that columns are replaced by points connected by a line. The line chart is ideal for illustrating trends over time. For example, Figure 8-4 is a line chart that shows the growth of the U.S. public debt from 1990 to 2003. The vertical *axis* represents the level of the debt and the horizontal axis shows the years. The line chart makes it easy to see how the federal debt has grown over time.

FIGURE 8-4
A line chart is ideal for illustrating trends of data over time

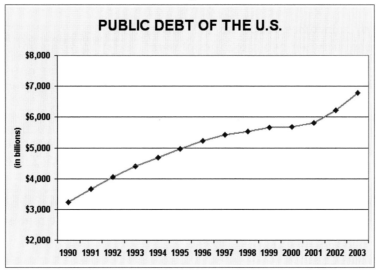

Pie Chart

A *pie chart* shows the relationship of a part to a whole. Each part is shown as a "slice" of the pie. For example, a teacher could create a pie chart of the distribution of grades in a class, as shown in Figure 8-5. Each slice represents the portion of grades given for each letter grade.

FIGURE 8-5
Each "slice" of a pie chart represents part of a larger group

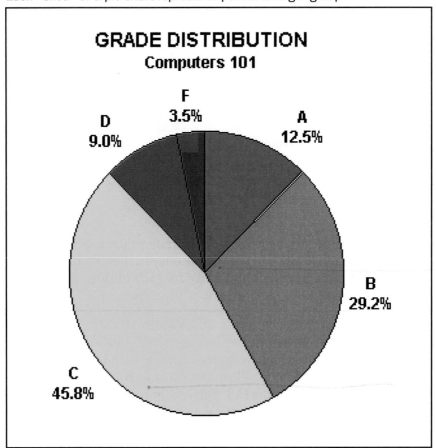

Scatter Chart

A *scatter chart*, sometimes called an *XY* chart, shows the relationship between two categories of data. One category is represented on the vertical (Y) axis, and the other category is represented on the horizontal (X) axis. It is not practical to connect the data points with a line because points on a scatter chart usually do not relate to each other as they do in a line chart. For example, the scatter chart in Figure 8-6 shows a data point for each of 12 individuals based on their heights and weights. In most cases, a tall person tends to be

> **Did You Know?**
>
> Businesses often use column, bar, and line charts to illustrate growth over several periods. For example, the changes in yearly production or income over a 10-year period can be shown easily in a column chart.

heavier than a short person. However, because some people are tall and skinny, and others are short and stocky, the relationship between height and weight cannot be represented by a line.

FIGURE 8-6
Scatter charts show the relationship between two categories of data

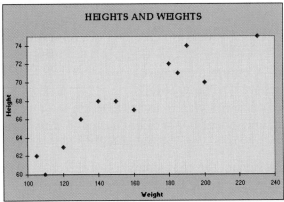

Creating a Chart from Worksheet Data

Y ou can create and display charts in two ways: by placing the chart on a chart sheet or by embedding the chart in the worksheet. A *chart sheet* is a separate sheet in the workbook on which you can create and store a chart. You can name the chart sheet to identify its contents and access it by clicking its tab. Use a chart sheet when it is inconvenient to have the chart and data on the same screen or when you plan to create more than one chart from the same data.

An *embedded chart* is created within the worksheet. The primary advantage of an embedded chart is that it can be viewed at the same time as the data from which it is created. When you print the worksheet, the chart is printed on the same page.

Creating a Chart Sheet

Create a chart sheet by first highlighting the data from the worksheet that is to be included in the chart. Open the Insert menu and choose Chart or click the Chart Wizard button on the toolbar. The *Chart*

Did You Know?

Businesses often use pie charts to indicate the magnitude of expenses in comparison to other expenses. Pie charts are also used to illustrate the company's market share in comparison to its competitors.

Hot Tip

To determine the name of a chart part, place the mouse pointer on the part. A ScreenTip with the name of the part appears next to the pointer.

Careers

Excel worksheets are used in education to evaluate and instruct students. Instructors use Excel worksheets to track student grades and to organize the number of hours spent on certain topics. Excel charts are used to illustrate numerical relationships to students.

Wizard, an on-screen guide that helps you prepare a chart, appears. The Chart Wizard presents four steps for preparing a chart:

■ **Step 1, Select the Chart Type**—Select a type of chart, such as column, line, or pie.

■ **Step 2, Chart Source Data**—Confirm the range of data to be included in the chart. The range should also include the textual data that you plan to use as labels in the chart. You can also designate whether there is more than one series of data to be charted. A *data series* is a group of related information in a column or row of a worksheet that will be plotted on a chart.

■ **Step 3, Chart Options**—Designate the characteristics of the chart. The parts of a worksheet chart are identified in Figure 8-7. Table 8-1 describes the chart options that are specified under a separate tab in the Step 3 dialog box of the Chart Wizard.

FIGURE 8-7
Parts of a worksheet chart

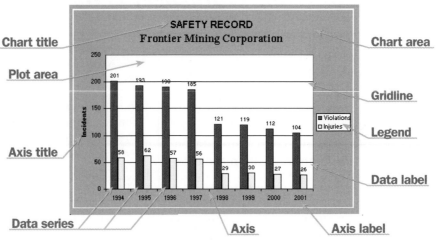

TABLE 8-1
Characteristics related to chart options

CHART OPTION TAB	OPTION FUNCTION
Titles	Headings that identify the contents of the chart or the axes in the chart; most charts have a chart title and titles for each axis
Axes	Lines that establish a relationship between data in a chart; most charts have a horizontal or X-axis and a vertical or Y-axis
Gridlines	Lines through a chart that relate the data in a chart to the axes
Legend	List that identifies patterns or symbols used in a chart
Data Labels	Text or numbers that identify the values depicted by the chart objects directly on the chart
Data Table	Data series values displayed in a grid below the chart

■ **Step 4, Chart Location**—Specify whether the chart is to be embedded within the worksheet or created on a separate sheet. When you create a chart on a separate sheet, the tab of the chart sheet appears directly to the left of the tab of the worksheet from which the chart was created. If you do not name the chart in Step 4 of the Chart Wizard, Excel names the first chart sheet Chart1. If additional charts are created from the worksheet, they become Chart2, Chart3, and so on.

> ### Did You Know?
>
> A chart is considered part of a workbook. When you save the workbook, you also save the charts you have created. Save the workbook by choosing **Save** on the **File** menu. It does not matter if you are on the worksheet containing the data or the chart sheet.

After you complete the Chart Wizard steps, a chart appears on the worksheet you specify.

STEP-BY-STEP 8.1

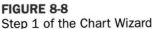

1. Open **IE Step8-1** from the data files. Save it as **Education Pays,** followed by your initials. Column A contains educational levels and column B contains the median incomes of those with corresponding levels of education.

2. Select the range **A3:B8.** This is the data to be charted.

3. Open the **Insert** menu and choose **Chart.** The *Step 1 of 4* Chart Wizard dialog box opens, as shown in Figure 8-8.

FIGURE 8-8
Step 1 of the Chart Wizard

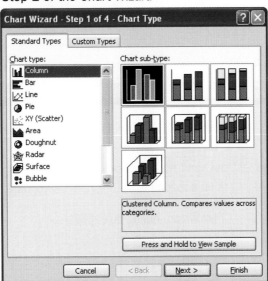

4. Click **Column** in the *Chart type* list, if it is not already selected.

5. From the *Chart sub-type* options, click the first chart sub-type box if it is not already selected. The description identifies the selected chart as *Clustered Column. Compares values across categories.*

STEP-BY-STEP 8.1 Continued

6. Preview the chart you are about to create by clicking and holding the **Press and Hold to View Sample** button.

7. Click **Next**. The *Step 2 of 4* Chart Wizard dialog box appears. In this dialog box, Excel has created a sample chart.

8. Click **Next**. The *Step 3 of 4* dialog box appears. The tabs at the top of the dialog box indicate chart options that you can change.

9. Click the **Titles** tab if it is not selected already.

10. In the *Chart title* text box, key **YOUR EDUCATION PAYS**; in the *Category (X) axis* text box, key **Education Level;** and in the *Value (Y) axis* text box, key **Median Income.** As you enter the titles, they appear in the sample chart area on the right side of the dialog box. When you finish, the dialog box should appear similar to Figure 8-9.

FIGURE 8-9
Enter chart titles on the Titles tab

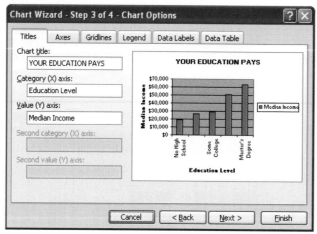

11. Click the **Legend** tab.

12. Click the **Show legend** text box until no check mark appears in the box. This chart uses only one series of data and does not need a legend to distinguish among data.

13. Click **Next**. The *Step 4 of 4* Chart Wizard dialog box appears.

14. Click **As new sheet.**

15. Enter **Column** in the text box. The dialog box should look similar to Figure 8-10.

STEP-BY-STEP 8.1 Continued

FIGURE 8-10
Step 4 of the Chart Wizard

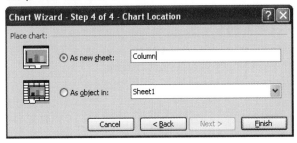

16. Click **Finish.** The chart appears on a chart sheet with a sheet tab named *Column*. The chart should appear similar to Figure 8-11. Leave the file open for the next Step-by-Step.

FIGURE 8-11
Finished chart sheet

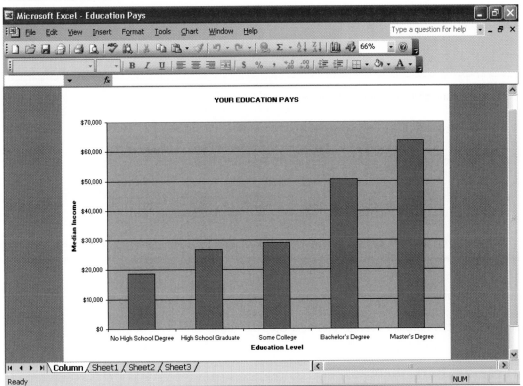

The chart illustrates the value of education in attaining higher income. Notice that the columns get higher on the right side of the chart, indicating that those who stay in school will be rewarded with higher incomes.

Switching Between Chart Sheets and Worksheets

A chart sheet is closely related to the worksheet data from which it is created. If you change the data in a worksheet, these changes are automatically made in the chart created from the worksheet.

To return to the worksheet from which a chart was created, click the tab of the worksheet. The chart can be accessed once again by clicking the sheet tab with the chart name on it.

Zoom Command

You can use the Zoom command on the View menu to enlarge a chart sheet or worksheet to see it in greater detail, or reduce it to see more on your screen. You can use the preset zoom settings or key your own between 10% and 400% of the actual size. When you choose the Fit Selection option, the sheet is automatically sized to fit the screen. You can choose the Zoom command on the View menu or the Zoom button on the toolbar.

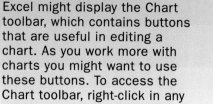

Hot Tip

Excel might display the Chart toolbar, which contains buttons that are useful in editing a chart. As you work more with charts you might want to use these buttons. To access the Chart toolbar, right-click in any existing toolbar and choose **Chart** from the shortcut menu. If you do not want the Chart toolbar displayed, you can close it.

S TEP-BY-STEP 8.2

1. Click the **Sheet1** tab. The worksheet appears.

2. Edit the contents of **A5** to be **High School Degree.**

3. Click the **Column** sheet tab. The chart sheet appears. The label for the second column has changed.

4. To see the labels more closely, click the arrow on the **Zoom** button. Click **75%.** Scroll to view all areas of the chart.

5. To reduce the sheet to fit the screen, open the **View** menu and choose **Zoom.** The Zoom dialog box appears.

6. Click **Fit selection** from the options. Click **OK.**

7. Save and leave the file open for the next Step-by-Step.

Renaming a Chart Sheet

Renaming a chart sheet is particularly useful after you have prepared several charts from the same data on a worksheet. These charts could become difficult to distinguish by their chart sheet number and are easier to recognize with more descriptive names. Change the name of the chart sheet by choosing the Sheet command on the Format menu and choosing Rename on the submenu. You can also change the name of the sheet by right-clicking the sheet tab and then clicking Rename on the shortcut menu (or double-click the tab, which highlights the name, and key the new name).

Hot Tip

You can delete chart sheets by right-clicking the chart sheet tab, and clicking **Delete** on the shortcut menu.

STEP-BY-STEP 8.3

1. Right-click the **Column** sheet tab.

2. Click **Rename** on the shortcut menu.

3. Key **Income Chart** on the sheet tab.

4. Click outside the sheet tab.

5. Save and leave the file open for the next Step-by-Step.

Previewing and Printing a Chart

You preview and print a chart the same way you do a worksheet. You can click the Print Preview button to preview the sheet. You click the Print button to send the sheet directly to the printer.

STEP-BY-STEP 8.4

1. Click the **Print Preview** button. The chart appears in the preview window.

2. Click the **Print** button in the Print Preview window.

3. Click **OK**.

4. Save and close the file.

Creating an Embedded Chart

An embedded chart appears within a worksheet rather than on a separate sheet. An embedded chart is created in the same way as a chart on a sheet with one exception. In the last step of the Chart Wizard (step 4), you click the *As object in* button rather than the *As new sheet* button, as shown in Figure 8-10.

Because embedded charts are displayed directly on the worksheet, there is the possibility that they can interfere with other worksheet data by covering it or by appearing in an area that is inconvenient for printing. You can move an embedded chart by dragging it to a different part of the worksheet. You can also change the size of an embedded chart by dragging the *image handles*, which are small black squares that appear at the corners and sides of an embedded chart.

> **Computer Concepts**
>
> Embedded charts are useful when you want to print a chart next to the data the chart illustrates. When a chart will be displayed or printed without the data used to create the chart, a separate chart sheet is usually more appropriate.

S TEP-BY-STEP 8.5

Great Plains Grains is a company that sells a variety of agricultural products. The managers would like to determine which products comprise the largest portion of their sales by illustrating the segment sales in a pie chart.

1. Open **IE Step8-5** from the data files, and save it as **Segment Sales,** followed by your initials.

2. Select the range **A7:B10.**

3. Click the **Chart Wizard** button on the Standard toolbar.

4. Click the **Pie** chart type.

5. Click the pie chart in the upper left corner of the *Chart sub-type* section, if it is not already selected. The description identifies the selected chart as *Pie. Displays the contribution of each value to a total.*

6. Click **Next.** The Step 2 Chart Wizard dialog box appears.

7. Click **Next.** The Step 3 Chart Wizard dialog box appears.

8. Click the **Titles** tab if it is not selected already, and key **Annual Sales by Segment** in the *Chart title* text box.

9. Click the **Legend** tab and make sure the **Show Legend** box is not checked.

10. Click the **Data Labels** tab and click the **Category name** and **Percentage** check boxes.

11. Click **Next.** The Step 4 Chart Wizard dialog box appears.

12. Click **As object in** if it is not already selected, and then click **Finish.**

13. Use the image handles to fit the chart within **C6:E14.** Then click outside of the chart. Your screen should look similar to Figure 8-12.

STEP-BY-STEP 8.5 Continued

FIGURE 8-12
Creating an embedded pie chart

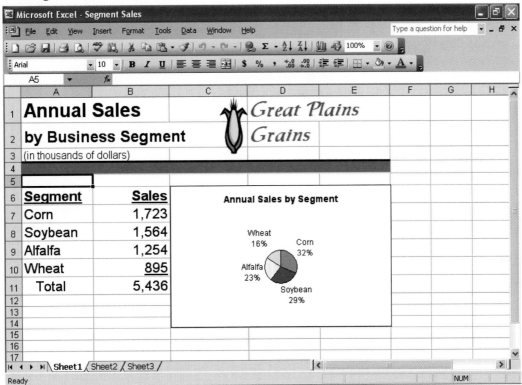

14. Save and print the file and leave the worksheet open for the next Step-by-Step.

Creating Other Types of Charts

In previous Step-by-Steps you created a column chart and a pie chart. Now you learn to create a three-dimensional chart and a scatter chart.

Three-Dimensional Charts

Excel enables you to make charts look as though they are three-dimensional. Area, bar, column, cone, cylinder, line, surface, pie, and pyramid charts are available in three-dimensional formats.

Hot Tip

You can print the chart with or without the worksheet data you used to create the chart. To print the chart only, select the chart by clicking it, and on the **File** menu, choose **Print**. To print the chart and the worksheet data, deselect the chart by clicking outside of it, and then open the **File** menu and choose **Print**.

STEP-BY-STEP 8.6

1. Save the Segment Sales workbook as **Segment Sales 3D,** followed by your initials.

2. Right-click the white space in the pie chart embedded in the worksheet. A shortcut menu appears.

3. Choose **Chart Type** on the menu. The Chart Type dialog box appears.

4. Click the middle chart in the top row of the *Chart sub-type* section. The chart description *Pie with a 3-D visual effect* appears at the bottom of the dialog box.

5. Click **OK.** You are returned to the worksheet. Click outside the chart to deselect it. Your screen should look similar to Figure 8-13.

FIGURE 8-13
3-D pie chart

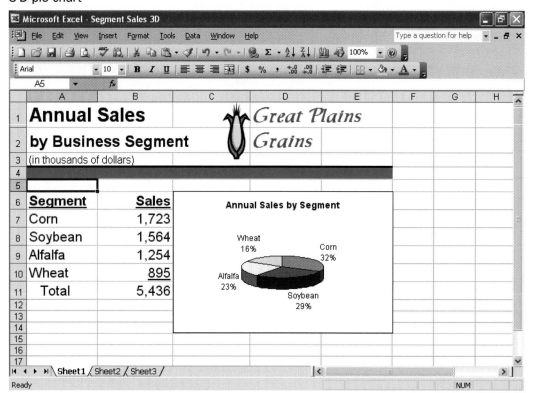

6. Save, print, and then close the worksheet.

Scatter charts are sometimes referred to as XY charts because they place data points between an X and Y axis. Scatter charts can be harder to prepare because you must designate which data should be used as a scale on each axis.

STEP-BY-STEP 8.7

Coronado Foundries produces manufactured goods. During the manufacturing process, a certain amount of scrap will be produced. Management expects that as more goods are produced, more scrap will also be produced. They would like to produce a chart to illustrate the expected relationship.

1. Open **IE Step8-7** from the data files, and save it as **Scrap Report,** followed by your initials.

2. Select the range **B6:C16.**

3. Open the **Insert** menu and choose **Chart.** The Step 1 Chart Wizard dialog box appears.

4. Click the chart type **XY (Scatter)** and then click the first chart sub-type if it is not already selected. The description identifies the selected chart as *Scatter. Compares pairs of values.*

5. Click **Next.** The Step 2 Chart Wizard dialog box appears.

6. Click **Next.** The Step 3 Chart Wizard dialog box appears.

7. Click the **Titles** tab if it is not selected already. In the *Chart title* box, key **Production and Scrap Report;** in the *Value (X) axis* box, key **Units of Production;** and in the *Value (Y) axis* box, key **Units of Scrap.**

8. Click the **Legend** tab, and make sure the **Show Legend** box is not checked.

9. Click **Next.** The Step 4 Chart Wizard dialog box appears.

10. Click **As new sheet** if it is not already selected.

11. Key **Scatter Chart** in the *As new sheet* text box.

12. Click **Finish.** A scatter chart appears on a chart sheet. You might be able to tell that factories with larger production also tend to generate more scrap. Notice that the data points are concentrated in the right portion of the chart. To spread the data out, you can adjust the scale of the chart.

13. To adjust the X-axis to the left, double-click the X (horizontal) axis. (*Hint*: To ensure that you double-click the correct chart part, point to the part to display its ScreenTip. For the horizontal axis, you should see the ScreenTip *Value (X) axis.*) The Format Axis dialog box appears.

14. Click the **Scale** tab, key **4000** in the *Minimum* box, and click **OK.** The portion of the chart to the left of 4000 on the X-axis, which did not have any data points, has been removed.

STEP-BY-STEP 8.7 Continued

15. To adjust the Y-axis downward, double-click the Y (vertical) axis. The Format Axis dialog box appears.

16. Click the **Scale** tab if necessary, key **250** in the *Maximum* box, and click **OK.** The portion of the chart above 250 is removed. The chart sheet on your screen should look similar to Figure 8-14.

FIGURE 8-14
Scatter charts can show labeled points between two axes

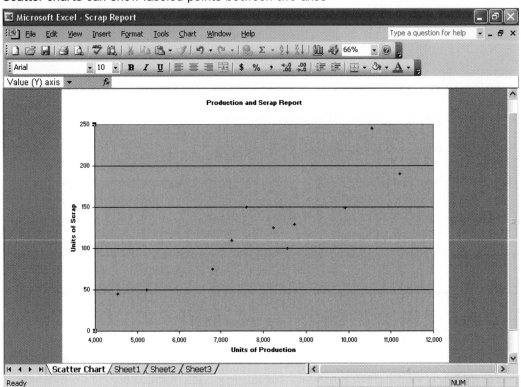

17. Save, print, and close the file.

Editing a Chart

The Chart Wizard is a quick and easy way to create professional-looking charts. However, you might want to edit the chart to suit your specific needs. For example, you might want to change a title font or the color of a column. Figure 8-15 shows six areas of the chart and some of the characteristics that can be changed. Clicking once on the part selects it; double-clicking it opens a dialog box in which you can make formatting changes. Each dialog box contains tabs with options for editing specific chart characteristics, as described in Table 8-2. Right-clicking a part displays a shortcut menu with options such as clearing data, inserting data, or changing chart types.

FIGURE 8-15
Six parts of the chart

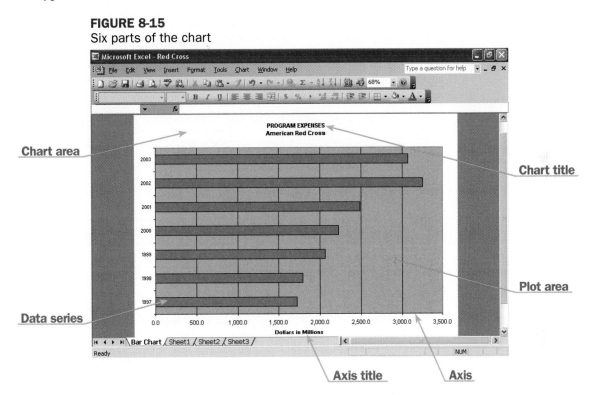

TABLE 8-2
Charts can be edited using one of six Format dialog boxes

FORMAT DIALOG BOX	TABS IN THE DIALOG BOX
Format Chart Title	Patterns—designates the border and color of the chart title
	Font—designates the font, font size, and color of characters in the chart title
	Alignment—designates the justification and orientation of the chart title
Format Axis Title	Patterns—designates the border and color of the axis title
	Font—designates the font and font size of characters in the axis title
	Alignment—designates the justification and orientation of the axis title
Format Axis	Patterns—designates the border and color of the axis
	Scale—designates characteristics of the axis scale
	Font—designates the font and font size of characters in the axis
	Number—designates the format of numbers in the labels in the axis (for example, currency, text, date)
	Alignment—designates the orientation of the labels in the axis
Format Data Series	Patterns—designates the border and color of the data series
	Axis—designates whether the data is plotted on a primary or secondary axis
	Y Error Bars—designates the treatment of points that extend beyond the scale of the chart
	Data Labels—designates the words or values that may appear on the points of a graph
	Series Order—designates which data series will appear first in clustered charts
	Options—designates the other characteristics unique to the chart type
Format Plot Area	Patterns—designates the border and color of the plot area
Format Chart Area	Patterns—designates the border and color of the chart background
	Font—designates the font and font size of characters in the chart area

STEP-BY-STEP 8.8

1. Open **IE Step8-8** from the data files, and save it as **Red Cross,** followed by your initials. This is a worksheet containing the program expenses of the American Red Cross.

2. Click the **Bar Chart** sheet tab. The sheet contains a chart that indicates the level of disaster services expense for each period.

3. To add a subtitle, click the chart title **PROGRAM EXPENSES.** A shaded border with handles surrounds the title.

4. Click to the right of the last *S* in the title. An insertion point appears.

5. Press **Enter.** The insertion point becomes centered under the first line of the title.

6. Key **American Red Cross.** The subtitle appears in the chart.

7. To change the font size of the horizontal axis labels, double-click the horizontal axis. The Format Axis dialog box appears.

8. Click the **Font** tab. The axis labels are currently 10 point.

9. Choose **12** in the *Size* box.

10. Click **OK.** You are returned to the chart sheet. The horizontal axis labels are now larger.

11. To change the color of the bars, right-click one of the bars and select **Format Data Series** on the shortcut menu. The Format Data Series dialog box appears.

12. Click the **Patterns** tab if it is not already selected.

13. Click any bright red in the *Area* box. A bright red color appears in the Sample box.

14. Click **OK**. You are returned to the chart sheet. The chart appears with bright red bars. Your screen should appear similar to Figure 8-15.

15. Leave the chart sheet open for the next Step-by-Step.

Changing the Type of Chart

After creating a chart, you can change it to a different type by choosing the Chart Type command on the Chart menu (or by right-clicking the chart area or plot area and then choosing the Chart Type command). The Chart Type dialog box is the same dialog box that appears in the *Step 1* Chart Wizard dialog box (see Figure 8-8).

> **Computer Concepts**
>
> Not all charts are interchangeable. For example, data that is suitable for a pie chart is often not logical in a scatter chart. However, most line charts are easily converted into column or bar charts.

S TEP-BY-STEP 8.9

1. Open the **Chart** menu and choose **Chart Type.**

2. Click **Line** in the *Chart type* box.

3. Click the middle box in the first column of the *Chart sub-type* section if it is not already selected. The description identifies the selected chart as *Line with markers displayed at each data value.*

4. Click **OK.** The new line chart appears.

5. Rename the chart sheet as **Line Chart.** Your line chart should appear as shown in Figure 8-16.

FIGURE 8-16
Changing a column chart to a line chart

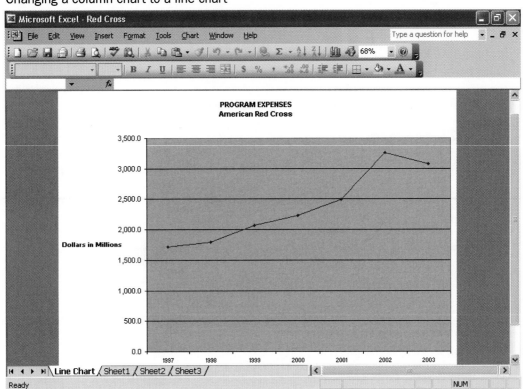

6. Save, print, and close the file.

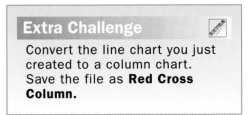

Extra Challenge

Convert the line chart you just created to a column chart. Save the file as **Red Cross Column.**

SUMMARY

In this lesson, you learned:

- A chart is a graphical representation of worksheet data. You can create several types of worksheet charts, including column, line, pie, and scatter charts. Several types of charts can also be created three-dimensionally.

- Charts can be embedded within a worksheet or created on a chart sheet. A chart sheet is an area separate from the Excel worksheet in which a chart is created and stored. An embedded chart is created within a worksheet.

- The Chart Wizard is a four-step, on-screen guide that helps you prepare a chart from an Excel worksheet. The Chart Wizard is used to prepare a chart whether the chart is to appear in the worksheet or in a chart sheet.

- A chart created from a worksheet is considered part of that worksheet. When you save the worksheet, you also save the charts you have created from the worksheet.

- You can edit your chart by clicking one of six areas of the chart that accesses a Format dialog box. You can change the type of chart in the Chart Type dialog box.

VOCABULARY *Review*

Define the following terms:

Axis	Column chart	Image handles
Chart	Data labels	Line chart
Chart sheet	Data series	Pie chart
Chart Wizard	Embedded chart	Scatter chart

REVIEW *Questions*

TRUE/FALSE

Circle T if the statement is true or F if the statement is false.

T   F   1. Charts are a graphical representation of worksheet data.

T   F   2. Column charts are the best way to represent data groups that are part of a whole.

T   F   3. Line charts are good for representing trends over a period of time.

T   F   4. A scatter chart produces a "cloud" of data points not connected by lines.

T   F   5. When the worksheet data changes, charts created from the worksheet also change.

FILL IN THE BLANK

Complete the following sentences by writing the correct word or words in the blanks provided.

1. A(n) _____ chart is represented by a circle divided into portions.

2. In a worksheet chart, the _____ shows patterns or symbols that identify the different types of data.

3. The _____ menu contains the command for renaming a chart sheet.

4. A(n) _____ chart is created on the same sheet as the data being charted.

5. _____ represent the values depicted by chart objects like data points or columns.

PROJECTS

 PROJECT 8-1

The file *IE Project8-1* contains the populations of the world's largest cities. Create a column chart to illustrate the data.

1. Open **IE Project8-1** from the data files, and save it as **Population,** followed by your initials.

2. Create a column chart from the data in **A5:B12** in a chart sheet.

3. Title the chart **World's Largest Cities.**

4. Title the Y-axis **Population in Millions.** No X-axis title is needed.

5. Include major horizontal gridlines. (*Hint*: Gridlines are specified under the **Gridlines** tab in *Step 3* of the Chart Wizard.)

6. Do not include a legend in the chart.

7. Name the chart sheet **Column Chart.**

8. Preview the chart.

9. Save, print, and close the file.

PROJECT 8-2

You have been running each morning to stay in shape. Over the past 10 weeks you have recorded your running times in file *IE Project8-2*.

1. Open **IE Project8-2** from the data files and save it as **Training,** followed by your initials.

2. Create an embedded line chart with markers at each data value from the data in **A5:B14.**

3. Do not include a chart title. *in a work sheet*

4. Title the Y-axis **Time in Minutes.** No X-axis title is needed.

5. Include major horizontal gridlines in the chart.

6. Do not include a legend in the chart.

7. Use the chart handles to position the chart in the range **C3:I15** on the worksheet.

8. Save the file. Print the worksheet with the embedded chart, and close the file.

 PROJECT 8-3

The file *IE Project8-3* contains the number of McDonald's hamburger restaurants in different regions of the world.

1. Open **IE Project8-3** from the data files, and save it as **McDonalds**, followed by your initials.

2. Create a pie chart in a chart sheet from the data in **A6:B10**.

3. Title the chart **Systemwide Locations.**

4. Place a legend on the right side of the chart that identifies each geographical region.

5. Include percentages as data labels next to each slice.

6. Name the chart sheet **Pie Chart.**

7. Edit font sizes so the chart title is **24** points, the slice percentages are **18** points, and the legend is **18** points.

8. Switch to the worksheet. Edit the content of **A8** to be **Other** rather than *APMEA*.

9. Switch back to the chart sheet to see that the legend has been updated with the edited data.

10. Save the file. Print the chart and close the file.

 PROJECT 8-4

The file *IE Project8-4* contains the monthly cash flow of a young family. To better explain their expenses to family members, a member of the household decides to create a pie chart in which each slice represents an expense category that contributes to total expenses.

1. Open **IE Project8-4** from the data files, and save it as **Family Expenses,** followed by your initials.

2. Create a three-dimensional pie chart on a chart sheet from the data in **A6:B13.**

3. Title the pie chart **Where Our Money Goes.**

4. Do not include a legend in the chart.

5. The pie chart should include the category names and percentages for each slice.

6. Name the chart sheet **3D Pie Chart.**

7. Change the font size of the chart title to **18** points.

8. Change the font size of the data labels to **14** points.

9. Preview the chart. As you view the chart determine in what areas you believe most spending occurs.

10. Save the file. Print the chart and close the file.

 PROJECT 8-5

The file *IE Project8-5* contains the study time and examination scores for several students. The instructor is attempting to determine if there is a relationship between study time and examination scores.

1. Open **IE Project8-5** from the data files, and save it as **Study Time,** followed by your initials.

2. Create a scatter chart without connecting lines in a chart sheet from the data in **B4:C21.**

3. Title the chart **Comparison of Exam Grades to Study Time.**

4. Title the X-axis **Hours of Study.**

5. Title the Y-axis **Examination Grades.**

6. Do not include gridlines, a legend, or data labels in the chart.

7. Name the chart sheet **Scatter Chart.**

8. Change the font size of the chart title to **20** points.

9. Change the font size of the axis titles to **14** points.

10. Change the font size of the axis labels to **12** points.

11. Change the minimum value of the vertical scale (Y-axis) to **50.**

12. Preview the chart. As you view the chart, determine whether you believe a relationship exists between study time and examination results.

13. Save the file. Print the chart and close the file.

PROJECT 8-6

You operate the concession stand at the home baseball games of Mountain College, and have noticed a decrease in popularity of certain items as the season has progressed. The sales for each game have been kept on a worksheet. Now you would like to use the worksheet to create a chart that illustrates the change in sales levels for each product during the season.

1. Open **IE Project8-6** from the data files, and save it as **Concession Sales,** followed by your initials.

2. Create a column chart on a chart sheet from the data in **A4:E9.**

3. Title the chart **Concession Sales.**

4. No X-axis title is needed. Title the Y-axis **Sales in Dollars.**

5. Include a legend at the right of the chart to identify the game number.

6. Name the chart sheet **Column Chart.**

7. Access the Format Plot Area dialog box and change the color in the *Area* box to white.

8. Change the font of the chart title to **18** points.

9. Change the font size of the X (horizontal) axis labels to **14** points and make them bold.

10. Change the font size of the Y (vertical) axis labels to **12** points.

11. Change the font size of the Y-axis title to **14** points.

12. Change the font size of the legend labels to **12** points.

13. Preview the chart. While you view the chart, determine which product has decreased in sales over the last four games.

14. Save the file. Print the chart and close the file.

 PROJECT 8-7

The file *IE Project8-7* contains the income statement of Radiation Software Corporation for several years. You want to illustrate the corporation's growth by charting the sales and income levels.

1. Open **IE Project8-7** from the data files and save it as **Radiation,** followed by your initials.

2. Create a line chart with markers in a chart sheet from the data in **A5:F7.**

3. Title the chart **Revenue and Income of Radiation Software Corporation.**

4. Title the Y-axis (**in Thousands**). No X-axis title is needed.

5. Place a legend that distinguishes revenue from income at the bottom of the chart.

6. Name the chart sheet **Revenue Chart.**

7. Change the font size of the chart title to **18** points.

8. Change the font size of the X (horizontal) axis and Y (vertical) axis labels to **14** points.

9. Change the font size of the Y-axis title to **12** points and make it bold.

10. Change the font size of the legend labels to **14** points.

11. Save the file. Print the chart. As you view the printed chart, determine whether the company's sales have decreased, increased, or remained stable.

12. Change the type of chart to a clustered column chart.

13. Save the file. Print the chart and close the file.

PROJECT 8-8

1. Open **IE Project8-8** from the data files and save it as **Temperature,** followed by your initials.

2. Create a line chart with markers in a chart sheet from the data in **A3:M5.**

3. Title the chart **Temperatures for Chico, California.**

4. Title the Y-axis **Temperatures in Fahrenheit.** No X-axis title is needed.

5. Place a legend on the right side of the chart that distinguishes the high and low temperatures.

6. Name the chart sheet **Line Chart.**

7. Change the font size of the chart title to **18** points.

8. Change the font size of the X (horizontal) axis and Y (vertical) axis labels to **14** points.

9. Change the font size of the Y-axis title to **16** points and make it bold.

10. Change the font size of the legend labels to **14** points.

11. Double-click the high temperature line to display the Format Data Series dialog box. Make the following changes:
    a. Click the **Patterns** tab if necessary. In the *Line* section, change the *Weight* to the heaviest line and the *Color* to red.
    b. In the *Marker* section, change the *Foreground* to red and the *Background* to red.

12. Click **OK** to close the Format Data Series dialog box.

13. Double-click the low temperature line to display the Format Data Series dialog box. Make the following changes:
    a. In the *Line* section (on the **Patterns** tab), change the *Weight* to heavy and *Color* to blue.
    b. In the *Marker* section, change the *Foreground* to blue and the *Background* to blue.

14. Click **OK** to close the Format Data Series dialog box.

15. Double-click the plot area of the chart to display the Format Plot Area dialog box. In the *Area* section of the dialog box, change the color to white.

16. Click **OK** to close the Format Plot Area dialog box.

17. Save the file. Print the chart and close the file.

CRITICAL *Thinking*

 ACTIVITY 8-1

 For each scenario, determine what type of worksheet chart you believe would be the most appropriate to represent the data. Justify your answer by describing why you believe that chart is most appropriate.

Scenario 1. A scientist has given varying amounts of water to 200 potted plants. Over 35 days, the height of the plant and the amount of water given to the plant are recorded in a worksheet.

Scenario 2. A corporation developed a new product last year. A manager in the corporation recorded the number of units sold each month. He noticed that sales in summer months are much higher than sales in the winter. He would like to prepare a chart to illustrate this to other sales managers.

Scenario 3. A high school principal has students who come from five middle schools. She has recorded the name of the middle school and the number of students from each of the middle schools. She would like to illustrate how some of the middle schools supply significantly more students than other middle schools.

 ACTIVITY 8-2

You recently opened a store that buys and sells used CDs and DVDs. Now that you have a small business, you are responsible for budgets, invoices, and inventory. Initially you kept track of inventory and budget data by writing them in a paper notebook. Now that the business is growing, this method has become too cumbersome. You decide to transfer the data into electronic format. All worksheets should contain the name of your store, Old Cee Dees, the current date, and a title describing the data.

1. Create a worksheet to track your inventory. The worksheet should include (a) the title of the CD or DVD, (b) the artist, (c) the quantity of each, and (d) the cost per item. Enter the data shown in Figure 8-17 in the worksheet and save the workbook as **Cee Dee Inventory**, followed by your initials.

FIGURE 8-17

Title	Artist	Quantity	Cost per Item
Heading Out	Art Burns	3	$5.50
Goin' Home	Art Burns	4	$4.75
Grass is Greener	Sally Clyde	5	$5.50
Blue Hearts	Sally Clyde	2	$5.75
Red Roses	Sally Clyde	7	$4.75
Wild Time	Turner McGrew	5	$5.75

2. Create another worksheet showing the expected income and expenses for the month. The rows of the worksheet should accommodate the (a) sales revenue, (b) purchases of used CDs/DVDs, (c) rent expense, (d) utilities expense, (e) tax expense, and (f) net income. The columns in your worksheet should include (a) budgeted amounts, (b) actual amounts, and (c) the variance (difference between budgeted and actual). Then, enter the data shown in Figure 8-18. For the Actual Net Income, enter a formula that subtracts the purchases and expenses from revenue. For the Budgeted Net Income, enter a formula that subtracts the purchases and expenses from revenue. Save the workbook as **Cee Dee Budget.**

FIGURE 8-18

	Actual	Budgeted
Revenue	$10,388	$9,000
Purchases of Used CDs/DVDs	$5,000	$4,500
Rent Expense	$500	$500
Utilities Expense	$350	$300
Tax Expense	$817	$666
Net Income		

INTRODUCTORY MICROSOFT EXCEL

COMMAND SUMMARY

FEATURE	MENU CHOICE	TOOLBAR BUTTON	LESSON
Align Data	Format, Cells, Alignment		2
Bold Data	Format, Cells, Font	**B**	2
Borders Around Cells	Format, Cells, Border	▦	2
Center Data Across Range of Cells	Format, Cells, Alignment, Center Across Selection	▦	2
Chart, Create a	Insert, Chart	▥	8
Chart, Preview a	File, Print Preview	▨	8
Color a Worksheet Tab	Format, Sheet, Tab Color		7
Column, Delete a	Edit, Delete, Entire column		3
Column, Hide	Format, Column, Hide		6
Column, Insert a	Insert, Columns		3
Column, Unhide	Format, Column, Unhide		6
Column Width, Automatic	Format, Column, AutoFit Selection		2
Column Width, Specific	Format, Column, Width		2
Copy by Filling	Edit, Fill		3
Clip Art, Insert	Insert, Picture, Clip Art		6
Data, Color	Format, Cells, Font	**A** ▾	2
Data, Copy	Edit, Copy	▤	3
Data, Filter	Data, Filter, AutoFilter		6
Data, Find	Edit, Find	▤	1
Data, Italicize	Format, Cells, Font	*I*	2
Data, Move	Edit, Cut, and then Edit, Paste	✂ ▤	3
Data, Paste	Edit, Paste	▤	3
Data Ascending, Sort	Data, Sort	▤	6
Data Descending, Sort	Data, Sort	▤	6
Data, Replace	Edit, Replace		1
Data, Rotating	Format, Cells, Alignment		2
Data, Underline	Format, Cells, Font	U	2
Data, Wrap	Format, Cells, Alignment, Wrap text		2

FEATURE	MENU CHOICE	TOOLBAR BUTTON	LESSON
Decimal, Decrease	Format, Cells, Number		2
Decimal, Increase	Format, Cells, Number		2
Delay Calculations	Tools, Options, Calculation		4
Design a Printed Page	File, Page Setup		3
Drawing Toolbar, Display the	View, Toolbars, Drawing		6
Fill a Cell with Color	Format, Cells, Patterns		2
Font, Change a	Format, Cells, Font	Arial	2
Font Size, Change the	Format, Cells, Font	10	2
Format Painting			2
Formulas, Show	Tools, Options, View		4
Function Formula, Insert a	Insert, Function		5
Hyperlink, Insert a	Insert, Hyperlink		6
Indention, Decrease			2
Indention, Increase			2
Picture from a File, Insert	Insert, Picture, from File		6
Research	Tools, Research		6
Row, Delete a	Edit, Delete		3
Row Height, Change	Format, Row, Height		2
Row, Hide	Format, Row, Hide		6
Row, Insert a	Insert, Rows		3
Row, Unhide	Format, Row, Unhide		6
Spelling, Check	Tools, Spelling		3
Sum a Range (AutoSum)	Insert, Function	Σ	4
Titles, Freeze the	Window, Freeze Panes		3
Titles, Unfreeze	Window, Unfreeze Panes		3
Worksheet, Delete	Edit, Delete Sheet		6
Worksheet, Move	Edit, Move or Copy Sheet		7
Worksheet, Name a	Format, Sheet, Rename		6
Worksheet, Open a	File, Open		1
Worksheet, Preview a	File, Print Preview		3
Worksheet, Print a	File, Print		1
Worksheet, Save a Named	File, Save		1
Worksheet, Save an Unnamed	File, Save As		1
Zoom	View, Zoom	100%	1

REVIEW *Questions*

TRUE/FALSE

Circle T if the statement is true or F if the statement is false.

T   F   1. The active cell reference will appear in the toolbar.

T   F   2. To select a group of cells, click each cell individually until all cells in the range have been selected.

T   F   3. The Save As dialog box appears every time you save a worksheet.

T   F   4. The formula =B$4+C$9 contains mixed cell references.

T   F   5. A chart can be printed from the chart sheet.

MATCHING

Match the description in Column 2 with the text position function in Column 1.

Column 1	Column 2
___ 1. Wrapping	**A.** Displays text at an angle
___ 2. Rotating	**B.** Aligns the text to the right, left, or center
___ 3. Indenting	**C.** Combines several cells into one and places the contents in the middle of the cell
___ 4. Justifying	**D.** Begins a new line within a cell
___ 5. Merge and Center	**E.** Moves the text several spaces to the right

FILL IN THE BLANK

Complete the following sentences by writing the correct word or words in the blanks provided.

1. A(n) _____ cell reference will remain the same when copied or moved.

2. The Manual button on the Calculation tab in the Options dialog box delays calculation until the _____ key is pressed.

3. The _____ toolbar button will add a range of numbers in a worksheet.

4. A(n) _____ chart uses bars to represent values in a worksheet.

5. The _____ tab in the Options dialog box is used to display formulas rather than values in the worksheet.

MATCHING

Match the correct result in Column 2 to the formula in Column 1. Assume the following values appear in the worksheet:

Cell	Value
B2	5
B3	6
B4	4
B5	7

Column 1	Column 2
___ 1. =10+B5	A. 2
___ 2. =B2*B4	B. 5
___ 3. =(B3+B4)/B2	C. 17
___ 4. =AVERAGE(B3:B4)	D. 20
___ 5. =SUM(B2:B5)	E. 22

PROJECTS

PROJECT 1

The worksheet in *IE Project1* is a daily sales report that is submitted by a gas station manager to the owner. Change the appearance of the worksheet to make it easier to read.

1. Open **IE Project1** from the data files, and save it as **Gas Sales,** followed by your initials.

2. Change the size of the text in **A1** to **16** points, and then bold it.

3. Change the width of column **A** to **20,** and the width of columns **B** through **D** to **15.**

4. Merge and center **A1:D1.**

5. Format **B2** as a date in which the month is alphabetic and the day and year are numeric (Month XX, XXXX).

6. Enter **May 28, 2006** in B2.

7. Merge and center **B2:D2.**

8. Format **B3** for time in which the hours and minutes are numeric and followed by AM or PM (XX:XX XM).

9. Enter **8:05 PM** in **B3**.

10. Merge and center **B3:D3**.

11. Change the size of the text in **A2:D8** to **14** points.

12. Wrap the text in **C5**.

13. Underline and center **B5:D5**.

14. Format **B6:B8** as a **Number** with a comma separator and no decimal places.

15. Format **C6:D8** for **Currency** with 2 decimal places.

16. Save, print, and close the file.

PROJECT 2

An income statement describes how profitable a company has been during a certain period of time. *IE Project2* is the income statement of Dole Food Company, Inc. Format the income statement in a way that makes it more readable to the financial statement user. The financial statement should have the following qualities:

■ The heading should be in a bold font that is larger than the font of the items in the body of the financial statement.

■ The heading should be separated from the body of the financial statement by at least one row.

■ Columns of the worksheet should be wide enough to view all of their contents.

■ The first (revenues) and last (net income) numbers in the financial statement should be preceded by dollar signs.

■ All numbers should use a comma as the 1000 separator.

■ Color and borders should be added to make the file visually appealing.

When you have finished, save the file as **Dole**, followed by your initials. Then, print and close the file.

PROJECT 3

The file *IE Project3* is a worksheet that contains a list of members of the Computer Science Club and service points the members earned during the year. In preparation for their end-of-year banquet, the club secretary would like to prepare a worksheet that identifies the exceptional members (those with service points exceeding 1,000) and outstanding members (those with service points between 800 and 1,000). Format the worksheet with the following qualities.

■ Sort the data by column B, the number of service points, with those with the most points at the top of the worksheet.

■ Add the title **Exceptional and Outstanding Members** at the top of the worksheet. The title should be bold and in a font larger than the other text in the worksheet.

■ Add the subtitle **Exceptional Members** above William Griffin's name and bold it.

■ Add the subtitle **Outstanding Members** above Matthew Carcello's name and bold it.

■ Add the subtitle **Other Active Members** above Mohamed Abdul's name and bold it.

■ The service points should be formatted as a Number with a comma separator and no decimal places.

■ The school colors are blue and red. Add these colors and bolding to make the worksheet visually appealing.

When you have finished, save the file as **CS Club**, followed by your initials. Then, print and close the file.

PROJECT 4

The revenue and expenses of Escape Computer Network Corporation are recorded in *IE Project4*. You want to illustrate the distribution of the corporation's costs for the year.

1. Open **IE Project4** from the data files, and save it as **Escape**, followed by your initials.

2. Create an exploded pie chart with three-dimensional effects in a chart sheet using the data in **A13:B19**.

3. Title the chart **Expenses for the Year**.

4. Place a legend at the bottom of the chart to identify the slices.

5. Include percentages next to each slice.

6. Name the chart sheet **Pie Chart**.

7. Edit font sizes so the chart title is **22** points, the slice percentages are **18** points, and the legend is **14** points.

8. Preview the chart. As you view the chart, determine the largest categories of expense.

9. Save the file, print the chart, and close the file.

SIMULATION

   You work at the Java Internet Café, which has been open a short time. The café serves coffee, other beverages, and pastries; and offers Internet access. Computers are set up on tables in the store so customers can come in, have a cup of coffee and a Danish, and explore the World Wide Web. You are asked to create a menu of coffee prices and computer prices. You will do this by integrating Microsoft Excel and Microsoft Word.

JOB 1

1. Open a new Excel workbook.

2. Key the data shown in Figure UR-1 in the worksheet.

FIGURE UR-1

	A	B	C	D
1	Coffee Prices			
2				
3	House coffee	$1.00	Café breve	$2.25
4				
5	Café au lait	$1.50	Café latte	$2.25
6				
7	Cappuccino	$1.75	Con panna	$2.50
8				
9	Espresso	$2.00	Espresso doppio	$2.75

3. Change the width of columns **A** and **C** to **29** and columns **B** and **D** to **9**.

4. Left-align data in columns **B** and **D**.

5. Change the font of all data to **Arial, 14** points.

6. Format the data in columns **B** and **D** for currency with 2 places to the right of the decimal.

7. Underline the data in **A1**.

8. Save the file as **Coffee Prices**, followed by your initials.

9. Highlight and copy **A1** through **D9**.

10. Open Word and the **IE Simulation** document from the data files.

11. Insert one blank line below the *Menu* heading and paste link the worksheet.

12. Save the document as **Java Café Menu**, followed by your initials.

13. Switch to Excel, and open **Computer** from the data files.

14. Rename and save it as **Computer Prices,** followed by your initials.

15. Highlight and copy **A1** through **B11.**

16. Switch to Word and **Java Café Menu.**

17. Insert a blank line after the *Coffee Prices* menu listings.

18. Paste link the **Computer Prices** worksheet.

19. Preview the document. Adjust the placement of data if necessary so that all data fits on one page.

20. Save, print, and close **Java Café Menu.**

21. Switch to Excel and close **Computer Prices** and **Coffee Prices** without saving changes.

JOB 2

The menu you created has been very successful. However, your manager asks you to make a few changes.

1. Open the **Coffee Prices** and **Computer Prices** files you saved in Job 1.

2. Make changes to the **Coffee Prices** and **Computer Prices** worksheets as shown in Figure UR-2.

FIGURE UR-2

Java Internet Café

2001 Zephyr Street
Boulder, CO 80302-2001
303.555.JAVA JavaCafe@Cybershop.com

The Java Internet Café is a coffee shop with a twist. As you can see, there are seven computers on tables at the north side of the café. These computers provide high-speed Internet access to our customers. Whether you're a regular on the Net or a novice, our system is designed to allow you easy exploration of the World Wide Web. You've heard about it; now give it a try. Ask your server to help you get started.

Menu

Paste Special
Edit

Coffee Prices

House coffee	$1.00 *.75*	Café breve	$2.25
Café au lait	$1.50	Café latte	$2.25
Cappuccino	$1.75 *2.00*	Con panna	$2.50
Espresso	$2.00	Espresso doppio	$2.75

Computer Prices

Membership fee -- includes own account with personal ID, password, and e-mail address	$10 per month
28,800 bps Internet access (members) -- includes World Wide Web, FTP, Telnet, and IRC plus e-mail	$4 per hour
28,800 bps Internet access (non-members) -- includes World Wide Web, FTP, Telnet, and IRC	$6 per hour
Color scanner -- includes Internet access, use of software and the CD-ROM library	$5 per 1/2 hour
Laser printer -- inquire about duplexing capabilities	$.25 per page

Sit back, sip your coffee, and surf the net.

3. Save and close **Coffee Prices** and **Computer Prices**. Exit Excel.

4. Switch to Word and open **Java Café Menu.**

5. Notice the file has been updated since you made changes to the two worksheet files. Make the correction in the footer.

6. Save the document as **Java Café Menu 2,** followed by your initials.

7. Print and close. Exit Word.

Advanced Microsoft® Excel

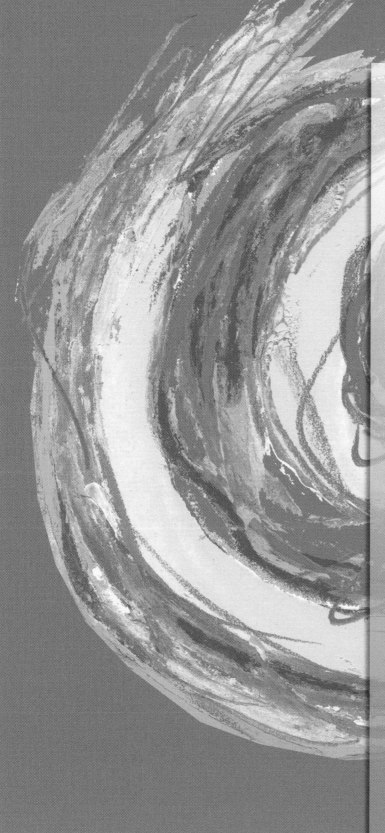

Unit

 Estimated Time for Unit: 19.5 hours

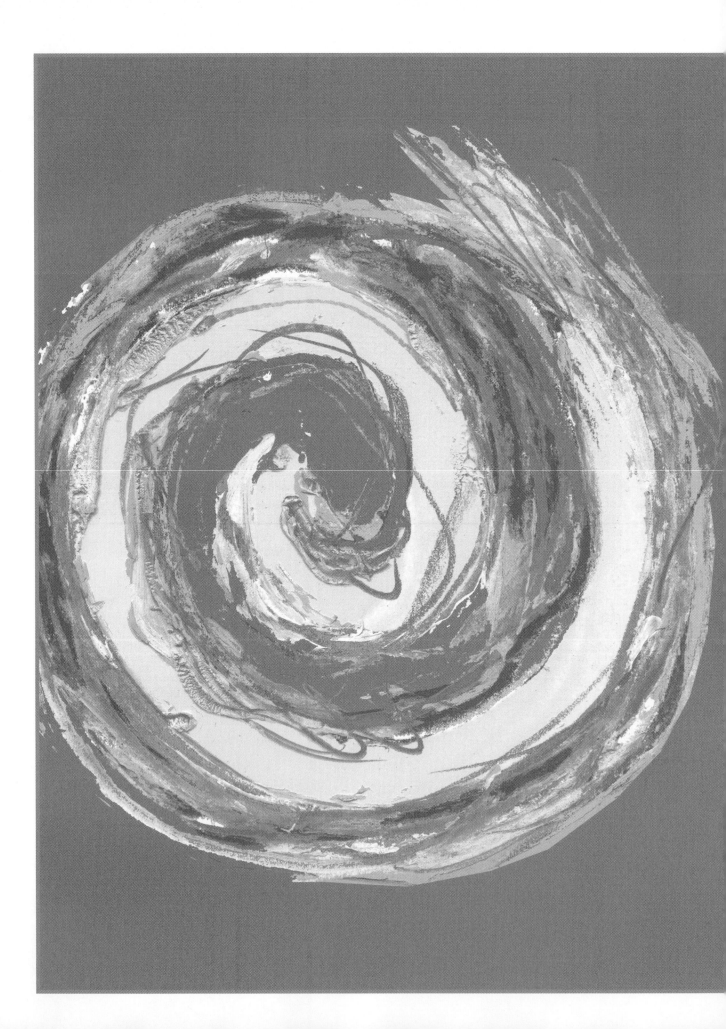

APPLYING ADVANCED WORKSHEET AND CHART OPTIONS

OBJECTIVES

Upon completion of this lesson, you will be able to:

■ Create a custom format.

■ Use AutoFormats.

■ Apply conditional formats.

■ Use styles and data validation.

■ Transpose data.

■ Copy formula results as values.

■ Modify Excel default settings.

■ Enhance the appearance of worksheet charts.

Estimated Time: 2.5 hours

VOCABULARY

Conditional formatting

Data table

Data validation

Default

Transpose

Value

Introduction

Microsoft Excel comes equipped with a number of advanced tools and features that empower you to create professional-looking spreadsheets that use advanced formatting and validation techniques. In this lesson, you will learn how to apply advanced features to data and charts on a worksheet.

Creating a Custom Format

There might be instances in which you need to apply a number format that is not already predefined. For example, the date format *Year-Month,* which would display a date in the format 2006-March, is not one of the formats available in Excel. You can create your own format by selecting the Custom option in the Category list on the *Number* tab.

Formats are actually composed of codes. These codes are simply strings of characters that represent the actual data, such as M for *month*, D for *day*, and Y for *year*. You can easily create your own codes by assembling these characters in a certain order. Table 9-1 describes the various character codes you can select.

TABLE 9-1
Format codes

FORMAT CODE	WHAT IT MEANS
0	Placeholder for a digit. If there is not a digit to fill this place, a zero will hold the place.
#	Placeholder for a digit. If there is not a digit to fill this place, nothing will appear in the place.
; (semicolon)	Divides the parts of the format code.
$	Puts a dollar sign with the number at the same location it appears in the format code.
%	Puts a percent sign with the number at the same location it appears in the format code.
, (comma)	Puts a comma with the number at the same location it appears in the format code.
. (decimal)	Puts a decimal with the number at the same location it appears in the format code.
M or m	Used for months in dates or minutes in time.
D or d	Used for days.
Y or y	Used for years.
H or h	Used for hours.
S or s	Used for seconds.
: (colon)	Used to separate hours, minutes, seconds.

$\mathcal{S}$TEP-BY-STEP 9.1

1. Open **AE Step9-1** from the data files and save the workbook as **Personnel,** followed by your initials.

2. Select the range **C5:C10.**

3. Choose the **Format** menu and select **Cells.**

4. Choose the **Number** tab, if necessary.

5. Select **Custom** from the *Category* list box.

STEP-BY-STEP 9.1 Continued

6. Highlight the text in the *Type* text box, and key **yyyy-d-mmmm.** (Entering four y's tells Excel to enter the complete year number—hence, the year will be displayed as 2006. Entering four m's tells Excel to spell out the complete month name instead of an abbreviation.) Your dialog box should appear similar to Figure 9-1.

FIGURE 9-1
Format Cells dialog box

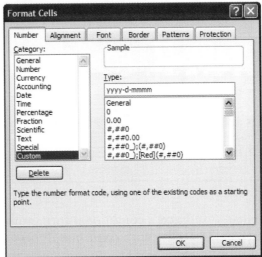

7. Click **OK** and look at your dates.

8. Now, let's modify this custom format. With the range **C5:C10** still selected, select the **Format** menu, click **Cells,** and then choose the **Number** tab, if necessary.

9. Select **Custom** from the *Category* list box, if necessary, and then click on the custom format you just created. Type one more **d** in the *Type* text box so your final format shows as yyyy-dd-mmmm.

10. Click **OK** and view the results. Notice how in every instance the day of the month has two digits instead of one.

11. Print the worksheet. Then save and close the workbook.

Using AutoFormat and Conditional Formatting

AutoFormat is a simple way to make your worksheet appear more professional. With AutoFormat, you can instantly format the entire worksheet at once. You don't need to select individual cells and apply individual formats; an AutoFormat is a complete format already designed for you. These formats include borders, cell shading, and data formatting. To apply an

AutoFormat, select the range of cells you want to format, and then select AutoFormat on the Format menu. The AutoFormat dialog box opens, as shown in Figure 9-2.

FIGURE 9-2
AutoFormat dialog box

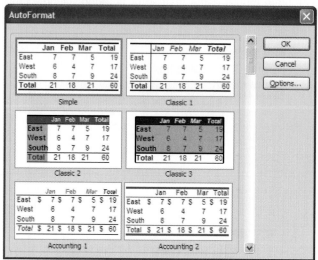

You may already be familiar with Excel's conditional formatting feature which enables you to quickly identify outstanding data in cells. With *conditional formatting,* you can apply certain formats to data that meets specified criteria. For example, if you wanted to highlight which products were your top sellers, you could specify that any product's sales that exceed a certain amount appear in red, boldface type.

STEP-BY-STEP 9.2

1. Open **AE Step9-2** from the data files, and save the workbook as **Formats,** followed by your initials.

2. You want to format the range A4:M11. Select any cell in this range.

3. Open the **Format** menu and then choose **AutoFormat.** The AutoFormat dialog box appears.

4. Scroll down and choose the **3D Effects 2** option from the **AutoFormat** list.

5. Click **OK.** Look at your worksheet; it should look similar to Figure 9-3. Instant formatting!

FIGURE 9-3
Applying an AutoFormat

	A	B	C	D	E	F	G	H	I	J	K	L
1	The Future Company											
2	Annual Budget											
3												
4		January	February	March	April	May	June	July	August	September	October	Novem
5	Sales	$ 53.50	$ 57.35	$ 61.20	$ 65.05	$ 68.90	$ 72.75	$ 76.60	$ 80.45	$ 84.30	$ 88.15	$ 92
6	Marketing	$ 65.00	$ 68.25	$ 71.50	$ 74.75	$ 78.00	$ 81.25	$ 84.50	$ 87.75	$ 91.00	$ 94.25	$ 97
7	Manufacturing	$ 99.00	$107.30	$115.60	$123.90	$132.20	$140.50	$148.80	$157.10	$ 165.40	$173.70	$ 182
8	Administrative	$ 45.50	$ 42.25	$ 39.00	$ 35.75	$ 32.50	$ 29.25	$ 26.00	$ 22.75	$ 19.50	$ 16.25	$ 13
9	Communications	$ 45.00	$ 46.75	$ 48.50	$ 50.25	$ 52.00	$ 53.75	$ 55.50	$ 57.25	$ 59.00	$ 60.75	$ 62
10	R&D	$ 67.00	$ 69.25	$ 71.50	$ 73.75	$ 76.00	$ 78.25	$ 80.50	$ 82.75	$ 85.00	$ 87.25	$ 89
11		$375.00	$391.15	$407.30	$423.45	$439.60	$455.75	$471.90	$488.05	$ 504.20	$520.35	$ 536

STEP-BY-STEP 9.2 Continued

6. Now, let's apply conditional formats to the data. You want to highlight budget figures that exceed $75.00 in any given month for any department. Select the range **B5:M10**.

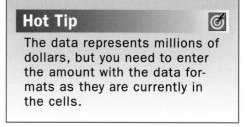

Hot Tip

The data represents millions of dollars, but you need to enter the amount with the data formats as they are currently in the cells.

7. Open the **Format** menu and select **Conditional Formatting.** The Conditional Formatting dialog box appears.

8. Click the drop-down arrow for the second text box and click **greater than.** Key **75.00** in the third text box.

FIGURE 9-4
Applying an AutoFormat

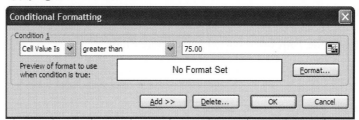

9. Click the **Format** button, and on the **Font** tab change the *Font style* to **Bold** and the *Color* to a **red**.

10. Click **OK** twice to close the Format Cells and the Conditional Formatting dialog boxes. Your screen should appear as shown in Figure 9-5.

FIGURE 9-5
Applying an AutoFormat

	A	B	C	D	E	F	G	H	I	J	K	L
1	The Future Company											
2	*Annual Budget*											
3												
4		January	February	March	April	May	June	July	August	September	October	Novem
5	Sales	$ 53.50	$ 57.35	$ 61.20	$ 65.05	$ 68.90	$ 72.75					
6	Marketing	$ 65.00	$ 68.25	$ 71.50	$ 74.75							
7	Manufacturing											
8	Administrative	$ 45.50	$ 42.25	$ 39.00	$ 35.75	$ 32.50	$ 29.25	$ 26.00	$ 22.75	$ 19.50	$ 16.25	$ 13
9	Communications	$ 45.00	$ 46.75	$ 48.50	$ 50.25	$ 52.00	$ 53.75	$ 55.50	$ 57.25	$ 59.00	$ 60.75	$ 62
10	R&D	$ 67.00	$ 69.25	$ 71.50	$ 73.75							
11		$375.00	$391.15	$407.30	$423.45	$439.60	$455.75	$471.90	$488.05	$ 504.20	$520.35	$ 536

11. Print the worksheet in landscape orientation and so the data fits on one page. Then save and close the file.

Using Styles and Data Validation

You can use styles for formats that recur. If you want your worksheet to have a consistent appearance and you don't want the hassle of applying the formats over and over, you can use styles. The big advantage of using a style is that if you modify a style, each cell that is formatted using this style will change to reflect the new style.

Excel's *data validation* feature helps ensure that accurate data is being entered into a cell. For example, you can use the data validation feature to alert users if an incorrect entry, such as an invalid date, is entered into a cell. You can create messages that will display when a person enters incorrect data. The message alerts the user about the invalid entry, and normally explains what data is valid.

You can also create a message that will display whenever a cell is selected. This message prompts the user as to what type of data should be entered into the cell.

S TEP-BY-STEP 9.3

1. Open **AE Step9-3** from the data files and save it as **Style,** followed by your initials.

2. Select cell **A3.**

3. Click the arrow on the **Fill Color** button and choose **Light Yellow.**

4. Click the arrow on the **Font Color** button and choose **Plum.**

5. Click the **Bold** button.

6. Open the **Format** menu and select **Style.**

7. Key **My Style** in the *Style name* box. The format options in the Style dialog box will change to reflect the new style, as shown in Figure 9-6.

FIGURE 9-6
Style dialog box

8. Click **OK.**

9. Select the range **B3:E3.**

10. Open the **Format** menu and select **Style.** In the Style dialog box, click the *Style name* arrow and choose **My Style.**

11. Click **OK** and view the results.

STEP-BY-STEP 9.3 Continued

12. Select the range **B4:B15.**

13. With this range selected, select the **Data** menu, click **Validation,** and select the **Settings** tab, if necessary.

14. Click the *Allow* drop-down list arrow and choose **Whole number.**

15. Click the *Data* drop-down list arrow and choose **between,** if necessary.

16. Enter **1** in the *Minimum* text box.

17. Enter **50** in the *Maximum* text box. This will allow employee numbers between 1 and 50 to be entered.

18. Click the **Error Alert** tab and key **Data Entry Mistake** in the *Title* box.

19. In the *Error message* box, key **Employee number must be between 1 and 50.**

20. Click the **Input Message** tab and key **Input Help** in the *Title* box.

21. In the *Input message* box, key **Please enter a number between 1 and 50.** Click **OK.**

22. In cell **A7,** enter the name **Brady Richardson** and press **Tab.** Notice how the input message displays. Key **55** in cell **B7** and press **Enter.** The error message should display.

23. Click **Retry.** Then, key **4** and press **Enter.** Notice how the error message does not display when a correct number is entered.

24. In cell **C7,** key **Sales;** in cell **D7,** key **US;** and in cell **E7,** key **Sales.**

25. Print the current sheet, and then save and close the workbook.

Hot Tip

With Excel's AutoComplete feature, as you key the first letter of Sales, the entire word appears in the cell. Once the word appears, you simply need to press Enter.

Computer Concepts

To remove a style, open the Style dialog box, select the style from the *Style name* drop-down list, and click the **Delete** button.

Transposing Data

There may be times when data is entered into a worksheet in columns or rows. Then, you find out later that it would be best to have the data in the opposite format. The transposition feature in Excel lets you copy and paste data into a different position. When you *transpose* data, you switch the order of the data. Tables 9-2 and 9-3 show an example of transposition from rows to columns.

TABLE 9-2
Worksheet data entered in rows

JANUARY	FEBRUARY	MARCH	APRIL	MAY
$14,533	$16,779	$14,106	$13,909	$19,224

TABLE 9-3
Worksheet data transposed into columns

January	$14,533
February	$16,779
March	$14,106
April	$13,909
May	$19,224

Excel makes transposing data a very simple process. The transpose option can be found in the Paste Special dialog box, as shown in Figure 9-7.

FIGURE 9-7
Paste Special

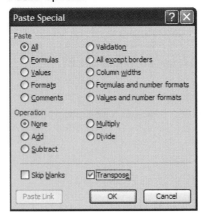

STEP-BY-STEP 9.4

1. Open the **AE Step9-4** workbook from the data files and save it as **Transpose** followed by your initials.

2. In Sheet1, select the range **A5:M24**.

3. Click the **Copy** button on the Standard toolbar.

4. Click on **Sheet2** tab and select cell **A5**. *Note:* You may copy into any cell. In this exercise, you copy into cell A5 to allow room for a worksheet title or subtitle if desired.

5. Choose the **Edit** menu and then select **Paste Special**.

6. Click the **Transpose** check box and then click **OK**.

> **Hot Tip** ◎
>
> You can also click the Paste button arrow and select Transpose.

7. Change each of the column widths at one time by selecting columns **A** through **T** and then double-clicking on the right edge of the last selected column heading, as shown in Figure 9-8. *Note:* You will need to select the entire column when changing multiple column widths.

FIGURE 9-8
Change Multiple Column Widths

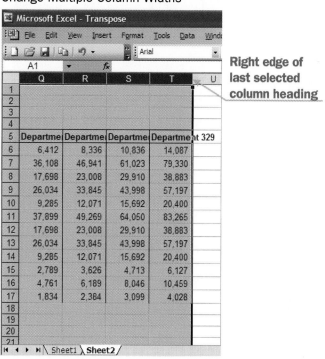

8. Print Sheet1 and Sheet2. Save and close the workbook.

Copying Values

There may be times when you simply need to copy values to a new location rather than copying values and any underlying formulas or links. *Value* is typically referred to as the result of a formula rather than the formula itself. For example, you may be preparing a year-end report and you just want the final numbers displayed in the report rather than many linked formulas that need to recalculate each time you open the year-end workbook. To accomplish this task, Excel lets you copy values by selecting **Values** from the *Paste* section of the Paste Special dialog box, as shown in Figure 9-9.

FIGURE 9-9
Paste Special dialog box

STEP-BY-STEP 9.5

1. Open the **AE Step9-5** workbook from the data files and save it as **Values,** followed by your initials.

2. Click in any cell with data in row 25 and note that these cells contain formulas.

3. Select the range **A5:G25.**

4. Click the **Copy** button on the Standard toolbar.

5. Click on **Sheet2** tab and select cell **A5.**

6. Choose the **Edit** menu and then select **Paste Special.**

7. Click the **Values** radio button and then click **OK.**

8. Click in any cell with data in row 25 and note that these cells contain values and not formulas. Change the column widths as necessary.

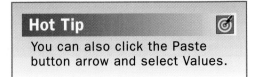

Hot Tip

You can also click the Paste button arrow and select Values.

9. Save the workbook and keep this file open for the next exercise.

Modifying Default Settings

When creating a new workbook in Excel, you've noticed that three worksheets automatically appear and the font is set as Arial, 10 point. These are referred to as *default* settings, which are the original settings loaded when you install the Excel program. But, you might need to create new workbooks that have more worksheets, such as one for each month of the year. Also, you might want the font set to Times New Roman. Excel lets you change these features in the **General** tab of the Options dialog box, which can be selected from the Tools menu. Figure 9-10 shows the **General** tab.

FIGURE 9-10
General Tab of the Options dialog box

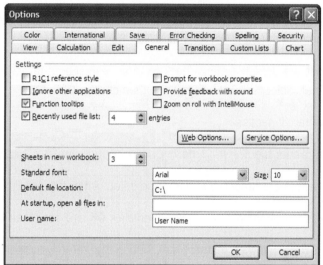

STEP-BY-STEP 9.6

1. Select the **Tools** menu and then choose **Options.**

2. Click the **General** tab, if necessary.

3. Click the up arrow for the **Sheets in new workbook** option until 5 appears.

4. Click the arrow next to the **Standard font** box and select **Times New Roman** from the list.

STEP-BY-STEP 9.6 Continued

5. Click **OK.** A message box will display, as shown in Figure 9-11, advising you that the default font changes will take place when you exit and then restart Excel. Click **OK.**

FIGURE 9-11
Microsoft Excel message box

6. Exit the Excel program and then restart Excel. Notice that five worksheets now appear in the new workbook and the default font is set for Times New Roman.

7. You will now reset the default settings back to three worksheets in new workbooks and reset the default font to Arial. Select the **Tools** menu and then choose **Options.**

8. Click the **General** tab, if necessary.

9. Click the down arrow for the *Sheets in new workbook* option until **3** appears.

10. Click the arrow next to the *Standard font* box and select **Arial** from the list.

11. Click **OK** to close the Options dialog box and then click **OK** again to close the message box.

12. Exit the Excel program and then restart Excel. Notice that three worksheets now appear in the new workbook and the default font is now reset for Arial. Remain in this screen for the next exercise.

Enhancing the Appearance of Charts

Charts are ideal for adding graphic flare and punch to the presentation of data. You can enhance the appearance of a chart in many ways, such as drop shadows and changing background colors.

Adding a Drop Shadow and Changing Background Color

A drop shadow adds dimension to a chart and creates a professional appearance. An example of a chart with a drop shadow is shown in Figure 9-12.

FIGURE 9-12
Chart with drop shadow

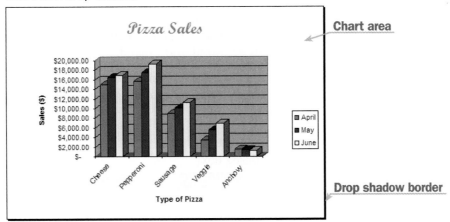

You can further customize the chart by changing the background color. The background color affects the chart area. The chart area is identified in Figure 9-12. Changes are made to the chart area in the Format Chart Area box shown in Figure 9-13.

FIGURE 9-13
Format Chart Area dialog box

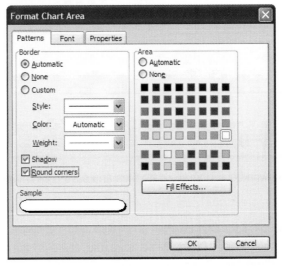

There are three options available on the tabs in the Format Chart Area dialog box:

1. **Patterns.** This option lets you choose the border style for the chart. Attributes you can apply include border color, thickness of line (weight), shadow, or rounded corners. You may also choose a background color or pattern for the chart area. The *Sample* box will display a preview of the selected options.

2. **Font.** Selected options in the Font tab affect selected text. You can change the font style and size as well as the color of the font.

3. **Properties.** You can select whether the chart will be printed with the worksheet. The default is set to allow the chart to be printed with worksheet data. You can also decide whether the chart can be sized or moved when worksheet cells are sized and moved.

Additionally, you can change an individual data series in the chart by double-clicking on the data series, which will then display the Format Data Series dialog box as shown in Figure 9-14. Then, you simply select the desired options.

FIGURE 9-14
Format Data Series dialog box

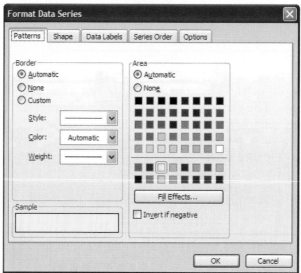

S TEP-BY-STEP 9.7

1. Open the **AE Step9-7** workbook from the data files and save it as **Bauer Pizza Chart,** followed by your initials.

2. Click the chart to select it. If the Chart toolbar is not displayed, right-click on any toolbar and then select **Chart.** Make sure the chart is still selected and choose **Chart Area**, if necessary, from the *Chart Objects* drop-down list on the Chart toolbar.

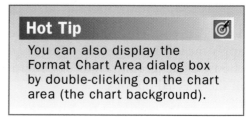

3. Click the **Format Chart Area** button on the Chart toolbar to display the Format Chart Area dialog box.

4. On the **Patterns** tab, click the **Shadow** option and then select the **Round corners** option from the Border section.

5. Choose a light color or shade from the *Area* color palette and click **OK.**

Hot Tip

You can also display the Format Chart Area dialog box by double-clicking on the chart area (the chart background).

STEP-BY-STEP 9.7 Continued

6. Double-click on the **April** data series and select the color **Red** as the new color for the series in the Format Data Series dialog box.

7. Click **OK**. Your screen should look similar to Figure 9-15.

FIGURE 9-15
Chart with drop shadow, background color and data series color

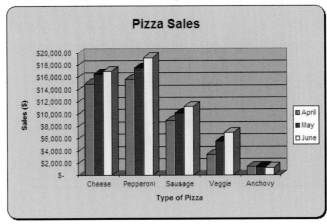

8. Save and print the worksheet. Remain in this worksheet for the next Step-by-Step.

Formatting Chart Text

Formatting text in a chart is very similar to formatting text in the worksheet. You can change the format of any text in the chart by first selecting the text and then clicking the buttons on the Formatting toolbar. Or you can double-click on the chart text to open its Format dialog box.

STEP-BY-STEP 9.8

1. Save the **Bauer Pizza Chart** file you created in Step-by-Step 9.7 as **Bauer Pizza Chart 2,** followed by your initials. Click on the chart title **Pizza Sales.**

2. Click the *Font Size* drop-down list arrow (on the Formatting toolbar) and choose **18.**

3. Click the *Font* drop-down list arrow and choose **Script MT Bold** (or a similar font).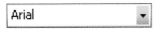

4. Click the *Font Color* drop-down list arrow and choose a color from the color palette. (Remember to select a different color than the chart background or the text will not be visible.)

5. On the Chart toolbar, click the *Chart Objects* drop-down list arrow and select **Category Axis.**

6. Click the **Angle Counterclockwise** button on the Chart toolbar. Notice how the text identifying the X axis is now displayed at an angle.

STEP-BY-STEP 9.8 Continued

7. Your screen should look similar to Figure 9-16. Save and then print the worksheet. Remain in this worksheet for the next Step-by-Step.

FIGURE 9-16
Chart with font enhancements

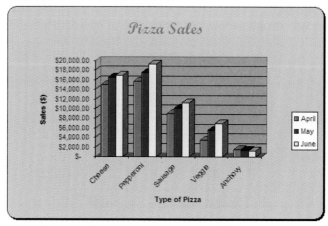

Adding a Data Table

A *data table* displays the worksheet data on the chart itself. This feature can be useful when your chart is on a separate sheet in the workbook, or for quickly referencing the worksheet data while viewing chart data series. To add a data table to a chart, simply click the Data Table button on the Chart toolbar.

STEP-BY-STEP 9.9

1. Save the **Bauer Pizza Chart 2** file you created in Step-by-Step 9.8 as **Bauer Pizza Chart 3,** followed by your initials. If necessary, click on the chart to select it.

2. Click the **Data Table** button on the **Chart** toolbar. Notice that the labels are no longer angled upward. When a data table is added to a chart, the axis labels return to a horizontal alignment.

3. Resize the chart so all the text is displayed. Click on the chart to select it, place your mouse pointer over a selection handle, and drag it to the right, left, up or down.

4. Select the legend object on the chart and press **Delete** to remove the legend. Your screen should appear similar to Figure 9-17.

> **Integration Tip**
>
> You can quickly copy an Excel chart into a Word document or a PowerPoint slide. Simply click on the chart to select it, click the **Copy** tool, switch to the location and click in the Word document or PowerPoint slide where you want the chart to appear and click the **Paste** tool. Then, you can resize the chart as desired.

STEP-BY-STEP 9.9 Continued

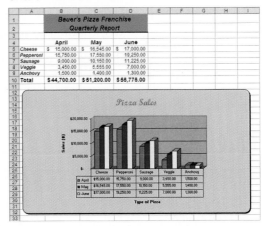

FIGURE 9-17
Chart with data table

5. Save and print the worksheet in landscape orientation.

6. Leave the workbook open for the next exercise.

Time Saver

You can create an instant chart in its own sheet with Excel's time saving function key F11.

STEP-BY-STEP 9.10

1. Select the text and data that make up the Bauer Pizza spreadsheet.

2. Press **F11**. A chart is automatically created.

3. Close the workbook without saving your changes.

SUMMARY

In this lesson, you learned:

■ You can create a custom format in a workbook and apply this format to data in the worksheet cells.

■ AutoFormats let you create instant worksheet formats.

■ Conditional formatting enables you to highlight data that meets specified criteria.

■ Styles let you apply the same formatting scheme over and over, thereby eliminating the time-consuming task of applying individual formats.

- Data validation can increase data entry accuracy.

- You can transpose data from column and row format into rows and columns.

- You can copy values, such as formula results, rather that copying entire formulas.

- Excel's default setting features can be changed. For example, you can change the number of worksheets that display when opening a new workbook and the default font.

- The appearance of worksheet charts can be enhanced by using the Chart toolbar and formatting techniques that you've also applied to worksheet data.

VOCABULARY *Review*

Define the following terms:

Conditional formatting	Data validation	Transpose
Data Table	Default	Value

REVIEW *Questions*

WRITTEN QUESTIONS

Write a brief answer to the following questions.

1. What is the difference between the following date codes: *dd-mmm-yy* and *dd-mmmm-yyyy*?

2. Which dialog box contains the Transpose feature?

3. How can AutoFormats save you time?

4. Explain the process to transpose data.

5. Explain the process for copying values instead of formulas.

6. Explain the difference between AutoFormats and Styles.

7. Which dialog box would you use to change the default number of worksheets in a workbook?

8. List the steps for creating a custom format.

9. Which button on the Chart toolbar lets you select a chart object to modify?

10. When would you use a style?

PROJECTS

PROJECT 9-1

1. Open **AE Project9-1** from the data files, and save the workbook as **Class Scores,** followed by your initials.

2. Change the date format in column A so your dates appear in the format March 14, 2006.

3. Format the range **C12:G14** as percentages with no decimal places.

4. Copy the range **C4:G14** as values into Sheet2 with the copy to range starting in cell C4. Increase the column widths as necessary.

5. Save the workbook.

6. Print the worksheet in Landscape orientation. Then, close the file.

PROJECT 9-2

1. Open **AE Project9-2** from the data files and save the workbook as **Pizza** followed by your initials.

2. Add a currency format to the sales figures with **$** sign and two decimal places.

3. Change the alignment of the month column headings to a 45-degree angle. Hint: Use Format, Cells, Alignment.

4. Center the title and subtitle across columns A through D using the Merge and Center button on the Formatting toolbar. Hint: Select the cell with the title and the cells that you want to merge. Then, click the Merge and Center button.

5. Transpose the data range **A4:D11** and put the transposed data into Sheet2. Change the column widths as necessary.

6. Save and print the workbook. Close the workbook.

PROJECT 9-3

1. Open the **AE Project9-3** workbook from the data files and save it as **Sales Chart** followed by your initials.

2. Add a data table to the chart.

3. Resize the chart as you feel appropriate.

4. Change the border style of the chart to a rounded border.

5. Save the workbook and then print it in landscape orientation and so all the data fits on one page. Close the workbook.

CRITICAL*Thinking*

 ACTIVITY 9-1

You are the new manager of the New Internet Products Corporation. After reviewing workbooks created by the former manager, you decide to enhance the data contained in the files by applying different formatting features.

1. Open the **AE Activity9-1** workbook from the data files and save it as **Trendy Resort Projected Sales** followed by your initials.

2. Format the First Year worksheet using the formatting features you learned about in this

lesson. Apply an AutoFormat to the projected sales data and use conditional formatting to highlight those projected sales figures that exceed $60,000 for any month and any division. Format the title and subtitle as desired.

3. Save and print the worksheet in landscape orientation and so all the data fits on one page. Then close the workbook.

SCANS ACTIVITY 9-2

1. Open the **AE Activity9-2** workbook from the data files and save it as **Project Value** followed by your initials.

2. Copy and transpose the values of the data and formula results from Sheet1 into Sheet2. Note: Make sure the values copy into Sheet2, not the formulas. Add currency format to the data.

3. Save and print the worksheet in landscape orientation and so all the data fits on one page. Then close the workbook.

SCANS ACTIVITY 9-3

Using Excel's Help system, find information on the different types of Number formats. Write a brief explanation of each format and give an example of when you would apply it to worksheet data.

USING LISTS

OBJECTIVES

Upon completion of this lesson, you should be able to:

- Create a list.
- Add records to a list.
- Edit records in a list.
- Delete list records.
- Sort a list.
- Search for records that meet certain criteria.

Estimated Time: 1 hour

VOCABULARY

Ascending order

Criteria

Descending order

Field

List

Record

Introducing Lists

You can sort and search data in a worksheet much as you do in a database. When data on a worksheet is set up as a list, it can be manipulated in a variety of ways. In this lesson, you will learn how to create and make changes to a list, such as editing and adding records. Then you will learn how to sort the list alphabetically and numerically and how to search for data that meets criteria you specify.

Creating a List

You can think of a list as a database table. *Lists* are used to organize, manage, and retrieve information. Thousands of examples of lists are in use today. For example, lists are used to organize payroll information, keep track of inventories, and manage customer information.

A list consists of columns and rows of data—in fact, it looks similar to other worksheets you've created. Lists are made up of records. A *record* is a collection of information about a particular object. The information could include a name, an address, and a telephone number. Records are further divided into *fields,* columns of information that contain one type of data. For the previous example, you would have a name field, an address field, and a telephone number field. You enter information in fields. A list with records and fields is shown in Figure 10-1.

FIGURE 10-1
List with records and fields

Last Name	First Name	Address	City	State
Keplinger	Jo Ann	P.O. Box 47654	Madison	Wisconsin
Thomsen	Barb	347 Edison Dr.	Madison	Wisconsin
Crawford	Ti	1423 First Street	Madison	Wisconsin
Bretzke	Dee	4400 Lake Dr.	Madison	Wisconsin
Fields	Shania	19 Harbor Ave.	Madison	Wisconsin
Pullis	Cheryl	10 North McDonald	Madison	Wisconsin
Arland	Juan	27 Knight Street	Madison	Wisconsin
Gonzalez	Lisa	Rt. 3, Box 157	Madison	Wisconsin
Goodwin	Sallye	43 First St.	Madison	Wisconsin
Loucini	Dwanda	4212 Woodbridge Lane	Madison	Wisconsin

Field names

Record

Field

The data in a list can be manipulated in various ways. For example, you can sort the list alphabetically or numerically by any column or field. Or you can search the list for records that meet specific requirements (criteria). You can also print the list and display the data visually in a graph.

A list must be set up according to a few simple guidelines:

■ The first row of the list (not including worksheet titles and subtitles) should contain the field names.

■ You can have blank rows above the field names or below the last record, and you can have blank columns to the right or left of the list. However, you cannot have a blank row or column within the list.

■ Every record must have the same fields.

■ Every field does not have to contain data.

■ You can use any of the usual formatting and editing techniques.

S TEP-BY-STEP 10.1

1. Start a new workbook, and enter the data shown in Figure 10-2. The actual list range is **A4:H14.** Worksheet titles and subtitles are not included in the list range, but field names are included.

2. Format the data so that it looks similar to the worksheet in Figure 10-2.

3. Save the workbook as **CTI Training,** followed by your initials, and remain in this screen for the next Step-by-Step.

Integration Tip

You can copy and paste a list into a Word document. When you paste a list into the Word document, Word recognizes it as a table. You can add rows and columns to the table as well as perform other table functions.

STEP-BY-STEP 10.1 Continued

FIGURE 10-2
Setting up a list

	A	B	C	D	E	F	G	H
1	Computer Technology Institute							
2	Training Department							
3								
4	**Last Name**	**First Name**	**Address**	**City**	**State**	**ZIP Code**	**Telephone**	**Area of Expertise**
5	Keplinger	Jo Ann	P.O. Box 47654	Madison	Wisconsin	53447	608-555-6712	Access
6	Thomsen	Barb	347 Edison Dr.	Madison	Wisconsin	53476	608-555-3345	Access
7	Crawford	Ti	1423 First Street	Madison	Wisconsin	53447	608-555-4303	Excel
8	Bretzke	Dee	4400 Lake Dr.	Madison	Wisconsin	54358	608-555-9938	Outlook
9	Fields	Shania	19 Harbor Ave.	Madison	Wisconsin	54358	608-555-7788	PowerPoint
10	Pullis	Cheryl	10 North McDonald	Madison	Wisconsin	53329	608-555-3455	PowerPoint
11	Arland	Juan	27 Knight Street	Madison	Wisconsin	54347	608-555-3601	Word
12	Gonzalez	Lisa	Rt. 3, Box 157	Madison	Wisconsin	54112	608-555-9987	Word
13	Goodwin	Sallye	43 First St.	Madison	Wisconsin	53446	608-555-8008	Word
14	Loucini	Dwanda	4212 Woodbridge Lane	Madison	Wisconsin	54347	608-555-4444	Word

Adding Records to a Data List

If you want to add a record to a list, you move to the row where you want to add the record, insert a row, and then key the data. You can also use the Data Form dialog box, shown in Figure 10-3, to enter your records.

FIGURE 10-3
Data Form dialog box

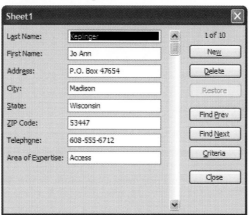

The Data Form dialog box lets you view records one at a time. You can also perform other functions, such as editing, when you use the Data Form dialog box. Records are added to the bottom of the data list when you use this dialog box. You can also delete and find records within the Data Form dialog box. The options available in it are as follows:

- New: Lets you add a new record

- Delete: Lets you delete the displayed record

- Restore: Lets you undo changes to the displayed record

> **Computer Concepts**
>
> You can also move to the previous or next records by using the up and down arrow keys on the slider bar alongside of the fields in the Data Form dialog box or by moving the slider within the bar.

- Find Prev: Goes to the record before the displayed record
- Find Next: Goes to the record after the displayed record
- Criteria: Lets you find records based on criteria you specify

STEP-BY-STEP 10.2

1. Add a record to the list. Select cell **A5,** and insert a row. Enter the following data in the appropriate fields:

    D.J.Mann

    4319 Bridge Rd.

    Madison, Wisconsin 54347

    608-555-1234

    Word

> **Hot Tip**
>
> If the inserted row assumes the same formatting as the preceding row, select the record by clicking on the row number and reformatting it appropriately.

    If necessary, format the record so it looks the same as the other records you've already entered.

2. Try another method for adding records. Select cell **A4** in the list range. (You need to select a cell in the list before you can get into the Data Form dialog box.) Open the **Data** menu and select **Form.** The Data Form dialog box appears. To move in the dialog box, click in the field's text box. You can also press **Tab** to move to the next field or **Shift+Tab** to move to a previous field.

3. Click the **New** button. The fields should now be blank and ready for you to enter the new data.

4. Key the following data in the appropriate fields:

    Susan Cod

    1617 Mockingbird

    Madison, Wisconsin 54358

    608-555-7792

    PowerPoint

5. Click the **Close** button. Make sure the new record appears at the end of the list.

6. Your screen should look similar to Figure 10-4. Save the file as **CTI Training-Revised,** followed by your initials. Print and close the workbook.

FIGURE 10-4
Adding records to a list

	A	B	C	D	E	F	G	H
1			**Computer Technology Institute**					
2			**Training Department**					
3								
4	**Last Name**	**First Name**	**Address**	**City**	**State**	**ZIP Code**	**Telephone**	**Area of Expertise**
5	Mann	D.J.	4319 Bridge Rd.	Madison	Wisconsin	54347	608-555-1234	Word
6	Keplinger	Jo Ann	P.O. Box 47654	Madison	Wisconsin	53447	608-555-6712	Access
7	Thomsen	Barb	347 Edison Dr.	Madison	Wisconsin	53476	608-555-3345	Access
8	Crawford	Ti	1423 First Street	Madison	Wisconsin	53447	608-555-4303	Excel
9	Bretzke	Dee	4400 Lake Dr.	Madison	Wisconsin	54358	608-555-9938	Outlook
10	Fields	Shania	19 Harbor Ave.	Madison	Wisconsin	54358	608-555-7788	PowerPoint
11	Pullis	Cheryl	10 North McDonald	Madison	Wisconsin	53329	608-555-3455	PowerPoint
12	Arland	Juan	27 Knight Street	Madison	Wisconsin	54347	608-555-3601	Word
13	Gonzalez	Lisa	Rt. 3, Box 157	Madison	Wisconsin	54112	608-555-9987	Word
14	Goodwin	Sallye	43 First St.	Madison	Wisconsin	53446	608-555-8008	Word
15	Loucini	Dwanda	4212 Woodbridge Lane	Madison	Wisconsin	54347	608-555-4444	Word
16	Cod	Susan	1617 Mockingbird	Madison	Wisconsin	54358	608-555-7792	PowerPoint

New records

Editing Records in a List

You can edit a data list record the same way you edit worksheet data. First, locate the cell you want to change and edit the data. You can also use the Data Form dialog box to make changes to a record.

STEP-BY-STEP 10.3

1. Open the **AE Step10-3** workbook from the data files, and save it as **CTI Payroll,** followed by your initials.

2. Select the cell containing the street address for Sallye Goodwin (43 First St.). Change the address to **2563 Middle Rd.** and press **Enter**.

3. Now change a record using the Data Form dialog box. Open the **Data** menu, and then select **Form**.

4. Click the **Find Next** button until you locate the record for **Ti Crawford.**

5. Click in the **Telephone** field. The old telephone number is 608-555-4303. Change it to **608-555-3199.**

6. Click the **Close** button. Locate the record for Ti Crawford, and view the change. Your screen should look similar to Figure 10-5.

> **Speech Recognition**
>
> If you have speech recognition capabilities, enable the Voice Command mode and say the appropriate series of commands to open the Data Form dialog box.

> **Hot Tip**
>
> If you move past a record in the Data Form dialog box, click the **Find Prev** button to go to the previous records.

FIGURE 10-5
Editing records in a list

	A	B	C	D	E	F	G	H
1			**Computer Technology Institute**					
2			**Training Department**					
3								
4	**Last Name**	**First Name**	**Address**	**City**	**State**	**ZIP Code**	**Telephone**	**Area of Expertise**
5	Mann	D.J.	4319 Bridge Rd.	Madison	Wisconsin	54347	608-555-1234	Word
6	Keplinger	Jo Ann	P.O. Box 47654	Madison	Wisconsin	53447	608-555-6712	Access
7	Thomsen	Barb	347 Edison Dr.	Madison	Wisconsin	53476	608-555-3345	Access
8	Crawford	Ti	1423 First Street	Madison	Wisconsin	53447	608-555-3199	Excel
9	Bretzke	Dee	4400 Lake Dr.	Madison	Wisconsin	54358	608-555-9938	Outlook
10	Fields	Shania	19 Harbor Ave.	Madison	Wisconsin	54358	608-555-7788	PowerPoint
11	Pullis	Cheryl	10 North McDonald	Madison	Wisconsin	53329	608-555-3455	PowerPoint
12	Arland	Juan	27 Knight Street	Madison	Wisconsin	54347	608-555-3601	Word
13	Gonzalez	Lisa	Rt. 3, Box 157	Madison	Wisconsin	54112	608-555-9987	Word
14	Goodwin	Sallye	2563 Middle Rd.	Madison	Wisconsin	53446	608-555-8008	Word
15	Loucini	Dwanda	4212 Woodbridge Lane	Madison	Wisconsin	54347	608-555-4444	Word
16	Cod	Susan	1617 Mockingbird	Madison	Wisconsin	54358	608-555-7792	PowerPoint

Changed records

7. Save, print, and close the workbook.

Deleting Records in a List

It is easy to delete a record in a list. You can delete a record by selecting a field in the record and deleting the entire row or by using the Data Form dialog box. If you mistakenly delete a record by deleting the row, you can click the **Undo** button to cancel the action.

If you are using the Data Form dialog box, Excel will display a message box alerting you that the record is about to be deleted permanently. You cannot use the **Undo** button to restore a record deleted in the Data Form dialog box.

S TEP-BY-STEP 10.4

1. Open the **AE Step10-4** workbook from the data files, and save it as **CTI Mailing List,** followed by your initials.

2. Select any field in the record for **Barb Thomsen.**

3. Open the **Edit** menu and select **Delete.**

4. Choose **Entire row** and click **OK.** The record for Barb Thomsen should be gone.

5. Delete another record. Open the **Data** menu and select **Form.**

6. If necessary, press the up and down arrow keys on the slider bar until the record for **D. J. Mann** is displayed.

7. Click the **Delete** button. A message box appears.

8. Click **OK** to confirm that you want to delete the record.

9. Click **Close.** The record for D. J. Mann should be gone. The revised data list should look similar to Figure 10-6.

Speech Recognition

If you have speech recognition capabilities, enable the Voice Command mode and say the appropriate series of commands to open the Data Form dialog box.

Computer Concepts

You can also click the scroll arrows in the Data Form dialog box to move between records.

FIGURE 10-6
Deleting records in a list

	A	B	C	D	E	F	G	H
1	**Computer Technology Institute**							
2	**Training Department**							
3								
4	**Last Name**	**First Name**	**Address**	**City**	**State**	**ZIP Code**	**Telephone**	**Area of Expertise**
5	Keplinger	Jo Ann	P.O. Box 47654	Madison	Wisconsin	53447	608-555-6712	Access
6	Crawford	Ti	1423 First Street	Madison	Wisconsin	53447	608-555-3199	Excel
7	Bretzke	Dee	4400 Lake Dr.	Madison	Wisconsin	54358	608-555-9938	Outlook
8	Fields	Shania	19 Harbor Ave.	Madison	Wisconsin	54358	608-555-7788	PowerPoint
9	Pullis	Cheryl	10 North McDonald	Madison	Wisconsin	53329	608-555-3455	PowerPoint
10	Arland	Juan	27 Knight Street	Madison	Wisconsin	54347	608-555-3601	Word
11	Gonzalez	Lisa	Rt. 3, Box 157	Madison	Wisconsin	54112	608-555-9987	Word
12	Goodwin	Sallye	2563 Middle Rd.	Madison	Wisconsin	53446	608-555-8008	Word
13	Loucini	Dwanda	4212 Woodbridge Lane	Madison	Wisconsin	54347	608-555-4444	Word
14	Cod	Susan	1617 Mockingbird	Madison	Wisconsin	54358	608-555-7792	PowerPoint

10. Save, print, and close the workbook.

Sorting a List

Sorting is used primarily in lists. You can quickly sort a list alphabetically or numerically using the **Sort Ascending** button ![] and the **Sort Descending** button ![] on the toolbar. **Ascending order** sorts alphabetically from A to Z; numerically, from the lowest to the highest number. **Descending order** sorts alphabetically from Z to A; numerically, from the highest to the lowest number. You can click the Undo button on the toolbar to undo a sort.

STEP-BY-STEP 10.5

1. Open the **AE Step10-5** workbook from the data files, and save it as **CTI Revised List,** followed by your initials.

2. Click on any cell in the **Last Name** column.

3. Click the **Sort Descending** button. Your records should be sorted by last name in descending order from Z to A. *Note*: You may need to add the Sort Descending button to the Standard toolbar or move the Formatting toolbar to its own line in order to view the Sort Descending button.

4. Save the workbook, and remain in this screen for the next Step-by-Step.

Sorting a List with the Sort Dialog Box

The sort buttons provide a quick method for sorting a data list. But you may need more flexibility in your sort. The Sort dialog box provides you with numerous sorting options. You can specify by which field you want the data sorted. For example, you may want an address list to appear alphabetically by last name. You also can sort by more than one field. For example, you could sort by the Last Name field or you could sort by the Last Name and First Name fields. In this type of sort, Excel will first sort all the records by the Last Name field; then if any records have the same last name, these records will be sorted alphabetically by first name.

To sort using the Sort dialog box, you choose Sort on the Data menu. The Sort dialog box appears, as shown in Figure 10-7.

FIGURE 10-7
The Sort dialog box

You can designate up to three fields by which to sort in the dialog box. The *Header row* options pertain to the row of column labels in a list. If the list has column labels as the top row, you'll want to select the *Header row* option in order to exclude this data from being included in a sort. If the list does not have a row of column headings, then click the *No header row* option to indicate that the first row should be included in the sort. Clicking the **Options** button provides additional sort selections. The Sort Options dialog box appears, similar to Figure 10-8.

FIGURE 10-8
The Sort Options dialog box

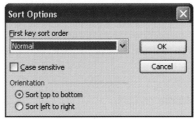

Four options are available in the Sort Options dialog box:

- *First key sort order.* Specify a sort order other than ascending or descending. For example, you might want to sort the months of the year, "January, February, March."

- *Case sensitive.* Sort the list by capitalization. Records that begin with a capital letter appear first, followed by records that begin with the same letter in lowercase.

- *Sort top to bottom.* Sort the list from the top to the bottom rather than from left to right.

- *Sort left to right.* Sort the list from the left side to the right side rather than from top to bottom.

S TEP-BY-STEP 10.6

1. Choose the **Data** menu and select **Sort**.

2. Click the first **Sort by** drop-down list arrow, and then scroll and select **Area of Expertise.** Choose **Ascending** as the sort order.

3. Click the **Then by** drop-down list arrow, and select **Last Name.** If necessary, choose **Ascending** as the sort order.

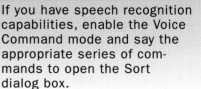

Speech Recognition

If you have speech recognition capabilities, enable the Voice Command mode and say the appropriate series of commands to open the Sort dialog box.

4. Be sure the **Header row** option is selected. This option instructs Excel to exclude the column labels from the sort.

5. Click **OK** to begin the sort. The records should be sorted alphabetically by area of expertise and then by last name.

6. Save the workbook; then print the sheet in landscape orientation and so all the data fits on one page. Close the workbook.

Searching for Records Meeting a Specific Criteria

Earlier in this lesson, you used the Data Form dialog box to find and edit records using very basic search procedures. With a large list, however, trying to find a record in this manner could take quite awhile. To save time and increase your productivity, you can use the Criteria button in the Data Form dialog box to find one or more records that meet specific *criteria*.

STEP-BY-STEP 10.7

1. Open the **AE Step10-7** workbook from the data files, and save it as **Arts & Crafts Data List,** followed by your initials.

2. Select a cell in the field name row. (Excel starts the search from this point.) Choose the **Data** menu, and then select **Form.**

3. Click the **Criteria** button. Your screen should look similar to Figure 10-9. Notice the word *Criteria* in the upper-right corner below the title bar. Also note that the **Form** button has replaced the **Criteria** button. Clicking the **Form** button returns you to the Data Form dialog box.

FIGURE 10-9
Criteria dialog box

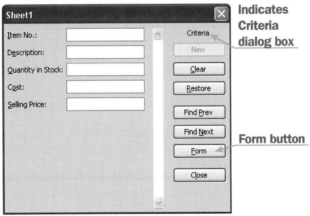

4. Click in the **Description** field, and key **Varnish - Satin.** *Note:* You will need to use the exact spacing.

5. Click the **Find Next** button. The record for Item No. 15-993 will be displayed. Notice that you are back in the Data Form, where you can make changes to the record.

6. Click the **Find Next** button again. You might hear a beep when you choose the **Find Next** button, indicating that this is the only record that meets the criteria.

7. Let's try another search. Click the **Criteria** button.

8. Click in the **Item No.** field and key **12-295.** *Note:* Make sure the Description field is blank.

9. Click the **Find Next** button. The record for **Paint - White** will be displayed.

STEP-BY-STEP 10.7 Continued

10. Click the **Find Next** button. There are no more records meeting the criteria.

11. Click **Close.** Save and close the workbook.

Time Saver

Excel lets you quickly select a range of cells even if you are not at the very beginning or end of the range. To quickly select a range of cells:

STEP-BY-STEP 10.8

1. Click anywhere in the range you wish to select.

2. Press **CTRL** + **Shift** + * (asterisk)

SUMMARY

In this lesson, you learned:

■ A data list consists of records and fields of information. The list must be set up according to the following guidelines: no blank rows or columns can be within the list, and every record must have the same fields.

■ You can add records to a list directly on a worksheet or in the Data Form dialog box.

■ You can edit and delete records in a list directly on a worksheet or in the Data Form dialog box. When you delete records in the Data Form dialog box, they are deleted permanently.

■ Lists are ideal for sorting worksheet data. You can sort data using the Sort Ascending and Sort Descending buttons or by selecting various options in the Sort dialog box.

VOCABULARY *Review*

Define the following terms:		
Ascending order	Descending order	List
Criteria	Field	Record

REVIEW *Questions*

WRITTEN QUESTIONS

Write a brief answer to the following questions.

1. What is a list?

2. Not including titles and subtitles, what does the first row of a list normally contain?

3. What is a record?

4. What is a field?

5. What are the guidelines for creating a list?

6. What are the two methods for adding a record to a list?

7. What is the advantage of using the Data Form dialog box to edit a record?

8. What are the two methods for deleting records?

9. What is the difference between ascending order and descending order?

10. What is a case-sensitive sort?

PROJECTS

PROJECT 10-1

1. Open the **AE Project10-1** workbook from the data files, and save it as **NL Corporation** followed by your initials.

2. Sort the list by **Division,** then by **Last Name,** and then by **First Name.**

3. Print each division on a separate page. Change the page setup to landscape orientation and so the data in rows 1 through 4 prints across the top of every page.

4. Save the workbook, and then close it.

PROJECT 10-2

You are starting a home remodeling business. You realize the importance of keeping accurate information about your subcontractors. You decide to create a data list of your subcontractors that contains their mailing addresses and ID numbers. Start a new workbook, and enter the information shown in Figure 10-10.

FIGURE 10-10
Project worksheet

	A	B	C	D	E	F	G	H	I
1				Subcontractor Mailing List					
2									
3									
4									
5									
6	ID No.	Company Name	Last Name	First Name	Address	City	State	ZIP	Phone Number
7	9010	It's a Smash	Joshua	Daniel	Crowther Way	Irving	TX	76221	214-555-1128
8	3006	Carpets and More	Cartwrite	Zachary	8 Johnstown Road	Brazos	TX	77822	713-555-1928
9	20550	Under Construction	Jameson	Marty	1924 Norton	Dallas	TX	76099	214-555-6600
10	18500	Sinks and Such	Taylor	Beverly	12 East St.	Grapevine	TX	76055	940-555-6698
11	17750	Roofs and More	Burke	Nathan	89 Chiaroscuro Rd.	Houston	TX	73303	713-555-4455
12	17250	Redo Time	Davidson	Annabelle	Fifth Ave.	Bossier City	LA	71223	210-555-2276
13	16400	Phil's Remodeling	Benntly	Lorna	52 Llano Largo	Shreveport	LA	75331	512-555-1926
14	16250	Paint, Paint, Paint	Fredrick	Helen	87 Polk St.	Southlake	TX	76056	940-555-2258
15	15665	One More Time Remodeling	Levinson	Victor	7 Main St.	Lewisville	TX	76055	940-555-2108
16	14750	New Carpets	Kennedy	Rosa	12 Orchestra Terrace	Riverside	TX	75234	214-555-6778
17	14650	New and Improved	Johnson	Sally	1900 Oak St.	San Antonio	TX	75443	210-555-6558
18	14500	Never Say New	Martin	Jose	1 Lorraine	Houston	TX	73302	713-555-4423
19	12330	Last Resort Furniture	Robinson	Pauline	67 Avenue Europe	El Paso	TX	73445	702-555-4435
20	1005	At Home Decorating	Smith	George	516 Main St.	Houston	TX	73301	713-555-2341
21	10005	Just a Little Touch	Anderson	Melissa	90 Maubel St.	Austin	TX	75377	512-555-0003

1. Format the data as you choose.

2. Sort the list by **State** and then by **City** so that you can quickly glance at the subcontractors available in a specific area.

3. Save the workbook as **Mailing List** followed by your initials.

4. Print the worksheet in landscape orientation, and then close the file.

CRITICAL *Thinking*

ACTIVITY 10-1

Ms. Emily Smith, your boss at Lincoln College Fan-Fair, a sports apparel shop for Lincoln College, has just handed you the inventory list shown in Figure 10-11. She asks you to key the items into a worksheet in a data list format with a title and subtitle.

FIGURE 10-11
Activity worksheet

	A	B	C	D	E
1		Lincoln College Fan-Fair			
2		Sports Apparel Shop			
3					
4	Item No.	Item Description	Size	Cost	Selling Price
5	SP-LC-XL	Sweat Pants - Lincoln College emblem	XL	$15.99	$ 19.99
6	SS-LC1-L	Sweat Shirt - Lincoln College emblem	L	$14.99	$ 19.99
7	SP-LC-L	Sweat Pants - Lincoln College emblem	L	$13.99	$ 17.99
8	SS-LC1-M	Sweat Shirt - Lincoln College emblem	M	$12.99	$ 17.99
9	Shorts-XL	Shorts	XL	$13.99	$ 15.99
10	SP-LC-M	Sweat Pants - Lincoln College emblem	M	$11.99	$ 15.99
11	SS-LC1-S	Sweat Shirt - Lincoln College emblem	S	$10.99	$ 15.99
12	Shorts-L	Shorts	L	$11.99	$ 13.99
13	SP-LC-S	Sweat Pants - Lincoln College emblem	S	$ 9.99	$ 13.99
14	Shorts-M	Shorts	M	$ 9.99	$ 11.99
15	TS-LC-L	Tee Shirt - Lincoln College emblem	L	$ 8.99	$ 10.99
16	Shorts-S	Shorts	S	$ 7.99	$ 9.99
17	Cap-XL	Baseball Cap	XL	$ 5.99	$ 8.99
18	TS-LC-M	Tee Shirt - Lincoln College emblem	M	$ 6.99	$ 8.99
19	Cap-L	Baseball Cap	L	$ 4.99	$ 7.99
20	TS-LC-S	Tee Shirt - Lincoln College emblem	S	$ 4.99	$ 6.99

After you enter the data, apply an AutoFormat to format the data list quickly. Then add currency format to all dollar values. Save the file as **Lincoln FF Inventory** followed by your initials.

Ms. Smith also asks that you sort the list in ascending order by Item No. Finally, Ms. Smith would like a printout of this information.

ACTIVITY 10-2

Use Excel's Help system to find information on list organization when creating a list.

FILTERING, EXTRACTING, AND USING DATABASE FUNCTIONS

OBJECTIVES

Upon completion of this lesson, you should be able to:

- Search a list using AutoFilter.

- Search for records using the Top 10 feature.

- Display records using custom filters and search operators.

- Display records using Advanced Filters.

- Use Advanced Filters to find Multiple Criteria.

- Use DSUM and DAVERAGE.

Estimated Time: 2 hours

VOCABULARY

AutoFilter

Copy to range

Criteria range

Custom filter

DSUM

DAVERAGE

Filter

Introduction

In the previous lesson, you learned how to create a list. Data was entered into a worksheet according to specific guidelines. When data is entered as a list, it can be manipulated in a variety of ways. In this lesson, you will learn how to *filter* (or find) records that meet certain criteria in a list.

Searching a List Using AutoFilter

AutoFilter is an Excel feature that lets you display only the records in a data list that meet specific criteria. When you apply the AutoFilter feature to your list, arrows appear in the cell for each column heading, as shown in Figure 11-1.

FIGURE 11-1
AutoFilter arrows

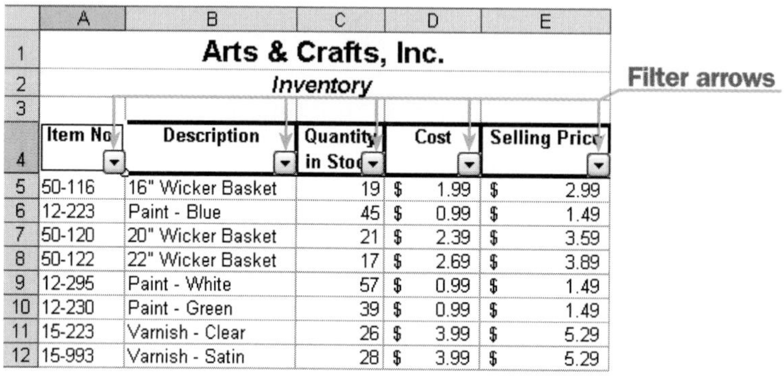

	A	B	C	D	E
1	Arts & Crafts, Inc.				
2	*Inventory*				
3					
4	Item No	Description	Quantity in Sto	Cost	Selling Pric
5	50-116	16" Wicker Basket	19	$ 1.99	$ 2.99
6	12-223	Paint - Blue	45	$ 0.99	$ 1.49
7	50-120	20" Wicker Basket	21	$ 2.39	$ 3.59
8	50-122	22" Wicker Basket	17	$ 2.69	$ 3.89
9	12-295	Paint - White	57	$ 0.99	$ 1.49
10	12-230	Paint - Green	39	$ 0.99	$ 1.49
11	15-223	Varnish - Clear	26	$ 3.99	$ 5.29
12	15-993	Varnish - Satin	28	$ 3.99	$ 5.29

Click on these arrows to display a drop-down list for that field, similar to that shown in Figure 11-2. The drop-down list contains the different entries in that field as well as other search options, such as *(Custom)*, which allows you to create your own search.

FIGURE 11-2
AutoFilter drop-down list

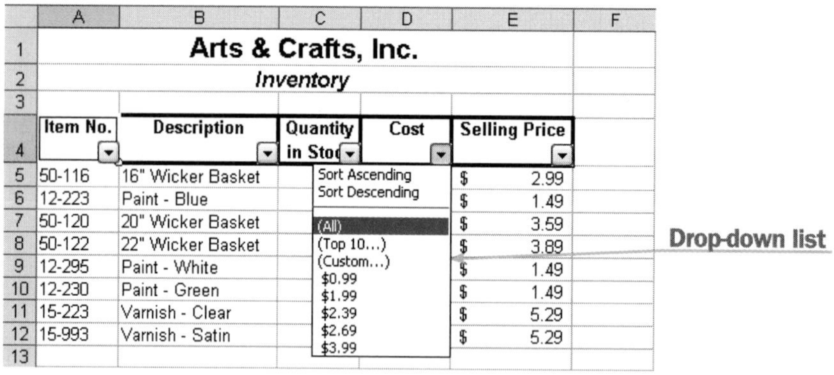

	A	B	C	D	E	F
1	Arts & Crafts, Inc.					
2	*Inventory*					
3						
4	Item No.	Description	Quantity in Sto	Cost	Selling Price	
5	50-116	16" Wicker Basket			$ 2.99	
6	12-223	Paint - Blue			$ 1.49	
7	50-120	20" Wicker Basket			$ 3.59	
8	50-122	22" Wicker Basket			$ 3.89	
9	12-295	Paint - White			$ 1.49	
10	12-230	Paint - Green			$ 1.49	
11	15-223	Varnish - Clear			$ 5.29	
12	15-993	Varnish - Satin			$ 5.29	
13						

Select an entry or one of the other search options from the drop-down list, and Excel displays only records that meet the selected criteria. For example, if you selected the $1.99 entry in the *Cost* drop-down list shown in Figure 11-2, Excel would display only those records that contain that value in the Cost field. The other records in the list are temporarily hidden from view. To redisplay them, click the AutoFilter arrow on the field you used to filter the records and select the *(All)* option at the top of the drop-down list. You can tell which field (or column) is filtered because the filter arrow will be a different color from the other arrows. You can edit or modify records in a filtered list, and you can print the worksheet with only the filtered list displayed.

STEP-BY-STEP 11.1

1. Open the **AE Step11-1** workbook from the data files and save it as **Stock Quantity.** followed by your initials.

2. Select a cell in the field name row. From the **Data** menu, select **Filter,** and then select **AutoFilter**.

3. Click the **Cost** filter arrow.

4. Click **$0.99**. Notice how only the records that have a cost of $0.99 are displayed.

5. To redisplay all the records, click the **Cost** filter arrow and select **(All)**.

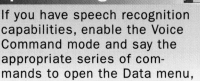

Speech Recognition

If you have speech recognition capabilities, enable the Voice Command mode and say the appropriate series of commands to open the Data menu, select Filter, and then select AutoFilter.

6. Let's try another filter. Click the **Selling Price** filter arrow.

7. Select **$5.29**. Note that only the records with a selling price of $5.29 are shown.

8. Print the filtered list. Then redisplay all records and remain in this screen for the next Step-by-Step.

Searching for Records Using Top 10

Excel's Top 10 feature offers you the ability to quickly display the highest or lowest values in a data list. For example, suppose you want to see the customers who have the highest account balances. You could quickly select these records using the *(Top 10...)* option from the AutoFilter list. Even though it's called the Top 10, you can display any number of records at the top or bottom of a list.

When you select the Top 10 feature, a dialog box appears, similar to Figure 11-3. The first *Show* option box in the Top 10 AutoFilter dialog box lets you choose the top or bottom of the list. The middle option box lets you select the number of records or the percentage of records to be displayed. The last option box lets you choose *Items* or *Percent,* meaning you can display a specific number of records to appear in the selected AutoFilter column or a percentage of records, such as the top 25%.

FIGURE 11-3
Top 10 AutoFilter dialog box

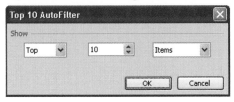

STEP-BY-STEP 11.2

1. Click the AutoFilter arrow for **Selling Price.**

2. Choose **(Top 10...).**

3. Click the down arrow next to the middle option box until **5** appears in the box.

4. Click **OK.** Five records with the highest selling prices will be displayed.

5. Let's try this again. Redisplay all the records.

6. Click the **Quantity in Stock** AutoFilter arrow and choose **(Top 10...).**

7. Click the up arrow for the middle option box until **25** is displayed.

8. Click the drop-down list arrow for the last option box and choose **Percent.**

9. Click **OK.** You should see two records that make up the top 25% of records containing the highest quantities in stock.

10. Save and close the workbook.

Displaying Records Using Custom Filters and Search Operators

So far, you've located records meeting specific criteria, such as items that cost $0.99. In some cases, though, you may need to find records that meet less specific criteria or that fall into a range. For example, you may want to find all the records that have a cost of $1.49 or greater. To search in this manner, you will use search operators. Excel's search operators and their descriptions are explained in Table 11-1.

Integration Tip

In order to put filtered data from an AutoFilter into a Word document, you will need to select the data and click the **Copy** tool, then switch to Word and click in the location where you want the data, and select the **Edit** menu and choose **Paste Special.** You will then need to select **Formatted Text (RTF)** in order for the filtered data to appear in a table.

TABLE 11-1
Search operators

OPERATOR	EXAMPLE	FIELD VALUE
equals	equals 10	10
does not equal	does not equal 10	all values but 10
is greater than	is greater than 10	11 or greater
is greater than or equal to	is greater than or equal to 10	10 or greater
is less than	is less than 10	9 or less
is less than or equal to	is less than or equal to 10	10 or less
begins with	begins with C	any value that begins with C or c
does not begin with	does not begin with C	any value that does not begin with C or c
ends with	ends with 7	any value that ends with a 7
does not end with	does not end with 7	any value that does not end with a 7
contains	contains 2005	any value that contains 2005 anywhere in them
does not contain	does not contain 2005	any value that does not contain 2005

Searching with Custom Filter

Custom filters let you search for values using the search operators, display rows that contain either one value or another, or display rows that meet more than one condition for a column. You select operators in the Custom AutoFilter dialog box, which is shown in Figure 11-4. Select an operator in the Search Operator list box by selecting from the drop-down list. Enter the search criteria in the Criteria text box to the right. We'll discuss the other options in the Custom AutoFilter dialog box later in this lesson.

FIGURE 11-4
Custom AutoFilter dialog box

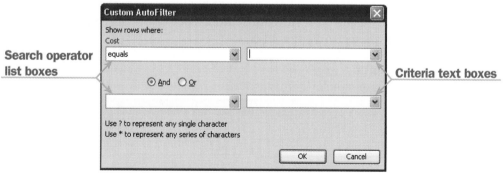

Search operator list boxes

Criteria text boxes

STEP-BY-STEP 11.3

1. Open the **AE Step11-3** workbook from the data files and save it as **Custom Filters,** followed by your initials.

2. Select a cell in the field name row. Open the **Data** menu, select **Filter,** and then select **AutoFilter.**

3. Click the **Cost** filter arrow.

4. Select **(Custom...).** The Custom AutoFilter dialog box appears, similar to Figure 11-4.

5. Click the drop-down list arrow next to the first Search Operator list text box and select **is greater than** from the list.

6. Click the drop-down list arrow for the first Criteria text box and select **$0.99.** This selection tells Excel to find all records with costs greater than $0.99.

7. Click **OK.** You will see records that have costs greater than $0.99.

8. Display all records.

9. Let's try this again. Select the **Selling Price** filter arrow and select **(Custom...).**

10. Select **is less than** as the search operator.

11. Select **$5.29** as the criteria and click **OK.** You will see six records that have a selling price less than $5.29.

12. Display all the records and remain in this screen for the next Step-by-Step.

Searching a List Using AND

There may be times when you want to locate records that meet two criteria. For example, you may want to locate customers who have account balances more than $200 and under $500. You can accomplish this by using AND in your search. You set up an AND search in the Custom AutoFilter dialog box, as shown in Figure 11-5.

FIGURE 11-5
Custom AutoFilter using AND

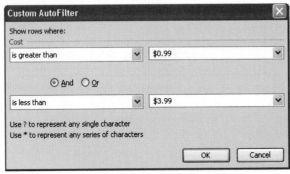

STEP-BY-STEP 11.4

1. Click the **Cost** filter arrow and choose **(Custom...)**.

2. Choose **is greater than** from the top Search Operator list box and select **$0.99** as the criteria.

3. Click **And** if it is not already selected.

4. Choose **is less than** from the bottom Search Operator list box and select **$3.99** as the criteria.

5. Click **OK**. You will see three records with costs greater than $0.99 and less than $3.99.

6. Save, print, and close the workbook.

Searching a List Using OR

Excel also allows you to search for records in a single field that meet one set of criteria or another. For example, you may want to search for all customers based in either California or Texas. To search for more than one value, you use the OR search operator. You set up an OR search in the Custom AutoFilter dialog box, as shown in Figure 11-6.

FIGURE 11-6
Custom AutoFilter using OR

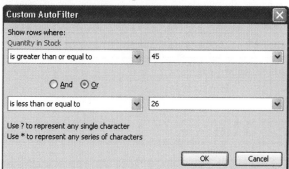

STEP-BY-STEP 11.5

1. Open the **AE Step11-5** workbook from the data files and save it as **Custom Filter2** followed by your initials.

2. Select a cell in the field name row. Open the **Data** menu, select **Filter,** and then select **AutoFilter**.

3. Click the **Quantity in Stock** filter arrow and choose **(Custom...)**.

4. Select **is greater than or equal to** from the Search Operator list box and select **45** as the criteria.

5. Click **Or.**

STEP-BY-STEP 11.5 Continued

6. Select **is less than or equal to** from the bottom Search Operator list box and select **26** as the criteria.

7. Click **OK.** You will see six records with a quantity in stock greater than or equal to 45 or less than or equal to 26.

8. Save, print, and close the workbook.

Searching a List Using Wildcards

So far, you've only searched for known values. But what if you don't know the exact value? This is where wildcards come in handy. Wildcards are used when you don't know the exact spelling of a word or name, or the exact value for which you are searching. For example, you might want to find all the records for employees whose last names begin with A.

The wildcard symbols are an asterisk (*) and a question mark (?). A question mark (?) represents a single character and the asterisk (*) represents one or more characters. Table 11-2 lists examples of the wildcards and how you could use them.

TABLE 11-2
Wildcards

IF YOU ENTER	EXCEL FINDS
A*	Apple, Aberdeen, Alabama
9??37	92237, 94537, 99937
a*h	accomplish, ash

STEP-BY-STEP 11.6

1. Open the **AE Step11-6** workbook from the data files and save it as **Wildcards,** followed by your initials.

2. Select a cell in the field name row. Open the **Data** menu, select **Filter,** and then select **AutoFilter.**

3. Click the **Item No.** filter arrow and choose **(Custom...).**

4. Key **50-*** in the top criteria text box and click **OK.** You will see three records with item numbers beginning with 50-.

5. Display all records.

6. Select the **Description** filter arrow and choose **(Custom...).**

7. Key **Paint - ?????** in the top Criteria text box. This will find records that begin with Paint and have five characters following the – (hyphen).

8. Click **OK.** You will see two records that meet the criteria.

9. Save and close the workbook.

Displaying Records Using Advanced Filters

In your previous searches, Excel would find records that met specific criteria and only display these records. Records not meeting these criteria would be temporarily removed from the screen. At times, however, you might want to continue viewing all data list records and have records that meet specific criteria copied to another location on the worksheet. Advanced Filters enable you to view the list records and the records that meet specific criteria at the same time. You will need to set up your worksheet for Advanced Filtering by creating a *Criteria Range* and a *Copy To Range*. The *Criteria Range* is the location where you will enter the information you want Excel to locate. The *Copy To Range* is the worksheet area where the records that meet the specific criteria will be copied. To create these ranges, you need to copy the field names (column headings) in the database list to the area where you want the *Criteria range* and *Copy To range* to appear in the worksheet. A sample worksheet using an Advanced Filter setup is shown in Figure 11-7.

FIGURE 11-7
Advanced Filter worksheet setup

	A	B	C	D	E	
1			Arts & Crafts, Inc.			
2			Inventory			
3						← List range
4	Item No.	Description	Quantity in Stock	Cost	Selling Price	
5	50-116	16" Wicker Basket	19	$ 1.99	$ 2.99	
6	12-223	Paint - Blue	45	$ 0.99	$ 1.49	
7	50-120	20" Wicker Basket	21	$ 2.39	$ 3.59	
8	50-122	22" Wicker Basket	17	$ 2.69	$ 3.89	
9	12-295	Paint - White	57	$ 0.99	$ 1.49	
10	12-230	Paint - Green	39	$ 0.99	$ 1.49	
11	15-223	Varnish - Clear	26	$ 3.99	$ 5.29	
12	15-993	Varnish - Satin	28	$ 3.99	$ 5.29	
13						
14						
15						← Criteria range
16	Item No.	Description	Quantity in Stock	Cost	Selling Price	
17						
18						
19						
20						
21						← Copy To range
22	Item No.	Description	Quantity in Stock	Cost	Selling Price	
23						
24						
25						
26						

The Advanced Filter feature searches for records meeting certain criteria and copies the records to the Copy To range. The original records are left intact.

After you enter search data in the criteria range, select the Data menu, Filter, and then Advanced Filter. In order to have Excel copy records to the copy to range, select the **Copy to another location** button and enter this range in the *Copy to* text box. The **Unique records only** option prevents duplicate records from being copied to the copy to range.

S TEP-BY-STEP 11.7

1. Open the **AE Step11-7** workbook from the data files and save it as **Advanced Filter** followed by your initials.

2. Create a criteria range. You will need to copy the data list field names to the criteria range. Select the range **A4:E4** (the field name row) and click the **Copy** button. When determining where the criteria range should be placed, try to allow enough blank rows below the list range so additional records can be added to the list in the future.

3. Select cell **A16** and click the **Paste** button.

4. Now let's create the copy to range. You will want to copy the list field names to this range as well. Select cell **A22** and click the **Paste** button.

5. Select cell **A17** in the criteria range and key **12-***. This tells Excel to search for all records with item numbers beginning with 12-.

6. Click anywhere in the original list, open the **Data** menu, select **Filter**, and then select **Advanced Filter**. The Advanced Filter dialog box appears, as shown in Figure 11-8.

FIGURE 11-8
Advanced Filter dialog box

7. Click the **Copy to another location** option. This option instructs Excel to copy the filtered records to the Copy to range.

STEP-BY-STEP 11.7 Continued

8. Verify that the list range **$A$4:$E$12** is in the *List range* text box.

9. In the *Criteria range* text box, key **A16:E17.** You need to include the criteria range field names and enough blank rows beneath the criteria field names to accommodate the criteria you are entering.

10. In the *Copy to* text box, key **A22:E35.** You need to include the field names and enough blank rows beneath the copy range field names to accommodate the records that Excel finds.

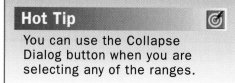

> **Hot Tip**
>
> You can use the Collapse Dialog button when you are selecting any of the ranges.

11. Click **OK**. Scroll to the copy to range. You will see three records with item numbers beginning with 12-, as shown in Figure 11-9.

FIGURE 11-9
Filtered records

	A	B	C	D	E	
1		**Arts & Crafts, Inc.**				
2		*Inventory*				← List range
3						
4	Item No.	Description	Quantity in Stock	Cost	Selling Price	
5	50-116	16" Wicker Basket	19	$ 1.99	$ 2.99	
6	12-223	Paint - Blue	45	$ 0.99	$ 1.49	
7	50-120	20" Wicker Basket	21	$ 2.39	$ 3.59	
8	50-122	22" Wicker Basket	17	$ 2.69	$ 3.89	
9	12-295	Paint - White	57	$ 0.99	$ 1.49	
10	12-230	Paint - Green	39	$ 0.99	$ 1.49	
11	15-223	Varnish - Clear	26	$ 3.99	$ 5.29	
12	15-993	Varnish - Satin	28	$ 3.99	$ 5.29	
13						
14						← Criteria range
15						
16	Item No.	Description	Quantity in Stock	Cost	Selling Price	
17	12-*					
18						
19						
20						← Copy To range
21						
22	Item No.	Description	Quantity in Stock	Cost	Selling Price	
23	12-223	Paint - Blue	45	$ 0.99	$ 1.49	
24	12-295	Paint - White	57	$ 0.99	$ 1.49	
25	12-230	Paint - Green	39	$ 0.99	$ 1.49	
26						

12. Save and close the workbook.

Using Advanced Filters to Find Multiple Criteria

When you looked for records that met two criteria with AutoFilter, you used the AND search option. You can use this same search option with advanced filters. To find records that meet two criteria, enter the criteria in the same row in the criteria range, as shown in Figure 11-10.

FIGURE 11-10
Using AND in an advanced filter

	Item No.	Description	Quantity in Stock	Cost	Selling Price	
16						
17	50-*			>$2.00		This item information AND
18						greater than this value
19						

To find records that met one search criteria or another, you used the OR search option in AutoFilter. To search for records meeting one criteria or another in an advanced filter, enter the criteria on separate rows as displayed in Figure 11-11.

FIGURE 11-11
Using OR in an advanced filter

	Item No.	Description	Quantity in Stock	Cost	Selling Price	
16						
17				$0.99		This value OR this value
18				$3.99		
19						

S TEP-BY-STEP 11.8

1. Open the **AE Step11-8** workbook from the data files and save the workbook as **Filter6,** followed by your initials.

2. Select cell **A17** and clear the contents of the cell. You must remove criteria from a previous search before you can start a new search.

3. Enter **50-*** in cell **A17.**

4. Select cell **D17** and enter **>$2.00.** This will find all records that have an item number beginning with 50- and that have a cost greater than $2.00.

5. Click in any cell in the data list, open the **Data** menu, select **Filter,** and select **Advanced Filter.**

6. Select **Copy to another location.**

7. Check the *List range, Criteria range,* and *Copy to* boxes. These ranges should still be entered correctly in the text boxes. If not, enter the correct ranges at this time.

8. Click **OK.** Look at the *Copy to* range. You should see the two records for item numbers beginning with 50- that have a cost greater than $2.00.

9. Let's try another advanced filter. Select the cells in the criteria range that you used in the previous search and clear the contents.

STEP-BY-STEP 11.8 Continued

10. Select cell **D17** and enter **$.99**.

11. Select cell **D18** and enter **$3.99**. (This will find all records that have a cost of either $0.99 or $3.99.)

12. Click in any cell in the data list, open the **Data** menu, select **Filter,** and then select **Advanced Filter.**

13. Click **Copy to another location.**

14. In the *Criteria range* text box, delete the current range and key **A16:E18.** (You need to expand the range one row because you've entered criteria on two rows in the criteria range.)

15. If necessary, key **A22:E35** in the *Copy to* text box.

16. Click **OK.** Look at the copy to range. You should see five records that have a cost of $0.99 or $3.99, as shown in Figure 11-12.

Hot Tip

The *List, Criteria,* and *Copy to* ranges typically display each time you open the Advanced Filter box, thereby saving you time.

FIGURE 11-12
Filtered Records

	Item No.	Description	Quantity in Stock	Cost	Selling Price
					Arts & Crafts, Inc.
					Inventory
5	50-116	16" Wicker Basket	19	$ 1.99	$ 2.99
6	12-223	Paint - Blue	45	$ 0.99	$ 1.49
7	50-120	20" Wicker Basket	21	$ 2.39	$ 3.59
8	50-122	22" Wicker Basket	17	$ 2.69	$ 3.89
9	12-295	Paint - White	57	$ 0.99	$ 1.49
10	12-230	Paint - Green	39	$ 0.99	$ 1.49
11	15-223	Varnish - Clear	26	$ 3.99	$ 5.29
12	15-993	Varnish - Satin	28	$ 3.99	$ 5.29

	Item No.	Description	Quantity in Stock	Cost	Selling Price
17				$0.99	← Criteria specified
18				$3.99	

	Item No.	Description	Quantity in Stock	Cost	Selling Price
23	12-223	Paint - Blue	45	$ 0.99	$ 1.49
24	12-295	Paint - White	57	$ 0.99	$ 1.49
25	12-230	Paint - Green	39	$ 0.99	$ 1.49
26	15-223	Varnish - Clear	26	$ 3.99	$ 5.29
27	15-993	Varnish - Satin	28	$ 3.99	$ 5.29

Search results →

17. Save the workbook.

18. Print the data, including the column headings, in the copy to range only. Close the workbook.

Speech Recognition

If you have speech recognition capabilities, enable the Voice Command mode and say the appropriate series of commands to print the worksheet.

Using DSUM and DAVERAGE

Y ou can use Excel's database functions to provide quick answers to your database questions, such as a sum or average of some of the values within the database. For example, you may have a sales database and you want to find out the sum of all of the sales of $10,000 for the day. In order to get a quick sum of the $10,000 sales sold on a day, you can use the *DSUM* function. In addition, you can find the average of values within a database by using the *DAVERAGE* function. Figures 11-13 and 11-14 display the DSUM and DAVERAGE Function Arguments dialog boxes.

FIGURE 11-13
DSUM Function Arguments dialog box

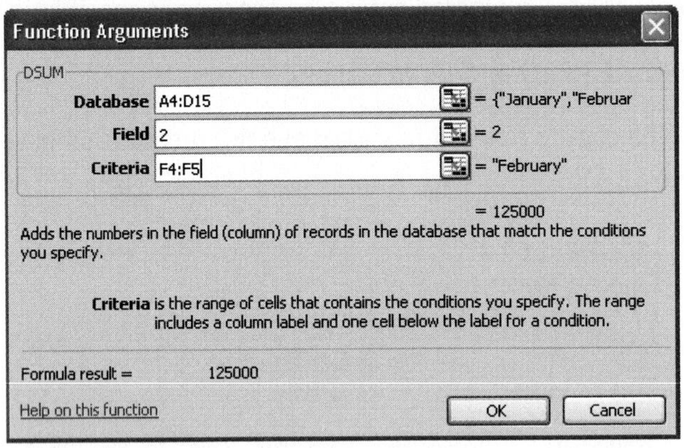

FIGURE 11-14
DAVERAGE Function Arguments dialog box

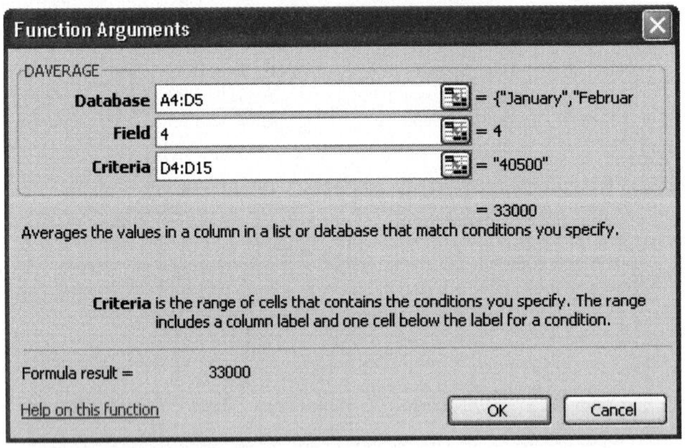

For each function you will first need to specify the database range in the *Database* text box as displayed in Figures 11-13 and 11-14. Then you will indicate the number of the field from which you want to sum or average. For example, if you wanted to find the sum of the $25,000 motorcycles that were sold in February, you would enter 2 for the field since February is the second field (column) in the database shown in Figure 11-15.

FIGURE 11-15
Database

	A	B	C	D	E	F	G	H	
1	Lynn's Motorcycle Sales								
2									
3									
4	January	February	March	April		February		125000	
5	$10,000.00	$ 2,000.00	$10,000.00	$33,000.00		$25,000			
6	$ 5,000.00	$ 3,000.00	$11,000.00	$44,000.00					
7	$10,000.00	$ 4,000.00	$12,000.00	$43,000.00					
8	$10,000.00	$ 5,000.00	$13,000.00	$35,000.00					
9	$10,000.00	$25,000.00	$14,000.00	$40,000.00					
10	$10,500.00	$25,000.00	$15,000.00	$40,500.00					
11	$11,000.00	$25,000.00	$16,000.00	$41,000.00					
12	$11,500.00	$25,000.00	$17,000.00	$41,500.00					
13	$12,000.00	$25,000.00	$18,000.00	$42,000.00					
14	$12,500.00	$10,000.00	$19,000.00	$42,500.00					
15	$13,000.00	$26,000.00	$20,000.00	$43,000.00					

Field 4
Field 3
Field 2
Field 1

Criteria range

Location of
DSUM
function

Field Name

Search Item

The criteria range needs to include both the field name and the search item as indicated in Figure 11-15. In this example, the criteria range would be F4:F5. You will need to select a cell outside the database range and the criteria range for the database function.

STEP-BY-STEP 11.9

1. Open the **AE Step11-9** workbook from the data files and save the workbook as **Filter7,** followed by your initials.

2. First, you will sum all of the $25,000 sales for the month of February; therefore, select cell **F4** and enter **February.** Then, select cell **F5** and enter **$25,000.**

3. Click in cell **H4,** select the **Insert** menu, and then choose **Function.**

4. Choose **All** from the *Or select a category* list box, and then click once in the *Select a function* list box.

5. Press the letter **D** and scroll down until you see DSUM, then select it and click **OK.**

6. Enter **A4:D15** for the *Database* text box.

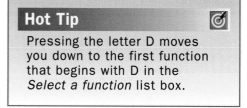

Hot Tip

Pressing the letter D moves you down to the first function that begins with D in the *Select a function* list box.

7. Enter **2** for the *Field* text box since you are looking for sales in February, which is the second field in the database.

8. Enter **F4:F5** in the *Criteria* text box, as this range is where you specified the deposit amounts for which you want to search. Then, click **OK.** The result will display in H4 as 125,000. This is the sum of the $25,000 sales in February.

9. Now, let's try the DAVERAGE function and find the average sales for April. Select cell **H10,** select the **Insert** menu and then choose **Function.**

STEP-BY-STEP 11.9 Continued

10. Choose **All** from the *Or select a category* list box, if necessary. Then, click once in the *Select a function* list box.

11. Press the letter **D** and scroll down until you see **DAVERAGE**, then select it and click **OK**.

12. Enter **A4:D15** in the *Database* text box.

13. Enter **4** in the *Field* text box since you are looking for sales in April, which is the fourth field in the database.

14. Enter **D4:D15** in the *Criteria* text box as the range and click **OK**. The result, 40,500, will display in H10. This is the average sales for the month of April.

15. Save and print the worksheet. Then close the workbook.

Time Saver

Sometimes if your hands are already on the keyboard, it's easier to make selections using the keys. For example, you can quickly select the AutoFilter list with your keyboard.

STEP-BY-STEP 11.10

1. Select the cell containing the desired column label and AutoFilter.

2. Press **Alt + down arrow**.

3. You can then move down and up in the list by pressing the **down arrow** and **up arrow**.

4. Press **Enter** to select an item.

SUMMARY

In this lesson, you learned:

- AutoFilter can be used to find records within a list that meet specific criteria. When you select AutoFilter on the Data menu, arrows are displayed in each field name's cell. Click the AutoFilter arrow for the field you want to search and select the entry or other search option from the drop-down list. Excel will display only those records containing the specified field criteria.

- Excel's search operators let you quickly create your search criteria. Use the AND search operator to find records that meet two criteria and the OR search operator to find records that meet one criteria or another.

- Custom filters allow you the flexibility to search for values using the search operators, to display rows that contain either one value or another, or to display rows that meet more than one condition for a column.

- Wildcard characters can be used when you're not sure about the complete value for which you're searching. The asterisk (*) wildcard is used to represent any number of characters or numbers. The question mark (?) wildcard is used to represent a single character or number.

- Advanced filters can be used to find records that meet more complex criteria. The results of the search can then be copied to another location on the worksheet.

- The DSUM and DAVERAGE functions allow you to sum and average values in your database.

VOCABULARY *Review*

Define the following terms:		
AutoFilter	Custom filter	DAVERAGE
Copy to range	DSUM	Filter
Criteria range		

REVIEW *Questions*

WRITTEN QUESTIONS

Write a brief answer to the following questions.

1. When would you use AND in a search?

2. When would you use OR in a search?

3. What is the difference between AutoFilter and Advanced Filter?

4. How do you indicate you want to find records meeting two criteria on different fields using advanced filters?

5. How do you find records meeting one criteria or another using advanced filters?

6. What AutoFilter option would you select to search for values using operators?

7. How do you redisplay data after you've filtered a column using AutoFilter?

8. What symbol can you use to find all records that start with a specific number, regardless of how many characters follow the first number?

9. What search criteria would you use to find words in a field that start with the letter A followed by three characters?

10. Which feature could you use to find the highest 25% of sales in a database field?

TRUE/FALSE

Circle T if the statement is true or F if the statement is false.

T F 1. AutoFilter lets you copy records found in a search to another range on the worksheet.

T F 2. You can use the AND operator in an advanced filter, but not in an AutoFilter.

T F 3. You would use the DSUM function to average a field of values in a database.

T F 4. If you select the *Top, 50,* and *Percent* options in the Top 10 dialog box, the first 50% of records will be displayed.

T F 5. If you enter the search operator *begins with* C, the filter would find records that begin with C or c.

PROJECTS

PROJECT 11-1

1. Open the **AE Project11-1** workbook from the data files and save it as **Pet Store Inventory,** followed by your initials.

2. Use AutoFilter to find products that cost less than $1.00. Print the filtered list so that all the data fits on one page.

3. Use an advanced filter to find records for all Kitten products with a quantity in stock of less than 100. Copy the found records to a range on the worksheet.

4. Print the entire worksheet so that all the data fits on one page.

5. Save and close the workbook.

PROJECT 11-2

1. Open the **AE Project11-2** workbook from the data files.

2. Use advanced filters to find records with the following criteria. Use a Copy to range.
   a. Products that are available in a small size. Save the file as **Sports Store Sales – Small Size,** followed by your initials. Print the results in portrait orientation.
   b. Products that have a sales price greater than $10.00 that are available in a large size. Save the file as **Sports Store Sales – Large Size,** followed by your initials. Print the results in portrait orientation.

3. Save and then close the workbook.

CRITICAL *Thinking*

SCANS **ACTIVITY 11-1**

You work in the sales department of New Horizons Engine Corporation and you've set up a list containing an extensive number of records. The list includes the names of salespersons and their individual sales. You want to find out exact sales amounts for company salespeople whose individual sales are more than $5,000. Describe how you would enter this criteria in the criteria range of an advanced filter.

SCANS **ACTIVITY 11-2**

Using Excel's Help system, explain the purpose of the wildcard character ~ (tilde).

ACTIVITY 11-3

Using Excel's Help system, find additional database functions other than DSUM and DAVERAGE.

WORKING WITH ANALYSIS TOOLS

Introduction

Excel features a number of tools that give you the power to manipulate, analyze, interpret, and predict worksheet data. Auditing is a powerful feature that lets you locate cells in formulas and trace formula errors. You can also add data validation to your worksheet cells to assist you in monitoring the accuracy of the data that's being entered. In addition, you can have Excel place circles around any invalid data.

Scenarios allow you to view what would happen to existing worksheet data if the value in one or more cells were changed. For example, if your company were expecting to receive increased revenues next year, you could use a scenario to see how your net income (bottom line) would be affected by this change. Goal Seek is a feature that lets you determine a value in order to meet a goal. Solver enables you to calculate several values in order to generate an optimal solution.

Correlation allows you to determine if a strong relationship exists between variables. If a strong relationship does exist, then you could perform a regression and use the regression equation to predict values. *Regression* is a statistical method used to describe the relationship between variables.

Using Excel's Auditing Feature

Excel's *auditing* feature identifies the cells that are referenced in a formula, thereby making it easier for you to determine where an error might occur in a formula. To use the auditing tools, you can select the Formula Auditing command on the Tools menu or you can display the Formula Auditing toolbar to access the commands via toolbar buttons.

The auditing feature lets you trace precedents and dependents. A *precedent* refers to the cells that are referenced in a formula. If you select a cell containing a formula and then click the **Trace Precedents** button on the Formula Auditing toolbar, Excel draws a line from the formula cell to each cell that is referenced in the formula.

A *dependent* refers to the cells that contain formulas that reference a selected cell. If you select a cell that contains a value and then click the Trace Dependents button on the Formula Auditing toolbar, Excel draws a line to each cell that contains a formula that references the selected cell.

Figure 12-1 illustrates how Excel traces precedents and Figure 12-2 shows how dependents are traced. In Figure 12-1, cell F5 contains a formula that references cells B5, C5, D5, and E5. These are its precedents, as identified by the blue Trace Precedents line through the cells and the blue box around the outside of the cells. In Figure 12-2, the value in cell B6 is used in formulas contained in cells B10, B14, and F6 as indicated by the arrows on the Trace Dependents lines.

FIGURE 12-1
Trace Precedents

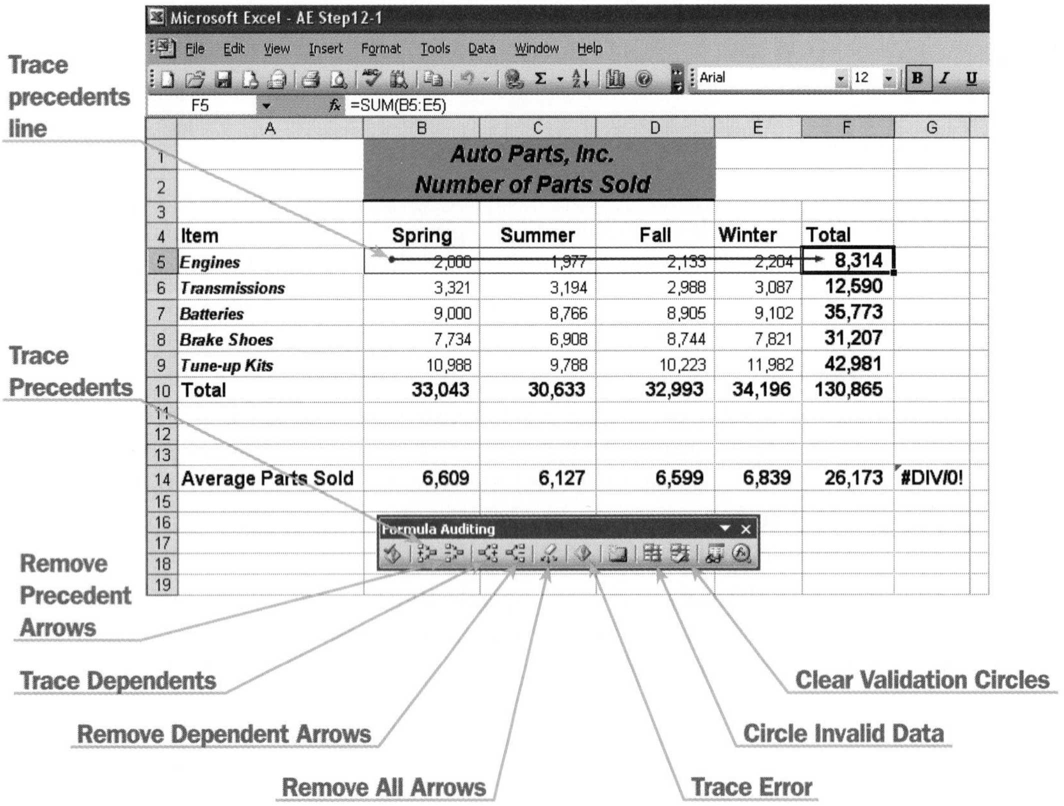

FIGURE 12-2
Trace Dependents

	A	B	C	D	E	F
1		Auto Parts, Inc.				
2		Number of Parts Sold				
3						
4	Item	Spring	Summer	Fall	Winter	Total
5	Engines	2,000	1,977	2,133	2,204	8,314
6	Transmissions	3,321	3,194	2,988	3,087	12,590
7	Batteries	9,000	8,766	8,905	9,102	35,773
8	Brake Shoes	7,734	6,908	8,744	7,821	31,207
9	Tune-up Kits	10,988	9,788	10,223	11,982	42,981
10	Total	33,043	30,633	32,993	34,196	130,865
11						
12						
13						
14	Average Parts Sold	6,609	6,127	6,599	6,839	26,173

Trace dependents arrows

Figure 12-1 also shows the Formula Auditing toolbar. You can remove the precedents and dependents lines by clicking either the Remove Precedent Arrows or Remove Dependent Arrows buttons. Or you can click the Remove All Arrows button. If a cell contains a message like #DIV/0!, indicating an error in the formula, you can select it and click the Trace Error button on the Formula Auditing toolbar. A red line is drawn to the cell(s) in which the problem occurs. The Circle Invalid Data and Clear Validation Circles buttons relate to finding cells that contain data that is outside the rules of validation that you've set.

STEP-BY-STEP 12.1

1. Open the **AE Step12-1** workbook from the data files and save it as **Auto Parts** followed by your initials.

2. Open the **Tools** menu, select **Formula Auditing,** and then choose **Show Formula Auditing Toolbar.** Move the toolbar, if necessary.

3. Click cell **F5**.

4. Click the **Trace Precedents** button. Your screen should look similar to Figure 12-1. Notice the line drawn through the cells contained in the formula, as well as the box drawn around them. An arrow is displayed in the cell with the formula.

5. Click cell **B6**.

6. Click the **Trace Dependents** button. Notice that an arrow appears in each cell containing a formula that references cell B6. You should have arrows in cells B10, B14, and F6.

STEP-BY-STEP 12.1 Continued

7. Notice that cell G14 contains the #DIV/0! error message. Select cell **G14** and then click the **Trace Error button**. A line from the cell extends to the cells G5:G9, which have a blue box around them. To determine the cause of the error, click the **Error Checking** tool. An Error Checking dialog box appears (as shown in Figure 12-3) with a message indicating the formula is trying to divide empty cells. Click **Next** and then click **OK**.

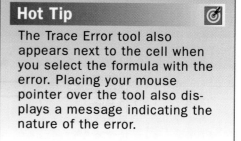

> ### Hot Tip
>
> The Trace Error tool also appears next to the cell when you select the formula with the error. Placing your mouse pointer over the tool also displays a message indicating the nature of the error.

FIGURE 12-3
Error Checking Dialog Box

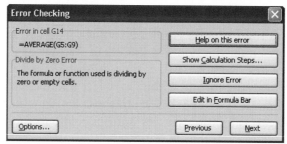

8. Edit cell **G14** so that the formula finds the average of the values in cells **B14:F14**. The error message is replaced by a correct value and the Trace Error arrows and the blue box are removed.

9. Click **Print Preview** to see how you could print this sheet with arrows displayed. Click **Close**.

10. Remove all arrows by clicking the **Remove All Arrows** button on the Formula Auditing toolbar, and then print the worksheet in landscape orientation.

11. Save and close the workbook.

Performing Data Validation and Circling Invalid Data

The *Data Validation* feature of Excel allows data to be entered according to certain rules that you specify. For example, you may have a worksheet containing a budget. If data exceeds a certain amount, you can have that data flagged. In addition, you can have an instructive message appear as data is entered into the cell and another message appear if the data does not meet the rules you specified. Additionally, Excel can circle any data that violates the rules you specify.

STEP-BY-STEP 12.2

First, let's apply data validation to the data. You want to circle budget figures that exceed $10,000 in any given month for any department.

1. Open the **AE Step12-2** workbook from the data files and save it as **Budget Analysis,** followed by your initials. Select the range **B5:G10.**

2. Open the **Data** menu and select **Validation.** The Data Validation dialog box appears as shown in Figure 12-4.

FIGURE 12-4
Data Validation dialog box

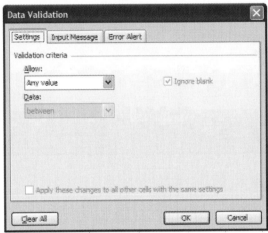

3. In the **Settings** tab, click the *Allow* drop-down arrow and select **Whole number.**

4. Click the *Data* drop-down arrow and choose **less than or equal to.** Selecting this option will allow numbers less than the number specified in the *Maximum* text box to be considered valid.

5. In the *Maximum* text box, key **$10,000.00.** The Data Validation dialog box should be shown as in Figure 12-5.

FIGURE 12-5
Completed Settings tab of the Data Validation dialog box

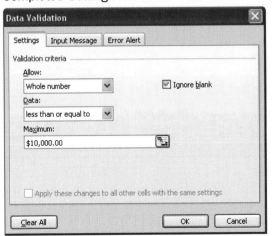

STEP-BY-STEP 12.2 Continued

6. Select the **Input Message** tab, click in the *Title* text box and key **Data Validation.**

7. Click in the *Input message* text box and key **Amounts should be $10,000 or less**. The **Input Message** tab should appear as shown in Figure 12-6.

FIGURE 12-6
Input Message tab of the Data Validation dialog box

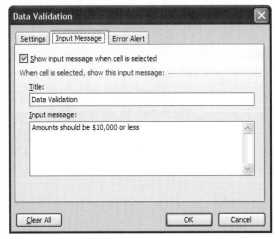

8. Click the **Error Alert** tab.

9. In the *Title* text box, key **Data Alert.** This text will appear on the title of the dialog box when invalid data is entered.

10. Click in the *Error message* text box and key **Amount exceeds budget limits**. This message will appear in the Error Message dialog box. Your **Error Alert** tab should appear similar to Figure 12-7.

FIGURE 12-7
Error Alert tab of the Data Validation dialog box

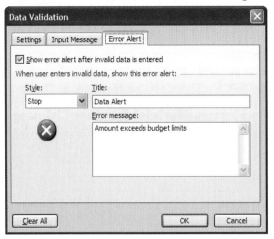

STEP-BY-STEP 12.2 Continued

11. Click **OK.**

12. Now, let's see how data validation works. Notice that B5:G10 is still selected and the input message appears over the range. Click in **B5,** key **$12,000,** and press **Enter.** The Error Alert dialog box appears. Click **Cancel** to remove the invalid new entry from the cell.

13. To have the invalid data (that was entered before the validation rule was established) circled, you will need to display the Formula Auditing toolbar. Display the Formula Auditing toolbar, if necessary, by opening the **Tools** menu, selecting **Formula Auditing,** and then choosing **Show Formula Auditing Toolbar.**

14. Click the **Circle Invalid Data** tool. The budget figures that exceed $10,000 are circled as displayed in Figure 12-8.

FIGURE 12-8
Invalid Data Circled

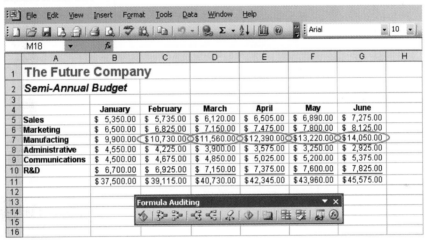

15. To remove the validation circles, click the **Clear Validation Circles** tool on the Formula Auditing toolbar.

16. Save and close the workbook.

Creating and Merging Scenarios

Ⓒ A *scenario* performs a "what-if" analysis in your worksheet. Scenarios are often used to develop budgets. For example, you may expect shipping or equipment expenses to increase next year. To find out how these increased expenses may affect your future budget, you can use the Scenario Manager to insert different values that generate different versions of the budget.

Creating Scenarios

To create scenarios, open the Scenario Manager dialog box, which is shown in Figure 12-9. Click **Add** to open the Add Scenario dialog box, shown in Figure 12-10. Note that **Prevent changes** is selected to stop unwanted changes to the new scenario.

FIGURE 12-9
Scenario Manager dialog box

FIGURE 12-10
Add Scenario dialog box

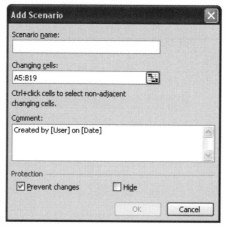

The Add Scenario dialog box is where you create a scenario. Key a name for the scenario and then determine which cells contain the values that can be changed to produce a different result. Click **OK** to create the scenario. After you've created your scenarios, the Scenario Manager can save them in a preset report format on a separate sheet in the workbook. Excel automatically names the sheet "Scenario Summary" and applies formatting to the data.

STEP-BY-STEP 12.3

1. Open the **AE Step12-3** workbook from the data files and save it as **International Income Statement,** followed by your initials.

2. View the current budget.

3. Select the range **A5:B19.**

4. Open the **Tools** menu and then select **Scenarios.**

5. Click the **Add** button in the Scenario Manager dialog box.

6. In the Add Scenario dialog box, key **Current Budget** in the *Scenario name* text box.

7. Click the **Collapse Dialog** button in the *Changing cells* box, select the range **B10:B16,** and then press **Enter**.

8. Click **OK**. The scenario values for the selected cells appear in the Scenario Values dialog box, as displayed in Figure 12-11. Click **OK**. You've now saved the original budget values.

FIGURE 12-11
Scenario Values dialog box

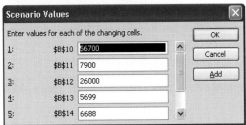

9. Click **Add** in the Scenario Manager dialog box.

10. Key **Increased Equipment and Shipping** in the Scenario name text box and click **OK.**

11. In the Scenario Values dialog box, select the value in the Equipment text box ($B$10), if necessary, and key **90000.**

12. Select the value in the Freight text box ($B$11) and key **9000.**

13. Select the value in the Postage text box ($B$14) and key **8000.**

14. Click **OK.**

15. Click **Add** in the Scenario Manager dialog box.

16. Key **Increased Shipping and Office Supplies** in the Scenario name text box and click OK.

17. Select the value in the Freight text box ($B$11) and key **10000.**

STEP-BY-STEP 12.3 Continued

18. Select the value in the Office Supplies ($B$13) text box and key **8500**.

19. Select the value in the Postage ($B$14) text box and key **8000**.

20. Click **OK.**

21. Now, you will create a summary of the scenarios. In the Scenario Manager dialog box, click **Summary.**

22. In the Scenario Summary dialog box, make sure **Scenario summary** is selected. Key **B17** in the Result cells text box, if necessary. This cell will display the Expense total. Click **OK.** The scenarios are placed on a new Scenario Summary worksheet in the workbook as shown in Figure 12-12.

FIGURE 12-12
Scenario Summary worksheet

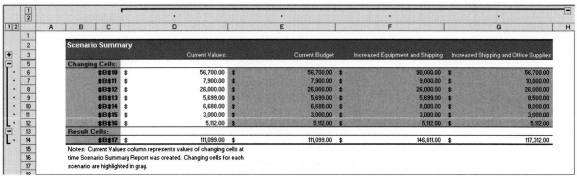

23. Click the **Income Statement** worksheet tab, select the range **A10:A16,** and click the **Copy** button.

24. Click the **Scenario Summary** worksheet tab, click in cell **A6,** and click the **Paste** button. Resize columns as necessary to display the data.

25. Print the Scenario Summary worksheet in landscape orientation and so all the data fits on one page. Save and close the workbook.

> **Speech Recognition**
>
> If you have speech recognition capabilities, enable the Voice Command mode and say the appropriate series of commands to print the scenario summary.

Merging Scenarios

Excel lets you merge scenarios from one workbook into another workbook in order to view them. This feature allows you to quickly and conveniently bring a scenario from one workbook into another simply by selecting the scenario's name.

STEP-BY-STEP 12.4

In this exercise, you will merge expenses from the source workbook into an active workbook in order to view a company's profits (or losses) using the merged expense scenario. You will create scenarios in two different workbooks and then you'll merge a scenario from one workbook into another.

1. Open the **AE Step12-4A** workbook from the data files and save it as **Region A,** followed by your initials. Open the **AE Step12-4B** workbook from the data files and save it as **Region B,** followed by your initials.

2. In the Region B workbook, select the range **A7:B10.**

3. Choose the **Tools** menu, select **Scenarios** and then click the **Add** button.

4. Key **Mini Calculation Scenario** in the *Scenario name* text box.

5. Key **B7:B9** in the *Changing cells* text box and then click **OK.** Choosing these cells allows you to change the cells that contain expenses. Click **OK** to close the Scenario Values dialog box.

6. Select **Close** to close the Scenario Manager dialog box. Save the workbook.

7. Go to the **Region A** workbook.

8. Select the range **A7:B10.**

9. Choose the **Tools** menu, select **Scenarios,** and then click the **Add** button.

10. Key **Mini Printing Systems Scenario** in the *Scenario name* text box.

11. Key **B7:B9** in the *Changing cells* text box and then click **OK.** Note that these are the same cells you chose to change in the previous scenario. Click **OK** to close the Scenario Values dialog box.

12. Select **Close** to close the Scenario Manager dialog box. Save the workbook.

13. Select cell **B7** to let Excel know that this cell can change in the Merge process. Click on the **Tools** menu, choose **Scenarios,** and then click on the **Merge** button. The Merge Scenarios dialog box will appear similar to Figure 12-13.

FIGURE 12-13
Merge Scenarios dialog box

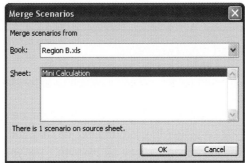

STEP-BY-STEP 12.4 Continued

14. Click **OK** to select the Mini Calculation scenario from the Region B workbook. Notice that both scenarios now appear in the Scenario Manager dialog box.

15. Click the **Mini Calculation Scenario** and click the **Show** button to see this scenario.

16. Click the **Mini Printing Systems Scenario** and click the **Show** button to see this scenario.

17. Click **Close** to close the Scenario Manager dialog box.

18. Save and close both workbooks.

Performing What-if Analysis Using Goal Seek

Formulas and functions usually perform mathematical calculations with known values to give you a result. Sometimes, however, you may know the result (goal), but you don't necessarily know the values needed to arrive at the goal. For example, you may want to save $15,000 for your first year of college five years from now. You need to know how much to save each month in order to meet this goal. The Goal Seek feature does this for you. Goal seek is referred to as a "what-if" analysis tool. *Goal Seek* allows you to adjust a value in a formula in order to reach a desired result or answer.

The Goal Seek dialog box is shown in Figure 12-14. In the *Set cell* box, you enter the cell that contains the formula. This lets Excel know what calculation to use when it is looking for the answer. You enter the desired goal in the *To value* box. In the *By changing cell* box, you enter the address for the cell in which you want the answer to be displayed.

FIGURE 12-14
Goal Seek dialog box

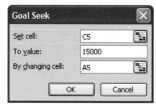

STEP-BY-STEP 12.5

1. Click the **New** button to start a new workbook.

2. Select cell **C5**. (*Note:* You could select any cell in which to enter the formula.)

3. Key **=A5*12*5**. (Using the above example with college funds, cell A5 will be the unknown monthly savings amount. Again, you can enter this information into any cell. This formula takes the unknown monthly amount in cell A5 and multiplies it by 12 payments per year for 5 years. You use Goal Seek to find the amount you need in cell A5 to come up with the result of $15,000. For simplicity's sake, let's ignore the interest rate.)

STEP-BY-STEP 12.5 Continued

4. Select cell **C5** (the cell with the formula), if necessary.

5. From the **Tools** menu, choose **Goal Seek**. Cell C5 should appear in the *Set cell* text box.

6. In the *To value* box, key **15000.** This is the goal value.

7. In the *By changing cell* box, key **A5.** This is the cell address of the unknown value.

8. Click **OK.** The Goal Seek Status dialog box appears to let you know that it has found a value.

9. Click **OK** in the Goal Seek Status dialog box and look at the value in cell A5. In this example, 250 should be in the cell. (To double-check if this is accurate, multiply $250 by 12 by 5 and, sure enough, you get $15,000.)

10. Save the file as **College Fund Goal,** followed by your initials and close the workbook.

11. Now, let's try another example. You will determine what growth rate is necessary for your company to achieve a projected sales amount. Start a new workbook.

12. Select cell **A3** and key **2005 Total Gross Sales.** Apply a bold format.

13. Select cell **A4** and key **2005 Projected Growth Rate.** Apply a bold format.

14. Select cell **A5** and key **2005 Projected Sales.** Apply a bold format.

15. Choose cell **C3** and key **850,000.** Apply the currency format with no decimal places. Widen the column widths as necessary to view the data and text.

16. Select cell **C5** and key **=C3*C4.** (This will calculate the projected sales once Goal Seek calculates a growth rate for cell C4.)

17. Select cell **C4** and give the cell a percentage format with two decimal places.

18. Select cell **C5**. This cell contains the formula for projected sales.

19. Open the **Tools** menu and then select **Goal Seek.**

20. In the *To value* box, key **1000000.** In the *By changing cell* box, key **C4.** (This action tells Excel to change the amount in cell C4 until the value in C5 is $1,000,000.)

21. Click **OK.** The value in cell C4 should be 117.65%, which indicates a 100% sales rate and a 17.65% growth rate is necessary to achieve the projected sales total. Click **OK** again to close the Goal Seek Status box. If necessary, format cell C5 as currency with no decimal places. Widen columns as necessary.

22. Save the workbook as **Projected Sales,** followed by your initials. Print the sheet and then close the workbook.

> **Speech Recognition**
>
> If you have speech recognition capabilities, enable the Voice Command mode and say the appropriate series of commands to print the worksheet.

Using Solver

Excel's Solver tool is used to determine two or more unknown values. For example, let's say you have a company that makes three sports products: baseball bats, footballs, and helmets. You need to sell $100,000 of sports equipment per year to break even. You want a general idea of how many of each item you need to sell. Solver can help you calculate how many of each item you need to sell to reach your goal. The Solver Parameters dialog box is shown in Figure 12-15.

FIGURE 12-15
Solver Parameter dialog box

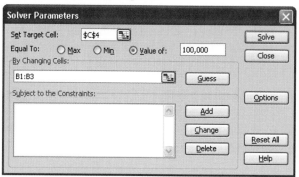

STEP-BY-STEP 12.6

1. Start a new workbook, and save it as **Solver**, followed by your initials.

2. Select cell **A1** and key **15** (the sales price for a baseball bat).

3. Select cell **A2** and key **8** (the sales price for a football).

4. Select cell **A3** and key **12** (the sales price for a helmet). Format cells **A1:A3** for currency.

5. Key **0** in cells **B1, B2,** and **B3.** (*Note*: These cells are where Solver will enter the quantity that should be produced.)

6. Select cell **C1** and key **=A1*B1** (this tells Excel to multiply the sales price by the quantity sold). Select cell **C2** and key **=A2*B2**. Select cell **C3** and key **=A3*B3**. *Note:* You can also use the AutoFill to copy the formula in C1 to cells C2 and C3.

7. Select cell **C4** and key **=SUM(C1:C3)** or click the **AutoSum** tool and press **Enter.** Entering this formula will total the dollar amount of sales. This cell will be set equal to the total dollar amount of sales you want.

8. For reference, let's enter the equipment item name in the row that contains data for the item. Select cell **D1** and key **Bat,** select cell **D2** and key **Football,** and select cell **D3** and key **Helmet.**

9. Select **C4.** Open the **Tools** menu and then select **Solver.**

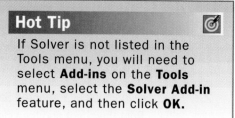

Hot Tip

If Solver is not listed in the Tools menu, you will need to select **Add-ins** on the **Tools** menu, select the **Solver Add-in** feature, and then click **OK.**

STEP-BY-STEP 12.6 Continued

10. Notice the **Max, Min,** and **Value of** buttons in the dialog box. The **Max** option increases the goal cell to the largest possible value. The **Min** option decreases the goal cell to the smallest possible value. The **Value of** option sets the goal cell value to the value you specify in the Value of text box. Select **Value of** and key **100,000** in the *Value of* text box.

11. In the *By Changing Cells* text box, key **B1:B3** (these are the cells that will be adjusted to reach the desired solution).

12. Click **Solve.** Click **OK** when the Solver Results dialog box lets you know it found a solution. Increase the column widths, if necessary.

13. Look at the values. Using the cost values as a guide, Solver determined the sales for each item that would total $100,000.

14. You can round the numbers in column **B** by selecting these cells and clicking the **Decrease Decimal** button for each decimal place you want to remove. For this exercise, decrease the decimal places until there are no decimal places. Format column **C** with currency format and two decimal places.

15. Print the sheet. Then save and close the workbook.

Projecting Values Using Correlation and Regression

In our everyday lives, we commonly make projections. For example, when we hear thunder and see lightning, we often predict that it will be followed by rain. We can make this prediction because we know that there is a strong relationship between these variables. We can also use Excel's analysis tools to determine if variables have a strong relationship. If a strong relationship is determined, then we can make predictions from the variables.

First, to determine if the variables have a strong relationship, we will use Excel's Correlation feature. When variables are highly correlated, they are said to have a strong relationship. As a general rule, if the correlation coefficient is *above* a plus (+) or minus (-) .70, then a strong correlation between the variables exists. Therefore, correlations of +0.85 or -0.85 would be considered strong correlations. A negative correlation indicates that as one variable increases, the other corresponding variable decreases. For example, the number of days a student is absent from school would probably be negatively correlated to the student's grade. The more days the student misses, the lower their grade will be.

> **Integration Tip**
>
> If you want part of an Excel worksheet that contains tracing arrows, such as trace precedent arrows, to be put into a Word document, simply select the area of the worksheet containing the data and the arrows and click the Paste tool. Then, select the location in the Word document where you want the information copied and click the Edit menu and select Paste Special. You will then need to select Picture to paste the information and arrows.

To run a correlation, simply choose the Tools menu, point to Data Analysis, and then select Correlation from the list. The Correlation dialog box is shown in Figure 12-16.

FIGURE 12-16
Correlation dialog box

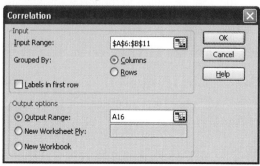

Using the above example, the input range would consist of the values for the Days Absent and Final Grade. The output range would be the location where you want the correlation results displayed, as shown in Figure 12-16.

If a strong correlation exists, then you can use Excel's regression analysis to produce a regression formula that can be used to make predictions of final grade based on the number of days absent. If there is not a high correlation, then you should not perform a regression analysis, since you could not use one variable to predict the other. Only variables with a high correlation should be used to make predictions and should have a regression analysis performed.

To have Excel perform a regression analysis, simply choose the Tools menu, click Data Analysis, and then select Regression from the Analysis Tools list. The Regression dialog box appears as shown in Figure 12-17.

FIGURE 12-17
Regression dialog box

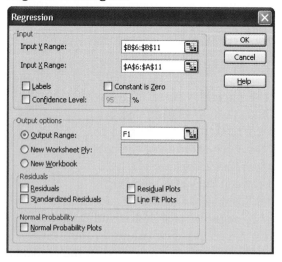

In the example shown in Figure 12-17, X is the variable that you would use to predict, in this case, days absent. Y is the variable that is predicted, in this case, final grade. After you perform the regression analysis you will see coefficients displayed (as well as a good deal of other information), as shown in Figure 12-18. These are the coefficients used to create the prediction formula. The -2.668 coefficient (rounded) is the X coefficient and will be placed in front of the X variable in the regression equation. The intercept coefficient is 96.784 (rounded) and will be placed after the plus sign in the regression equation. The intercept is where the line created by this formula would cross the y-axis.

FIGURE 12-18
Regression results

	A	B	C	D	E	F	G	H	I	J	K	L	M	N
1	**Final Grades**					SUMMARY OUTPUT								
2														
3						*Regression Statistics*								
4						Multiple R	0.980682							
5	**Number of Absences**	**Final Grade**				R Square	0.961737							
6	10	70				Adjusted R	0.952171							
7	12	65				Standard E	2.77555							
8	2	96				Observatio	6							
9	0	94												
10	8	75				ANOVA								
11	5	82					*df*	*SS*	*MS*	*F*	*ignificance F*			
12						Regression	1	774.5186	774.5186	100.5388	0.000556			
13						Residual	4	30.8147	7.703675					
14						Total	5	805.3333						
15														
16		*Column 1*	*Column 2*				*Coefficient*	*tandard Err*	*t Stat*	*P-value*	*Lower 95%*	*Upper 95%*	*ower 95.0%*	*pper 95.0%*
17	Column 1	1				Intercept	96.78407	1.993918	48.53964	1.08E-06	91.24807	102.3201	91.24807	102.3201
18	Column 2	-0.980681759	1			X Variable	-2.66769	0.266053	-10.0269	0.000556	-3.40637	-1.92901	-3.40637	-1.92901
19														
20														

Intercept coefficient   **X coefficient**

The regression equation that would be created from these coefficients (rounded) would be:

Y = -2.668X + 96.784

Notice the minus sign in front of the X variable and be certain that you multiply the X value by -2.668. Therefore, if you wanted to predict the final grade for a student based on their number of days absent, simply put in the days absent as X and then do the calculation.

STEP-BY-STEP 12.7

1. Open the **AE Step12-7** workbook from the data files and save it as **Final Grades,** followed by your initials. Notice that column A contains the years of experience variable and column B contains the salary variable.

2. Select the **Tools** menu and then choose **Data Analysis.**

3. Select **Correlation** from the **Analysis Tools** list box and click **OK.**

4. Click in the **Input Range** text box and then drag through the range **A6:B11.**

> **Hot Tip**
>
> If Data Analysis is not an option on the Tools menu, you will need to add the feature. To add the Analysis ToolPak, choose the **Tools** menu, select **Add-ins,** click the checkbox for **Analysis ToolPak,** and then click on **OK.**

STEP-BY-STEP 12.7 Continued

5. Select the **Output Range** option and click in the **Output Range** text box.

6. Key **A16** as the cell for the start of the output range.

7. Click **OK.** The correlation is -0.98 (rounded). Since this correlation is well above -0.70, it is considered very significant; and, therefore, a regression can now be performed. Once again, since the correlation is high, there is a strong relationship between days absent and final grade.

8. Select the **Tools** menu and then choose **Data Analysis.**

9. Select **Regression** from the Analysis Tools list box and click **OK.**

10. Click in the Input Y Range text box and then select the range **B6:B11.**

11. Click in the Input X Range text box and then select the range **A6:A11.**

12. Select the **Output Range** option and click in the **Output Range** text box.

13. Select cell **F1** and click **OK.** Increase the column widths as necessary. Your worksheet should appear similar to Figure 12-18.

14. The regression equation from the regression results would be Y=−2.668X + 96.784. To predict a student's final grade with 4 days of absences, simply replace the X with 4 and calculate the results. In this case, you would calculate Y = −2.668(4) + 96.784, which equals 86.112 or a predicted final grade of 86 (rounded).

Time Saver

You can calculate a person's age by selecting cell a cell and keying in their birthday. Then, in another cell, just key in the formula to calculate their age.

STEP-BY-STEP 12.8

1. In cell **A1**, key in *your birth date* separating the day/month/year with slashes.

2. Select cell **A2** and key **=DATEDIF(A1,TODAY(),"y")**

3. Press **Enter**.

SUMMARY

In this lesson, you learned:

■ The auditing feature assists in dependencies, precedents, and identifying errors in formulas.

■ You can add data validation to cell data to assist with the entry of data and to alert you when data is not entered according to the rules you specify.

■ Invalid data can also be circled so that you can review data that violates the validation rules.

■ Scenarios let you enter possible variations to values in a formula, and display in a Summary Sheet how the various values affect the outcome. You can also merge scenarios from one workbook into another.

■ Goal Seek and Solver let you determine unknown values that would result in a specified goal or value.

■ Correlation allows you to determine if a strong relationship exists between variables. If a strong relationship does exist, then you could perform a regression and use a regression equation to predict values.

VOCABULARY *Review*

Define the following terms:

Auditing	Dependent	Regression
Correlation	Goal Seek	Scenario
Data validation	Precedent	

REVIEW *Questions*

TRUE/FALSE

Circle T if the statement is true or F if the statement is false.

T   F   1. When you trace dependents of a cell, you are identifying the cells that contain formulas that reference the specified cell.

T   F   2. You can create only one additional scenario for a set of values.

T   F   3. If two variables are not correlated, then a strong relationship between the variables does exist.

T   F   4. In a regression equation, Y is the variable that is predicted.

T   F   5. Use Goal Seek in order to reorganize data to provide you with a different perspective on the data.

WRITTEN QUESTIONS

Write a brief answer to the following questions.

1. Which analysis feature would you use to predict how future changes in sales and expenses would affect your company's income?

2. Which analysis needs to be completed first, before performing a regression analysis?

3. Explain the difference between a dependent and a precedent.

4. What analysis tool would you use to determine if a relationship exists between variables?

5. What analysis tool would you use to determine two or more unknown values?

PROJECTS

PROJECT 12-1

1. Open the **AE Project12-1** workbook from the data files and save it as **International Sales,** followed by your initials.

2. Select the range **A5:B19**. Create a scenario named **Increased Lease and Utilities Expense.** For the changing cells, key the range **B10:B16**. Enter the following expenses into the scenario:
   B10 (Lease): 75000
   B11 (Utilities): 9000

3. Click **OK,** select the **Show** button, and then click the **Close** button. This action "shows" the scenario directly on the worksheet.

4. Print the Income Statement sheet and then save and close the workbook.

PROJECT 12-2

1. Open the **AE Project12-2** workbook from the data files and save it as **Student Debate,** followed by your initials.

2. A debate instructor wants to determine if there is a relationship between the number of years that a student has been in debate programs and the number of championships they win. First, enter the following data into a worksheet. Perform a correlation analysis on the data.

Years of Experience	Championships Won
3	5
9	14
2	12
5	21
1	8

3. Explain the results of this analysis.

4. Print the worksheet. Then save and close the workbook.

CRITICAL *Thinking*

 ACTIVITY 12-1

As the accountant for a major corporation, you decide to assist your clerks with their data entry. You will add data validation features to existing worksheets and then check for any invalid data that may have already been entered.

1. Open the **AE Activity12-1** workbook from the data files and save it as **Data Validation Review,** followed by your initials.

2. Select the range **B7:E14** and set data validation for the numbers with decimals in this range with 0 as the minimum value and 1875 as the maximum value.

3. Enter an **Input Message** with the title **Data Input** and the message **Value should be between $0 and $1875.**

4. Enter an **Error Message** with the title **Data Error** and the message **Costs must be between $0 and $1875.** Try to enter invalid data in this range to be certain data validation is working.

5. Use the Circle Invalid Data feature to place a circle around any invalid data.

6. Save and print the worksheet. Close the workbook.

SCANS ACTIVITY 12-2

A superintendent of a school district wants to see if years of experience can be used to predict an administrator's salary. The data for years of experience and administrators' salaries appears in the table below. Determine if a relationship exists. If a relationship does exist, run a regression and write out the corresponding regression equation. Save the workbook as **Administrator Salary.**

YEARS OF EXPERIENCE	ADMINISTRATIVE SALARY
22	200,000
14	140,000
31	540,000
36	630,000
9	170,000
41	710,000
19	230,000

SCANS ACTIVITY 12-3

Using Excel's Help system, find out what would cause tracer arrows to disappear on your worksheet.

CREATING PIVOTTABLES AND PIVOTCHARTS

Introduction

Excel gives you a unique method for changing the way data is displayed with the PivotTable feature. A *PivotTable* lets you rearrange how data in a PivotList is organized. You can drag fields (or columns) to different locations in the PivotTable report in order to present the data in new ways. These changes can be made instantly while you are presenting the information simply by dragging the data fields to new positions. You can also graphically display the PivotTable using a *PivotChart*.

Creating a PivotList and PivotTable Report

A PivotTable report is a powerful Excel tool that lets you rearrange and summarize data in a PivotList (data list) in order to analyze or interpret it in a different manner. It is an *interactive* feature, meaning you control how data is displayed by dragging items in the PivotTable window. For example, say you have a worksheet on employees that includes fields (or columns) for Last Name, First Name, Division, Starting Date, and Salary. You decide you want to see salary totals by division. You can use the PivotTable feature to quickly reorganize the data in an easy-to-read report format.

You can place the PivotTable report on a separate worksheet in the workbook or in another location within the same worksheet. You can also create a PivotChart from the report, which is discussed later in this lesson. Figure 13-1 shows a worksheet containing a data list. Since this is going to be made into a PivotTable, we will refer to this list as the PivotList. Figure 13-2 shows a PivotTable report created from the list. The PivotTable toolbar automatically appears when you create a PivotTable or PivotChart. Also notice the PivotTable Field List that contains the field names (column headings) from your worksheet. You will drag the fields from the PivotTable Field List that you want to appear in the PivotTable. The PivotTable toolbar buttons perform the tasks listed in Table 13-1.

FIGURE 13-1
PivotList

	A	B	C	D	E
1	**Cellular Sales**				
2	*Employee List*				
3					
4					
5					
6	**Last Name**	**First Name**	**Division**	**Start Date**	**Salary**
7	Baines	Bill	Marketing	December 31, 2003	$ 30,000.00
8	Caldwell	Sue	Marketing	June 30, 2000	$ 75,000.00
9	Dominquez	David	Sales	March 14, 2000	$ 95,000.00
10	Giraddelli	Lilly	Accounting	February 15, 1987	$ 83,000.00
11	Holder	Howard	Sales	December 31, 1999	$ 125,000.00
12	Johnson	Jack	Accounting	May 24, 1990	$ 26,000.00
13	Tanquez	Trevor	Marketing	February 15, 1987	$ 52,000.00
14	Vegas	Vivala	Sales	July 27, 2000	$ 135,000.00
15	Crawford	Katie	Clerical	January 28, 2001	$ 29,000.00
16	Dominquez	Gary	Sales	August 1, 2001	$ 145,000.00
17	Gonzalez	Lisa	Accounting	February 2, 2002	$ 29,000.00
18	Goodwin	Sallye	Marketing	August 6, 2002	$ 34,000.00
19	Keplinger	Miller	Marketing	August 6, 2002	$ 100,000.00
20	Keplinger	JoAnn	Marketing	February 7, 2003	$ 100,000.00
21	Khorjin	Fugi	Marketing	August 11, 2003	$ 40,000.00
22	Langford	Kate	Accounting	February 12, 2004	$ 35,000.00
23	Lanquez	JoAnne	Clerical	August 15, 2004	$ 19,000.00
24	Pullis	Cheryl	Sales	February 16, 2005	$ 124,000.00
25	Rigola	Carol	Clerical	August 20, 2005	$ 26,000.00
26	Rosenberg	Carol	Clerical	February 21, 2006	$ 98,000.00
27	Smith	Sally	Sales	August 25, 2006	$ 124,000.00
28	Thomsen	Barb	Clerical	February 26, 2007	$ 67,000.00
29	Wong	Sue	Accounting	August 30, 2007	$ 35,000.00

FIGURE 13-2
PivotTable report

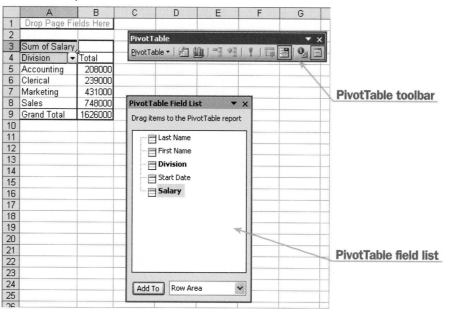

TABLE 13-1
PivotTable toolbar buttons

TOOLBAR BUTTON NAME	BUTTON	ACTION PERFORMED
PivotTable	PivotTable ▾	Takes you back to the PivotTable Wizard and lets you change table options.
Format Report		Contains predefined formats for PivotTables from which you can select.
ChartWizard		Lets you choose chart styles, enter titles and change other chart features.
Hide Detail		Hides field data behind the totals.
Show Detail		Displays field data for the selected item.
Refresh Data		Changes the PivotTable or PivotChart to correspond with changes in the worksheet.
Include Hidden Items in Totals		Hidden items are not normally included in totals; therefore, this feature allows them to be computed with the totals.
Always Display Items		Hiding an item in a page field removes it both from the report and from the drop-down list for the field. This tool keeps items displayed.
Field Settings		Lets you format data and change the calculations, such as from Sum to Average.
Hide/Display Field List		Removes or displays the PivotTable list areas that appear on the layout screen in a gray font.

The PivotTable and PivotChart Wizard will take you step-by-step through the process of creating a PivotTable report. If you make changes to data in a worksheet, you must click the **Refresh Data** button located in the PivotTable toolbar before the changes will be shown in the report.

S TEP-BY-STEP 13.1

In this first step-by-step exercise, you will create a PivotTable that shows total employee salary by department.

1. Start a new workbook and enter the PivotList information shown in Figure 13-3. Save the workbook as **Cellular Sales PivotTable** followed by your initials.

FIGURE 13-3
Exercise PivotList

	A	B	C	D	E
1			Cellular Sales		
2			Employee List		
3					
4					
5					
6	Last Name	First Name	Division	Start Date	Salary
7	Baines	Bill	Marketing	December 31, 2003	$ 30,000.00
8	Caldwell	Sue	Marketing	June 30, 2000	$ 75,000.00
9	Dominquez	David	Sales	March 14, 2000	$ 95,000.00
10	Giraddelli	Lilly	Accounting	February 15, 1987	$ 83,000.00
11	Holder	Howard	Sales	December 31, 1999	$ 125,000.00
12	Johnson	Jack	Accounting	May 24, 1990	$ 26,000.00
13	Tanquez	Trevor	Marketing	February 15, 1987	$ 52,000.00
14	Vegas	Vivala	Sales	July 27, 2000	$ 135,000.00
15	Crawford	Katie	Clerical	January 28, 2001	$ 29,000.00
16	Dominquez	Gary	Sales	August 1, 2001	$ 145,000.00
17	Gonzalez	Lisa	Accounting	February 2, 2002	$ 29,000.00
18	Goodwin	Sallye	Marketing	August 6, 2002	$ 34,000.00
19	Keplinger	Miller	Marketing	August 6, 2002	$ 100,000.00
20	Keplinger	JoAnn	Marketing	February 7, 2003	$ 100,000.00
21	Khorjin	Fugi	Marketing	August 11, 2003	$ 40,000.00
22	Langford	Kate	Accounting	February 12, 2004	$ 35,000.00
23	Lanquez	JoAnne	Clerical	August 15, 2004	$ 19,000.00
24	Pullis	Cheryl	Sales	February 16, 2005	$ 124,000.00
25	Rigola	Carol	Clerical	August 20, 2005	$ 26,000.00
26	Rosenberg	Carol	Clerical	February 21, 2006	$ 98,000.00
27	Smith	Sally	Sales	August 25, 2006	$ 124,000.00
28	Thomsen	Barb	Clerical	February 26, 2007	$ 67,000.00
29	Wong	Sue	Accounting	August 30, 2007	$ 35,000.00

2. Click in any cell in the PivotList.

3. Open the **Data** menu and select **PivotTable and PivotChart Report.** The PivotTable and PivotChart Wizard - Step 1 of 3 dialog box appears, as shown in Figure 13-4.

Speech Recognition

If you have speech recognition capabilities, enable the Voice Command mode and say the appropriate series of commands to open the Data menu and select PivotTable and PivotChart Report.

STEP-BY-STEP 13.1 Continued

FIGURE 13-4
PivotTable and PivotChart Wizard – Step 1 of 3

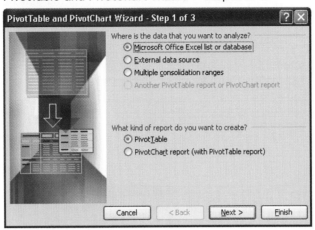

4. If necessary, select **Microsoft Office Excel list or database** and choose **PivotTable.**

5. Click **Next.** The PivotTable and PivotChart Wizard - Step 2 of 3 dialog box appears, as shown in Figure 13-5.

FIGURE 13-5
PivotTable and PivotChart Wizard – Step 2 of 3

6. The range **A6:E29** should be displayed in the *Range* text box. Click **Next.** The PivotTable and PivotChart Wizard - Step 3 of 3 dialog box appears, as shown in Figure 13-6.

FIGURE 13-6
PivotTable and PivotChart Wizard – Step 3 of 3

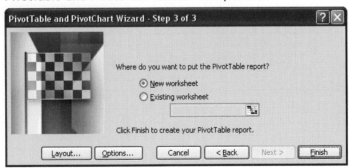

STEP-BY-STEP 13.1 Continued

7. Be sure that **New worksheet** is selected and click **Finish.** Notice that the PivotTable report is placed in a new worksheet, typically named Sheet4. Excel will name the new worksheet automatically with the next available sheet tab number. Your screen should appear similar to Figure 13-7.

FIGURE 13-7
PivotTable Report screen

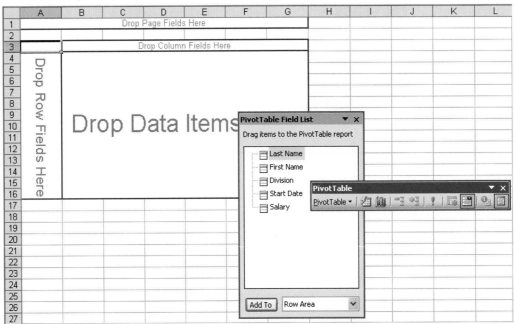

8. If necessary, move the PivotTable toolbar and PivotTable Field List so that you can clearly view the PivotTable layout. Drag the **Division** field item from the PivotTable Field List to the *Drop Row Fields Here* area as displayed in Figure 13-8.

FIGURE 13-8
PivotTable Layout screen

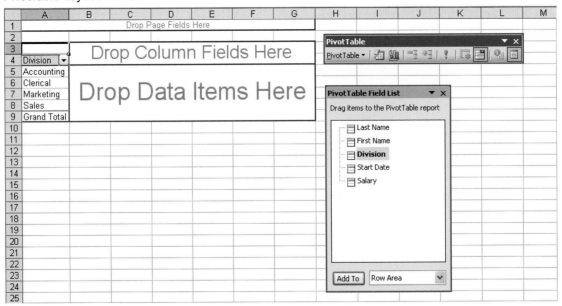

STEP-BY-STEP 13.1 Continued

9. Drag the **Salary** field item on the PivotTable Field List to the *Drop Data Items Here* area. The PivotTable report should instantly appear as shown in Figure 13-9.

FIGURE 13-9
PivotTable report

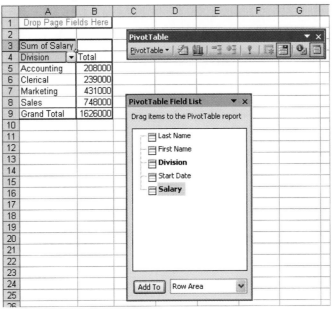

Now, let's rearrange the data for a different view.

10. Click the **PivotTable** button in the PivotTable toolbar and select **PivotTable Wizard** from the pop-up menu. The PivotTable and PivotChart Wizard - Step 3 of 3 dialog box opens.

11. Click the **Layout** button. The PivotTable and PivotChart Wizard – Layout dialog box appears. Drag the existing field items (Division and Sum of Salary) off the table diagram to clear it.

> ### Integration Tip
>
> To copy a PivotChart into a PowerPoint presentation, simply hold down the **SHIFT** key and select the **Edit** menu. You'll notice the option Copy Picture on the Edit menu. Select **Copy Picture**; choose whether you want the chart to appear as it is shown on your screen or how it appears when printed, choose the location in the PowerPoint presentation you want the chart to appear and then click the **Paste** tool.

STEP-BY-STEP 13.1 Continued

12. Drag the **Division** field item to the Page section. Drag the **Last Name** field item to the *Row* section. Drag the **Salary** field item to the *Data* section. Your screen should appear similar to Figure 13-10.

FIGURE 13-10
PivotTable Layout

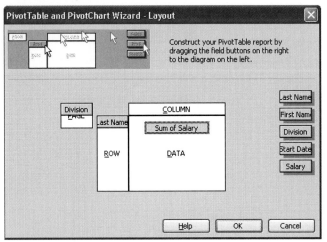

13. Click **OK** to close the PivotTable and PivotChart Wizard - Layout dialog box, and then click **Finish** to close the wizard. Your PivotTable report should look like that shown in Figure 13-11.

FIGURE 13-11
Rearranged PivotTable report

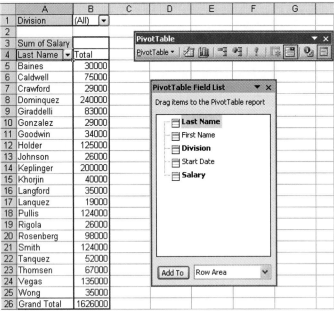

STEP-BY-STEP 13.1 Continued

14. Click the arrow shown in cell B1 for Division. Select **Marketing,** and click **OK.** Notice how only the Marketing personnel salaries are now displayed.

15. Format the range B5:B11 as **Currency** with no decimal places.

16. Select the **Format Report** tool on the PivotTable toolbar and choose the **Report 4** format from the AutoFormat dialog box. Click **OK.**

> **Hot Tip**
>
> PivotTable reports can be formatted automatically using the **Format Report** button on the PivotTable toolbar. When you click the button, an AutoFormat dialog box opens, displaying a number of preset formats from which you can choose.

17. Print Sheet4 of the workbook. Save and then close the workbook.

Creating Interactive PivotTables for the Web

Excel's interactive PivotTable feature lets users interact with the PivotTable data in Microsoft's browser program, Internet Explorer. You can rearrange the data in the Web page by dragging fields, just as you do in a regular PivotTable. You can also publish a PivotTable as a noninteractive Web page by simply saving it in HTML format. Doing so will prevent others from changing its layout or the way data is displayed.

STEP-BY-STEP 13.2

1. Open the **AE Step13-2** workbook from the data files.

2. Save the workbook as an HTML file by opening the **File** menu and selecting **Save As Web Page.**

3. Enter **Division Analysis,** followed by your initials for the filename. Click the **Publish** button.

4. Click the drop-down arrow next to the *Choose* text box and select **Items on Sheet4.**

5. Choose **PivotTable** in the list box below the *Choose* text box.

6. Click the **Add interactivity with** option and select **PivotTable functionality** if necessary.

STEP-BY-STEP 13.2 Continued

7. Click the **Open published web page in browser** option if necessary. Your dialog box should be displayed as in Figure 13-12.

FIGURE 13-12
Publish as Web Page dialog box

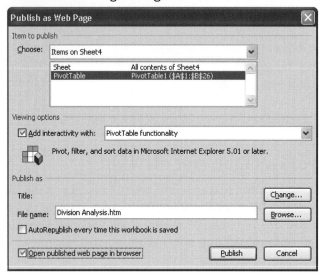

8. Click **Publish.** Microsoft Internet Explorer starts and the PivotTable appears in the Explorer window.

Since you requested that this PivotTable be interactive, you can make changes to it.

9. Place your mouse pointer over the **Division** field in the upper-left corner of the PivotTable. Your mouse pointer will appear with a four-headed arrow. Drag the **Division** field to the *Drop Column Fields Here* section in the PivotTable. The PivotTable now displays all of the Divisions at one time. Your screen should appear similar to Figure 13-13.

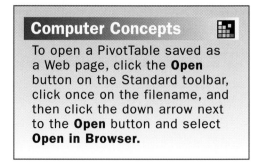

Computer Concepts

To open a PivotTable saved as a Web page, click the **Open** button on the Standard toolbar, click once on the filename, and then click the down arrow next to the **Open** button and select **Open in Browser.**

STEP-BY-STEP 13.2 Continued

FIGURE 13-13
Interactive PivotTable in Web Page

PivotTable1						
Drop Filter Fields Here						
	Division ▾					
	Accounting	Clerical	Marketing	Sales	Grand Total	
Last Name ▾	Sum of Salary	Sum of Salary	Sum of Salary	Sum of Salary	Sum of Salary	
Baines			$ 30,000		$ 30,000	
Caldwell			$ 75,000		$ 75,000	
Crawford		$ 29,000			$ 29,000	
Dominquez				$ 240,000	$ 240,000	
Giraddelli	$ 83,000				$ 83,000	
Gonzalez	$ 29,000				$ 29,000	
Goodwin			$ 34,000		$ 34,000	
Holder				$ 125,000	$ 125,000	
Johnson	$ 26,000				$ 26,000	
Keplinger			$ 200,000		$ 200,000	
Khorjin			$ 40,000		$ 40,000	
Langford	$ 35,000				$ 35,000	
Lanquez		$ 19,000			$ 19,000	
Pullis				$ 124,000	$ 124,000	
Rigola		$ 26,000			$ 26,000	
Rosenberg		$ 98,000			$ 98,000	
Smith				$ 124,000	$ 124,000	
Tanquez			$ 52,000		$ 52,000	
Thomsen		$ 67,000			$ 67,000	
Vegas				$ 135,000	$ 135,000	
Wong	$ 35,000				$ 35,000	
Grand Total	$ 208,000	$ 239,000	$ 431,000	$ 748,000	$ 1,626,000	

10. Close Microsoft Internet Explorer and then close the workbook without saving changes.

Creating a PivotChart

Not only can you rearrange the data in a worksheet by creating PivotTable reports, you can create a visual representation of this data in a PivotChart. A PivotChart report must be associated with a PivotTable report in the same workbook. Therefore, if a change is made to the PivotTable, the associated PivotChart changes as well.

You use the PivotTable and PivotChart Report Wizard to create the PivotChart. The wizard lets you specify the type of the data you want to use, set options for how the data is used, and lay out the chart elements.

When you create a PivotChart report that is based on an existing PivotTable report, the information in the chart is laid out like the data in the PivotTable report: Row data in the table becomes category data (typically the X-axis data) in the chart, and column data in the table becomes series data (typically the Y-axis) in the chart.

Before creating a PivotChart, let's review the parts of a chart, as shown in Figure 13-14. These are described in Table 13-2.

FIGURE 13-14
PivotChart

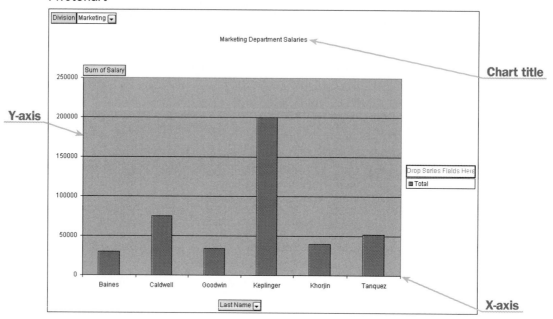

TABLE 13-2
Parts of a chart

TABLE PART	DESCRIPTION
Chart title	Explains the purpose of the chart
X-axis	Typically the horizontal axis, which usually displays the categories of data
Y-axis	Typically the vertical axis, which usually displays the numeric chart data

With the exception of the pie-type charts, each chart type has two axes: a horizontal axis and a vertical axis. The horizontal axis normally plots the categories along the bottom of the chart. The vertical axis normally plots values (such as dollar amounts) along the left side of the chart.

STEP-BY-STEP 13.3

1. Open the **AE Step13-3** workbook from the data files and save it as **Cellular Sales PivotChart**, followed by your initials.

2. Click any cell in the PivotList (data list).

3. Open the **Data** menu and select **PivotTable and PivotChart Report.**

4. If necessary, select **Microsoft Office Excel list or database** and then choose **PivotChart report (with PivotTable report).** The PivotTable and PivotChart Wizard - Step 1 of 3 dialog box should appear as shown in Figure 13-15.

STEP-BY-STEP 13.3 Continued

FIGURE 13-15
PivotTable and PivotChart Wizard – Step 1 of 3

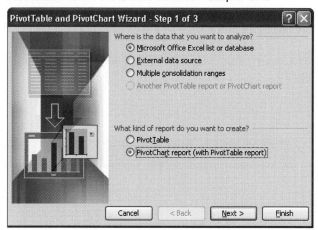

5. Click **Next**. The PivotTable and PivotChart Wizard - Step 2 of 3 dialog box appears. The range A6:E29 should be displayed in the *Range* text box.

6. Click **Next**. The PivotTable and PivotChart Wizard - Step 3 of 3 dialog box appears.

7. Be sure that **New worksheet** is selected and click **Finish.** Your screen should appear similar to Figure 13-16.

FIGURE 13-16
PivotChart window

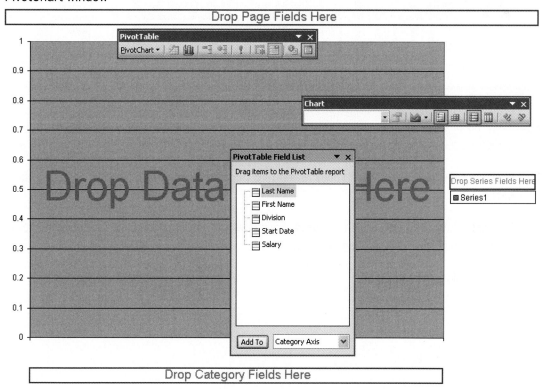

STEP-BY-STEP 13.3 Continued

8. Drag the **Division** field item from the PivotTable Field List to the *Drop Page Fields Here* area (located at the top).

9. Drag the **Last Name** field item to the *Drop Category Fields Here* area (located at the bottom).

10. Drag the **Salary** field to the *Drop Data Items Here* area. The PivotChart should instantly appear, as shown in Figure 13-17.

FIGURE 13-17
PivotChart

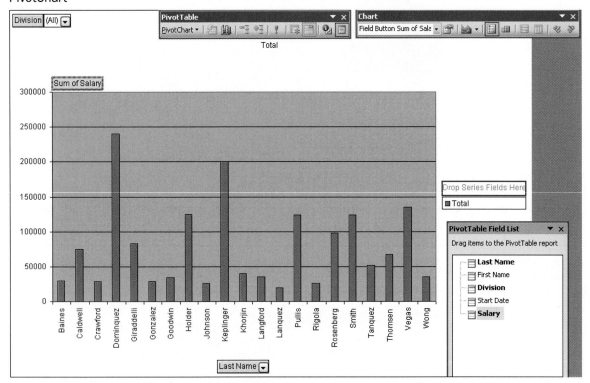

11. Click the arrow next to the Division heading and select **Marketing.** Click **OK.** Notice that only the Marketing personnel and their salaries are now displayed.

12. Click on the **Chart Title** and then key **Marketing Department Salaries** for the new chart title. Press **Enter.**

13. Print the Chart1 sheet. Click the **Sheet4** worksheet tab. Notice how Excel automatically created a PivotTable report which corresponds to the PivotChart as well.

14. Save and close the workbook.

Time Saver

You can quickly group and ungroup items in a PivotTable using the keyboard.

STEP-BY-STEP 13.4

1. Press **Alt** + **Shift** + **right arrow** to group Pivot Table items

2. To ungroup items, press **Alt** + **Shift** + **left arrow**.

SUMMARY

In this lesson, you learned:

- PivotTables let you easily and quickly rearrange and summarize data.
- Excel's interactive PivotTable feature lets you interact with PivotTable data in Microsoft's browser program, Internet Explorer.
- PivotCharts are ideal for graphically illustrating the data in a PivotTable report.

VOCABULARY *Review*

Define the following terms:		
Interactive	PivotChart	PivotTable

REVIEW *Questions*

TRUE/FALSE

Circle T if the statement is true or F if the statement is false.

T   F   1. A PivotChart report must be associated with a PivotTable report in the same workbook.

T   F   2. You can place the PivotTable report on a separate worksheet in the workbook or in another location within the same worksheet.

T   F   3. You can change the layout of a PivotTable after it has been created in the PivotTable and PivotChart Wizard.

T   F   4. Excel automatically creates a PivotTable report when you create a PivotChart.

T   F   5. When you create a PivotChart report that is based on an existing PivotTable report, the information in the chart is laid out like the data in the PivotTable report.

WRITTEN QUESTIONS

Write a brief answer to the following questions.

1.   Why are PivotTables and PivotCharts referred to as *interactive?*

2.   Which feature would you use to rearrange a PivotList (data list) in order to view another perspective of the data?

3.   What is the purpose of a PivotTable report?

4.   Give a brief explanation of each of the following parts of a chart:
     (a) Chart title

     (b) X-axis

     (c) Y-axis

5.   Explain what happens to a PivotChart when you make changes to the PivotTable from which the PivotChart was created?

PROJECTS

PROJECT 13-1

You will create a PivotTable that shows the total sales amounts of products in each of two stock areas.1.

1. Open the **AE Project13-1** workbook from the data files and save it as **P&K Industries,** followed by your initials.

2. Create a PivotTable with the following setup:

   ROW: **Stock Area**

   DATA: **Cost**

3. Add a currency format to the total amounts. (Adjust the column widths if necessary.)

4. Print the PivotTable. Save and close the workbook.

PROJECT 13-2

You will create a PivotTable that shows grade point averages for students by their last name.

1. Open the **AE Project13-2** workbook from the data files and save it as **Student List,** followed by your initials.

2. Create a PivotTable with the following setup:

   PAGE: **Class**

   ROW: **Last Name**

   DATA: **Grade Point Average**

3. Modify the layout of the PivotTable so that a grand total is not displayed. (Display the PivotTable and PivotChart Wizard - Step 3 of 3 dialog box, click the **Options** button, and deselect the **Grand totals for columns** and **Grand totals for rows** options. Click **OK** to close the Options dialog box and then click **Finish** to redisplay the PivotTable.)

4. Select **Senior** from the Page list. Click **OK.**

5. Print Sheet4. Then save and close the workbook.

CRITICAL*Thinking*

ACTIVITY 13-1

You are the manager for P&K Industries. You will be giving a presentation to the owner this afternoon and you want to create a PivotChart that shows the total sales amounts in each of the stock areas in order to show the owner the amount available for potential sales.

1. Open the **AE Activity13-1** workbook from the data files and save it as **P&K Chart,** followed by your initials.

2. Create a PivotChart which shows the total product value for each of the stock areas. Change the chart title to read **Total Product Value in Inventory by Stock Area.**

3. Change the chart type to a three-dimensional column chart by selecting the **Chart Wizard** on the PivotTable toolbar and then selecting the desired type.

4. Save and print the chart. Then close the workbook.

 ## ACTIVITY 13-2

Using Excel's Help system, find information on how you can change PivotTable data to various number formats using the **Field Settings** button on the PivotTable toolbar. Write a brief explanation of this procedure.

CREATING MACROS AND MENUS

OBJECTIVES

Upon completion of this lesson, you should be able to:

- Discuss the purpose of macros.
- Create, record, and run a macro.
- Edit a macro.
- Change macro settings.
- Customize a toolbar by adding macro buttons.
- Assign a macro to a command button.
- Create a custom menu.

Estimated Time: 1.5 hours

VOCABULARY

Commands

Macro

Visual Basic

Introduction

A *macro* is simply a way to automate some of the common, repetitive tasks you perform in Excel, thereby saving valuable time. In this lesson, you will learn how to create macros. When you create a macro, Excel converts the automated tasks you've entered into a macro language. An entire book could be devoted to macro programming. If you'll be spending a considerable amount of time creating detailed macros, you'll find the study of macro language a rewarding experience. But, if you just want to use macros to speed up some basic, repetitive tasks, you just need to learn the basics of creating and editing a macro—which is the focus of this lesson. In addition, you will learn how to add a macro as a button on a toolbar. Then you will add a macro to a button you create within a worksheet.

You will also learn how to create a new menu containing frequently used *commands* or tools. You can add a new menu to the menu bar, to an existing toolbar, or to a new toolbar.

Understanding Macros

A macro is simply a way of recording the actions necessary to complete a certain task. For example, you may need all the titles on your worksheets to be in a bold, large font, and centered across columns. It can be time consuming to do these steps over and over each time you create a new worksheet. Macros can simplify these steps.

When you create a macro, Excel records the menu selections you make and keystrokes you use to complete a task. When you are ready to use the macro, you tell Excel to play back the macro by pressing a key combination (usually the Ctrl key plus another key) that you assign to the macro. As the macro is played back, the previously recorded steps are performed automatically.

Creating, Recording, and Running a Macro

 Creating a macro involves a few basic steps.

1. Name the macro and assign any shortcut keys (keys that quickly start the macro).
2. Turn on the recorder.
3. Perform the sequence of actions you want recorded (you can choose commands from the menus, click on toolbar buttons, or use shortcut keys).
4. Turn off the recorder.
5. When you're ready to use the macro, press the shortcut keys assigned to the macro.

To create a new macro, select Record New Macro from the Macro submenu on the Tools menu. The Record Macro dialog box appears as shown in Figure 14-1. You can enter a name and description for the macro. The options in the Record Macro dialog box are explained in Table 14-1.

FIGURE 14-1
Record Macro dialog box

TABLE 14-1
Record Macro dialog box options

RECORD MACRO OPTIONS	DESCRIPTION
Macro name	Enter an easily identifiable name for the macro. This name should be descriptive.
Shortcut key	Assign a key combination that you can press to start a macro. This is an optional setting.
Store macro in	From the drop-down list, you can choose to store the macro in the Personal Macro Workbook, which makes it available in other workbooks. You can also select to store the macro in This Workbook so it is available when the current workbook is opened, or you can store the macro in a New Workbook.
Description	Key a brief description to use for future reference. This is an optional setting.

STEP-BY-STEP 14.1

1. Open the **AE Step14-1** workbook from the data files and save it as **Fonts,** followed by your initials.

2. Open the **Tools** menu, select **Macro,** and then select **Record New Macro.**

3. In the Record Macro dialog box, key **Fonts** in the *Macro name* box.

4. Click in the *Description* text box, highlight the existing text, and key **Applies fonts and formats.**

5. Click in the *Shortcut key* text box. In this box you enter the letter you want to use in combination with the **Ctrl** key to start your macro. You may use a single letter between A and Z as a shortcut key. Try to avoid using letters already assigned to shortcut keys, such as **Ctrl+C** (which is the same as the Copy command on the Edit menu). You can glance through the menus to see what shortcut keys have already been assigned to commands. Enter **t** in the text box next to *Ctrl+*.

6. Choose **This Workbook** from the *Store macro in* drop-down list, if necessary.

7. Click **OK.** Notice that the word *Recording* is displayed on the status bar. Also note the Stop Recording toolbar, shown in Figure 14-2, is displayed on the worksheet.

FIGURE 14-2
Stop Recording toolbar

Stop Recording button

8. Open the **Format** menu, and then select **Cells.**

9. Select the **Font** tab. Choose the **Bold Italic** font style and select a size of **14.**

STEP-BY-STEP 14.1 Continued

10. Choose the **Border** tab. Select the fifth line style option in the right column of line styles, and then choose **Outline** in the *Presets* section. Click **OK.**

11. Click the **Stop Recording** button (or open the **Tools** menu, select **Macro**, and then select **Stop Recording**). Notice that the formats were actually applied during the recording of the macro.

    Let's see how this macro works.

12. Select cell **A2.**

13. Press **Ctrl+t.** The subtitle should now be in a large, bold, italic font with an outline border. Adjust the column width, if necessary.

    Let's create another macro.

14. Select cell **A5.** Open the **Tools** menu, select **Macro,** and then select **Record New Macro.**

15. Key **Font2** in the *Macro name* box and key **Italic underlined font** in the *Description* text box.

16. Enter **r** in the *Shortcut key* text box next to *Ctrl+*. Click **OK.**

17. Click the **Borders** button drop-down list arrow and choose the **No Border** option to remove any borders. Click the **Underline** button and then the **Italic** button.

18. Click the **Stop Recording** button.

    Now let's run the macro.

19. Select the range **A6:A9** and press **Ctrl+r.** You should see formatting changes of the new macro added to these cells.

20. Select the range **A13:A15** and press **Ctrl+r.**

21. Save the workbook and keep it open for the next Step-by-Step.

Editing a Macro

After you've created a macro, you can make changes to it if necessary. For example, you may have selected a dotted line as a cell border and you decide that you really want a solid line.

Excel stores the macro in a macro language called ***Visual Basic.*** Macro language is frequently referred to as macro code. To edit a macro, open the Visual Basic Editor, as shown in Figure 14-3. The macro language or code in Visual Basic looks and reads like actual text. You can make changes to the Visual Basic code just as you would edit text.

> **Hot Tip**
>
> You can delete a macro by selecting the Tools menu, Macro, and then Macros. In the Macro dialog box, click on the macro's name and click **Delete.**

FIGURE 14-3
Visual Basic Editor

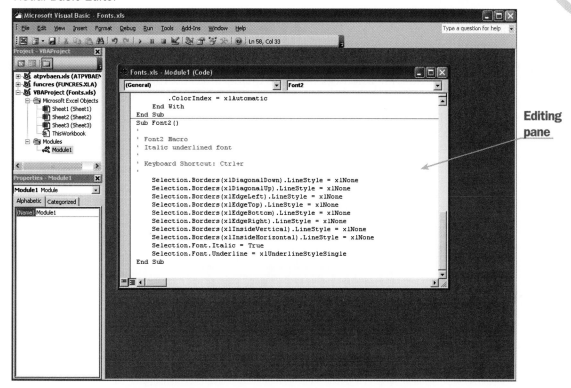

Editing pane

S TEP-BY-STEP 14.2

1. Open the **Tools** menu, select **Macro,** and then click **Macros.**

2. Select the **Font2** macro and then click the **Edit** button.

3. Scroll down through the Font2 code until you reach the line *Selection.Font.Italic = True*. Click at the end of the line and then press **Enter.**

4. Key **Selection.Font.Bold = True.**

5. Click the **Save** button.

6. Open the **File** menu and choose **Close and Return to Microsoft Excel.**

7. Select the range **A5:A9** and press **Ctrl+r.** Select the range **A13:A15** and press **Ctrl+r.** You should see the new formatting of the macro added to these cells.

8. Print the worksheet. Then save the workbook and remain in this screen for the next exercise.

Speech Recognition

If your computer has Speech Recognition capabilities, enable the Voice Command mode and say the steps necessary to open the Macros dialog box.

Changing Macro Settings

You may find that when you try to run a macro or open a workbook containing macros, you have difficulty because the macro security level is set to High. Typically, changing the macro security setting to **Medium** will allow you to run most macros. By setting the security level to **Medium,** you will be asked when opening a workbook containing macros whether you want to Enable or Disable the macros in the workbook before it opens. However, since some viruses can enter your computer as macros, it is not advisable to change the macro security setting to **Low.** The Macro Security dialog box is shown in Figure 14-4.

FIGURE 14-4
Macro Security dialog box

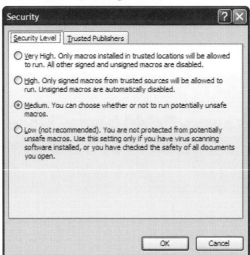

STEP-BY-STEP 14.3

1. Choose the **Tools** menu and then select **Macro.**

2. Select **Security** from the Macros menu. Notice that you have four security settings, Very High, High, Medium, and Low, with a description explaining the purpose of the security level.

3. Choose the **Medium** security level, if necessary, and click **OK.**

4. Save and close the workbook.

Integration Tip

You can quickly open a Word file or other file that you may need to view with an Excel file that you're working on by creating a hyperlink. To create a hyperlink, simply select the cell where you want the hyperlink to appear, select the **Insert** menu, choose **Hyperlink**, and then select the desired file. After you click **OK**, you'll notice that the file location and name within the cell is underlined and in a different color than the data. To test the hyperlink, place your mouse pointer over the hyperlink until a hand appears and then click. The hyperlinked file should open.

Customize a Toolbar by Adding Macro Buttons

 You may find you use a macro so frequently that you would like to place it as a button on the toolbar. That way, all you have to do is click the macro button to run the macro. Plus, the macro will then be available in any Excel workbook you open. Since a toolbar is available at anytime, you won't have to worry if your workbook contains the macro you need as it will be on the toolbar. To add a button to a toolbar, you simply need to customize the toolbar.

> **Hot Tip**
>
> To quickly display or hide a toolbar, place your mouse pointer over any toolbar and click your right mouse button. This action shows the toolbar list. Simply select or deselect the desired toolbar.

*S*TEP-BY-STEP 14.4

1. Open the **AE Step14-4** workbook from the data files. A message box may appear, asking if you want to disable or enable macros. Click the **Enable Macros** button and then save the file as **Macro1,** followed by your initials.

2. Open the **View** menu, select **Toolbars,** and then select **Customize.**

3. Select the **Commands** tab, if necessary.

4. Select **Macros** from the *Categories* list box. The **Commands** tab appears, similar to Figure 14-5.

> **Hot Tip**
>
> If a message box opens telling you that macros are disabled because the security level is high, click **OK** to close the message box. Then, open the **Tools** menu, click **Options,** and then click the **Security** tab. Click the **Macro Security** button and change the macro security level to **Medium** on the **Security Level** tab.)

FIGURE 14-5
Commands tab in the Customize dialog box

STEP-BY-STEP 14.4 Continued

5. Click **Custom Button** in the *Commands* list box and drag it from the dialog box to the **Formatting** toolbar, placing it between the **Underline** and **Left Align** buttons.

6. Place your mouse pointer over the Custom button on the toolbar and click the right mouse button. Choose **Assign Macro** on the shortcut menu. The Assign Macro dialog box appears, as shown in Figure 14-6. The file name and module number may appear in the Assign Macro dialog box.

> **Speech Recognition**
>
> If your computer has Speech Recognition capabilities, enable the Voice Command mode and say the steps necessary to open the Customize dialog box.

FIGURE 14-6
Assign Macro dialog box

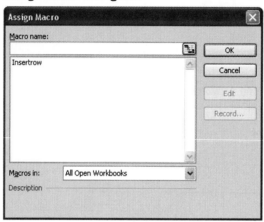

7. Click the **InsertRow** macro and click **OK.** Click **Close** in the Customize dialog box. The new button should look similar to that shown in Figure 14-7.

FIGURE 14-7
Macro button on a toolbar

Macro Button

8. To see how the button works, click cell **A6.**

9. Click the **Custom Button** button. You should see a new row inserted. Save the workbook and keep it open for the next Step-by-Step.

Removing a Button from a Toolbar

You can easily remove a button from the toolbar. Open the Customize dialog box, select the **Commands** tab, and simply drag the button off the toolbar.

STEP-BY-STEP 14.5

1. Open the **View** menu, select **Toolbars**, and then choose **Customize.**

2. Drag the **Custom Button** button to any spot off the toolbar. Look at the Formatting toolbar. The macro button should be gone.

3. Click **Close** in the Customize dialog box. Keep the workbook open for the next Step-by-Step.

Assigning a Macro to a Command Button

When you add a macro button to a toolbar, the button remains on the toolbar even as you work in different Excel files. You may, however, only need this macro for a specific workbook. A macro button placed directly on the worksheet will be available each time you open the workbook and provides easy access to a macro. The macro button appears only when the workbook is opened. Macro buttons also allow other users to run the macro without their having to know the macro's name.

A macro button can be created anywhere in a workbook. You can create a macro button in any shape, such as a rectangle or a circle. After creating the shape for the button, simply place the mouse pointer over the object, click the right mouse button, and choose **Assign Macro.**

Click the name of the macro you want to assign to the button and click **OK.** To add a name to a macro button, right-click the macro button again and choose **Add Text** on the shortcut menu. An insertion point will appear in the object where you can start typing the text. You will learn more about formatting objects on the worksheet in a later lesson.

STEP-BY-STEP 14.6

1. Save the Macro1 workbook as **Macro2,** followed by your initials.

2. If necessary, display the Drawing toolbar by opening the **View** menu, selecting **Toolbars,** and then selecting **Drawing.**

3. Click the **Rectangle** button. Notice how the mouse pointer changes into a crosshair as you move the mouse pointer within the worksheet window.

> **Speech Recognition**
>
> If your computer has Speech Recognition capabilities, enable the Voice Command mode and say the steps necessary to access the Drawing toolbar.

4. Place your mouse pointer in the upper-left corner of cell **E2,** press and hold the mouse button down, and drag to the lower-right corner of the cell. Release the mouse button. The rectangle should now be drawn in cell E2.

STEP-BY-STEP 14.6 Continued

5. Place your mouse pointer over the rectangle object in cell E2 and click the right mouse button. Choose **Assign Macro** on the shortcut menu.

6. Click the **InsertRow** macro in the Assign Macro dialog box and click **OK.** The macro is now assigned to the rectangle object. This object is now considered a macro button.

7. Place your mouse pointer over the macro button, click the right mouse button, and choose **Add Text.** The insertion point should now be inside the macro button. Key **New Row.**

8. With the macro button still selected, click the **3-D Style** button on the Drawing toolbar and choose a 3-D shape of your choice. (*Note:* If the button's text is not displayed after you select the 3-D option, simply click the right mouse button while the macro is selected and select **Send to Back.** This option sends the 3-D feature to the back and lets the text appear in front.)

9. Click anywhere outside the macro button to deselect it. The macro button should look similar to Figure 14-8.

FIGURE 14-8
Macro button within a worksheet

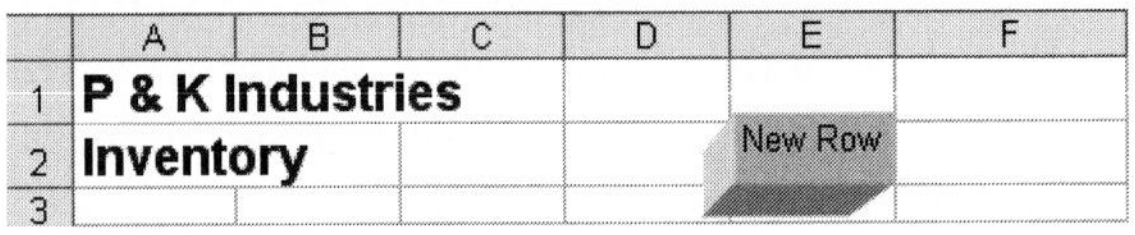

10. To see how this macro button works, select cell **A1** and click the **New Row** macro button. You should see a newly inserted row.

11. Print the sheet. Save the workbook and remain in this screen for the next exercise.

Creating a Custom Menu

Although Excel offers built-in menus, you might find that over time you use several commands or tools frequently. However, these commands may be found on separate menus or toolbars. With Excel's **New Menu** option, you can create a menu that contains your most frequently used commands.

You can add a new menu to the menu bar or to an existing toolbar, such as the Standard or Formatting toolbar. In addition, you can create a new toolbar and add a new menu to it. If you choose to add a menu to the menu bar or an existing toolbar, the menu will be available in any worksheet. If you place the new menu on a separate toolbar, it, too, is available in any worksheet you open, and you can display or hide this toolbar as desired.

If a new menu is added to a toolbar, you may leave the toolbar floating within the worksheet or you can dock (or place) the toolbar alongside the Standard or Formatting toolbar. To dock the toolbar, simply place your mouse pointer over the title bar of the toolbar and drag it to the side of any docked toolbar or to any side of your window.

STEP-BY-STEP 14.7

1. Choose the **View** menu, select **Toolbars,** and then select **Customize.**

2. Click the **Toolbars** tab and then click the **New** button.

3. Enter **My Toolbar,** followed by your initials, in the New Toolbar dialog box. Click **OK.** You will notice a small toolbar located to the side of the Customize dialog box, as shown in Figure 14-9.

FIGURE 14-9
New My Toolbar

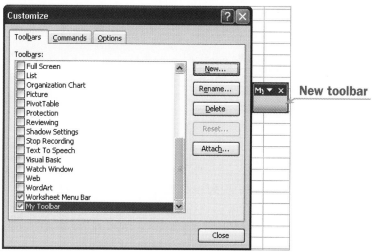

4. Click the **Commands** tab and scroll down the *Categories* list until you see New Menu.

5. Click the **New Menu** option in the *Categories* box. Drag the **New Menu** option from the *Commands* list to the My Toolbar and release the mouse button. You should see New Menu added to the toolbar as shown in Figure 14-10.

FIGURE 14-10
New Menu option on My Toolbar

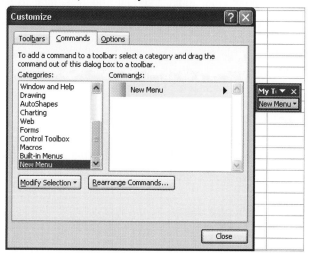

STEP-BY-STEP 14.7 Continued

6. To add commands to the new menu, click the arrow to the right of New Menu on My Toolbar. You should see a small menu box appear.

7. Choose the **AutoShapes** category from the *Categories* list in the Customize dialog box. Drag the **Line, Arrow,** and **WordArt** commands to the small menu box. After this step, your toolbar should appear similar to Figure 14-11.

FIGURE 14-11
My Toolbar with New Menu

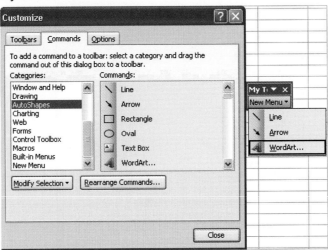

8. To change the new menu's name while the Customize dialog box is open, simply click the right mouse button over **New Menu** in the toolbar. A shortcut menu should appear. Click in the **Name** text box and delete the words *New Menu*. Key **My Menu** for the menu name and press **Enter.**

9. Close the Customize dialog box.

10. To dock the toolbar, simply place your mouse pointer over the title bar of My Toolbar and drag it to the side of the Formatting toolbar. (Your toolbar should appear similar to Figure 14-12.) A customized toolbar can be docked in a variety of positions, such as to the side of a window or with any toolbar.

FIGURE 14-12
Custom menu

11. To hide the toolbar, place your mouse pointer over any toolbar and click the right mouse button to display the shortcut menu. Deselect **My Toolbar.**

12. Save and close the workbook.

Time Saver

Excel lets you create macros using relative referencing rather than absolute referencing.

> **Computer Concepts**
>
> You can quickly display the Macro dialog box using the keystrokes **Alt** + **F8**.

STEP-BY-STEP 14.8

1. First, display the Stop Recording toolbar by selecting the **View** menu, **Toolbars**, **Customize**, choosing the **Toolbars** tab and then selecting the **Stop Recording** toolbar.

2. Click the **Relative Reference** button.

3. Start recording your macro.

SUMMARY

In this lesson, you learned:

- Macros are a method by which you can automate frequently used tasks.

- Excel records macros in a code called Visual Basic. To edit a macro, you make changes to this code in the Visual Basic editing window. Edit the code as you would edit text.

- Macro settings may be changed to increase or decrease the protection against viruses.

- You can run a macro by selecting it in the Macro dialog box or by pressing the shortcut keys (if a key was assigned). You can also run a macro if it is saved as a button on a toolbar or as a command button on a worksheet.

- You can create custom menus on the menu bar or on a toolbar allowing you to quickly access frequently used commands on a single menu.

VOCABULARY *Review*

Define the following terms:

Commands	Macro	Visual Basic

REVIEW *Questions*

WRITTEN QUESTIONS

Write a brief answer to the following questions.

1.   What is a macro?

2.   How do you delete a macro?

3.   What's the primary difference between placing a macro button on a toolbar and placing it directly on a worksheet?

4.   How do you edit a macro?

5.   How do you return to your worksheet from the Visual Basic Editor window?

MATCHING

Determine the correct sequence of procedures in creating and running a macro by matching the letter of the step number in the right column with the procedure listed in the left column.

Column 1	Column 2
___ 1. Execute the sequence of actions you want to record.	A. Step 1
___ 2. Turn the recorder on.	B. Step 2
___ 3. Use the macro by pressing the shortcut key assigned to the macro.	C. Step 3
___ 4. Turn the recorder off.	D. Step 4
___ 5. Name the macro and assign any shortcut keys.	E. Step 5

PROJECTS

PROJECT 14-1

1. Open the **AE Project14-1** workbook from the data files and save it as **Insert Column Macro,** followed by your initials.

2. Create a macro that inserts a blank column. Name the macro **InsrtCol** and assign a shortcut key of your choice. Be sure to look at the shortcut keys on each menu before you assign a shortcut key to the macro.

3. Run the macro to be certain it works.

4. Print the current sheet in landscape orientation, and then save and close the workbook.

PROJECT 14-2

1. Open the **AE Project14-2** workbook from the data files. Select **Enable Macros** and save the file as **New Fonts,** followed by your initials.

2. Edit the **Filefmt** macro to include italics and bold.

3. Test the macro on ranges **A5:A11, B4:G4,** and **B12:G12.**

4. Print the current sheet. Then save and close the workbook.

CRITICAL*Thinking*

ACTIVITY 14-1

You are preparing an Excel worksheet for your company's month-end close. Open the **AE Activity14-1** workbook from the data files and save it as **Month End,** followed by your initials. Create a macro that totals each month's expenses and places them in the Total row. (*Hint:* When referencing cells for the formula, use the arrow keys on your keyboard to select them. Macros record your exact actions and do not adjust for relative cell references.) Print the sheet when you are done.

ACTIVITY 14-2

Create a toolbar named **Art Tools** and add any drawing or AutoShape commands as desired.

ACTIVITY 14-3

Use Excel's Help system to obtain more information on using Visual Basic to edit macros.

IMPORTING AND EXPORTING

OBJECTIVES

Upon completion of this lesson, you should be able to:

■ Import data into Excel.

■ Import data from other data sources.

■ Export Excel data.

■ Export structured data.

■ Publish Excel worksheets and workbooks in HTML format.

Estimated Time: 1 hour

VOCABULARY

Export

Import

HTML

Structured data

Introduction

You can exchange data between Excel files, as well as other Office programs and the Web through the import and export features. In this lesson, you will learn how to import data using several import data sources. In addition, Excel data and structured data will be exported to other applications.

Importing Data

To *import* data means to bring information from another compatible program into Excel. One of the primary benefits of importing data into an Excel file is the ability to then use Excel's formula and data analysis tools with this data. You can also create PivotTable reports from imported data. Excel can read files created in other programs as well as those saved in various formats. Following is a list of some of the more common types of files Excel can read:

■ Microsoft Access

■ dBASE

■ Microsoft Works 2.0

■ XML files

- Lotus 1-2-3

- Quattro Pro

- Text files

- Other third-party providers

To import a text file into an Excel workbook, click the File menu and then select Open. From the *Files of type* drop-down list box, select Text Files. As you import this text file, the Text Import Wizard will start automatically as shown in Figure 15-1. The Wizard takes you step by step through the process of importing a text file into Excel. When a file is imported into Excel, you can add and edit the data, create charts, format the worksheet, and print the data as you would any other Excel file.

FIGURE 15-1
Text Import Wizard – Step 1

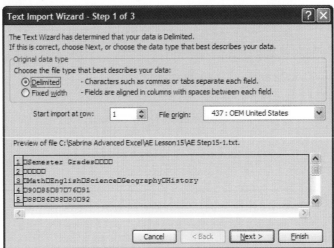

In the following Step-by-Step, you will import data from Word that has been saved as a text file. The text file is placed in a new Excel workbook file that assumes the same name as the text file. The worksheet tab is also labeled according to the text filename.

STEP-BY-STEP 15.1

1. Start Excel, if necessary, and click the **Open** button.

2. From the *Files of type* drop-down list in the Open dialog box, select **Text Files**.

3. Open the **AE Step15-1** text file from the data files.

4. The Text Import Wizard - Step 1 of 3 dialog box appears. (See Figure 15-1.) If necessary, click **Delimited** (the most common text type), and then click **Next**.

STEP-BY-STEP 15.1 Continued

5. The Text Import Wizard - Step 2 of 3 dialog box appears, as shown in Figure 15-2. Make sure **Tab** is selected in the *Delimiters* section. A sample of how the data will appear is displayed in the *Data preview* window. Click **Next**.

FIGURE 15-2
Text Import Wizard – Step 2

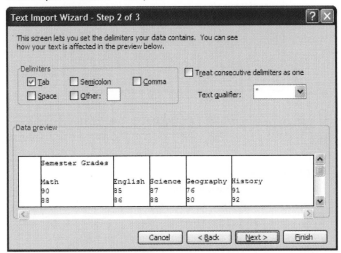

6. The Text Import Wizard - Step 3 of 3 dialog box appears, as shown in Figure 15-3. In this dialog box, you can change the data format, if necessary. Click the **Advanced** button to open the Advanced Text Import Settings dialog box shown in Figure 15-4. This dialog box allows you to add decimal places and a comma between thousands. Click **Cancel** to close the dialog box without making any changes. Click **Finish** in the Step 3 of 3 dialog box.

FIGURE 15-3
Text Import Wizard – Step 3

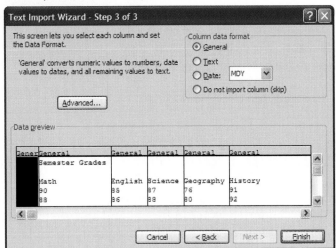

STEP-BY-STEP 15.1 Continued

FIGURE 15-4
Advanced Text Import Settings dialog box

7. Your worksheet should appear similar to Figure 15-5. Adjust the column widths as necessary to display all of the text.

FIGURE 15-5
Imported text file worksheet

	A	B	C	D	E	F	G
1		Semester Grades					
2							
3		Math	English	Science	Geography	History	
4		90	85	87	76	91	
5		88	86	88	80	92	
6		87	70	99	82	78	
7		88	72	99	79	67	
8		76	91	84	88	87	
9		82		87		88	
10				88		94	
11	Course Average						
12	Highest Grade						
13	Lowest Grade						
14							

8. Select the **File** menu and then choose **Save As**. Enter **Semester Grades** followed by your initials as the filename, click the down arrow for *Save as type* and select **Microsoft Office Excel Workbook**, and then click **Save**. These steps save the file as an Excel workbook.

9. Print the active sheet and then close the workbook.

Speech Recognition

If your computer has Speech Recognition capabilities, enable the Voice Command mode and say the steps necessary to close the workbook.

Importing External Data from Other Data Sources

Excel allows you to import external data from the Web or from other data sources, such as Access. After data is imported, you can format and analyze the data as desired. With certain imported data, you may even create PivotTable reports. After selecting the Data menu, Import External Data, and New Database Query, the Choose Data Source dialog box will appear. (*Note:* If this feature is not installed, you will need to install it at this time.)

If you leave the *Use the Query Wizard to create/edit queries* option selected, Excel will take you step by step through the process of importing MS Access data. You're then asked to choose the database file and columns you wish to import.

STEP-BY-STEP 15.2

1. Start a new blank workbook.

2. Open the **Data** menu, choose **Import External Data**, and then select **New Database Query**. The Choose Data Source dialog box appears as shown in Figure 15-6. (If this feature is not installed, you will be asked to install it at this time.)

FIGURE 15-6
Choose Data Source dialog box

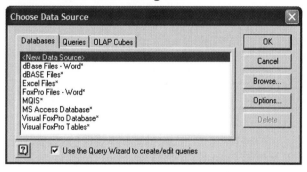

3. In the Choose Data Source dialog box, choose **MS Access Database**. If necessary, choose the **Use the Query Wizard to create/edit queries** option and click **OK**. The Select Database dialog box appears as in Figure 15-7; however, your student directory may differ from the one shown.

FIGURE 15-7
Select Database dialog box

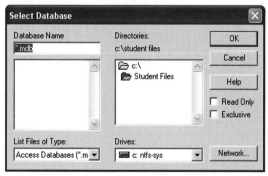

4. In the Select Database dialog box, choose the drive and folder (directory) where the data files are located.

5. Select the **AE Step15-2** Access database from the data files. Click **OK**.

STEP-BY-STEP 15.2 Continued

6. Click the **plus sign** for the Products table in the Query Wizard – Choose Columns dialog box as indicated in Figure 15-8. Click **Product ID** and then click the right arrow button to move this column into the *Columns in your query* box. Continue to click the right arrow button until the **Product Description**, **Price**, and **Stock on Hand** columns are in the *Columns in your query* box. Click **Next**.

FIGURE 15-8
Query Wizard – Choose Columns dialog box

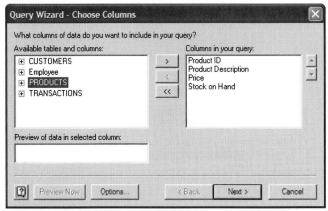

7. You have the option to filter for specific records with Query Wizard – Filter Data, which appears in Figure 15-9; however, for this Step-by-Step, simply click **Next**.

FIGURE 15-9
Query Wizard – Filter Data dialog box

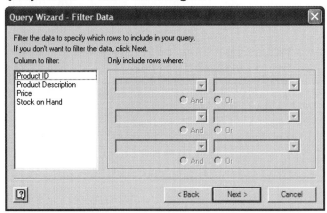

8. Click the *Sort by* down arrow in the Query Wizard – Sort Order dialog box and choose **Product ID**. If necessary, select **Ascending** as displayed in Figure 15-10. Click **Next**.

STEP-BY-STEP 15.2 Continued

FIGURE 15-10
Query Wizard – Sort Order dialog box

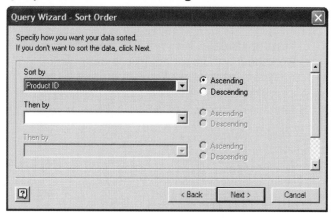

9. Make sure that *Return Data to Microsoft Office Excel* in the Query Wizard – Finish dialog box is displayed as shown in Figure 15-11. Click **Finish**. The Import Data dialog box appears as shown in Figure 15-12.

FIGURE 15-11
Query Wizard – Finish

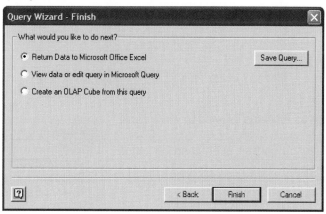

FIGURE 15-12
Import Data dialog box

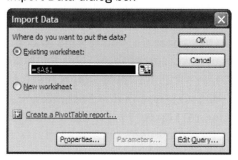

STEP-BY-STEP 15.2 Continued

10. Notice that the Collapse Dialog button is available for selecting the desired starting cell where the imported data will appear. If necessary, select cell **A1** and click **OK**. Your screen should look like that shown in Figure 15-13.

FIGURE 15-13
Worksheet with imported Access data

	A	B	C	D
1	Product ID	Product Description	Price	Stock on Hand
2	150	Wonder Diet - Dogs	11.923	560
3	162	Nail Trimmer - Small	11.025	205
4	230	Wonder Diet - Cats	6.256	256
5	245	Flea Shampoo	5.621	658
6	301	Clippers - Hair	25.369	56
7	318	Silkie Shampoo	7.856	632
8	323	Linatone for Coats	17.56	248
9	326	Dog Vitamins	15.626	77
10	340	Nail Trimmer - Large	17.658	963
11	347	Rawhide Bone - Small	3.896	145
12	349	Bird Bell	15.236	65
13	358	Lory Nectar - Small	4.998	25
14	415	Bird Seed - Parakeets	8.741	36
15	417	Cat Vitamins	14.895	79
16	486	Flea Collar - Cats	3.214	130
17	532	Groomer Brush	17.239	985
18	547	Rawhide Bone - Medium	5.239	452
19	574	Bird Seed Mix - Parrots	12.659	38
20	599	Plastic Toys - Assorted	1.987	98
21	600	Flea Collar - Dogs, Small	5.658	125
22	641	Plastic Ball	1.236	150
23	676	Catnip Mouse	6.347	142
24	847	Groomer Comb	22.965	120
25	856	Rawhide Bone - Large	7.239	985
26	872	Lory Nectar - Large	9.998	65
27	925	Flea Collar - Dogs, Large	9.293	125
28	930	Silkie Conditioner	5.236	360

11. Save the workbook as **Products** followed by your initials.

12. Print the worksheet in portrait orientation and then close the workbook.

> ### Speech Recognition
> If your computer has Speech Recognition capabilities, enable the Voice Command mode and say the steps necessary to save, print, and close the workbook.

Importing Real Time Data (RTD)

With Excel's New Web Query feature, you're able to connect to the Internet and import information directly into an Excel spreadsheet. This feature enables you to quickly get Real Time Data (RTD) from the Web for currency rates, major indices, stock quotes, and other data.

When you first start a New Web Query, a dialog box appears displaying your current Internet browser and home page, similar to Figure 15-14. Since many Internet browsers and service providers are available, your screen may not appear exactly as shown in the figures, but your options will be the same.

FIGURE 15-14
New Web Query dialog box

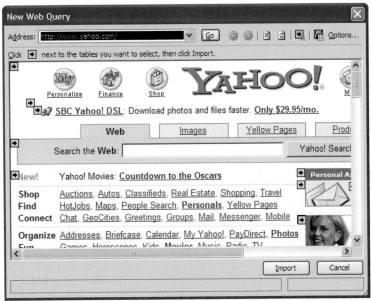

From the New Web Query dialog box, you may now enter the desired Web address in the Address box and click Go. For example, if you enter the Web address for MSN Money Central Investor Stock Quotes, your screen will appear similar to Figure 15-15.

FIGURE 15-15
MSN Money Central Investor Stock Quotes

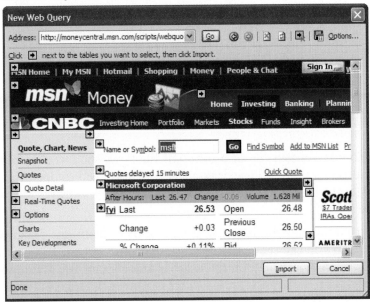

In this Step-by-Step, you will locate a stock quote for Wal-Mart. The stock symbol for Wal-Mart is wmt.

STEP-BY-STEP 15.3

1. Start a new workbook.

2. Start your Web browser.

3. Switch back to your workbook by clicking the **Excel** button on the Windows taskbar.

4. Open the **Data** menu, choose **Import External Data**, and then select **New Web Query**.

5. Click in the *Address* box and enter **http://moneycentral.msn.com/investor/home.asp**.

6. Click **Go**. After a brief pause, the MSN Money Central Investor screen should appear in the dialog box (similar to that shown in Figure 15-15). Notice that arrows appear to the left of various screen options. Selecting one or more of these arrows allows you to view or import specific information.

> **Speech Recognition**
>
> If your computer has Speech Recognition capabilities, enable the Voice Command mode and say the steps necessary to open the New Web Query dialog box.

7. Select the arrow to the left of the **Symbol** box. (This arrow may be at the far left of the entire bar.) You will now see the arrow change into a check mark indicating that you wish to view stock symbol information. Enter **wmt** in the *Symbol* box and click **Go**.

8. Click the arrow to the left of *Last* in the stock table to select this table for import. Click the **Import** button.

9. With cell **A1** selected in the Import Data dialog box, click **OK**. The imported data will appear in your worksheet. (Depending upon the speed of your Internet connection, the data may seem to appear instantaneously, or it may take a few seconds.)

10. Save the workbook as **Stock Quote** followed by your initials and then print and close the workbook.

Using Drag-and-Drop to Import Data

You may also insert a text file or a different file type, such as a graphic object, by using the drag-and-drop method. To use drag-and-drop, you need to open the file in the application from which you are importing data as well as the Excel workbook where you want the imported data to be placed.

One of the most popular methods to use drag-and-drop from one program to another is to position the windows so you can see both applications on the screen. To display both application windows, right-click in an empty area on the taskbar and choose Tile Windows Vertically on the shortcut menu.

Now you're ready for importing. You will select the data you want to import, hold down the Ctrl key to copy the data, and drag it to the Excel worksheet.

S TEP-BY-STEP 15.4

1. Open a new workbook in Excel.

2. Start the Microsoft Word program and open the **AE Step15-4** document from the data files.

3. Right-click an empty area (not over a program button, tool, or button) on your Desktop taskbar, and choose **Tile Windows Vertically** on the shortcut menu. Make sure you can see cell B5 in the Excel worksheet.

4. Click anywhere in the table in the Word document. Open the **Table** menu, choose **Select**, and then choose **Table**.

5. Place your mouse pointer over the table, then press and hold down the mouse button while holding down the **Ctrl** key. Pressing the Ctrl key will copy the table instead of moving it.

6. Drag the data to cell **B5** in the Excel worksheet. Release the mouse button and then release the **Ctrl** key. Be sure to release the mouse button first before releasing the Ctrl key or the data may be moved instead of copied.

7. Using Excel's **AutoFit** option (double-click the right edge of the column heading), change the column widths to accommodate the data.

8. Save the Excel workbook as **Addresses** followed by your initials. Print the sheet in landscape orientation.

9. Close the Excel workbook file and then close the Word document without saving changes.

Exporting Excel Data

Data created in Excel can be saved in various file formats so that it can be opened in another application. Also, with the compatibility features in Microsoft Office, you're able to copy and drag structured information between Office programs. *Structured data* typically indicates information that's entered into an Excel worksheet in a data list format. This can be copied, for example, into Word as a table.

Export refers to taking information from Excel and using it in another program. To save a file for use in another program, click the File menu and select Save As. In the Save As dialog box, click the *Save as type* drop-down list arrow and choose the desired format. Workbook files can be saved in many formats, such as:

- Web Page (single file or page)
- Text (Tab delimited)
- Formatted Text (space delimited)
- Unicode Text (for multilingual document creation)

- CSV (Comma delimited)
- WK*
- DBF
- XML spreadsheet
- XML data
- Template

In this Step-by-Step, you will export structured data using the drag-and-drop feature.

STEP-BY-STEP 15.5

1. Open the **AE Step15-5** workbook from the data files. If necessary, start the Microsoft Word program and click the **New** button to start a new document.

2. Return to the **AE Step15-5** workbook by clicking its button on the taskbar.

3. Select the range **A1:E19**.

4. Click the **Copy** button.

5. Click the **Microsoft Word** button on the taskbar.

6. Click in the Word document and click the **Paste** button. The student loan information is copied in a table format to the Word document. Now you could enter any text that explains the table and use your word-processing tools to edit and format it. Adjust column width if necessary by double-clicking Excel information and dragging the column lines.

7. Save the Word document as **Student Loan** followed by your initials. Print and then close the document. Close the Excel workbook without saving changes.

Now let's try saving an Excel file in a .txt format to be opened in Microsoft Word.

8. Open the **AE Step 15-5** workbook from the data files.

9. Save the workbook as **Student Loan – Text Format** and select **Text (Tab delimited)** from the *Save as type* list.

10. Click **OK** to save the first worksheet of this workbook in this format. Click **Yes** to let Excel know that you want to keep the selected format. Close the workbook.

11. Click the **Microsoft Word** button on the taskbar.

12. Click the **Open** tool in Word, choose the directory where the **Student Loan – Text Format** file is located, and select **All Files** from the *Files as type* list. Select the **Student Loan – Text Format** file and click **Open**.

13. View the file in text format. Then close the file in Word.

Publishing Excel Worksheets and Workbooks in HTML Format

It's easy to create a Web page from worksheet data or a chart and then publish this information on the World Wide Web. To create a Web page, you need to save the data in *HTML* (HyperText Markup Language) file format. When you save a worksheet or workbook for use on the Web, Excel also creates a folder to store these files.

To save a worksheet for viewing on the Web, you first need to open the desired worksheet. Next, select Save as Web Page from the File menu and choose OK. Your worksheet is now available to view on the Web. You could also save the workbook and select Web Page from the *Save as type* list in the Save dialog box as discussed previously.

STEP-BY-STEP 15.6

1. Open the **AE Step15-6** workbook from the data files.

2. Open the **File** menu and select **Save as Web Page**.

3. Click the **Selection: Sheet** option. This action will publish only the active worksheet as a Web page rather than the entire workbook.

4. In the *File name* box, key **Home Sales** followed by your initials and then click the **Save** button.

5. To view the Web page, click the **File** menu and then select **Web Page Preview**. You can also view the Web page by starting Internet Explorer (or another Web browser), choosing the **File** menu, selecting **Open**, clicking the **Browse** button, and locating and opening the **Home Sales** file. The worksheet data should be displayed, as shown in Figure 15-16.

FIGURE 15-16
Web page preview

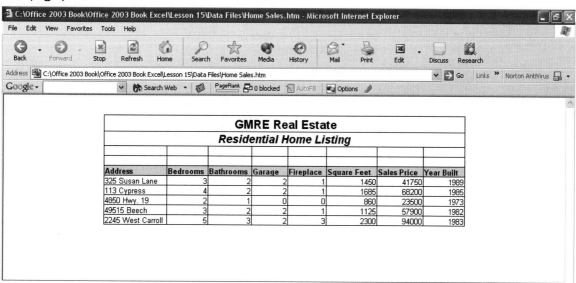

STEP-BY-STEP 15.6 Continued

6. Close the Web page window and your workbook without saving changes.

7. Open the **AE Step 15-6** workbook from the data files.

8. Click the **Sheet2** tab. Select cell **A1** and enter your full name, select cell **A2** and enter your street address, and select cell **A3** and enter your telephone number.

9. Open the **File** menu and click **Save as Web Page**.

10. Select **Entire Workbook**, if necessary. Then enter **Realtor Sales** followed by your initials for the filename.

11. Click **Save** and then click **Yes** in the message box.

12. Select the **File** menu and then choose **Web Page Preview**.

13. Click the **Sheet1** tab and then the **Sheet2** tab.

14. Close the Web page window, and then close the workbook.

Time Saver

You can quickly close all open workbooks at one time. When you are closing multiple workbooks, Excel will ask you if you want to save changes if it recognizes that one of the workbooks has not been saved since last updated.

STEP-BY-STEP 15-7

1. Open the **Stock Quote** and **Products** workbooks from the solution files you created in this lesson.

2. Hold down the **Shift** key.

3. Click on the **File** menu. Notice the option *Close All* now appears on the File menu.

4. Select **Close All**.

> ### Integration Tip
>
> After importing text and data, you might need to apply similar formats throughout the worksheet that were not imported with the data and text. To quickly apply the same format to many locations throughout the worksheet, simply click on a cell containing the desired format, double-click on the **Format Painter** tool, and click or select each location where you want the format. Double-clicking on the Format Painter keeps it active. To turn off the Format Painter tool, simply click once on it.

SUMMARY

In this lesson, you learned:

■ Data from other applications, such as Microsoft Word, Microsoft Access, and the World Wide Web, may be imported into Excel. You can then edit, format, and perform calculations and data analysis on this imported data using any Excel tools or features.

■ Excel files can be saved in various formats so that they can exported to other applications.

■ Worksheet data is easily saved in an HTML format for publishing to the Web.

VOCABULARY *Review*

Define the following terms:

Export   HTML   Structured data
Import

REVIEW *Questions*

TRUE/FALSE

Circle T if the statement is true or F if the statement is false.

T F 1. Excel can only import and export data between other Microsoft Office software applications.

T F 2. Once a file has been imported to Excel, you cannot make changes to it.

T F 3. Files in text (.txt) format are the only type of file format that can be imported into Excel.

T F 4. One of the benefits of importing data into Excel is the ability to use Excel's calculation and data analysis tools on the data.

T F 5. The Save as Web Page feature allows you to save Excel worksheets in a format that may be viewed on the Web.

WRITTEN QUESTIONS

Write a brief answer to the following questions.

1. Does the Text Import Wizard start when any file in Excel is opened that was created in another program? Why or why not?

2. Why would you want to import a table with numbers from Word into Excel?

3. What are three file types that can be imported into Excel?

4. What are three file types that Excel files can be saved as before they are exported from Excel?

5. What are the steps for saving a worksheet as a Web page?

PROJECTS

PROJECT 15-1

1. Import the **AE Project15-1** text file from the data files into an Excel worksheet. Select **Delimited** as the file type that best describes the data. Choose **Tab delimited** and leave the other defaults as they appear.

2. Adjust column widths wherever necessary. Apply any formats that you think are appropriate.

3. Save the workbook as **Address List** followed by your initials in Microsoft Office Excel Workbook file format.

4. Print the active sheet and then close the workbook.

PROJECT 15-2

1.   Open the **AE Project15-2** workbook from the data files.

2.   Select all the data and copy this information to a new blank document in Microsoft Word.

3.   Save the Word document as **NL Employee List** followed by your initials.

4.   Insert four blank lines above (outside of) the table. On the first line, key **NL Corporation**; on the second line, key **Employee List**. Format the heading as you think is appropriate.

5.   Modify the column widths and format the table as you think is appropriate. (*Hint:* Select the entire table and open the Table Properties dialog box by double-clicking the table selection handle. You can then adjust the column widths one by one without having to select each individually and reopen the Table Properties dialog box.)

6.   Print the document and then close it. Close the Excel workbook without saving changes.

CRITICAL *Thinking*

 ACTIVITY 15-1

Import the text file **AE Activity15-1** from the data files into a new workbook. Save the workbook as **A&C Imported File** followed by your initials. Calculate totals in the worksheet that you think are necessary. Add any formats that you think will enhance the appearance of the worksheet. Print the sheet and then close the workbook.

 ACTIVITY 15-2

You have imported a text file into Excel that contains the names, ID numbers, and salaries of all employees at your company. You know that you would like the imported data to change if any modifications are made to it in the original file. Use Excel's Help system to find information on updating or refreshing imported data. Write a brief essay on how you would proceed.

USING TEMPLATES AND PROTECTION

OBJECTIVES

Upon completion of this lesson, you should be able to:

- Create a template.
- Save a template.
- Open and use a template.
- Edit a template.
- View additional templates.
- Add protection options to a cell, worksheet, and workbook.
- Change the default location for templates.

Estimated Time: 1 hour

VOCABULARY

Protection

Template

Introduction

A template may be used many times to create new workbooks that follow the same format but require different data. A template normally contains titles, subtitles, formats, and formulas but no specific data values. In this lesson, you'll learn to create, save, and edit templates.

In addition to being able to create your own templates, Excel also provides preformatted templates, such as the Invoice template, that let you quickly prepare customized workbooks. Templates are automatically saved to a default location. This location, however, can be changed for easier access or so that the template files can be shared with others.

In addition to learning about templates in this lesson, you'll also learn how to add protection features to workbooks, worksheets, and cells. These features will help prevent unwanted changes in your workbooks.

Creating and Saving a Template

A *template* can save you valuable time. For example, you may need to prepare a budget report each month. The budgetary text and formats in the workbook remain the same from month to month, but the numbers change. Rather than entering the same text and formulas over and over, you can create a template and then "fill in the blanks" with numbers.

To create a template, enter titles, subtitles, formats, and formulas. In other words, you enter everything but the data values. You then save the workbook as a template file; Excel saves the template in a default folder specifically for templates. Since you are constructing the template, Excel refers to it as a User-Created Template and makes them available on the General tab of the Templates dialog box. When you want to create a workbook based on the template, simply click the File menu and select New. Then, you will choose *On my computer* under the Templates options to view your templates. From there, you simply open the template file and then save it as an Excel workbook with a new name. This action maintains the template in its original form so that you may use it again.

STEP-BY-STEP 16.1

1. Start a new workbook.

2. Select cell **A1** and enter the title **Miss Bessie's Cookies**.

3. Continue by entering the following text in the corresponding cells.

Cell	Enter
A2	**Monthly Cookie Sales**
B5	**Chocolate Chip**
B6	**Oatmeal Raisin**
B7	**Sugar**
B8	**Peanut Blossom**
B9	**Chocolate/ Macadamia**
B10	**Total Sales**

4. Select cell **C10** and enter a formula that will sum the range C5:C9. Apply the **Currency** format to **C5:C10**, if necessary.

5. For the format, bold all the text you have entered. Change the text size of the title to **16** points and the size of the subtitle to **12** points. Add italics and underline to the subtitle. Widen column B to accommodate the data, if necessary.

6. On the **File** menu, select **Save As**.

7. Click the *Save as type* drop-down list arrow and scroll in this list until you see Template. (Your file list may or may not display file extensions, depending on your default settings.) The *Save as type* list displays, similar to Figure 16-1.

STEP-BY-STEP 16.1 Continued

FIGURE 16-1
Save as type list box

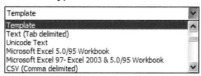

8. Select **Template**.

9. For the purpose of this course, locate the folder with your exercise solution files and save the template in this folder. Enter **Monthly Cookie Sales Template** followed by your initials as the filename.

10. Click **Save** and then close the template.

Speech Recognition

If your computer has speech recognition capabilities, enable the Voice Command mode and say the appropriate steps to save and close the template.

Opening and Using a Template

Now that you've created a template, it is ready to use. After you open a template and fill in the new data, you save it as a regular Excel workbook file. This leaves the original template intact for future use. To open the template, simply click the File menu, select New, and then choose *On my computer* under the *Templates* options in the New Workbook task pane.

You'll notice that the icon identifying a template file is different from that for an Excel workbook file. Figure 16-2 shows both the icon for a template and the icon for an Excel workbook file.

FIGURE 16-2
File type icons

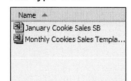

STEP-BY-STEP 16.2

1. Open the **Monthly Cookie Sales Template** file.

2. Save the file as **January Cookie Sales** followed by your initials and choose **Microsoft Office Excel Workbook** from the *Save as type* drop-down list.

STEP-BY-STEP 16.2 Continued

3. Enter the following data. Your worksheet should look similar to Figure 16-3.

Cell	Enter
A3	**January**
C5	**2544**
C6	**238**
C7	**878**
C8	**1433**
C9	**1052**

FIGURE 16-3
January Cookie Sales worksheet

	A	B	C
1	Miss Bessie's Cookies		
2	*Monthly Cookie Sales*		
3	January		
4			
5		Chocolate Chip	$2,544.00
6		Oatmeal Raisin	$238.00
7		Sugar	$878.00
8		Peanut Blossom	$1,433.00
9		Chocolate/Macadamia	$1,052.00
10		Total Sales	$6,145.00

4. Save the file.

5. Print the worksheet and then close the workbook.

Speech Recognition

If your computer has speech recognition capabilities, enable the Voice Command mode and say the appropriate steps to print and close the workbook.

Editing a Template

You can quickly make changes to a workbook template. Just open the template, make your changes, and save with the same filename. Make sure you select Template as the file type.

STEP-BY-STEP 16.3

1. Open the **Monthly Cookie Sales Template** file.

2. Change the title to a font size of **18**.

3. Insert a row after the subtitle and add the text **Unaudited Sales Report** to cell A3. Add italics to cell A3 if necessary with a font size of **12**. Remove the bold and underline format, if necessary.

4. Click the **File** menu, choose **Save As**, enter the filename **Monthly Cookie Sales Template–revised** followed by your initials, and select **Template** from the *Save as type* list box if necessary. Be sure to save this template in your exercise file folder.

5. Close the template file.

Using Predefined Templates

Excel provides a variety of preformatted templates to help you prepare workbooks quickly and efficiently. These templates allow you to create such items as invoices, balance sheets, purchase orders, and expense statements simply by filling in the blanks. And if you have access to the World Wide Web, you can access additional Excel templates in Template on Office Online located at *www.microsoft.com*. On the Web, you'll find templates designed for tasks such as planning personal and business finances. The template files available locally to you are determined by the options selected at installation.

The Sales Invoice and Balance Sheet templates are typically found on the Spreadsheet Solutions tab and appear similar to Figures 16-4 and 16-5.

FIGURE 16-4
Sales Invoice template

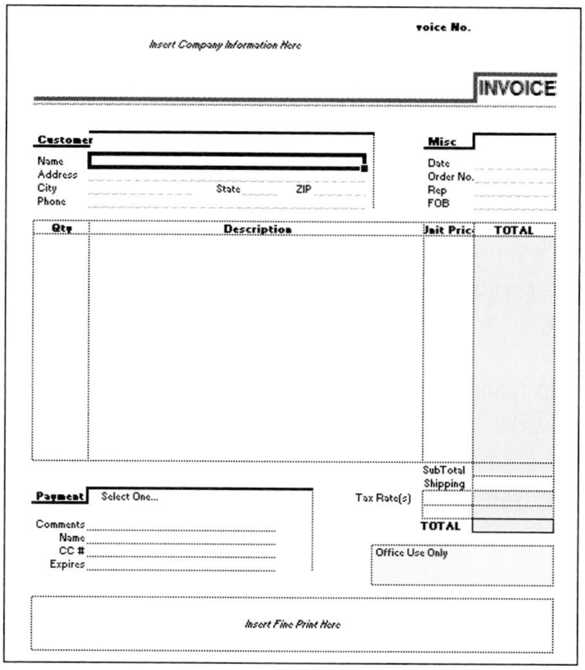

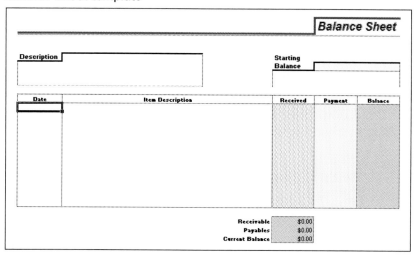

FIGURE 16-5
Balance Sheet template

You can choose to add the information entered in the template as a new record in a database associated with the template by using the Template Wizard add-in feature.

To use the templates, select *On my computer* in the *Templates* section of the New Workbook task pane, and view the templates that are available on the Spreadsheet Solutions tab.

Next, double-click a template to open it. (You may see a message box about enabling macros. To continue, click Enable Macros.) Shaded areas will be displayed on some of the templates. These areas contain formulas and other predefined calculations. You do not enter any information into the shaded areas of a template.

STEP-BY-STEP 16.4

1. Click the **File** menu and then select **New**. Choose **On my computer** from the *Templates* section of the New Workbook task pane.

2. Click the **General** tab if necessary. Note that this is the location in which you would find the Monthly Cookie Sales template if you had not specified that it be stored with your other files.

3. Select the **Spreadsheet Solutions** tab.

4. Open the **Loan Amortization** template. Note that Excel may need to install this template after you select it. Notice that when you open one of these templates, it automatically changes the name of the file (adds a number) and the file type defaults to a workbook so that you do not accidentally overwrite the template file.

5. Select various cells to familiarize yourself with the template. Enter values in the cells if you wish to see the template at work.

6. Close the template without saving any changes.

Adding Protection Options

Although sharing workbooks is a practical way to update data and incorporate changes made by those who use the workbook, there are times when you won't want to allow changes by anyone else.

With Excel's *protection* features, you can protect a single cell of data from being changed or deleted, you can protect all the data on a worksheet, or you can protect the entire workbook. After the data is protected, it cannot be altered. Excel refers to protected cells as locked cells. To understand this concept, visualize an imaginary lock on the cell that can't be opened to change data. You may also remove the protection feature from a cell, worksheet, or workbook.

You'll find the Protection option on the Tools menu. After a worksheet is protected, you may remove the protection by choosing Unprotect Worksheet on the Tools menu.

STEP-BY-STEP 16.5

1. Open the **AE Step16-5** template from the data files. Save the file as a template with the filename **Pie Sales – Protected** followed by your initials.

2. Select the range **B5:B10**.

3. Click the **Format** menu, select **Cells**, and then click the **Protection** tab.

4. Click in the **Locked** check box to deselect the *Locked* option. This action will allow these cells to remain unlocked so that data can be entered in the cells after the worksheet is protected.

5. Click **OK**.

6. To protect the worksheet, select the **Tools** menu, click **Protection**, and then select **Protect Sheet**. The Protect Sheet dialog box appears as shown in Figure 16-6. Notice that you can select options to allow users to format columns and rows, insert columns and rows, and so on. You may also enter a password that would be required to unprotect the worksheet.

FIGURE 16-6
Protect Sheet dialog box

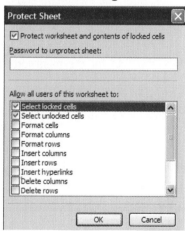

7. Click **OK**. Your entire worksheet is now protected (except B5:B10).

8. To see how this protection works, select cell **B5**. Enter 678. Since this is an unprotected (unlocked) cell, you are able to enter data.

9. Now select cell **A1**. Enter **New Pie Sales**. As soon as you begin keying text, a warning message appears indicating that this is a protected cell in the worksheet. Click **OK**.

10. To remove the protection, open the **Tools** menu, select **Protection**, and then click **Unprotect Sheet**.

> **Speech Recognition**
>
> If your computer has Speech Recognition capabilities, enable the Voice Command mode and say the appropriate steps to unprotect the Worksheet.

11. To see how the protection is now removed, click in cell **A10** and enter **Zucchini**.

12. Save, print, and close the workbook.

Protecting Workbooks

You can also add a higher level of protection to a workbook. For example, when you protect a worksheet, someone else can still open the workbook file. However, you may not want someone to view the information in your workbook. To prevent a workbook file from being opened by an unauthorized person, you can password-protect the workbook. If the person does not know the password, he or she cannot open the file.

Another protection option is read-only protection. This option lets another user open the file, but if changes are made, the workbook must be saved with another name. The password and read-only features can be applied by clicking the Tools button arrow in the Save As dialog box and then selecting General Options. You can add or remove password and read-only protections in the Save Options dialog box.

STEP-BY-STEP 16.6

1. Open the **AE Step16-6** workbook from the data files and save it as **Quarterly Sales** followed by your initials.

2. To password-protect the workbook, open the **File** menu and choose **Save As**.

3. Click the arrow on the **Tools** button in the dialog box's toolbar, and choose **General Options**.

4. In the Save Options dialog box, key **CAT** for the password in the *Password to open* text box and click **OK**.

5. Key **CAT** again in the Confirm Password dialog box. Click **OK**.

6. Click **Save** in the Save As dialog box. A message box appears asking if you want to replace the existing file named Quarterly Sales. Click **Yes**.

7. Let's see how password protection works. Close the Quarterly Sales workbook. Reopen the **Quarterly Sales** workbook. The Password dialog box appears, as shown in Figure 16-7.

> **Hot Tip**
>
> Passwords are case-sensitive. In other words, if a password contains capital letters, you will need to enter the password using the same capital letters. For example, if you enter CAT as the password, CAT (not cat or Cat, etc.) must be entered to open the workbook.

STEP-BY-STEP 16.6 Continued

FIGURE 16-7
Password dialog box

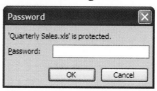

8. Key **CAT** and click **OK**.

9. Now remove the workbook protection. Select the **File** menu and then choose **Save As**.

10. Click the drop-down arrow on the **Tools** button and choose **General Options**. The highlight should be in the *Password to open* text box.

11. Press the **Delete** key to remove the password, and click **OK**.

12. Click **Save**. Click **Yes** when asked if you want to replace the existing file named Quarterly Sales. Remain in this screen for the next exercise.

Changing Default File Location of Templates

Excel saves templates in the default folder for templates in Microsoft Office 2003. However, you may want to save your templates in another folder for quicker access, to share with others, or to keep others from having access to the template. You can change the default location folder for saving and opening templates on the General tab of the Options dialog box.

STEP-BY-STEP 16.7

1. Click the **Tools** menu and then select **Options**.

2. Choose the **General** tab, if necessary.

3. In the *At startup, open all files in* text box, enter **C:\MutiUse Documents**. By entering another location for your files, Excel will look for your templates in this new location. For the purposes of this exercise, you will now cancel this dialog box in order that the template files will be saved in your student folder.

4. Click **Cancel**.

5. Close the workbook.

Time Savers

When making multiple copies of a worksheet, using the Copy and Paste funtions will copy the data to another worksheet, but not necessarily copy the formats. However, Excel lets you instantly make multiple copies of a worksheet and preserve the formatting.

STEP-BY-STEP 16-8

1. Open a new document.

2. Key **January 2007 Budget** in cell A1.

3. Select cell **A1**, change the font to bold and italicized, and increase the font size to **14**. Change the background color of the cell to light blue.

4. Place your mouse pointer over the **Sheet1** worksheet tab and click the left mouse button.

5. Hold down the **Ctrl** key and drag to the location next to Sheet1.

6. Release the mouse button and then release the **Ctrl** key. You will see a worksheet appear named Sheet1 (2).

7. Click on the **Sheet1** and **Sheet1 (2)** tabs and view the contents of the worksheets. Notice how the text, data and formats were copied.

8. Close the workbook without saving any changes.

You can easily control line breaks within a single Excel cell.

STEP-BY-STEP 16-9

1. Open a new document.

2. Type your first name and press **Alt+Enter**.

3. Type your last name.

4. Press **Enter**. Notice how your first and last names are on different lines of the cell.

5. Close the document without saving any changes.

SUMMARY

In this lesson, you learned:

- Templates are a timesaving feature that can increase your productivity. You discovered how to enter titles, subtitles, formats, and formulas into a template.

- When you open a template, you should save it immediately with a new filename. Then you can start entering data.

- Excel has a number of built-in templates, or you can go to *microsoft.com* on the Web to locate additional templates.

- Protection options can be added to a cell, worksheet, and workbook.

- The default location for templates can be changed.

VOCABULARY *Review*

Define the following terms:

Protection   Template

REVIEW *Questions*

TRUE/FALSE

Circle T if the statement is true or F if the statement is false.

T   F   1. When creating a template, you enter data and save the file as a workbook.

T   F   2. You can protect cells, worksheets, and workbooks in Excel.

T   F   3. You cannot add formulas to an existing Excel template.

T   F   4. A password for a workbook would be entered in the Save Options dialog box.

T   F   5. Once you create and save a new template in Excel, you cannot modify or edit the template workbook.

WRITTEN QUESTIONS

Write a brief answer to the following questions.

1. What is the purpose of a template?

2. What information is typically entered when creating a template?

3. Would you enter data into a template when creating it? Why or why not?

4. Why do you save a template with data entered into it as a workbook file instead of saving it as a template?

5. Describe two advantages of protecting a worksheet.

PROJECTS

PROJECT 16-1

1. Create a template for the Lazy Dayse Pie Factory with the information below. You will use the template to create a new workbook that will contain three months of data.

Cell	Enter
A1	Lazy Dayse Pie Factory
A2	Quarterly Sales:
A4	Type of Pie
A6	Apple
A7	Cherry
A8	Lemon
A9	Pumpkin
A10	Blueberry

2. Add formatting to the text. You can add bold and change the size of the title and subtitle. Select the range **B6:D10** and apply currency formatting with no decimals.

3. Save the template as **Pie Sales - Template** followed by your initials. Remember to save the template in the same directory and folder as your course files.

4. Close the template.

5. Reopen the template and enter the data for the first quarter. Key **First Quarter** in cell C2.

6. Enter the months **January, February,** and **March** in the range B4:D4. Widen the columns as necessary.

7. Enter the following sales data:

Type of Pie	January	February	March
Apple	900	723	1056
Cherry	459	649	576
Lemon	341	376	471
Pumpkin	298	277	240
Blueberry	197	188	160

8. Save the workbook as **Pie Sales** followed by your initials. (Be sure you're saving this as a workbook.)

9. Print the worksheet and then close the workbook.

PROJECT 16-2

1. Open the **AE Project16-2** workbook from the data files.

2. Save the workbook as **GMRE Real Estate** followed by your initials.

3. Password-protect the workbook with the password **CAT**.

CRITICAL *Thinking*

ACTIVITY 16-1

Ms. Emily Smith, your boss at Lincoln College Fan-Fair, a sports apparel shop for Lincoln College, has just handed you the inventory list shown below. She wants you to create a workbook template file containing the information and formatted as you think appropriate. Enter a formula in the *Value* field that multiplies the value in the *Quantity in Stock* column by the *Cost* column. This will indicate the value of the inventory. Save the template as **Lincoln FF Inventory Template** followed by your initials.

Item No.	Item Description	Size	Quantity in Stock	Cost	Value
SS-LC1-S	Sweat Shirt-Lincoln College emblem	S			
SS-LC1-M	Sweat Shirt-Lincoln College emblem	M			
SS-LC1-L	Sweat Shirt-Lincoln College emblem	L			
Cap-L	Baseball Cap	L			
Cap-XL	Baseball Cap	XL			
TS-LC-S	Tee Shirt-Lincoln College emblem	S			
TS-LC-M	Tee Shirt-Lincoln College emblem	M			
TS-LC-L	Tee Shirt-Lincoln College emblem	L			
Shorts-S	Shorts	S			
Shorts-M	Shorts	M			
Shorts-L	Shorts	L			
Shorts-XL	Shorts	XL			
SP-LC-S	Sweat Pants-Lincoln College emblem	S			
SP-LC-M	Sweat Pants-Lincoln College emblem	M			
SP-LC-L	Sweat Pants-Lincoln College emblem	L			
SP-LC-XL	Sweat Pants-Lincoln College emblem	XL			

Create a new workbook from the **Lincoln FF Inventory Template** file for the January inventory data. Input the Cost and Quantity in Stock data, as shown below. Save the workbook as **Lincoln FF January Inventory** followed by your initials. Then print and close the workbook.

Item No.	Item Description	Size	Quantity in Stock	Cost	Value
SS-LC1-S	Sweat Shirt-Lincoln College emblem	S	45	$10.99	
SS-LC1-M	Sweat Shirt-Lincoln College emblem	M	62	12.99	
SS-LC1-L	Sweat Shirt-Lincoln College emblem	L	39	14.99	
Cap-L	Baseball Cap	L	489	4.99	
Cap-XL	Baseball Cap	XL	234	5.99	
TS-LC-S	Tee Shirt-Lincoln College emblem	S	65	4.99	
TS-LC-M	Tee Shirt-Lincoln College emblem	M	42	6.99	
TS-LC-L	Tee Shirt-Lincoln College emblem	L	97	8.99	
Shorts-S	Shorts	S	48	7.99	
Shorts-M	Shorts	M	22	9.99	
Shorts-L	Shorts	L	19	11.99	
Shorts-XL	Shorts	XL	7	13.99	
SP-LC-S	Sweat Pants-Lincoln College emblem	S	56	9.99	
SP-LC-M	Sweat Pants-Lincoln College emblem	M	31	11.99	

| SP-LC-L | Sweat Pants-Lincoln College emblem | L | 33 | 13.99 |
| SP-LC-XL | Sweat Pants-Lincoln College emblem | XL | 21 | 15.99 |

 ACTIVITY 16-2

You've been using Excel templates for a variety of tasks at your office. However, you notice that one of the files you thought you had saved as a template is actually saved as a regular Excel workbook. Use the Excel Help system to troubleshoot the problem and discover why it might have occurred. Write a short essay on how you should proceed.

WORKING WITH MULTIPLE WORKSHEETS AND WORKBOOKS

OBJECTIVES

Upon completion of this lesson, you should be able to:

- Name a range and use it in a formula.
- Copy and move data between worksheets.
- Copy an entire worksheet.
- Consolidate data from multiple worksheets.
- Move between open workbooks.
- Save a workspace.
- Define and modify workbook properties.

Estimated Time: 1.5 hours

VOCABULARY

Consolidating

Named range

Introduction

Just as you copy and move data within a worksheet, Excel lets you copy and move data between various worksheets. In this lesson, you will learn how to copy and move data between multiple worksheets and copy an entire worksheet with formats. You'll also discover how to save several workbooks together as a workspace.

When working with several worksheets, you may find it necessary to combine data from these worksheets and show the data total on a summary worksheet. You can easily combine data by using Excel's consolidation feature. The consolidation works much more easily if the range of data to be combined is a *named range*. As you will see, naming ranges proves to be very handy when creating formulas.

In addition, Excel lets you set file properties such as a file title, subject, and author to help you identify and find a file. Information such as the file size and date the file was created or modified are automatically saved for you.

Naming Ranges and Using in Formulas

Assigning names to specified ranges is another method for identifying and organizing data. Range names are especially useful in formulas. For example, you might have entered sales data for the month of April in the range B15:B20. To reference the data in a formula, as you've learned, you key the range of cells or select the range. By assigning a name, such as April, to the range, all you have to do is key the range of cells in place of the range address. For example, to sum the April data using a named range, you would enter =SUM(April). For most of us, April is much easier to key than B15:B20.

You assign a range name by selecting the range, choosing Name on the Insert menu, and then defining the range name in the Define Name dialog box.

> ### Hot Tip
> A shortcut for naming a range is to select the range you want to name, click the **Name** box in the Formula bar, key the range name, and press **Enter**. Be sure to press Enter as your last step or the name will not be entered.

STEP-BY-STEP 17.1

1. Open the **AE Step17-1** workbook from the data files, and save it as **Pizza Quarterly Sales** followed by your initials.

2. Select the range **B5:B9**.

3. Open the **Insert** menu, point to **Name**, and choose **Define**.

4. In the Define Name dialog box, the word *April* may already appear in the *Names in workbook* text box. Excel automatically looks for a range name by locating word(s) above the selected range. If the name does not appear, key **April** in the top box. Your screen should appear similar to Figure 17-1.

FIGURE 17-1
Define Name dialog box

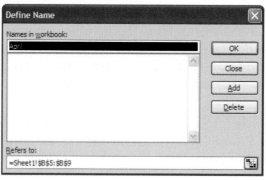

5. Click **Add** and then click **OK**.

STEP-BY-STEP 17.1 Continued

6. Select the range **C5:C9** and follow steps 3–5 to name this range **May**.

7. Select the range **D5:D9** and follow steps 3–5 to name this range **June**.

8. Click in cell **B10** and enter the formula **=SUM(April)**.

9. Click in cell **C10** and enter the formula **=SUM(May)**.

10. Click in cell **D10** and enter the formula **=SUM(June)**.

11. Save, print, and close the workbook.

> **Speech Recognition**
>
> If your computer has speech recognition capabilities, enable the Voice Command mode and say the appropriate steps to save and close the workbook.

> **Hot Tip**
>
> You can delete a range name by opening the Define Name dialog box, selecting the name, and clicking the **Delete** button.

Copying Data Between Worksheets

Copying data between worksheets in a workbook is similar to copying data within a worksheet. First, you select the cell or range of cells to be copied, click the Copy button (or choose Copy on the Edit menu), click in the location where you want the copied cell or range to appear, and then choose Paste.

In Excel, you can also copy data between worksheets by using the mouse in combination with the keyboard. To copy data using the mouse/keyboard combination, first select the range to be copied. Then place the mouse pointer on the border of the selected cell or range until it turns into an arrow, and hold down the left mouse button. While pressing the mouse button, press and hold down the Ctrl and Alt keys simultaneously. Drag the selection to the tab of the worksheet where you want the data copied. When you place your mouse pointer on the worksheet tab, that sheet becomes active. Then position the range where you want the data copied. The most important technique to remember is not to release the mouse button or the Ctrl and Alt keys until you are at the location in the worksheet where you want the data copied. Release the mouse button first and then release the other keys.

STEP-BY-STEP 17.2

1. Open the **AE Step17-2** workbook from the data files and save it as **Complete College Budget** followed by your initials. In this workbook, you want to create worksheets that show your budget for the Second Year, Third Year, and Fourth Year of college.

STEP-BY-STEP 17.2 Continued

2. Rename the worksheet tab Sheet1 as **First Year**, rename Sheet2 as **Second Year**, rename Sheet3 as **Third Year**, and rename Sheet4 as **Fourth Year**. Click the **First Year** worksheet tab to return to the worksheet with data. Your worksheet should appear as shown in Figure 17-2.

FIGURE 17-2
Complete College Budget worksheet

	A	B	C	D	E	F	G	H	I	J	K
1	College Budget										
2	First Year										
3											
4		Jan	Feb	Mar	Apr	May	Jun	Jul	Aug	Sep	Oct
5	Dorm Fee	$ 500.00	$500.00	$500.00	$500.00	$ -	$ 500.00	$500.00	$ -	$ 500.00	$500.0
6	Tuition	1,750.00	-	-	-	-	1,500.00	-	-	1,750.00	-
7	Books	200.00	-	-	-	-	150.00	-	-	200.00	-
8	Meals	200.00	200.00	200.00	200.00	-	200.00	200.00	-	200.00	200.0
9	Clothes	200.00	-	-	-	-	200.00	-	-	200.00	-
10	Gas	25.00	25.00	25.00	25.00	25.00	25.00	25.00	25.00	25.00	25.0
11	Misc.	100.00	100.00	100.00	100.00	100.00	100.00	100.00	100.00	100.00	100.0
12		$2,975.00	$825.00	$825.00	$825.00	$125.00	$2,675.00	$825.00	$125.00	$2,975.00	$825.0

First Year / Second Year / Third Year / Fourth Year /

3. Select the range **A1:M12** in the First Year worksheet and click the **Copy** button.

4. Select the **Second Year** worksheet and click in cell **A1**, if necessary.

5. Click the **Paste** button. Excel still retains the copied data on the Clipboard; therefore, you can paste this data again.

6. Select the **Third Year** worksheet. Select cell **A1** and click the **Paste** button.

7. Now let's try using the mouse/keyboard method for copying data between worksheets. Click the **First Year** worksheet tab.

> **Hot Tip**
>
> If you were copying to another open workbook, you would select the workbook on the Window menu, and then select the sheet to which you wanted to copy the data.

8. You will copy the expenses in two parts to get more practice using this method. Select the range **A1:G12**.

9. Place your mouse pointer over the border of the selected range until it turns into an arrow. When you see the arrow, press and hold down the left mouse button.

STEP-BY-STEP 17.2 Continued

10. While still holding down the left mouse button, press the **Ctrl** and **Alt** keys. Drag down to the **Fourth Year** worksheet tab. Notice how the Fourth Year worksheet becomes active. Drag the outline of the range until the range is located at **A1:G12**. Release the mouse button and then release the Ctrl and Alt keys. Your data should now be copied.

11. When using this method of copying, the range you are copying needs to be visible. Therefore, in the Fourth Year worksheet, scroll until columns H through M are visible, if necessary.

12. Click the **First Year** worksheet tab. Select the range **H4:M12**.

13. Repeat steps 9 and 10, dragging the range until you see the range H4:M12 displayed in the outline. Release the mouse button and then release the Ctrl and Alt keys. Your data should now be copied.

14. Click the **Second Year** worksheet tab, click in cell **A2**, and enter **Second Year**.

15. Click the **Third Year** worksheet tab, click in cell **A2**, and enter **Third Year**.

16. Click the **Fourth Year** worksheet tab, click in cell **A2**, and enter **Fourth Year**. Resize the columns in each worksheet to accommodate data.

17. Save, print, and close the workbook.

> **Hot Tip**
>
> To move data between worksheets, you first need to select the data you wish to move. Then, press and hold down the **Alt** key while dragging the selection to the worksheet tab and worksheet area where the data is to be pasted. Finally, release the mouse button and then release the Alt key.

Copying an Entire Worksheet

Various worksheets in a workbook often follow a similar format. For example, some companies keep monthly budgets that summarize income and expenses. Each month's figures are entered on a separate worksheet using the same titles, row headings, and column headings. Rather than reentering identical information over and over again, you can copy the contents of one worksheet to another. This process is a little different from the copy and paste functions you've been using.

When you copy an entire worksheet, you copy not only the data but all the formats as well. Excel actually inserts a new worksheet into the workbook to which the data and formats are copied. The worksheet tab of the new worksheet contains the name of the copied worksheet plus a (2), or the next available number, after the name to identify it as a duplicate. You can rename the new worksheet tab by double-clicking on it, typing a new name, and pressing Enter.

STEP-BY-STEP 17.3

1. Open the **AE Step17-3** workbook from the data files and save it as **Degree Budget** followed by your initials.

2. Click the **Fourth Year** tab.

3. Press and hold down the **Ctrl** key, place the mouse pointer over the **Fourth Year** sheet tab, and drag until you see a page icon to the right of the Fourth Year tab. Release the mouse button and then release the Ctrl key.

4. Click the **Fourth Year (2)** tab, if necessary. The worksheet should be identical to the Fourth Year worksheet.

5. Double-click the **Fourth Year (2)** sheet tab, key **Total Expenses** as the new sheet name, and press **Enter**.

6. In the Total Expenses worksheet, select cell **A2** and key **Total Expenses**.

7. Select the range **B5:M11** and press the **Delete** key. You will learn how to enter total expenses in the Consolidating Data section of this lesson.

8. Save and close the workbook.

Printing Multiple Worksheets

You can print multiple worksheets in a workbook by grouping the sheets. To group two or more worksheets together, click the tab of the first sheet in the group, hold down the Shift key, and click the tab of the last worksheet in the group. You'll notice that the tabs of the sheets in a group are selected. Also note that the word *Group* appears in parentheses in the title bar.

Print options, such as Landscape, may still be selected in the Page Setup dialog box. The selected print options will apply to each sheet in the group. To print the group, make sure the Active sheet(s) feature is selected in the Print dialog box.

STEP-BY-STEP 17.4

1. Open the **AE Step17-4** workbook from the data files and save it as **Budget Print** followed by your initials.

2. Select all four worksheets. Click the **First Year** sheet tab, hold down the **Shift** key, and click the **Fourth Year** tab. All sheet tabs should now be selected (grouped). Your worksheets should be displayed as shown in Figure 17-3.

STEP-BY-STEP 17.4 Continued

FIGURE 17-3
Grouped worksheets

	A	B	C	D	E	F	G	H	I	J	K
1	*College Budget*										
2	*First Year*										
3											
4		Jan	Feb	Mar	Apr	May	Jun	Jul	Aug	Sep	Oct
5	Dorm Fee	$ 500.00	$500.00	$500.00	$500.00	$ -	$ 500.00	$500.00	$ -	$ 500.00	$500.0
6	Tuition	1,750.00	-	-	-	-	1,500.00	-	-	1,750.00	-
7	Books	200.00	-	-	-	-	150.00	-	-	200.00	-
8	Meals	200.00	200.00	200.00	200.00		200.00	200.00	-	200.00	200.0
9	Clothes	200.00	-	-	-	-	200.00	-	-	200.00	-
10	Gas	25.00	25.00	25.00	25.00	25.00	25.00	25.00	25.00	25.00	25.0
11	Misc.	100.00	100.00	100.00	100.00	100.00	100.00	100.00	100.00	100.00	100.0
12		$2,975.00	$825.00	$825.00	$825.00	$125.00	$2,675.00	$825.00	$125.00	$2,975.00	$825.0
13											
14											
15											
16											
17											
18											
19											
20											
21											

First Year / Second Year / Third Year / Fourth Year /

Grouped Worksheets

3. Click the **File** menu and select **Page Setup**.

4. Select **Landscape Orientation** and select **Fit to**. Enter **1** in the *page(s) wide* box and **1** in the *tall* box if necessary. Click **OK**.

5. Click the **File** menu and choose **Print**.

6. Choose the **Active sheet(s)** option, if necessary, in the Print dialog box and click **OK**. Notice how each worksheet prints on a separate page with the data displayed.

> **Speech Recognition**
>
> If your computer has speech recognition capabilities, enable the Voice Command mode and say the appropriate steps to save and close the workbook.

7. Click any sheet tab to remove the grouped sheet feature.

8. Save and close the workbook.

Consolidating Data

Consolidating data is a method for bringing data from several worksheets into one worksheet. The consolidated data may be summed, averaged, counted, and so on. Excel provides several methods for consolidating data. First, you can use 3-D worksheet references in formulas, as you learned in the Introduction section. You can also combine values in several ranges of data from various worksheets. For example, if you have a worksheet of sales data for each of your regional offices, you can use the consolidation feature to summarize the data from each regional office into a total corporate sales worksheet.

You can also consolidate data by position and by category. Consolidating by position is simple to perform if the data within each worksheet area is arranged in the same order and location. This arrangement is typical if you've created worksheets from a template. Consolidating data by category combines data with matching labels from each worksheet. You can also consolidate data using named worksheet ranges.

In this exercise, you will learn how to combine data using named worksheet ranges. When you're finished consolidating the data, notice that the data in the Total Expenses worksheet does not contain formulas, just totals. You also will learn that consolidating data sets up the worksheet as an outline. To update the consolidation table automatically when the source data changes, you will need to select the *Create links to source data* check box.

S TEP-BY-STEP 17.5

1. Open the **AE Step17-5** workbook from the data files and save it as **Consolidated School Budget** followed by your initials.

2. Click each of the worksheet tabs to familiarize yourself with the worksheets, if necessary. No matter which sheet you are looking at, on the **Insert** menu, point to **Name**, and then choose **Define**. The ranges containing the data for each worksheet, B5:M11, are already named. Close the Define Name dialog box.

3. Click in cell **B5** in the Total Expenses worksheet.

4. Click the **Data** menu and choose **Consolidate**. The Consolidate dialog box appears as shown in Figure 17-4.

FIGURE 17-4
Consolidate dialog box

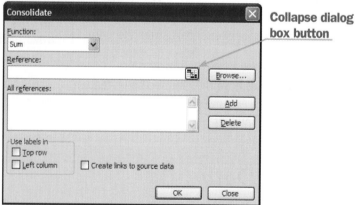

5. Click the **Collapse Dialog Box** button next to the *Reference* option.

6. Click the **First Year** worksheet tab and then type **FirstYear** (the range name for data) after the worksheet name.

7. Click the **Expand Dialog Box** button or press **Enter**.

8. Click the **Add** button. Notice how this reference now appears in the *All references* box.

STEP-BY-STEP 17.5 Continued

9. Click the **Collapse Dialog Box** button.

10. Click the **Second Year** worksheet tab. Key **SecondYear** after the worksheet name, if necessary. Excel may remember the range B5:M11 from the First Year worksheet. If so, you do not need to enter the range name as the range already appears.

11. Click the **Expand Dialog Box** button or press **Enter**.

12. Click the **Add** button.

13. Click the **Collapse Dialog Box** button.

14. Click the **Third Year** worksheet tab. Key **ThirdYear** after the worksheet name, if necessary. Excel may remember the range B5:M11 from the Second Year worksheet. If so, you do not need to enter the range name as the range already appears.

15. Press **Enter** or click the **Expand Dialog Box** button.

16. Click the **Add** button.

17. Click the **Collapse Dialog Box** button.

18. Click the **Fourth Year** worksheet tab. Key **FourthYear** after the worksheet name, if necessary. Excel may remember the range B5:M11 from the Third Year worksheet. If so, you do not need to enter the range name as the range already appears.

19. Press **Enter** or click the **Expand Dialog Box** button.

20. Click the **Add** button.

21. Click **OK**. Resize the columns in each worksheet to accommodate the data.

22. Print the Total Expense worksheet to fit on one page in Landscape orientation. You may want to change the Zoom option to view all of the worksheet on screen.

23. Save and close the workbook.

> **Hot Tip**
>
> After you have established a range in the Consolidate dialog box, you don't need to keep collapsing and expanding the dialog box. You can just click the appropriate tab, then click the **Add** button. Then, click the next tab and click the **Add** button.

Moving Between Workbooks

Just as you can move between worksheets within a workbook, you can also move between open workbooks. Excel lets you use the menu bar or the keyboard to move between workbooks. To use the menu bar, click the Window menu and then choose the desired workbook. To move between open workbooks using the keyboard, simply press Ctrl+F6. If you're able to view the taskbar, you can also move between workbooks by clicking on the button that displays the name of the desired workbook. (If the taskbar is full, there may be a single button for the Excel application which will open a submenu that contains a list of all the open Excel workbooks.)

STEP-BY-STEP 17.6

1. Open the **AE Step17-6a** and **AE Step17-6b** workbooks from the data files.

2. To move to the AE Step17-6a workbook, open the **Window** menu and then choose the **AE Step17-6a** workbook, which should be listed near the bottom of the Window menu.

> **Hot Tip** ⌖
>
> You can open multiple files at one time from the Open dialog box by holding down the **Ctrl** key while you select all of the files you want to open.

3. Press **Ctrl+F6** to move to the AE Step17-6b workbook. Remain in this screen for the next Step-by-Step.

Saving a Workspace

Excel's workspace feature is designed to save you time and increase your efficiency. For example, you may have a workbook that contains the sales information for your company and another workbook that contains inventory information. You like to have both workbooks open at the same time when making changes. Rather than going through the steps to open one workbook at a time, you can group the workbooks as a workspace instead. Then when you want to open the workbooks, you only have to open the workspace file. The workspace file appears in your file list with the workspace icon.

All the workbooks grouped in the workspace are displayed automatically when the workspace file is opened. The workbooks still remain as separate files that you can open individually if you prefer. The workspace saves information on window sizes, screen magnification, print areas, and other display settings. However, if the workbook files within the workspace are renamed or are moved, the workspace will not work.

Once a workspace is open, you can access each workbook by choosing its name from the Window menu within Excel, selecting from the taskbar, or by pressing Ctrl+F6. To close multiple workbooks simultaneously, hold down the Shift key and click the File menu. You will see that instead of the Close option, you now have the Close All option.

S TEP-BY-STEP 17.7

1. Open the **File** menu and choose **Save Workspace**. The Save Workspace dialog box appears.

2. Key **Semester Workspace** followed by your initials in the *File name* text box and click **Save**.

3. Close both workbooks.

4. Open the workspace by clicking the **Open** button and choosing **Semester Workspace**. Your screen should look similar to Figure 17-5.

FIGURE 17-5
Semester Workspace

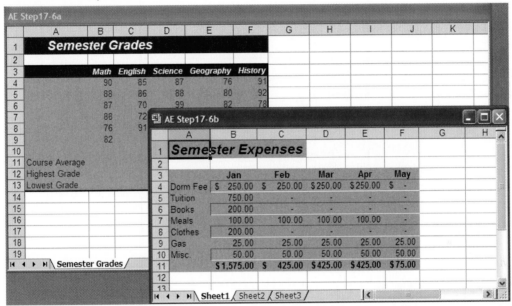

5. Check the taskbar and click each workbook to see that both workbooks are open independently.

6. Close both workbooks by pressing the **Shift** key, clicking on the **File** menu, and then choosing **Close All**.

Defining and Modifying Workbook Properties

Excel lets you set file properties that can help you identify and find a file. Information such as the file size and date the file was created or modified are automatically saved for you. However, you can add additional information about the file such as file title, subject, author, and company. This property information is entered in the Properties dialog box as shown in Figure 17-6.

FIGURE 17-6
Properties dialog box

STEP-BY-STEP 17.8

1. Open the **AE Step17-8** workbook from the data files and save it as **Sales Data** followed by your initials.

2. Select the **File** menu and then choose **Properties**.

3. Choose the **Summary** tab, if necessary, and delete any default information in the text boxes. Click in the *Author* text box and enter your name, and then click in the *Title* text box and enter **Quarterly Sales**.

4. Click **OK** to close the Properties dialog box.

5. Save and close the workbook.

Time Saver

Y̶ou can quickly select range names to enter into a formula, without having to type the range names, by pressing F3.

S̲TEP-BY-STEP 17-9

1. Open the **Pizza Quarterly Sales** workbook from your solution files.

2. Select cell **B12**.

3. Key **=AVERAGE(**

4. Press **F3**.

5. Select **April**.

6. Click **OK**.

7. Key **)** (close parenthesis).

8. Press **Enter**. Notice how the formula is now complete!

9. Close the file without saving any changes.

Integration Tip

You can quickly copy text and data from an Excel worksheet into a Word document. First, display both Excel and Word on your screen at the same time. Then, select the Excel range, hold down the **Ctrl** key, place your mouse pointer over the border of the range until you see a plus sign appear next to the arrow, and then drag into the Word document where you want the copied information to appear. Release the mouse button and then release the Ctrl key.

SUMMARY

In this lesson, you learned:

■ You can copy and move data between worksheets using the Cut, Copy, and Paste commands or by using the mouse and keyboard to drag and drop.

■ You can assign a range a name that may be used in formulas.

■ Multiple worksheets can be printed at the same time.

■ Consolidating data lets you sum, average, or use other functions to bring data from several worksheets into one.

■ You can move between open workbooks.

■ By saving files as a workspace, you can open many files at one time by choosing the workspace name.

■ File properties can be added to a file to help identify information such as the author, title, subject, or company.

VOCABULARY *Review*

Define the following terms:
Consolidating   Named range

REVIEW *Questions*

TRUE/FALSE

Circle T if the statement is true or F if the statement is false.

T   F   1. Named ranges may be used in formulas.

T   F   2. A workspace saves information about window sizes, print settings, screen magnifications, and other display settings.

T   F   3. Grouped worksheets may be printed as a group, with each worksheet being printed after the previous worksheet is printed.

T   F   4. Using the Ctrl and Alt keys in combination with the mouse lets you copy information from one worksheet to another.

T   F   5. Consolidating data brings data from several worksheets into one worksheet.

WRITTEN QUESTIONS

Write a brief answer to the following questions.

1. What are two methods for copying data between worksheets?

2. What is the purpose of data consolidation?

3. What is the purpose of a workspace?

4. Why would you want to group worksheets?

5. How would you open an individual worksheet after it has been saved in a workspace?

PROJECTS

PROJECT 17-1

1. Open the **AE Project17-1** workbook and save it as **2007 Monthly Payroll** followed by your initials.

2. Create a worksheet for each month of the year by copying the January worksheet and making the necessary changes.

3. Save, print, and close the workbook.

PROJECT 17-2

1. Open the **AE Project17-2a** and **AE Project17-2b** workbooks from the data files. Name the workspace **Payroll Workspace**, followed by your initials.

2. Close all workbooks.

3. Open the **Payroll Workspace**.

4. Check to be certain both workbooks opened.

5. Close any open workbooks.

CRITICAL *Thinking*

 ACTIVITY 17-1

Open the **AE Activity17-1** workbook. Consolidate the data to sum the Quarterly Totals figures for each department on the Year-End Report worksheet. Save the workbook as **Sales Review** followed by your initials and print the Year-End Report worksheet.

 ACTIVITY 17-2

As a manager in the personnel department of a major corporation, you are responsible for updating a number of Excel workbooks every week. You maintain workbooks on payroll, vacation schedules, health insurance benefits, time sheets, and expenses. Explain how you could use the Workspace feature in Excel to work more efficiently with these workbooks.

WORKING WITH SHARED WORKBOOKS

OBJECTIVES

Upon completion of this lesson, you should be able to:

- Create and modify a shared workbook.

- Merge shared workbooks.

- Track changes.

- Add password protection to a workbook.

Estimated Time: 1 hour

VOCABULARY

Case-sensitive

Merge

Password

Track changes

Introduction

Shared workbooks allow you to work with other users in the same workbook at the same time. After each has made their desired changes, you can integrate the changes from each user back into the main workbook. If multiple people are working on the same workbook, whether shared or not, as a safety feature you might want Excel to keep track of the changes made to the document using the Track Changes feature. For additional security, you can add password protection to workbooks. This allows others to view documents but not change them unless they know the password. These safety options prevent unwanted changes to workbooks being viewed and edited by multiple users.

Creating and Modifying a Shared Workbook

There may be a situation when several people need to work in a workbook at the same time. For example, an airline may have a workbook containing reservation rate information that is used by several Rate Analysis personnel. By allowing multiple Rate Analysis personnel to view and make changes to this file at one time, company efficiency is maximized.

If several people need to work in a file at the same time, you can save the file as a shared workbook and then make it available in a shared folder or on a shared network drive. To create a shared workbook, open the Tools menu and select Share Workbook. In the Share Workbook dialog box, select the Editing tab, which appears similar to Figure 18-1.

FIGURE 18-1
Editing tab in the Share Workbook dialog box

In order for users to work within a shared file simultaneously, select the *Allow changes by more than one user at the same time* option. This option also allows individual changes in a shared workbook to be merged.

Each time you open the shared workbook, Excel makes a copy of this file "behind the scenes" and you actually work in the copied file. When you're ready to bring the changes into one workbook, you **merge** the changes. The merging process combines changes from the copied files into a main workbook.

With a shared workbook, you can choose to track the changes made to the workbook by individual users. You can then choose to accept or reject these changes while merging.

The Advanced tab in the Share Workbook dialog box, shown in Figure 18-2, gives you options for managing changes to the workbook. These options are described in Table 18-1.

FIGURE 18-2
Advanced tab in the Share Workbook dialog box

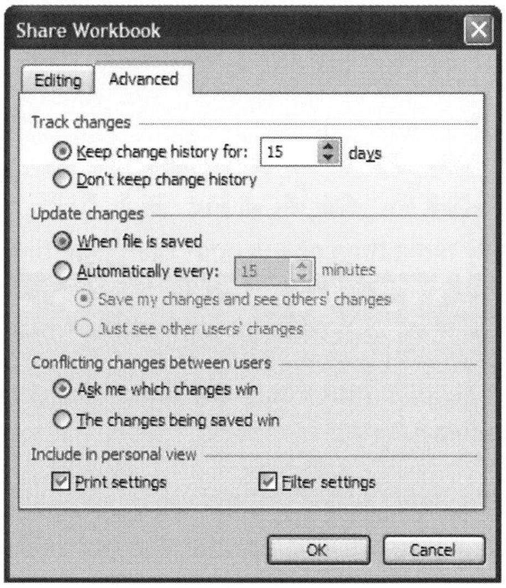

TABLE 18-1
Advanced Options in the Share Workbook dialog box

OPTION	DESCRIPTION
Track changes	The *Track changes* option maintains a history of changes made to the shared file based on the number of days selected. This option needs to be selected in order to merge changes from multiple copies of the same workbook. If you select the second option in this section, no history of changes will be kept.
Update changes	This option lets you update changes automatically or when the file is saved.
Conflicting changes between users	This first option displays the Resolve Conflict dialog box so that you may see which changes caused a conflict. You can then decide which changes to keep. Alternatively, you can choose the second option, which automatically keeps the changes made within the document being saved.
Include in personal view	The options in this section let you keep your personal print option, such as page breaks, as well as any filter settings.

When using shared workbooks, it's best to keep one copy of the shared workbook in a separate folder or drive. It can be used to merge changes. By using this procedure, you eliminate confusion as to which workbook is the final version with merged changes.

In this first Step-by-Step, you will create a shared workbook and make changes to it. This exercise uses the files on your hard drive since you may or may not have access to a network drive. The variation between creating shared workbooks on your hard drive versus a network drive is noted in the exercise.

STEP-BY-STEP 18.1

1. Open the **AE Step18-1** workbook from the data files and save it as **Airline Rates 1** followed by your initials.

2. Click the **Tools** menu, choose **Share Workbook**, and select the **Editing** tab in the Share Workbook dialog box, if necessary.

3. Click the **Allow changes by more than one user at the same time** option.

4. Click the **Advanced** tab.

5. Under the *Track changes* section, make sure the **Keep change history for** option is selected and enter **15** for the number of days.

6. Click **OK**. A message box appears telling you the workbook will now be saved. Click **OK**. Notice that the title bar of the workbook displays *[Shared]* after the workbook name as shown in Figure 18-3.

FIGURE 18-3
Shared workbook

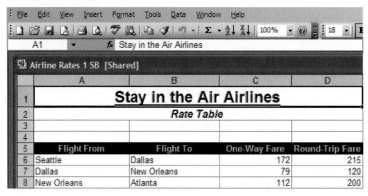

7. Save the **Airline Rates 1** shared workbook as **Airline Rates 2** followed by your initials. (*Note:* When using a shared workbook on a network, you would simply open and use the shared workbook.)

8. Save the **Airline Rates 2** shared workbook as **Airline Rates 3** followed by your initials.

9. Save the **Airline Rates 3** shared workbook as **Airline Rates Merged** followed by your initials.

10. Close all open workbooks.

STEP-BY-STEP 18.1 Continued

11. Open the **Airline Rates 1** shared workbook and make the following changes for the flight from Seattle to Dallas.

One-Way Fare	Round-Trip Fare
319	600

12. Save and close the workbook.

13. Open the **Airline Rates 2** shared workbook and make the following changes for the flight from New York to Chicago.

One-Way Fare	Round-Trip Fare
420	720

14. Save and close the workbook.

15. Open the **Airline Rates 3** shared workbook and make the following changes for the flight from Chicago to New York.

One-Way Fare	Round-Trip Fare
400	750

16. While still in the **Airline Rates 3** workbook, make the following changes for the flight from Los Angeles to Chicago.

One-Way Fare	Round-Trip Fare
125	250

17. Save and close the workbook.

> **Speech Recognition**
>
> If your computer has speech recognition capabilities, enable the Voice Command mode and say the appropriate steps to save and close the workbook.

Merging Shared Workbooks

To merge workbooks, simply select Compare and Merge Workbooks from the Tools menu. A list will appear from which you choose the copies of the shared workbooks to merge. After choosing the files you wish to merge, click OK. If any conflicting changes occur, such as two people who made a change within the same cell, you will be asked which change should be kept.

> **Hot Tip**
>
> You may select files that are not adjacent by using the Ctrl key when clicking on the filenames.

STEP-BY-STEP 18.2

1. Open the **Airline Rates Merged** workbook you saved in Step-by-Step 18.1.

2. Click the **Tools** menu and then select **Compare and Merge Workbooks**. The Select Files to Merge Into Current Workbook dialog box should appear.

3. Select the files **Airline Rates 1**, **Airline Rates 2**, and **Airline Rates 3** from the file list by first clicking the **Airlines Rates 1** file, holding down the **Shift** key, and then clicking **Airline Rates 3**. This action selects all three files. The Select Files to Merge Into Current Workbook dialog box should look similar to Figure 18-4.

FIGURE 18-4
Select Files to Merge into Current Workbook dialog box

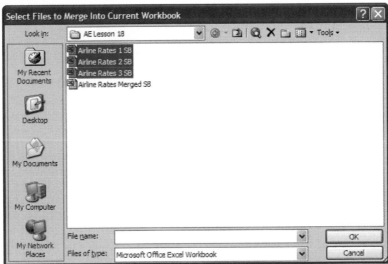

4. Click **OK**. If there are no conflicts, the merge will take place and no message boxes will be displayed. However, if there are conflicts, such as two people making changes to the same cell, you will be asked which change needs to be kept if you're using a shared network drive.

5. Print the merged workbook.

6. Save and close all workbooks.

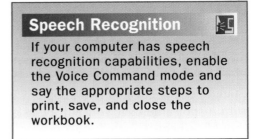

Speech Recognition

If your computer has speech recognition capabilities, enable the Voice Command mode and say the appropriate steps to print, save, and close the workbook.

Tracking Changes

When the *Track Changes* feature is turned on, Excel keeps track of changes made to cell contents, moves or copies, and insertions and deletions of rows or columns. Therefore, as you or other users make changes to a workbook, the changes are tracked. You or a reviewer may decide whether to accept or reject the changes. However, after you close your workbook and reopen it, the changes you have previously accepted will no longer appear with comments. Excel assumes that if you accepted the comments, you wanted to make them permanent and no longer recognizes them as changes.

After selecting Track Changes from the Tools menu, you choose Accept or Reject Changes. You can accept or reject each change one at a time, or you can accept or reject all changes at once by clicking Accept All or Reject All.

A few changes that Excel does not track are changes to sheet names, formats applied to cells or data, comments, and hidden rows or columns. However, you may select various tracking options in the Highlight Changes dialog box, such as whose changes you want to track, when you want to start tracking, and which cells may contain possible changes.

STEP-BY-STEP 18.3

1. Open the **AE Step18-3** workbook from the data files and save it as **Airline Rates – Track Changes** followed by your initials.

2. To have Excel track the changes that are made in this workbook, open the **Tools** menu, choose **Track Changes**, and then select **Highlight Changes**.

3. Select **Track changes while editing**. Notice the sentence after this option which indicates that selecting this option also shares your workbook. Then, choose the **Highlight changes on screen** option, if necessary.

4. Click the check box in front of *When* and select **All** from the drop-down list, if necessary.

5. Click the check box in front of *Who* and select **Everyone** from the drop-down list, if necessary.

STEP-BY-STEP 18.3 Continued

6. Click the check box in front of *Where*, click the **Collapse Dialog** button, and select the range **C6:D14**. Click the **Expand Dialog** button to return to the dialog box. Your screen should look like Figure 18-5. Press **Enter** or click **OK**.

FIGURE 18-5
Highlight Changes dialog box

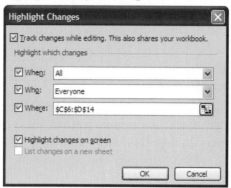

7. Click **OK** when asked to save the file.

8. Select cell **C7** and enter **377**. Select cell **D7** and enter **644**. Notice that comments are added to these cells with information about the change. The comment appears as a triangle in the upper left corner and a colored border is placed around the cell. To view the comment, place your mouse pointer over the changed cell.

9. Select cell **C9** and enter **555**.

10. Save the workbook. Your screen should appear similar to Figure 18-6.

FIGURE 18-6
Exercise worksheet showing tracked changes

	A	B	C	D
1	**Stay in the Air Airlines**			
2	*Rate Table*			
3				
4				
5	**Flight From**	**Flight To**	**One-Way Fare**	**Round-Trip Fare**
6	Seattle	Dallas	172	215
7	Dallas	New Orleans	377	644
8	New Orleans	Atlanta	112	200
9	Atlanta	Houston	555	400
10	Houston	San Francisco	354	715
11	San Francisco	Los Angeles	79	113
12	Los Angeles	Chicago	220	435
13	Chicago	New York	215	360
14	New York	Chicago	172	299
15				
16				
17				

STEP-BY-STEP 18.3 Continued

11. To accept or reject the changes, open the **Tools** menu, select **Track Changes**, and then choose **Accept or Reject Changes**. The Select Changes to Accept or Reject dialog box opens.

12. Click **OK** to begin the process. You should now see the Accept or Reject Changes dialog box similar to that shown in Figure 18-7.

FIGURE 18-7
Accept or Reject Changes dialog box

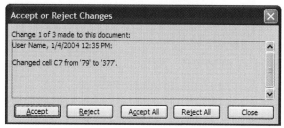

13. Click **Accept** for the changes in cells C7 and D7. Click **Reject** for the change to cell C9. Look at the comments on cells C7 and D7. These comments let you know that a change has taken place. Note that if you were to close this workbook and reopen it, the changes you previously accepted will no longer appear with comments.

14. Print, save, and close the workbook.

Adding Password Protection

To prevent a workbook file from being opened by an unauthorized person, you can password-protect a workbook. Then a person who does not know the password cannot open the file. A *password* refers to a sequence of characters, known only by you, that is required for access to the file. Passwords are *case-sensitive*. In other words, if a password contains capital letters, you will need to enter the password using the same capital letters. For example, if you enter CAT as the password, CAT (not cat or Cat) must be entered to open the workbook.

You can also use a password to prevent a file from being modified. Therefore, a person could open the workbook file, but they could not make any changes to it without knowing the correct password. In addition, both the password to open the file and a password to modify the file can be used together so that a person must know both passwords in order to open and make changes to the file.

A password can be set by clicking the Tools button arrow in the Save As dialog box and then selecting General Options. You may then add or remove password protection by selecting these options in the Save Options dialog box as shown in Figure 18-8. Also note that if you want to keep the previous version of a workbook as a backup, you can select the *Always create backup* option in the Save Options dialog box.

FIGURE 18-8
Save Options dialog box

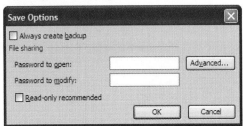

STEP-BY-STEP 18.4

1. Open the **AE Step18-4** workbook from the data files and save it as **Inventory – Password Protect** followed by your initials.

2. To password-protect a workbook, open the **File** menu and choose **Save As**.

3. Click the arrow on the **Tools** button in the dialog box's toolbar, and choose **General Options**.

4. In the Save Options dialog box, key **CAT** for the password in the *Password to open* text box and click **OK**.

5. Key **CAT** again in the Confirm Password dialog box. Click **OK**.

6. Choose **Save** in the Save As dialog box. A message box appears asking if you want to replace the existing file. Click **Yes**.

7. To see how password protection works, close the Inventory – Password Protect workbook. Reopen the **Inventory – Password Protect** workbook.

8. In the Password dialog box, key **CAT** and click **OK**. Your file should open.

9. To remove the workbook protection, Select **Save As** on the **File** menu.

STEP-BY-STEP 18.4 Continued

10. Click the drop-down arrow on the **Tools** button and choose **General Options**. The highlight should be in the *Password to open* text box.

11. Press the **Delete** key to remove the password from the *Password to open* text box and click **OK**.

12. Click **Save** to close the Save As dialog box and click **Yes** when asked if you want to replace the existing file. Then close the workbook.

Speech Recognition

If your computer has speech recognition capabilities, enable the Voice Command mode and say the appropriate steps to save the workbook.

Time Saver

You can quickly color-code worksheet tabs for easier identification or for grouping of related sheets.

1. Open a new workbook.

2. Right-click on the worksheet tab for **Sheet1**.

3. Choose **Tab Color**.

4. Select any blue color.

5. Click **OK**.

6. Close the workbook without saving any changes.

Integration Tip

You can save an Excel file in a Text (Tab delimited) (*.txt) format and then open the file in Microsoft Word. Some of the formats may not appear in the opened Word document, but you can quickly add formatting.

SUMMARY

In this lesson, you learned:

- A shared workbook allows several users to make changes to a file at the same time.

- Shared workbooks are merged so that the changes made by individual users may be combined and reflected in one file.

- Tracking changes gives you the option to accept or reject changes made to the file by other people using the file.

- Excel provides password protection for workbooks. If a person does not know the password, he or she will not be able to open the file.

VOCABULARY

Define the following terms:		
Case-sensitive	Password	Track changes
Merge		

REVIEW *Questions*

TRUE/FALSE

Circle T if the statement is true or F if the statement is false.

T F 1. Excel keeps the track changes history for only 15 days.

T F 2. Password protection on a file lets you open the file, but you cannot make changes to it.

T F 3. A shared workbook lets several people work in the same workbook at the same time.

T F 4. You select General Options from the Tools button menu in the Save As dialog box when you wish to enter a password to protect a file.

T F 5. The Merge Workbooks feature does not let you accept or reject a change if there is a conflict.

WRITTEN QUESTIONS

Write a brief answer to the following questions.

1. Explain what is meant by a shared workbook.

2. How many days will Excel keep a history of changes to a shared workbook?

3. When a file is opened, how can you tell whether it is a shared workbook?

4. In a shared workbook, what information does a comment display?

5. What option needs to be selected from the Tools menu to begin the merge shared workbook process?

PROJECTS

PROJECT 18-1

1. Open the **AE Project18-1** workbook from the data files and save it as a shared workbook with the filename **GMRE Real Estate 1** followed by your initials.

2. Create additional shared workbooks named **GMRE Real Estate 2, GMRE Real Estate 3,** and **GMRE Real Estate – Merged.**

3. Open all four workbooks and make the following sales price changes:

WORKBOOK NAME	CELL	CHANGE
GMRE Real Estate 1	H9	1992
GMRE Real Estate 2	G8	115000
GMRE Real Estate 2	I6	Sold
GMRE Real Estate 3	G6	130000

4. Save the workbooks. Close the edited workbooks. Merge the changed workbooks into **GMRE Real Estate – Merged.** Print the workbook.

5. Save and close all the workbooks.

PROJECT 18-2

1. Open the **AE Project18-2** workbook from the data files and save it as **Cost and Sales Table** followed by your initials.

2. Password-protect the workbook with the password **PASSWORD.**

3. Save and close the workbook.

4. Reopen the **Cost and Sales Table** workbook.

5. Type the password.

6. Close the workbook.

CRITICAL*Thinking*

ACTIVITY 18-1

You decide to create a shared workbook for people on your team. The team successfully uses the shared workbook for more than six months. Using Excel's Help system, explain how you would create a shared workbook for your team on a computer network.

ACTIVITY 18-2

Simon's Diamonds is a company owned by two brothers. As the accountant for this diamond company, you make changes to the diamond prices on a regular basis. Both brothers want to review your changes and they want the changed data to appear in a worksheet so they can review the new information. You decide to add the track changes options to your workbook, **AE Activity18-2**. You've just received the diamond price changes as shown below. Turn on the tracking feature and then make these changes. When you are done, save and print the worksheet. Save the workbook as **Simons Diamonds Price List** followed by your initials.

CELL	CHANGE
B6	2430.00
B11	9075.00

USING OUTLINES, SUBTOTALS, AND VALIDATION

Introduction

In this lesson you will learn about several Excel features that enable you to work with Excel in the most efficient ways possible. Outlines allow you to control which data in the worksheet is displayed or printed. In a large worksheet, grouping and outlining structured data lets you view important totals on your screen without displaying all the detail. And—best of all—Excel creates outlines for you in an instant! Another feature, the subtotal feature, automatically displays totals and subtotals for your data in the worksheet. This feature can save you time and increase your efficiency.

Adding Data Validation to your worksheet cells can assist you in monitoring the accuracy of the data that's being entered. Excel can even place circles around any invalid data to make sure that they stand out.

Excel will also let you step through the various parts of a formula to determine its accuracy. This tool, coupled with the Error Checking feature, helps you locate the error in your formula if the results of your formula are not appearing correctly in the cell.

Creating Outlines

An *outline* is especially helpful in large worksheets when you want to display only parts of a worksheet. For example, you may want to view column headings and totals in the worksheet. By applying the outline feature, detailed data is temporarily removed from display. You can then focus on the column totals.

Outlines are used in worksheets containing structured data, such as a data list or PivotTable list. Excel looks for column/row headings and formulas when creating outlines. An example of an outlined worksheet is shown in Figure 19-1.

FIGURE 19-1
Worksheet with outlined data

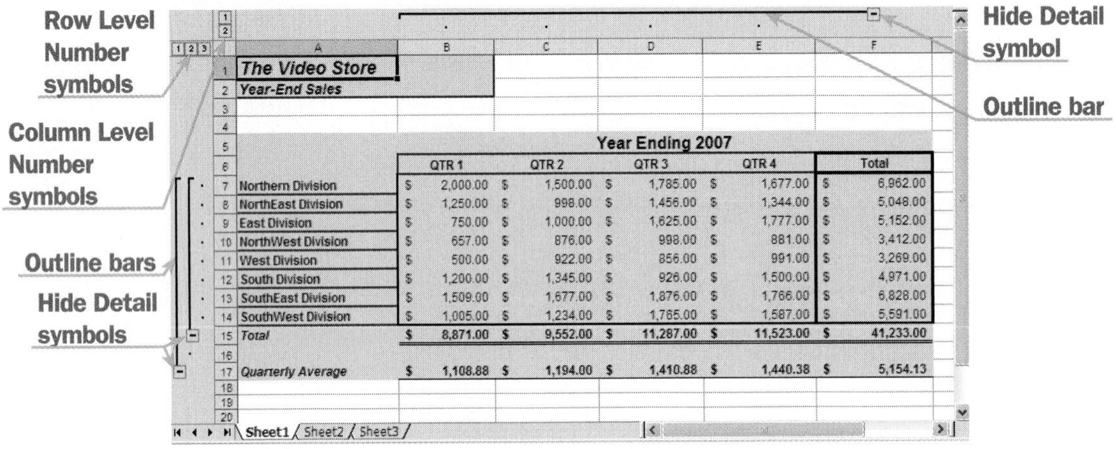

Notice the bars and symbols displayed to the left of rows and at the top of columns. These outline features let you control the amount of detail displayed. The bars show where the formulas are located within a worksheet. Clicking the Hide Detail symbol (the minus sign) hides data from view. The Show Detail symbol (the plus sign—not shown in Figure 19-1) lets you display the detailed data.

The column and row level symbols are the numbered symbols. The column level number symbols are displayed vertically and the row level symbols are displayed horizontally. These symbols let you display or hide details for the entire outline. For example, clicking 1 displays the least amount of detail. Clicking 3 shows the most detail.

STEP-BY-STEP 19.1

1. Open the **AE Step19-1** workbook from the data files and save it as **Video Store Outline** followed by your initials.

2. Click in any data list cell. Open the **Data** menu, point to **Group and Outline**, and then choose **Auto Outline** on the submenu. You should now see the outline symbols within the worksheet.

3. Click the **1** row level symbol. You should see the column headings and Quarterly Average row.

4. Click the **2** row level symbol. You should see the column headings, Total row, and Quarterly Average row.

5. Click the **Show Detail** symbol for the Total row. All the data should be displayed.

6. Click the **Hide Detail** symbol for the Quarterly Average row.

7. Save the workbook and then print the worksheet in landscape orientation. Remain in this screen for the next Step-by-Step.

Removing an Outline

Just as quickly as an outline can be displayed, it can be removed. When an outline is removed, worksheet data appears as it did originally, without the symbols and bars.

STEP-BY-STEP 19.2

1. Select any cell in the data list (in the Quarterly Average row). Open the **Data** menu, point to **Group and Outline**, and then choose **Clear Outline** on the submenu.

2. Save the workbook as **Video Store Outline - Removed**, followed by your initials.

3. Close the workbook.

> **Hot Tip**
>
> It's best to sort the structured data before adding outlines and subtotals.

Creating Subtotals

Excel instantly calculates column and row totals within the worksheet data with its subtotal feature. Subtotals are useful when you want to view results of the worksheet data but you don't want formulas permanently entered into the worksheet. For example, in a large worksheet containing formulas, it may take some time for the formulas to recalculate when worksheet data is changed. These recalculations can slow you down. Subtotals, however, calculate totals and grand totals, but they can be removed when you're finished viewing or printing.

When creating subtotals, Excel automatically puts the worksheet in an outline format to make it easier to view the location of the subtotals. Since your worksheet will be in an outline format, the Hide Detail and Show Detail symbols appear on your screen. Figure 19-2 shows a worksheet before subtotals are calculated and Figure 19-3 shows a worksheet where subtotals are applied. Notice how subtotals appear after each department.

FIGURE 19-2
Worksheet without subtotals

	A	B	C	D	E	F	G	H	I	J	K
1		P & K Industries									
2		Inventory									
3											
4	Stock Area	Item #	Description	Cost	Selling Price	Quantity in Stock	Total Product Value in Inventory				
5	K	K-CL04	Kitten Collar - 4"	$ 2.99	$ 5.50	45	$ 247.50				
6	K	K-CL04	Kitten Collar - 4"	$ 2.99	$ 5.50	86	$ 473.00				
7	K	K-CL04	Kitten Collar - 4"	$ 2.99	$ 5.50	554	$ 3,047.00				
8	K	K-CL04	Kitten Collar - 4"	$ 2.99	$ 5.50	252	$ 1,386.00				
9	K	K-CL05	Kitten Collar - 5"	$ 3.99	$ 6.50	66	$ 429.00				
10	K	K-CL05	Kitten Collar - 5"	$ 3.99	$ 6.50	123	$ 799.50				
11	K	K-CL05	Kitten Collar - 5"	$ 3.99	$ 6.50	504	$ 3,276.00				
12	K	K-CL05	Kitten Collar - 5"	$ 3.99	$ 6.50	279	$ 1,813.50				
13	K	K-KNLG	KittenNip - Large Bag	$ 7.00	$ 8.50	37	$ 316.58				
14	K	K-KNLG	KittenNip - Large Bag	$ 7.00	$ 8.50	308	$ 2,618.00				
15	K	K-KNLG	KittenNip - Large Bag	$ 7.00	$ 8.50	254	$ 2,159.00				
16	K	K-KNLG	KittenNip - Large Bag	$ 7.00	$ 8.50	414	$ 3,519.00				
17	K	K-KNSM	KittenNip - Small Bag	$ 4.50	$ 6.00	42	$ 252.37				
18	K	K-KNSM	KittenNip - Small Bag	$ 4.50	$ 6.00	271	$ 1,626.00				
19	K	K-KNSM	KittenNip - Small Bag	$ 4.50	$ 6.00	302	$ 1,812.00				
20	K	K-KNSM	KittenNip - Small Bag	$ 4.50	$ 6.00	387	$ 2,322.00				
21	K	K-TOYM	Kitten Toy - Mouse	$ 0.99	$ 2.10	28	$ 57.98				
22	K	K-TOYM	Kitten Toy - Mouse	$ 0.99	$ 2.10	382	$ 802.20				
23	K	K-TOYM	Kitten Toy - Mouse	$ 0.99	$ 2.10	111	$ 233.10				
24	K	K-TOYM	Kitten Toy - Mouse	$ 0.99	$ 2.10	468	$ 982.80				
25	P	P-CL05	Puppy Collar - 5"	$ 2.99	$ 5.50	100	$ 550.00				
26	P	P-CL05	Puppy Collar - 5"	$ 2.99	$ 5.50	23	$ 125.37				
27	P	P-CL05	Puppy Collar - 5"	$ 2.99	$ 5.50	419	$ 2,304.50				
28	P	P-CL05	Puppy Collar - 5"	$ 2.99	$ 5.50	90	$ 495.00				
29	P	P-CL07	Puppy Collar - 7"	$ 3.99	$ 6.50	156	$ 1,014.00				
30	P	P-CL07	Puppy Collar - 7"	$ 3.99	$ 6.50	600	$ 3,900.00				
31	P	P-CL07	Puppy Collar - 7"	$ 3.99	$ 6.50	456	$ 2,964.00				
32	P	P-CL07	Puppy Collar - 7"	$ 3.99	$ 6.50	117	$ 760.50				
33	P	P-CL10	Puppy Collar - 10"	$ 4.99	$ 7.50	27	$ 202.50				
34	P	P-CL10	Puppy Collar - 10"	$ 4.99	$ 7.50	54	$ 405.00				
35	P	P-CL10	Puppy Collar - 10"	$ 4.99	$ 7.50	493	$ 3,697.50				

FIGURE 19-3
Worksheet with subtotals

Subtotals

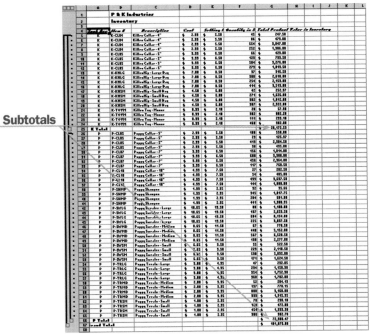

To use the Subtotals feature, select the Subtotals option on the Data menu. The Subtotal dialog box opens, as shown in Figure 19-4.

FIGURE 19-4
Subtotal dialog box

The options available in the Subtotal dialog box are described in Table 19-1.

TABLE 19-1
Options in the Subtotal dialog box

OPTION	DESCRIPTION
At each change in	This option lets you select the column of data that will determine how data is grouped for subtotaling. At each change in the values appearing in the column, a subtotal is entered.
Use function	This option lets you select the summary calculation to be performed. You may choose Sum, Average, Count, Min, Max, Product, or one of several statistical calculations.
Add subtotal to	This option determines in which column the subtotal will be placed.
Replace current subtotals	When subtotals already exist, this option replaces existing subtotals.
Page break between groups	This option creates a page break between each group subtotal.
Summary below data	This option inserts subtotals and a grand total below the detailed data.

S TEP-BY-STEP 19.3

1. Open the **AE Step19-3** workbook from the data files and save it as **P&K Inventory Totals** followed by your initials.

2. Now sort the data by Stock Area. Click in the data list and click **Sort** from the **Data** menu.

3. Select **Stock Area** in the *Sort by* box and choose **Item#** in the *Then by* box. Click **OK**.

4. Open the **Data** menu and then select **Subtotals**. The Subtotals dialog box opens.

5. Select **Stock Area**, if necessary, in the *At each change in* text box. This means a subtotal will calculate at each change in the Stock Area column.

6. Choose the Sum function if necessary in the *Use function* list box to calculate the subtotals.

7. Choose **Total Product Value in Inventory**, if necessary, in the *Add subtotal to* box. Click **OK**.

> **Hot Tip**
>
> You may sort data in a list by using the Sort Ascending or Sort Descending symbols on the toolbar or by opening the Sort dialog box.

STEP-BY-STEP 19.3 Continued

8. Click the **2** row level symbol to display only the subtotals and grand total. Your worksheet should appear similar to Figure 19-5.

FIGURE 19-5
Subtotals in worksheet

1 2 3		A	B	C	D	E	F	G	H	I
	1		P & K Industries							
	2		Inventory							
	3									
	4	Stock Area	Item #	Description	Cost	Selling Price	Quantity in Stock	Total Product Value in Inventory		
+	25	K Total						$ 28,172.53		
+	66	P Total						$ 72,900.47		
−	67	Grand Total						$ 101,073.00		

Show Detail symbols

9. Save the workbook and then print the worksheet. The worksheet should print as it appears on your screen. Remain in this screen for the next Step-by-Step.

Removing Subtotals

When subtotals are removed, the worksheet is displayed as it was before the subtotals were applied. You may remove the subtotals by selecting the Subtotals option on the Data menu and then clicking Remove All.

STEP-BY-STEP 19.4

1. Click the **3** row level symbol to redisplay all of the data.

2. To remove the subtotals, open the **Data** menu, select **Subtotals**, and then click the **Remove All** button in the Subtotal dialog box.

3. Save the workbook as **P&K Inventory Totals – Removed** followed by your initials. Then close the workbook.

Grouping Data

 The outline and subtotal features automatically determine your groups and add functions, such as SUM. There may be times, however, when you want to create your own groups. Excel's grouping feature lets you select items, such as rows or columns, and then *group* the data together for easier viewing. You may then add your own functions, such as Count, to any column in the list. The Count function counts the number of items.

STEP-BY-STEP 19.5

1. Open the **AE Step19-5** workbook from the data files and save it as **NL Corp–Grouped by City** followed by your initials.

2. Sort the data by city and then by last name. Make sure you have a cell selected in the data list, open the **Data** menu, and then choose **Sort**.

3. Select **City** in the *Sort by* box and choose **Last Name** in the *Then by* box. Click **OK**.

4. Insert a blank row at row 39 and also at row 42 to insert a blank row after the records located in Celina, Ohio and Edgerton, Ohio. (Right-click row heading **39** and choose **Insert** from the shortcut menu. Repeat this procedure for row 42.)

5. Select the range **A5:A38** to select the records located in Celina, Ohio. Open the **Data** menu, select **Group and Outline**, and then choose **Group** to open the Group dialog box. If necessary, select **Rows** from the Group dialog box and click **OK**. Notice how the outline symbols appear.

6. Repeat the grouping procedure in step 5 for the ranges **A40:A41** and **A43:A44**.

7. Select the range **A5:H44**. Open the **Data** menu and then select **Subtotals**. Click **Yes** when asked to include the column heading row. Select **City** in the *At each change in* text box. Choose **Count** if necessary in the *Use function* box. Then select **Zip Code** in the *Add subtotal to* box and deselect any other options that may be selected in this list. Click **OK**.

8. Click the **2** row level symbol to display only the subtotals and grand total. Your worksheet should appear as shown in Figure 19-6.

FIGURE 19-6
Group and Count data in worksheets

1 2 3		A	B	C	D	E	F	G	H
	1				**New Lock Corporation**				
	2				Employee List				
	3								
	4	Last Name	First Name	Address	City	State	Zip Code	Telephone	Division
+	39				Celina Count		34		
.	40								
+	43				Edgerton Count		2		
.	44								
+	47				Janesville Count		2		
−	48				Grand Count		38		
	49								

9. Save and print the worksheet.

10. Close the workbook and exit Excel.

Using Data Validation

 When you are entering data, or if someone else will add or change data in a worksheet, you may want to add Data Validation to the worksheet cells where values will be entered. *Validation* ensures that the data is entered as accurately as possible. For example, an inventory sheet may contain cells with cost values. If you know that the costs for the products is always between a certain range of values, you can put this range of values in Data Validation. Excel will alert the person entering the data if the cost value does not fall within the range specified. If the *Stop* style is selected in the Error Alert tab, you will not be allowed to enter any value that does not meet the criteria. Choosing the *Warning* style displays a warning dialog box, but allows the data to be entered. The *Information* style option also allows data to be entered, but simply displays an information box with a message that the data entered is invalid. Data Validation also lets you display a customized message when a cell is selected that tells the person entering data how the data should be entered or what values are acceptable.

STEP-BY-STEP 19.6

1. Open **AE Step19-6** from the data files and save the file as **Data Validation** followed by your initials.

2. Select the range **E6:E21**.

3. Click the **Data** menu and select **Validation**. The Data Validation dialog box opens with the Settings tab displayed.

4. In the Settings tab, click the drop-down arrow for the *Allow* list box and choose **Decimal**. This feature allows numbers with decimal places to be validated.

5. In the *Minimum* text box, enter **0** and in the *Maximum* text box, enter **15.00**. Adding these options allows for costs amounts between and including $0 and $15.00 to be entered in this range. The Settings tab should appear as shown in Figure 19-7.

FIGURE 19-7
Settings tab of the Data Validation dialog box

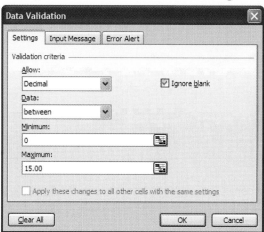

STEP-BY-STEP 19.6 Continued

6. Select the **Input Message** tab, click in the *Title* text box, and enter **Data Entry**.

7. Press the **Tab** key to move to the *Input message* text box and enter **Costs should be entered between $0.00 and $15.00.** as shown in Figure 19-8.

FIGURE 19-8
Input message tab of the Data Validation dialog box

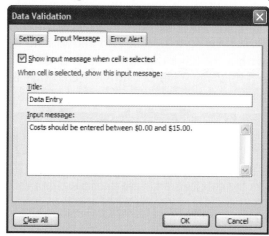

8. Click the **Error Alert** tab of the Data Validation dialog box, click in the *Title* text box, and enter **Error**.

9. Click in the *Error message* text box and enter **Costs must be between $0.00 and $15.00.** The Error Alert tab should look similar to Figure 19-9.

FIGURE 19-9
Error Alert tab of the Data Validation dialog box

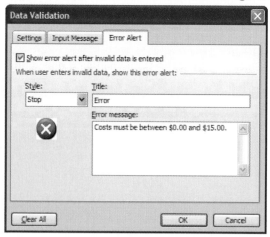

10. Click **OK**. Click in any cell in the range and notice how the input message is displayed.

STEP-BY-STEP 19.6 Continued

11. Click in cell **E7** and try to enter **120.00**. As soon as you press Enter or try to move from the cell, the Error dialog box displays as shown in Figure 19-10.

FIGURE 19-10
Error dialog box

12. Click **Retry** and then press **ESC** to cancel the editing of cell E7.

13. Save your workbook and remain in this screen for the next exercise.

Circling Invalid Data

If you choose an Error Alert to show a warning or an information message instead of a Stop message, then values outside of the criteria can be entered. In order to ensure that these invalid values are brought to your attention, you can have Excel circle cells that contain invalid data. This feature enables you to, at a glance, view the data on your worksheet that is outside the validation range. This is also useful in situations where a validation range has been added after data has already been entered. You can quickly and easily spot if any existing data is outside of the specified range.

To have cells with invalid data circled, simply select the Circle Invalid Data tool on the Formula Auditing toolbar. When you're finished viewing these cells, you can remove the circles by clicking the Clear Validation Circles tool. Also, closing the workbook will remove the validation circles.

STEP-BY-STEP 19.7

1. To display the Formula Auditing toolbar, if necessary, click the **Tools** menu, choose **Formula Auditing**, and then select **Show Formula Auditing Toolbar**.

2. Click the **Circle Invalid Data** tool so that the invalid data may be easily viewed. You will notice circles are placed around the cells containing the costs higher than $15.00 and less than $0.00 (the negative cost amount) that were incorrectly entered before the data validation rules were in place as shown in Figure 19-11.

FIGURE 19-11
Invalid data circled

	A	B	C	D	E	F	G	H
1		State of Texas College Fan-Fair						
2		Inventory						
3								
4								
5	Item No.	Item Description	Size	Quantity in Stock	Cost	Value		
6	SS-LC1-S	Sweat Shirt - State of Texas College College emblem	S	45	$ 10.99	$ 494.55		
7	SS-LC1-M	Sweat Shirt - State of Texas College College emblem	M	62	$ 12.99	$ 805.38		
8	SS-LC1-L	Sweat Shirt - State of Texas College College emblem	L	39	$			
9	Cap-L	Baseball Cap	L	489	$			
10	Cap-XL	Baseball Cap	XL	234	$			
11	TS-LC-S	Tee Shirt - State of Texas College College emblem	S	65	$			
12	TS-LC-M	Tee Shirt - State of Texas College College emblem	M	42	$			
13	TS-LC-L	Tee Shirt - State of Texas College College emblem	L	97	$ 8.99	$ 872.03		
14	Shorts-S	Shorts	S	48	$ 70.99	$3,407.52		
15	Shorts-M	Shorts	M	22	$ 9.99	$ 219.78		
16	Shorts-L	Shorts	L	19	$ 11.99	$ 227.81		
17	Shorts-XL	Shorts	XL	7	$ 13.99	$ 97.93		
18	SP-LC-S	Sweat Pants - State of Texas College College emblem	S	56	$ 9.99	$ 559.44		
19	SP-LC-M	Sweat Pants - State of Texas College College emblem	M	31	$ 11.99	$ 371.69		
20	SP-LC-L	Sweat Pants - State of Texas College College emblem	L	33	$ 13.99	$ 461.67		
21	SP-LC-XL	Sweat Pants - State of Texas College College emblem	XL	21	$ (0.99)	$ (20.79)		
22								
23								
24								

Data Entry
Costs should be entered between $0.00 and $15.00.

Input message

Invalid data circled

3. Select cell **E14** and enter **7.99**, and then select cell **E21** and enter **14.99**.

4. Save and close the workbook.

Hot Tip

If you want to remove the circles without changing the data, click the **Clear Validation Circles** tool on the Formula Auditing toolbar.

Placing a Watch on a Cell

 The *Cell Watch* feature in Excel lets you view the results of a cell in a separate window that appears within the worksheet. You may want to place a watch on a cell that contains a total if this cell is located out of view. For example, if you have an inventory worksheet and the cell with the total inventory cost is located at the bottom of the worksheet, you can have Excel display this total in a window using Cell Watch as shown in Figure 19-12. By simply clicking Show Watch Window on the Formula Auditing toolbar, you can easily keep on eye on total inventory costs.

You can have items in the Watch Window from multiple worksheets and workbooks. Simply double-clicking on an item being watched automatically takes you to that worksheet and the watched cell.

The Watch Window stays open as you move between different worksheets as well as different workbooks. The items being watched remain in the watch window until the worksheet is closed and reappear whenever the window is opened.

FIGURE 19-12
Cell Watch window

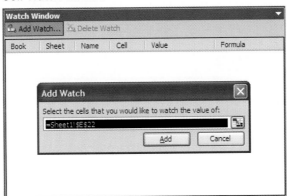

STEP-BY-STEP 19.8

1. Open **AE Step19-8** from the data files and save the file as **Cell Watch** followed by your initials.

2. If necessary, click the **Tools** menu, choose **Formula Auditing**, and then select **Show Formula Auditing Toolbar** to display the Formula Auditing toolbar.

3. Click the **Show Watch Window** button on the Formula Auditing toolbar to open the Watch Window dialog box.

4. Select cell **E22**.

5. Click the **Add Watch** option located under the title bar of the Watch Window dialog box. The correct information for cell E22 should be displayed in the Add Watch dialog box. Click **Add**. Your screen should appear similar to Figure 19-12 shown previously.

STEP-BY-STEP 19.8 Continued

6. To remove the cells being watched from the Watch Window, click the line in the Watch Window dialog box that displays the formula and its results, and then click the **Delete Watch** option.

7. To close the Watch Window, click the **Close** button in the upper-right corner of the Watch Window dialog box or click the **Show Watch Window** button on the Formula Auditing toolbar.

8. Remain in this screen for the next exercise.

Evaluating a Formula

 You can use the Evaluate Formula dialog box to step through a formula that is not giving you an error, but may not be producing the results that you're expecting. However, if your formula is producing an error, you can use the Error Checking feature in Excel to move through a formula one step at a time in order to find out why a formula isn't working. The Error Checking feature lets you move between the steps of the formula and move to the next or previous error. In the next exercise, you will use both features to review a formula.

STEP-BY-STEP 19.9

1. The Formula Auditing toolbar should still be displayed. (If not, select the **Tools** menu, choose **Formula Auditing**, and then select **Show Formula Auditing toolbar**.)

2. Select cell **G5** and enter the formula **=AVERAGE(C5:C21)*AVERAGE(D5:D21)**. Be sure to press **Enter** after typing the formula.

3. Select cell **G5** again and then click the **Evaluate Formula** tool on the Formula Auditing toolbar. You should see the formula displayed in the Evaluate Formula dialog box as shown in Figure 19-13. Notice that part of the formula is underlined—this underline represents the part of the formula that will be evaluated next.

FIGURE 19-13
Evaluate Formula dialog box

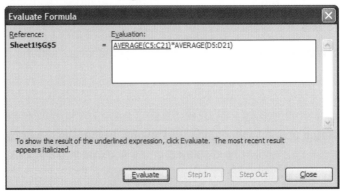

STEP-BY-STEP 19.9 Continued

4. Click the **Evaluate** button. Notice that the results of the first part of the formula are displayed and the second part is underlined.

5. Click the **Evaluate** button again. Notice that the results of the second part of the formula are now displayed (as well as the first part) as shown in Figure 19-14.

FIGURE 19-14
Evaluate Formula dialog box

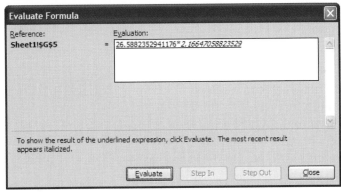

6. Click the **Evaluate** button once again and notice that the total formula results are now displayed.

7. Click **Close**.

8. Now let's use Error Checking to step through a formula. Select cell **H5** and enter the formula **=AVERAGE(C5:C21)*(D:D21)**. Be sure to press **Enter** after typing the formula. This cell should now contain #NAME? indicating a formula error.

9. Select cell **H5** again and then click the **Error Checking** tool on the Formula Auditing toolbar. The Error Checking dialog box appears as shown in Figure 19-15.

FIGURE 19-15
Error Checking dialog box

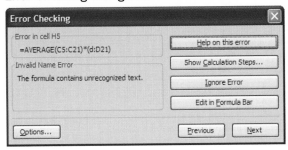

10. Click the **Show Calculation Steps** button and the Evaluate Formula dialog box appears.

11. Select the **Evaluate** button. Notice that the results of the first part of the formula are displayed; however, #NAME? appears in the second part of the formula indicating that this part of the formula is the problem.

STEP-BY-STEP 19.9 Continued

12. Click **Close** to close the Evaluate Formula dialog box and then select the **Edit in Formula Bar** button in the Error Checking dialog box.

13. Click in the Formula bar and edit the formula until it appears as **=AVERAGE(C5:C21)*(D5:D21)** and then click the **Resume** button in the Error Checking dialog box.

14. A message should appear indicating that the error check is complete for the entire sheet. Click **OK**.

15. Save and close the workbook.

Time Savers

Some of your formulas may contain a combination of relative and absolute references. Absolute reference is indicated by the $ symbol. When you enter a formula, you can easily change the column and row references between relative and absolute by pressing the F4 key. This key toggles you through each of the relative and absolute reference combinations.

> **Integration Tip**
>
> You can copy a range of data from Excel into Word or PowerPoint as a picture. First, select the range. Second, hold down the **Shift** key when selecting the **Edit** menu. And then select **Copy Picture**.

STEP-BY-STEP 19.10

1. Open a new spreadsheet.

2. Key **=B5** and do *not* press Enter.

3. Press **F4** several times to see how the referencing changes each time you press F4.

4. Close the spreadsheet.

You can quickly display or hide outline symbols on your screen using the keyboard.

S TEP-BY-STEP 19.11

1. Open the **Video Store Outline** workbook from your solution files that you saved previously.

2. Press **Ctrl+8** to hide the outline symbols.

3. Press **Ctrl+8** to redisplay the outline symbols.

4. Close the workbook without saving any changes.

SUMMARY

I n this lesson, you learned:

■ An outline is one method of organizing vast amounts of data in a worksheet. You can display as much or as little of the worksheet data as necessary.

■ Data can also be grouped in order to separate data for easier viewing.

■ Using the Subtotals feature is another method of handling large worksheets. Excel can quickly display totals, averages, and various other calculations without your having to enter these formulas.

■ Data Validation assists you by guiding you to enter accurate data and displaying a message if the data entered does not meet the validation criteria.

■ After setting Data Validation criteria, you can have Excel circle any invalid data that appears in the worksheet.

■ Cell Watch displays a formula and its results in a separate window in the worksheet so that you can watch the values in specific cells while you work in other areas of the worksheet or in other workbooks.

■ The Evaluate Formula and Error Checking features let you step through each part of a formula to review the results.

VOCABULARY

Define the following terms:		
Cell Watch	Outline	Validation
Group		

REVIEW *Questions*

TRUE/FALSE

Circle T if the statement is true or F if the statement is false.

T   F   1. You typically outline a worksheet that contains just a few rows of data.

T   F   2. You cannot print data that is outlined.

T   F   3. An outline lets you hide rows of data, but not columns.

T   F   4. You can total a group of data using the Subtotals feature.

T   F   5. Grouping gives you control over which type of data is put together in a worksheet.

T   F   6. Invalid data can be circled after the Data Validation criteria has been set.

T   F   7. The Evaluate Formula dialog box only displays the results of the formula.

T   F   8. The Error Checking dialog box gives you an option to edit the formula in the Formula bar.

T   F   9. You would select Data Validation to review the steps of a formula if #VALUE! is displayed in the cell.

T   F   10. You can remove a cell from being watched in the Watch Window.

WRITTEN QUESTIONS

Write a brief answer to the following questions.

1. What format does worksheet data need to be in before you can create an outline?

2. What is the purpose of an outline?

3. What is the greatest advantage of the Subtotals feature?

4. Why would you want to place a watch on a cell?

5. Describe the purpose of the level 1 symbol in an outlined worksheet.

PROJECTS

PROJECT 19-1

1. Open the **AE Project19-1** workbook from the data files and save it as **Outline Review** followed by your initials.

2. Create an outline for the worksheet data and hide the Spring, Summer, Fall, and Winter data. Your worksheet should display the Item and its Total, and the average Parts Sold.

3. Save and print the worksheet. Close the workbook.

PROJECT 19-2

1. Open the **AE Project19-2** workbook from the data files and save it as **Subtotals Review** followed by your initials.

2. Insert a column before column A. In cell **A5**, key **Region**.

3. In cell **A6**, key **NW** for Northwest region. Copy the contents of cell **A6** to **A7:A20**. Do the same for the other three regions, using **SW** for Southwest, **SE** for Southeast, and **NE** for Northeast.

4. Select the range **A5:E20** and use the Subtotal feature to Count the item numbers. Repeat this process for each region. (*Hint:* You need to select the range for the subtotals because there are blank rows between the regions.)

5. Click the **2** symbol.

6. Save and print the worksheet. Close the workbook.

PROJECT 19-3

1. Open **AE Project19-3** workbook from the data files and save it as **Data Validation Review** followed by your initials.

2. Select the range **B7:E14** and set data validation for the numbers with decimals in this range with **0** as the minimum value and **1875** as the maximum value.

3. Enter an **Input Message** with the title **Data Input** and the message **Value should be between $0 and $1875.**

4. Enter an **Error Alert** with the title **Data Error** and the message **Costs must be between $0 and $1875.** Try to enter invalid data in this range to be certain data validation is working.

5. Use the **Circle Invalid Data** feature to place a circle around any invalid data.

6. Save and print the worksheet. Close the workbook.

CRITICAL *Thinking*

ACTIVITY 19-1

In a new Excel workbook, create a data list of large household items. Include columns for item categories, item names, the year purchased, and the estimated value of the item. Format the data as desired. Use the outlining and subtotaling features to show and hide various levels of data and functions. Save the workbook as **Household Inventory**. A sample household inventory is shown in Figure 19-16.

FIGURE 19-16
Example of Household Inventory worksheet

	A	B	C	D
1	**Household Inventory**			
2				
3	*Category*	*Name*	*Year Purchased*	*Estimated Value*
4	Electronics	Television	2003	$ 2,500.00
5	Electronics	Stereo	2005	$ 1,400.00
6	Electronics	CD Player	2007	$ 450.00
7	Electronics	Speakers	2006	$ 1,800.00
8	**Electronics Total**			$ 6,150.00
9	Furniture	Living Room	2004	$ 3,500.00
10	Furniture	Bedroom 1	2002	$ 1,500.00
11	Furniture	Bedroom 2	2002	$ 1,750.00
12	Furniture	Armoire	2007	$ 1,800.00
13	Furniture	Dining Room	2006	$ 2,350.00
14	Furniture	Master Bedroom	2005	$ 1,600.00
15	**Furniture Total**			$ 12,500.00
16	Appliances	Stove	2007	$ 1,785.00
17	Appliances	Refrig	2005	$ 1,200.00
18	**Appliances Total**			$ 2,985.00
19	**Grand Total**			$ 21,635.00
20				

Sheet1 / Sheet2 / Sheet3 /

ACTIVITY 19-2

Using Excel's Help system, find the various features about correcting formulas.

USING ADVANCED EXCEL TOOLS

Introduction

Excel offers a variety of powerful tools that allow you to increase your productivity by calculating, predicting, and sharing information. This lesson discusses a number of these extremely useful tools.

The LOOKUP feature actually locates data for you based on the formula you enter. Trendlines are a terrific feature that can be added to charts to display the progression of data, which may be used to predict future data. Saving Excel data as XML lets others bring XML into Excel in the same format as the original file. Graphics can add a professional touch to your spreadsheets. Graphic images can be controlled by changing the contrast and brightness of the image and cropping out portions of the picture that you don't want to appear. And finally, digital signatures provide security for a file to let others know that the file has not been modified.

Creating LOOKUP Functions

LOOKUP functions allow you to find data that already exists rather than entering it yourself. For example, suppose you need to decide on the bonus amounts for your sales personnel. Their bonuses are based on their total sales for the quarter. Rather than calculating the bonuses yourself, you can let Excel's VLOOKUP function compare total sales to the bonus table and determine each salesperson's bonus. You use the VLOOKUP function when your table data is listed vertically from the top down. Use the HLOOKUP function when the data is listed horizontally from left to right.

In Figure 20-1, for example, salesperson Brenner's total sales for the first quarter were $374,220. Comparing these sales with the bonus table, you will see that Brenner's sales are above $350,000 and below $400,000. Therefore, Brenner should get a bonus of $18,000.

FIGURE 20-1
Worksheet with VLOOKUP function

	A	B	C	D	E	F	G	H	I
1			PCI, Inc.						
2									
3									
4			First Quarter Sales					Bonus Table	
5	Last Name	January	February	March	Total Sales	Bonus		Sales	Bonus
6	Brenner	$ 123,070.00	$ 122,590.00	$ 128,560.00	$ 374,220.00	$ 18,000.00		$ 250,000.00	$ 12,000.00
7	Guiterreux	$ 131,445.00	$ 127,220.00	$ 155,600.00	$ 414,265.00	$ 21,000.00		$ 300,000.00	$ 15,000.00
8	Larson	$ 139,820.00	$ 131,850.00	$ 182,640.00	$ 454,310.00	$ 24,000.00		$ 350,000.00	$ 18,000.00
9	Lichtenberg	$ 148,195.00	$ 136,480.00	$ 209,680.00	$ 494,355.00	$ 24,000.00		$ 400,000.00	$ 21,000.00
10	Stein	$ 156,570.00	$ 141,110.00	$ 236,720.00	$ 534,400.00	$ 27,000.00		$ 450,000.00	$ 24,000.00
11	Yoshida	$ 90,870.00	$ 110,990.00	$ 131,110.00	$ 332,970.00	$ 15,000.00		$ 500,000.00	$ 27,000.00
12	Total Sales	$ 789,970.00	$ 770,240.00	$ 1,044,310.00	$ 2,604,520.00			$ 550,000.00	$ 30,000.00
13									
14									
15									

STEP-BY-STEP 20.1

1. Open **AE Step20-1** from the data files and save it as **PCI Bonuses-First Quarter** followed by your initials.

2. Name the ranges to be used in the VLOOKUP formula. Select the range **E6:E11**.

3. Open the **Insert** menu, point to **Name**, and then click **Define**.

4. Enter **Total_Sales** in the *Names in workbook* text box, if necessary. Excel may already display this name since it appears above the selected cells.

5. Click **Add** and then click **OK**.

6. Select the range **H4:I12**.

7. Open the **Insert** menu, point to **Name**, and then click **Define**.

STEP-BY-STEP 20.1 Continued

8. Enter **Bonus_Table** in the *Names in workbook* text box, if necessary.

9. Click **Add** and then click **OK**.

10. Select cell **F6**.

11. Click the **Insert Function** button on the Formula bar. The Insert Function dialog box appears as shown in Figure 20-2.

FIGURE 20-2
Insert Function dialog box

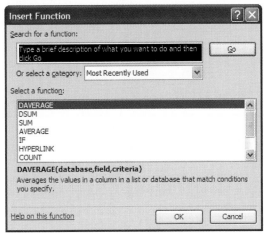

12. Key **lookup** in the *Search for a function* text box and click **Go**.

13. Select **VLOOKUP** in the *Select a function* list box and click **OK**.

14. In the Function Arguments dialog box, key **Total_Sales** in the *Lookup_value* text box. This is the range containing the total sales value that you want Excel to look up. (Notice that the total sales value for Brenner appears next to the *Lookup_value* text box.)

15. Key **Bonus_Table** in the *Table_array* text box. This is where the amounts are that you want Excel to compare with the sales amount.

STEP-BY-STEP 20.1 Continued

16. Key **2** in the *Col_index_num* text box. This represents the column number in the bonus table containing the data to be entered in cell F6. The completed dialog box should appear, as shown in Figure 20-3.

FIGURE 20-3
Function Arguments dialog box for VLOOKUP

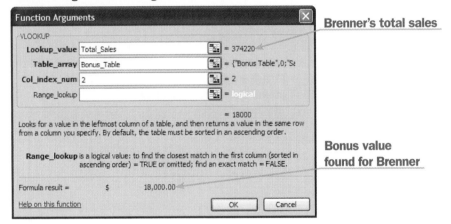

17. Click **OK**. Copy the formula in cell F6 to **F7:F11**.

18. Print the worksheet. Save and close the workbook.

Using the FORECAST Function and Adding Trendlines

Trendlines let you graphically display tendencies in data and, therefore, predict future values. A trendline can display a trend in data with such functions as FORECAST. FORECAST uses regression analysis to predict new values by assessing patterns in data, predicting future data. You can then display this data in a chart with a trendline. A *trendline* is a graphic presentation of movement in a data series. The Options tab in the Add Trendlines dialog box lets you choose future or backward units to also display in your chart.

In Figure 20-4, you may notice that several orders and the number of employees it took to fill those orders are shown at the top of the worksheet. At the bottom of the worksheet are order quantities. By using FORECAST, Excel predicts the number of employees it will take to fill orders of various quantities. These predictions should assist you in future planning when your company's orders start increasing.

FIGURE 20-4
Worksheet before the FORECAST function is applied

	A	B	C
1	**SCC Equipment Sales**		
2	*Projection of Number of Employees to Fill Orders*		
3			
4	*Number of Employees*	*Order Quantity*	
5	60	200	
6	70	280	
7	90	310	
8	150	380	
9	210	400	
10			
11	*Projected Number of Employees*	*Order Quantity*	
12		500	
13		600	
14		700	
15		800	
16		900	
17		1000	

STEP-BY-STEP 20.2

1. Open **AE Step 20-2** from the data files and save it as **SCC Employee Projection** followed by your initials.

2. Select cell **A12** and click the **Insert Function** button on the Formula bar.

3. Key **forecast** in the *Search for a function* text box and click **Go**.

4. Select **FORECAST** in the *Select a function* list box, if necessary. Click **OK**.

5. In the Function Arguments dialog box, key or select cell **B12** in the *X* text box.

6. Key **$A$5:$A$9** in the *Known_y's* text box.

STEP-BY-STEP 20.2 Continued

7. Key **$B$5:$B$9** in the *Known_x's* text box. The completed dialog box should look like Figure 20-5.

FIGURE 20-5
Function Arguments dialog box for FORECAST

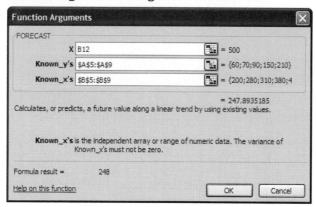

8. Click **OK**. Copy the formula in cell A12 to the range **A13:A17**. Your worksheet should appear similar to Figure 20-6.

FIGURE 20-6
Worksheet with FORECAST predictions

	A	B	C
1	**SCC Equipment Sales**		
2	*Projection of Number of Employees to Fill Orders*		
3			
4	*Number of Employees*	*Order Quantity*	
5	60	200	
6	70	280	
7	90	310	
8	150	380	
9	210	400	
10			
11	*Projected Number of Employees*	*Order Quantity*	
12	248	500	
13	319	600	
14	390	700	
15	461	800	
16	532	900	
17	602	1000	

9. To create a chart from the forecasted data, select the range **A11:B17**. Press **F11**. An instant chart appears.

10. To add a trendline to your chart, open the **Chart** menu and select **Add Trendline**. The Add Trendline dialog box is displayed.

11. Select **Linear**, if necessary.

STEP-BY-STEP 20.2 Continued

12. Click **OK**. Your chart and trendline should appear as shown in Figure 20-7.

FIGURE 20-7
Chart with trendline

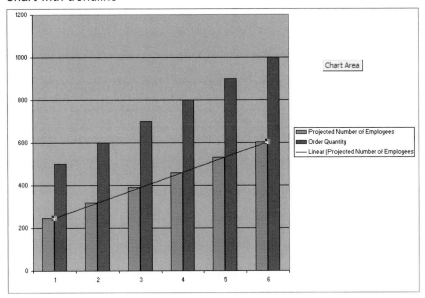

13. Save the workbook. Print the forecast worksheet and the chart.

14. Close the workbook.

Using XML to Share Data on the Web

In addition to a variety of other formats (some of which have been discussed in previous lessons), Excel supports Extensible Markup Language (XML). *XML* places structured data (such as data lists) in a format that can be read in a variety of applications. It is considered a universal format for data on the Web. You can load XML data from the Web directly into Excel. You may also save your Excel data in an XML format so that it can be exported to the Web. You can also modify the XML file as you would an Excel workbook.

In the following Step-by-Step, you will save structured data in a workbook as an XML file. Then you'll start your Internet browser and display the XML information. You are also going to view an XML file on the Web from your data files.

STEP-BY-STEP 20.3

1. Open **AE Step20-3** from the data files. Notice that the data is in a structured format with column headings and data listed below these headings as shown in Figure 20-8.

FIGURE 20-8
Worksheet with structured data

	A	B	C	D	E	F	G
1	Code	Description	Employee_ID	Order_Date	Order_Number	Price	Quantity
2	BP-BT	Beginning Computers	N440	4/4/05	3001	$ 15.95	67
3	BP-AT	Advanced Computers	N440	4/4/05	3002	$ 19.95	67
4	TT-TT	Advanced Spreadsheets	N550	4/6/05	3005	$ 19.95	65
5	BP-BP	Advanced Word Processing	S330	4/6/05	3006	$ 15.95	390
6	TT-BE	Beginning Presentations	S880	4/7/05	3007	$ 15.95	62
7	TT-AE	Advanced Presentations	S605	4/7/05	3008	$ 19.95	62
8	DB-DT	Beginning Database	S535	4/8/05	3009	$ 15.95	70
9	DB-BD	Beginning Web Sites	S535	4/12/05	3010	$ 15.95	80
10	DB-AD	Advanced Web Sites	S535	4/12/05	3011	$ 19.95	80
11	DP-DP	Desktop Web Sites for Beginners	N522	4/12/05	3012	$ 19.95	315
12	TT-BE	Beginning Presentations	N750	4/13/05	3013	$ 15.95	67
13	TT-AE	Advanced Presentations	N205	4/13/05	3014	$ 19.95	67
14	GR-CG	Computer Artist	N175	4/14/05	3015	$ 12.50	60
15	BP-BP	Word Processing for Professional	N522	4/15/05	3017	$ 15.95	90
16	BP-BT	Beginning Databases	N445	4/18/05	3018	$ 15.95	62
17	BP-AT	Advanced Databases	N175	4/18/05	3019	$ 19.95	62
18	DB-BD	Beginning Web Sites	N522	4/21/05	3020	$ 15.95	55
19	DB-AD	Advanced Web Sites	N522	4/21/05	3021	$ 19.95	55
20	BP-BT	Beginning Computers	N550	4/26/05	3022	$ 15.95	62
21	BP-AT	Advanced Computers	N175	4/26/05	3023	$ 19.95	62
22	CG-HM	History of Microcomputers	N660	4/27/05	3024	$ 9.95	60
23	DP-DP	Desktop Web Sites for Beginners	N445	4/27/05	3025	$ 19.95	95

2. You will now save this data file in an XML format. Open the **File** menu and choose **Save As**. Click the *Save as type* list arrow and select **XML Spreadsheet** as shown in Figure 20-9. Key **XML Exercise** followed by your initials in the *File name* text box and click **Save**. This file is now ready to share its data on the Web.

FIGURE 20-9
Save as type list box

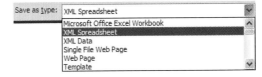

3. Select cell **B14** and change the description from *Computer Artist* to **Computer Graphics**.

4. Select range **A23:G23** and then click the **Cut** tool to cut this data. Then, choose cell **A15** and click the **Paste** tool to paste the cut data to replace the existing data. Change the order number to **3017** and the date of the order to **4/15/05**.

5. Choose cell **C7** and enter **S535** to change this employee's ID.

STEP-BY-STEP 20.3 Continued

6. Select the range **A23:G23**. While this range is selected, add the following data to the range by entering the data for a cell and then pressing **Enter** to move to the next selected cell in the range.

Cell	Data
A23	TT-BE
B23	Beginning Presentations
C23	N522
D23	4/28/05 (*Note*: Change the format if necessary.)
E23	3025
F23	13.95
G23	127

7. Save the file. XML Spreadsheet is the file type by default since the spreadsheet has already been saved as such. Then, close the file.

Now let's view the XML Exercise in the browser.

8. To open this file, go to Windows Explorer and select the folder with the location of the **XML Exercise** solution file you just saved. Right-click the file and select **Open With**. Then, select **Internet Explorer**.

9. You can now make changes to the file while you are viewing it. Select **Beginning Computers** in cell **B2** and change this description to read **Getting Started with Computers**.

10. You've now found out that the order in row **20** has been cancelled; therefore, click in cell **A20**, select the **Edit** menu, and then select **Delete**. Choose **Entire row** from the dialog box and click **OK**.

11. In addition, you found out the order date in cell **D6** is incorrect. The date should be **4/27/05**. Change the date.

12. Now, let's move row 6 to row 22 to put it in order by date. Select the range **A6:G6** and click the **Cut** tool. Select cell **A22** and click the **Paste** tool to replace the existing data.

13. To delete row 6, click in cell **A6**, select the **Edit** menu, and then select **Delete**. Choose **Entire row** from the dialog box and click **OK**.

14. To save the file, click the **File** menu, choose **Save As**, and save the file as **XML Exercise-2** followed by your initials.

15. Close your browser.

16. To see how this file has been changed, go into the Excel program, if necessary. Click **File**, **Open** and choose **XML Exercise-2**. View the changes.

17. Close the file.

Managing Attributes and Maps in XML Workbooks

XML saves structured data into a file that follows certain standard guidelines. Information about the structure and attributes of the file are contained in XML schemas and maps.

When using XML, you first create a workbook and then attach a custom XML schema to the workbook. After you attach the schema, an object called an XML map is automatically created. XML maps manage the elements between the XML schema and the XML data. The XML schema contains information about the structure of the worksheet data. Actually creating an XML schema from scratch is beyond the scope of this manual, but explanations for this effort can be found on the Microsoft Web site at *www.microsoft.com*.

In the following exercise, you will add headings in a worksheet and then map data from an XML data source into your worksheet under these headings. You will also change the heading attribute option, since you will be adding your own.

S TEP-BY-STEP 20.4

1. Open **AE Step20-4** from the data files and when the Open XML dialog box appears, choose **Use the XML Source task pane** and click **OK**. A message may appear letting you know that Excel will create a schema for you. Click **OK**. (AE Step20-4 is an empty worksheet that has been saved as an XML file.) If the List toolbar appears, simply close it since you will not be using it in this exercise.

2. To change the view options, click the **Options** button in the XML Source task pane and deselect **My Data Has Headings**, since you will be keying your own headings.

3. Enter the following headings into the indicated cells and increase column widths as necessary.

Cell	Heading
A1	Department
A3	Account
B3	Description
C3	Total

   Now you will begin mapping the data from the source information by dragging it to the desired location. *Note:* This data file contains a schema source since Excel automatically created a schema and map when you opened the file.

4. In the XML Source task pane, place your mouse pointer over **ns1:Department** and drag it to cell **C1**. Click in another cell and notice that cell C1 has a highlighted border. This border indicates that the cell is mapped.

5. Drag the following XML sources to the indicated cells.

Cell	XML Source
A4	ns1:Account
B4	ns1:Description
C4	ns1:Total

STEP-BY-STEP 20.4 Continued

6. Save the file as **My XML map** followed by your initials. Your screen should appear similar to Figure 20-10. *Note:* The down arrows in the cells let you sort the data.

FIGURE 20-10
XML mapping

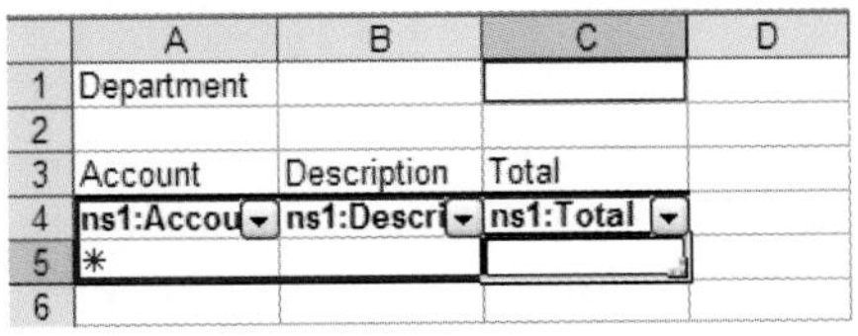

7. You have created the headings for the data you want to be brought in from the schema. Now, to import the actual data into these mapped cells, click the **Data** menu, choose **XML**, and then select **Import**. The Import XML dialog box appears.

8. Select **AE Step20-4** to import the data from the schema into the mapped locations you just created and then click **Import**. Notice how Excel populated the mapped fields. Your worksheet should look like Figure 20-11. *Note:* This data file includes a schema that contains the data you are about to import.

FIGURE 20-11
Worksheet with data mapped into it

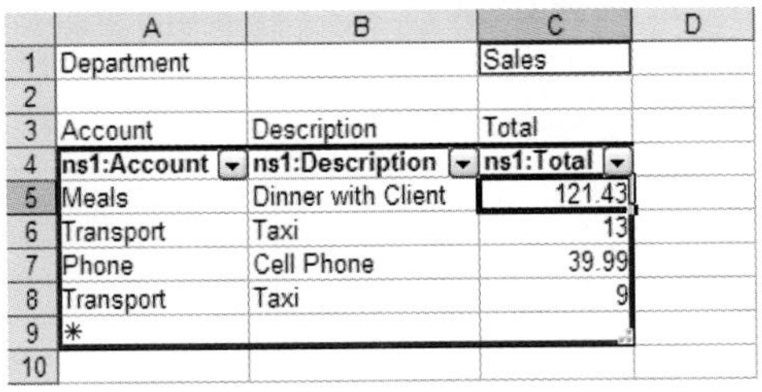

9. Save your workbook.

Mapped data can also be exported from Excel.

10. To export this data, click the **Data** menu, select **XML**, and then click **Export**.

11. Enter **XML Export** followed by your initials as the filename and click **Export**.

You can make changes to the mapped data. For example, to remove Description from the map, simply click the right mouse button while it is over the column heading of column **B** and choose **Delete** from the shortcut menu.

12. To delete a map from the worksheet, click the **XML Maps** button from the XML Source task pane. Select the map from the list in the XML Maps dialog box and then click the **Delete** button. Excel gives you a warning message that if you delete the XML map, you will no longer be able to import or export data using the XML map.

13. Choose **OK** to delete the map. Notice that the map is now removed from the XML Maps dialog box.

14. Click **OK** to close the XML Maps dialog box. Notice that the XML Source task pane is emptied.

15. Close the file without saving the changes.

Reformatting Graphics

Graphics can add a professional touch to your worksheets. You may enhance a worksheet that will be used in a presentation with graphics or you may want to stress a total on a worksheet. Excel includes default graphics with its program or you can import a picture into a workbook. After a graphic is inserted or a picture is imported, it can be resized to fit the desired location. The image may also be controlled by changing its contrast and brightness. If you want only a portion of the picture to appear, you can crop the picture.

The Drawing toolbar provides quick access to many reformatting options. For example, if you want to rotate a graphic, you can do so by simply clicking on the graphic to select it, choosing Draw from the Drawing toolbar, pointing to Rotate or Flip, and then selecting the desired action.

The most important step to editing graphics is to be sure that you select the graphic first. You can tell a graphic is selected when small selection handles (either circles or squares depending upon the type of graphic) appear on the corners and on the top and bottom of the graphic as shown in Figure 20-12. In the next exercise, you will add a graphic to a worksheet and then import and make changes to a picture.

FIGURE 20-12
Graphic with selection handles

Graphic with selection handles / Free Rotate handle

STEP-BY-STEP 20.5

1. Open the **AE Step20-5** workbook from the data files and save it as **Real Estate Acreage** followed by your initials.

Notice the red arrow that points to New Listings. You will now create arrows that point to the two new listings of 15.5 acres and 22 acres.

2. If necessary, display the Drawing toolbar by placing your mouse pointer over any toolbar, clicking the right mouse button, and then selecting **Drawing**.

STEP-BY-STEP 20.5 Continued

3. Click the **AutoShapes** button and then select **Block Arrows**.

4. Select the second arrow from the left on the top row (looks similar to the arrow already appearing on the screen).

5. Place your mouse pointer in cell **D9** at the left side, press and hold the mouse button down, and then drag about 1" to the right and slightly down to create a three-dimensional arrow. Then, release the mouse button.

6. If you need to move the arrow, click the arrow to select it, if necessary. Point to the arrow and you will see your cursor become a four-headed arrow. Press and hold the mouse button down and then drag the arrow to the desired location.

7. To resize the arrow, click the arrow to select it, if necessary. Place your mouse pointer over one of the selection boxes until your mouse pointer turns into a double-headed arrow. Then, drag the mouse until the arrow is the desired size.

8. To change the color of the arrow, place you mouse pointer over the arrow and double-click. The Format AutoShape dialog box appears, similar to Figure 20-13.

FIGURE 20-13
Format AutoShape dialog box

9. Select the **Colors and Lines** tab, if necessary, and click the arrow next to *Color* under the *Fill* section. Select a color of your choice and then click **OK**.

Now, let's make a copy of the arrow and place it in cell D10.

10. With the arrow still selected, click the **Copy** tool. Then, select cell **D10** and click the **Paste** tool. Move the graphic, if necessary, so that it is directly underneath the arrow in cell D9 and pointing to C10.

STEP-BY-STEP 20.5 Continued

11. First, rotate the graphic left. Click **Draw** on the Drawing toolbar, select **Rotate or Flip**, and then select **Rotate Left 90°**. Put the graphic back in its original position by choosing **Draw** again, selecting **Rotate or Flip**, and then selecting **Rotate Right 90°**.

To add a picture to a worksheet you must first select the cell where you want the picture to be placed and then insert the picture. You will now add a picture of the acreage that is for sale.

Hot Tip

You can also rotate a graphic by selecting the Free Rotate handle on the graphic and dragging the graphic to the desired rotation. The Free Rotate handle typically appears as a small green circle above a selection handle.

12. Select cell **F1**.

13. Select the **Insert** menu, choose **Picture**, and then click **From File**. Browse to select the folder with the data files for this lesson. You should see a graphic with the filename **J0144391.jpg**. Select this file and then click **Insert**. Notice the selection handles located around the picture. Practice moving and resizing this picture just as you did the graphic.

14. To change the brightness and contrast of the picture, place your mouse pointer over the picture and click your right mouse button to display the shortcut menu. Then, choose **Format Picture** and the Format Picture dialog box is displayed similar to Figure 20-14.

FIGURE 20-14
Format Picture dialog box

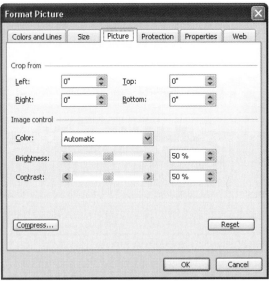

Notice the Brightness and Contrast bars located in the dialog box. By clicking the right or left arrows located to the side of these bars, you can increase or decrease the brightness and contrast.

15. Let's increase the brightness of the picture by clicking the right arrow on the *Brightness* bar until a brightness of **65%** appears in the *Brightness* text box. To increase the contrast, or differences between the colors, click the right arrow of the *Contrast* bar until **60%** appears in the *Contrast* text box.

STEP-BY-STEP 20.5 Continued

16. Click **OK**. View the results. Continue to change the brightness and contrast until the picture appears the way you desire.

17. Now try cropping the picture. If necessary, select the picture. Click the **Crop** tool from the Picture toolbar.

18. Place your mouse pointer over the middle top selection handle and drag down slightly to remove part of the sky.

19. Save and close the workbook.

Using Digital Signatures

Digital signatures are a security feature. They are added to a file when you want to let others know that a particular file was created by you and has not been modified. Files that have digital signatures can be viewed and modified. However, you cannot save any changes to the signed workbook without invalidating the signature. Digital signatures let everyone know that a file has not been changed from the point at which it was signed. This can be useful if you are sending files to others or if you want to verify the authenticity of a file coming from someone else.

One step that must occur before you can add a digital signature to a file is that you must create your own Digital Signature Certificate. This is done through a program called SelfCert that comes with your Office application. Once this has been done, the digital signature is available to all the Office applications. You should note that multiple digital signatures can be created on one personal computer and you should also note that someone else could create a certificate with your name.

Once a digital signature has been added to a file, making any change in the workbook and then trying to save the workbook will result in the digital signature being removed. Likewise, if you try to save the workbook (with the same name or with a different name) the digital signature will be removed. Before the digital signature is removed a message box appears to warn you that your action will result in the digital signature being removed.

In this next exercise, you will first create your own digital signature and then you will add it to a workbook file.

STEP-BY-STEP 20.6

1. Open the **AE Step20-6** workbook.

First you will create a digital signature for your Office applications.

2. Click the **Start** menu and then select **Run**.

3. Choose the **Browse** button in the Run dialog box and then locate the **Selfcert.exe** file. Typically, this file is located in C:\Program Files\Microsoft Office\Office 11\Selfcert.exe. If Microsoft Office is installed in another location, simply choose the path where it is located.

4. After selecting the Selfcert.exe file, click **Open** in the Browse dialog box and click **OK** in the Run dialog box. The Create Digital Signature dialog box appears.

5. Type your first and last name in the *Your name* text box and then click **OK**. The SelfCert Success dialog box will appear to let you know that the signature was successfully created. Click **OK**.

Your digital signature has been created and is available to all Office applications. Now you will attach it to the open workbook.

6. To add the digital signature to your workbook, click the **Tools** menu and then select **Options**.

7. Click the **Security** tab and then choose **Digital Signatures** to display the Digital Signatures dialog box.

8. Click the **Add** button, choose *digital signature with your name*, and then click **OK**.

9. Choose **OK** to close the Digital Signatures dialog box and then click **OK** again to close the Options dialog box.

10. Close your workbook without saving the changes.

Time Saver

You can instantly create random numbers in Excel. These random numbers are typically generated as numbers between 1 and 50 or 1 and 100.

Integration Tip

To take a picture of what's currently on your computer screen and put it into another document, simply press **PrintScreen** (**PrtSc**) and paste it into Word or PowerPoint. You can then resize and crop the graphic as desired.

STEP-BY-STEP 20.7

1. Open a new workbook.

2. In cell **A1**, key **=rand()*50**. Press **Enter**.

3. Select cell **A1**.

4. Place your mouse pointer over the selection handle in the lower right corner of the cell and drag to cell A10 to copy the formula. Notice how random numbers between 1 and 50 appear in the cells where the formula was entered and copied.

5. Close the workbook without saving any changes.

> **Hot Tip**
>
> To create random numbers between 1 and 100, key **=rand()*100**. Be sure to press **Enter** after you type the formula.

SUMMARY

In this lesson, you learned:

- LOOKUP functions find and compare worksheet data providing results based upon values found in specific regions of the worksheet.

- A trendline in a chart shows tendencies in data and predicts future values.

- XML is a universal format for structured data on the Web. Worksheets can be saved in an XML format and then shared on the Web.

- XML data can be mapped into a worksheet.

- Graphics can be added to a worksheet to enhance its appearance or to highlight certain elements. Once added, a graphic can be cropped and reformatted for brightness, contrast, and size.

- Digital signatures are a security feature that lets everyone who opens a file know that it has not been modified.

VOCABULARY

Define the following terms:

Trendline	XML

REVIEW *Questions*

TRUE/FALSE

Circle T if the statement is true or F if the statement is false.

T   F   1. VLOOKUP locates data in a range that displays vertically.

T   F   2. Structured data may be saved as an XML spreadsheet.

T   F   3. A trendline is added to a chart after the chart is created.

T   F   4. The FORECAST function can help predict future requirements, such as number of employees needed.

T   F   5. Graphics can be cropped and resized from their original format.

WRITTEN QUESTIONS

Write a brief answer to the following questions.

1. What format must worksheet data be in before you can save it as an XML spreadsheet?

2. What is the difference between the LOOKUP functions?

3. What are the steps for adding a trendline to a chart?

4. Describe two methods for rotating graphics.

5. What is the purpose of the mapping function for XML data?

PROJECTS

PROJECT 20-1

1. Open the **AE Project20-1** workbook from the data files and save it as an XML Spreadsheet named **CCI Company Addresses** followed by your initials. Close the file.

2. Open the **CCI Company Addresses** file in your browser by going to Windows Explorer, selecting **Open With,** and then choosing **Internet Explorer.**

3. Change the El Paso city to Ysletta.

4. Save the file as **CCI Shared Data** followed by your initials, and close the workbook.

5. Open the **CCI Shared Data** file in Excel and view the changes.

6. Close any open workbooks.

PROJECT 20-2

1. Open the **AE Project20-2** workbook from the data files and save it as **Trendline Review** followed by your initials.

2. Use the **FORECAST** function to predict the number of refrigerator mechanics needed.

3. Create a Bar chart for the forecasted data on a separate sheet.

4. Add a linear trendline to the chart.

5. Save and print the worksheet. Close the workbook.

CRITICAL *Thinking*

SCANS ACTIVITY 20-1

Your boss at Houston Eastern/Central Oil asks you to create LOOKUP functions in the company's program management report indicating the incentive pay for each program manager as his or her projects are completed on time. The company's program management report is located in **AE Activity20-1.** Save the workbook as **Houston Eastern Central Oil** followed by your initials. You will need to name the *Total Project Completion in Dollars* range **Project_Dollars** and the *Incentive Table* range **Incentive_Table** in order to use these named ranges in your LOOKUP formula.

SCANS ACTIVITY 20-2

As the new manager of a hospital management company, you discover that the company shares information about the individual hospitals on the Web using XML. You want to find more information about XML. Use Excel's Help feature to locate information about the XML language. Write a brief essay describing XML.

ADVANCED MICROSOFT EXCEL

COMMAND SUMMARY

FEATURE	MENU COMMAND	TOOLBAR BUTTON	LESSON
Angle Counterclockwise	Format, Cells, Alignment		9
Chart Creation	Insert, Chart		20
Clear Validation Circles			12, 19
Circle Invalid Data			12, 19
Comma Format	Format, Cells, Number		9
Currency Format	Format, Cells, Number		9
Data Table			9
Decrease Decimal	Format, Cells, Number		9
Fill Cell with Color	Format, Cells, Patterns		9
Font	Format, Cells, Font	Arial	9
Font Color	Format, Cells, Font		9
Font Size	Format, Cells, Font	10	9
Format Chart Area	Format, Selected Chart Area		9
Hide Detail	Data, Group and Outline, Hide Detail		19
Increase Decimal	Format, Cells, Number		9
Percent	Format, Cells, Number		9
Print Preview	File, Print Preview		10
Remove Arrows	Tools, Formula Auditing, Remove All Arrows		13
Remove Dependent Arrows	Tools, Formula Auditing, Show Formula Auditing Toolbar		13
Remove Precedent Arrows	Tools, Formula Auditing, Show Formula Auditing Toolbar		13
Show Detail	Data, Group and Outline, Show Detail		19
Show Watch Window			19
Sort Ascending	Data, Sort		11
Sort Descending	Data, Sort		11

FEATURE	MENU COMMAND	TOOLBAR BUTTON	LESSON
Trace Dependents	Tools, Formula Auditing, Remove Arrows		13
Trace Error	Tools, Formula Auditing, Remove Arrows		13
Trace Precedents	Tools, Formula Auditing, Remove Arrows		13
Undo	Edit, Undo		9

REVIEW *Questions*

TRUE/FALSE

Circle T if the statement is true or F if the statement is false.

T F   1.   If you use the Subtotals feature to place totals within a worksheet, the totals cannot be removed.

T F   2.   A workspace typically contains two or more related workbook files.

T F   3.   Protection may be added to cells, worksheets, or an entire workbook.

T F   4.   A template usually contains titles, subtitles, formats, and formulas, but not data.

T F   5.   Excel may be shared with external users by saving a structured worksheet as an XML file.

FILL IN THE BLANK

Complete the following sentences by writing the correct word or words in the blanks provided.

1.   You save a worksheet as _____ if you want to publish it on the Web.

2.   A(n) _____ may be created and saved as a toolbar button to automate repetitive tasks.

3.   The _____ _____ feature can display a message stating that the data entered is not valid.

4.   _____ _____ allow(s) you to enter data in a criteria range and copy the records that meet this criterion into another range in the worksheet.

5.   To trace cells that refer to a formula, to locate errors, or to find a formula that uses a specific cell, use the _____ tools.

PROJECTS

PROJECT 1

A data list containing employee information for the New Western Sales Company appears in **AE Project1**. You will want to filter information about the employees from time to time. Therefore, you will set up the worksheet for Advanced Filtering.

1. Open the **AE Project1** workbook from the data files and save it as **New Western Sales Filter** followed by your initials.

2. Copy the column headings from **A4:H4** to **A45:H45** as the headings for the *Criteria* range.

3. Copy the column headings from **A4:H4** to **A50:H50** as the headings for the *Copy to* range.

4. You want to find the records for the employees working for the Southwest region. Key **Southwest** in cell **H46** of the criteria range.

5. Save the workbook.

6. Start the **Advanced Filter** process and use **A45:H46** for the *Criteria* range.

7. Use **A50:H70** for the *Copy to* range.

8. You should see nine records for employees working for the Southwest region as displayed in Figure UR-1.

FIGURE UR-1

	A	B	C	D	E	F	G	H
45	Last Name	First Name	Address	City	State	Zip Code	Telephone	Division
46								Southwest
47								
48								
49								
50	Last Name	First Name	Address	City	State	Zip Code	Telephone	Division
51	Dominquez	Gary	Rt.4. Box 332	Fairfield	Wisconsin	72279	292-555-0089	Southwest
52	Gonzalez	Lisa	Rt.3. Box 157	Fairfield	Wisconsin	72291	292-555-9987	Southwest
53	Hernandez	Sally	19 West Travis	Fairfield	Wisconsin	72300	292-555-4607	Southwest
54	Hix	JoAnne	5656 Rain Forest	Fairfield	Wisconsin	72303	292-555-8411	Southwest
55	Holder	Howard	P.O. Box 1910	Fairfield	Wisconsin	72306	292-555-2705	Southwest
56	Hussam	Ali	Rt.3. Box 9090	Fairfield	Wisconsin	72309	292-555-5875	Southwest
57	Linebarger	Sallye	Rt. 5	Fairfield	Wisconsin	72330	292-555-7143	Southwest
58	Tanquez	Trevor	Rt. 4. Box 798	Fairfield	Wisconsin	72357	292-555-3339	Southwest
59	Thomsen	Barb	347 Edison Dr	Fairfield	Wisconsin	72360	292-555-3345	Southwest

9. Print the worksheet.

10. Save the workbook as **New Western Sales Southwest Region** followed by your initials.

11. Create another **Advanced Filter** to display employees in the **Northwest Region** in the *Copy to* range. You will need to increase the size of the **Copy To** range to row **75**.

12. Save the workbook as **New Western Sales Northwest Region** followed by your initials. You should see 21 records displayed.

13. Print and close the workbook.

PROJECT 2

Two workbooks, **AE Project2a** and **AE Project2b**, contain information about the employees of Virginia Manufacturing Corporation. Since you use these files together on a frequent basis, you will create a workspace for these files.

1. Create a workspace for the **AE Project2a** and **AE Project2b** workbooks from the data files. Name the workspace **Salaries Workspace**, followed by your initials.

2. Close all workbooks.

3. Open Salaries Workspace.

4. Check to be certain both workbooks opened.

5. Close any open workbooks.

PROJECT 3

The expenses for your school budget are recorded in **AE Project3**. You want to create a macro that will format titles and subtitles for each worksheet in the workbook.

1. Open the **AE Project3** workbook from the data files and save it as **School Budget** followed by your initials.

2. Create a macro named **Titles** to add formats to titles and subtitles in the workbook.
    A. Make the macro add **bold, 16-point, dark blue** formats to the worksheet title.
    B. Make the macro add **bold, 12-point, italic, black** formats to the worksheet subtitles.

3. Add a **dark blue** font color to the ranges **A6:A12** and **B5:L5**.

4. Use the macro to add the title and subtitle formats to each worksheet in the workbook.

5. Save, print, and close the workbook.

PROJECT 4

The **AE Project4** file is an income statement. You will create a scenario for lease and utility expense variances.

1. Open the **AE Project4** workbook from the data files and save it as **Forestry Services Scenarios** followed by your initials.

2. Create a scenario named **Current Expenses** using the expenses currently showing on your screen.

3. Create a scenario named **Lease and Utilities Variance**. Enter the following expenses into the scenario.
    Cell B10 (Lease): **83725**
    Cell B11 (Utilities): **6625**

4. Click the **Show** button and then click the **Close** button. This action displays the scenario directly on the worksheet.

5. Print the **Income Statement** sheet. Save and then close the workbook.

CRITICAL *Thinking*

JOB 1

You are the owner of a T-shirt screen-printing corporation called Corporate Tees. Your company designs and screen-prints T-shirts for schools, companies, and travel agencies. For each sale, you would like Excel to print an invoice that includes the sales price, the quantity sold, and the total sale. The invoice will also display your company's logo and address. Use the following steps to complete the invoice.

1. Open the **AE Job1** workbook from the data files.

2. Enter a formula in cell **E18** that multiplies **quantity** by **price** for a **total price**.

3. Change the font size for the invoice information you've entered to **12** points, if necessary.

4. Save this file as a *template* with the filename **Corporate Tees** followed by your initials. Save this file in the folder containing your other files (not the Templates folder).

5. Resave the **Corporate Tees** template as a workbook with the filename **Evansville High School Sale** followed by your initials.

6. Add the invoice information shown in Figure UR-2. Remember that you don't need to enter the total price, as the formula you entered previously should calculate this total.

FIGURE UR-2

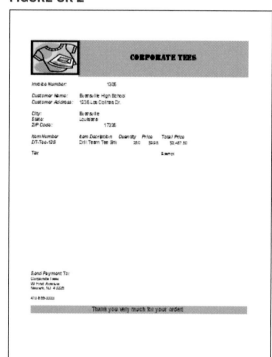

7. Save the workbook and print the invoice.

8. Close the workbook.

 JOB 2

Joe Emblem, your boss at Football 2007, a sports apparel shop, has just handed you the January inventory list. He would like you to enter the items into Excel. Since you will be maintaining a monthly inventory, you decide to create a template file.

1. Key the data shown in Figure UR-3.

FIGURE UR-3

	A	B	C	D	E
1					
2					
3					
4					
5					
6	Item No.	Item Description	Size	Cost	Selling Price
7	SS-LC1-S	Exercise Shirt-Football 2005 emblem	S		
8	SS-LC1-M	Exercise Shirt-Football 2005 emblem	M		
9	SS-LC1-L	Exercise Shirt-Football 2005 emblem	L		
10	Cap-L	Cap	L		
11	Cap-XL	Cap	XL		
12	TS-LC-S	Polo Shirt-Football 2005 Emblem	S		
13	TS-LC-M	Polo Shirt-Football 2005 Emblem	M		
14	TS-LC-L	Polo Shirt-Football 2005 Emblem	L		
15	Shorts-S	Walking Shorts	S		
16	Shorts-M	Walking Shorts	M		
17	Shorts-L	Walking Shorts	L		
18	Shorts-XL	Walking Shorts	XL		
19	SP-LC-S	Exercise Pants-Football 2005 Emblem	S		
20	SP-LC-M	Exercise Pants-Football 2005 Emblem	M		
21	SP-LC-L	Exercise Pants-Football 2005 Emblem	L		
22	SP-LC-XL	Exercise Pants-Football 2005 Emblem	XL		

2. Add the title **Football 2007** in cell A1. Change the font to **16** points and add a bold format.

3. Add the subtitle **Monthly Inventory** in cell A2. Change the font to **12** points and add bold and italic formats.

4. Merge and center both the title and subtitle across columns A through E.

5. Add a pale blue background color to the merged cells containing the title and subtitle.

6. Place a thick box border outlining the merged cells with the title and subtitle.

7. Add a border to each cell containing the column headings.

8. Save the file as a *template* with the filename **Football 2007 Monthly Inventory**. Save the template file in the folder with your data files.

9. Save the **Football 2007 Monthly Inventory** template as a workbook with the filename **Football 2007 – January Inventory**.

10. Add the *Cost* and *Selling* information for January shown in Figure UR-4.

FIGURE UR-4

	A	B	C	D	E	F
1		Football 2007				
2		Monthly Inventory				
3						
4						
5						
6	Item No.	Item Description	Size	Cost	Selling Price	
7	SS-LC1-S	Exercise Shirt-Football 2995 emblem	S	$ 10.99	$ 15.99	
8	SS-LC1-M	Exercise Shirt-Football 2995 emblem	M	$ 12.99	$ 17.99	
9	SS-LC1-L	Exercise Shirt-Football 2995 emblem	L	$ 14.99	$ 19.99	
10	Cap-L	Cap	L	$ 4.99	$ 7.99	
11	Cap-XL	Cap	XL	$ 5.99	$ 8.99	
12	TS-LC-S	Polo Shirt-Football 2995 Emblem	S	$ 4.99	$ 6.99	
13	TS-LC-M	Polo Shirt-Football 2995 Emblem	M	$ 6.99	$ 8.99	
14	TS-LC-L	Polo Shirt-Football 2995 Emblem	L	$ 8.99	$ 10.99	
15	Shorts-S	Walking Shorts	S	$ 7.99	$ 9.99	
16	Shorts-M	Walking Shorts	M	$ 9.99	$ 11.99	
17	Shorts-L	Walking Shorts	L	$ 11.99	$ 13.99	
18	Shorts-XL	Walking Shorts	XL	$ 13.99	$ 15.99	
19	SP-LC-S	Exercise Pants-Football 2995 Emblem	S	$ 9.99	$ 13.99	
20	SP-LC-M	Exercise Pants-Football 2995 Emblem	M	$ 11.99	$ 15.99	
21	SP-LC-L	Exercise Pants-Football 2995 Emblem	L	$ 13.99	$ 17.99	
22	SP-LC-XL	Exercise Pants-Football 2995 Emblem	XL	$ 15.99	$ 19.99	
23						

11. Apply the **Currency** format to the *Cost* and *Selling* data.

12. Save and print the workbook. Close the workbook.

 JOB 3

The Home Design Corporation has hired you to review its human resources department. After looking over the organizational structure, you decide to analyze management salary. You want to see if the salary correlates to the number of years of experience to be certain that the salaries reflect time-in-service.

1. Key the data shown in Table UR-1.

TABLE UR-1

YEARS OF EXPERIENCE	MANAGER'S SALARY
3	$55,000
14	$120,000
31	$320,000
36	$340,000
8	$75,000
43	$490,000
19	$180,000

2. Save the Workbook as **Human Resource Analysis** followed by your initials.

3. Run a correlation analysis of the years of experience and the salaries.

4. Write a brief statement regarding whether or not years of experience and salary are correlated and why you came to this conclusion.

5. Save and print the workbook. Close the workbook.

SCANS JOB 4

You are the Inventory Supervisor for a college bookstore. In an effort to assure that your assistant enters correct information when he is entering products into the inventory workbook, you decide to add data validation to the workbook. The data validation will display a message when the cell is selected explaining how the data should be entered. In addition, you will have an error message appear if the cost entered does not meet the validation criteria.

1. Open the **AE Job4** workbook from the data files and save it with the filename **Cost Validation** followed by your initials.

2. Select the range **E6:E25** and set data validation for the numbers within it. Allow decimal numbers between $0 and $25.00.

3. Save an Input Message with the title **Data Input** and the message **Value should be between $0 and $25.00**.

4. Save an Error Message with the title **Data Error** and the message **Costs must be between $0 and $25.00**. This should be a **Stop** style error message.

5. Try to change a cost amount to **$27.00** to be certain that the validation is working correctly.

6. Save and print the workbook. Close the workbook.

APPENDIX A

WINDOWS BASICS

OBJECTIVES

Upon completion of this lesson, you should be able to:

- Organize your desktop.
- Open programs using the Start button.
- Shut down your computer.
- Move, resize, open, and close a window.
- Use scroll bars.
- Use menus.
- Use Windows Help.

VOCABULARY

Mouse
Pointer
Desktop
Channels
Scroll bar
Scroll box
Scroll arrows
Maximize button
Minimize button
Close button
Restore Down button
Menus
Dialog box
Drop-down menu
Mnemonic
Link
Folder

This appendix will familiarize you with the Windows 2000 and Windows XP operating systems. It contains the basic information you need to move around your desktop and manage the files, folders, and other resources you work with every day. It also discusses the Windows Help system.

Starting Windows

If Windows is already installed, it should start automatically when you turn on the computer. If your computer is on a network, you may need some help from your instructor.

STEP-BY-STEP A.1

1. Turn on the computer.

2. After a few moments, Windows 2000 or Windows XP appears.

Navigating in Windows

The Mouse

A *mouse* is a device that rolls on a flat surface and has one or more buttons on it. The mouse allows you to communicate with the computer by pointing to and manipulating graphics and text on the screen. The *pointer*, which appears as an arrow on the screen, indicates the position of the mouse. The four most common mouse operations are point, click, double-click, and drag.

OPERATION	DESCRIPTION
Point	Moving the mouse pointer to a specific item on the screen.
Click	Pressing the mouse button and quickly releasing it while pointing to an item on the screen. (The term *click* comes from the noise you hear when you press and release the button.)
Double-click	Clicking the mouse button twice quickly while keeping the mouse still.
Drag	Pointing to an object on the screen, pressing and holding the left mouse button, and moving the pointer while the button is pressed. Releasing the button ends the drag operation.

The Desktop

When Windows starts up, the desktop displays on the screen. The *desktop* is the space where you access and work with programs and files. Figure A-1 illustrates a typical desktop screen. Your screen may vary slightly from that shown in the figure. For example, your screen may display icons that were installed with Windows or shortcut icons you've created. You can customize and organize your desktop by creating files, folders, and shortcuts.

FIGURE A-1
Typical desktop screen

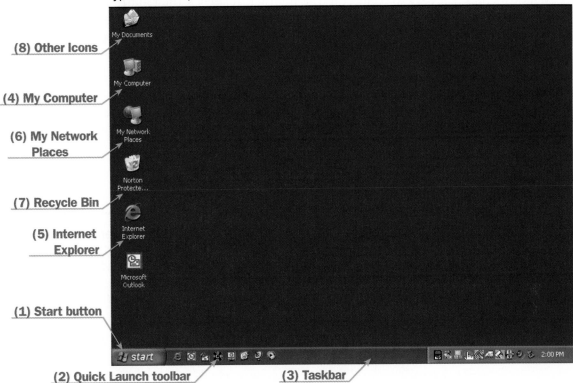

The main features of the desktop screen are labeled and numbered on the figure and discussed below:

1. The Start button brings up menus that give you a variety of options, such as starting a program, opening a document, finding help, or shutting down the computer.

2. The Quick Launch toolbar to the right of the Start button contains icons so you can display the desktop or quickly start frequently used programs.

3. The taskbar, located at the bottom of the screen, tells you the names of all open programs.

4. My Computer is a program that allows you to see what files and folders are located on your computer.

5. Internet Explorer is a Web browser that allows you to surf the Internet, read e-mail, or download your favorite Web sites right to your desktop.

6. My Network Places shows all the folders and printers that are available to you through the network connection, if you have one.

7. The Recycle Bin is a place to get rid of files or folders that are no longer needed.

8. Other icons, or small pictures, represent programs waiting to be opened.

9. Windows makes it easy to connect to the Internet. Just click the Launch Internet Explorer Browser button on the Quick Launch toolbar. The Quick Launch toolbar also has buttons so you can launch Outlook Express, view channels, and show the desktop.

With Windows you can incorporate Web content into your work by using the Active Desktop, an interface that lets you put "active items" from the Internet on your desktop. You can use *channels* to customize the information delivered from the Internet to your computer. By displaying the Channel bar on your desktop you can add, subscribe to, or view channels.

S TEP-BY-STEP A.2

1. Click the **Launch Internet Explorer Browser** button on the Quick Launch toolbar.

2. Click the **Show Desktop** button on the Quick Launch toolbar to display the Windows desktop.

Desktop

3. Click the **Internet Explorer** button on the taskbar to return to the browser window.

4. Choose **Close** on the **File** menu to close Internet Explorer.

5. Point to the **Start** button.

6. Click the left mouse button. A menu of choices appears above the Start button, as shown in Figure A-2.

FIGURE A-2
Start menu in Windows XP

7. If you are using *Windows 2000*, Point to **Settings** and then click **Control Panel** on the submenu. If you are using *Windows XP*, click **Control Panel** on the menu. A new window appears. The title bar at the top tells you that Control Panel is the name of the open window. If necessary, click the button in the Task pane that says **Switch to Classic View**. Leave this window open for the next Task.

Using Windows

Many of the windows you will work with have similar features. You can work more efficiently by familiarizing yourself with some of the common elements, as shown in Figure A-3 and explained below.

FIGURE A-3
Window elements

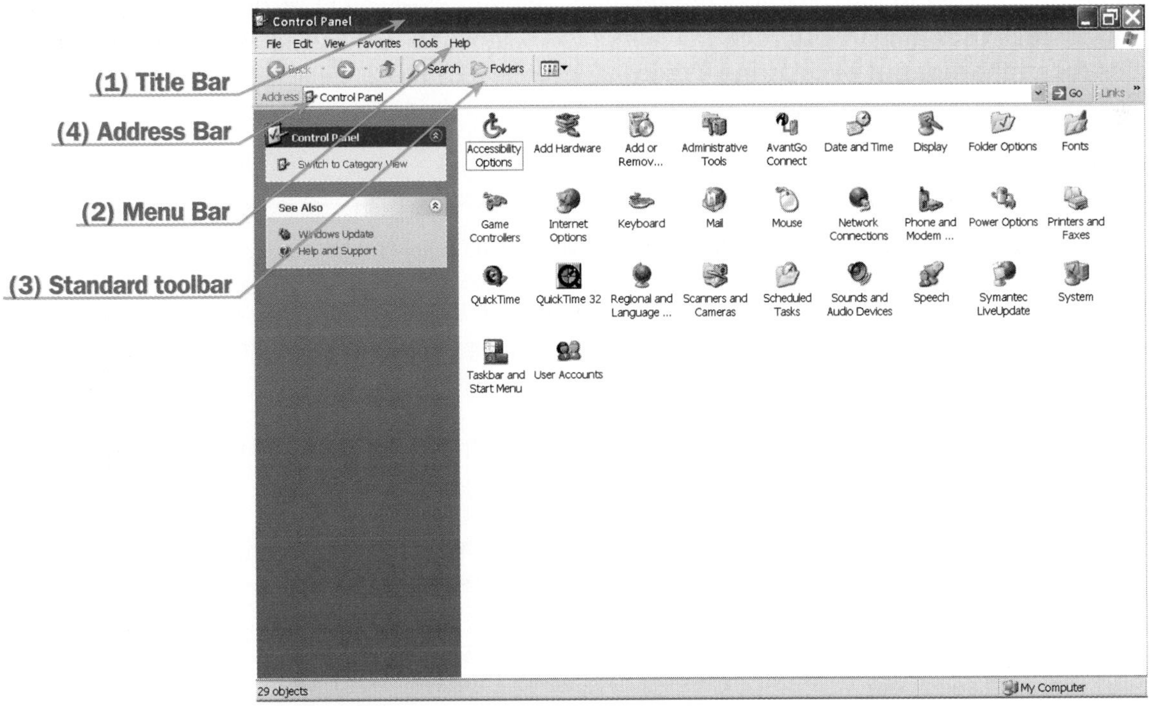

1. A title bar is at the top of every window and contains the name of the open program, window, document, or folder.

2. The menu bar lists available menus from which you can choose a variety of commands. Every option that is available for the current window is accessible through a menu.

3. The standard toolbar, located directly below the menu bar, contains common commands you can use by simply clicking the correct button.

4. The Address bar tells you which folder's contents are being displayed. You can also key a Web address in the Address bar without first opening your browser.

5. At the bottom of the window is the status bar that gives you directions on how to access menus and summarizes the actions of the commands that you choose. If the status bar does not appear on your screen, open the **View** menu and choose **Status Bar**.

Moving and Resizing Windows

Sometimes you will have several windows open on the screen at the same time. To work more effectively, you may need to move or change the size of a window. To move a window, click the title bar and drag the window to another location. You can resize a window by dragging the window borders. When you position the pointer on a horizontal border, it changes to a vertical two-headed arrow. When you position the pointer on a vertical border, it changes to a horizontal two-headed arrow. You can then click and drag the border to change the width or height of the window. It is also possible to resize two sides of a window at the same time. When you move the pointer to a corner of the window's border, it becomes a two-headed arrow pointing diagonally. You can then click and drag to resize the window's height and width at the same time. This maintains the proportions of the existing window.

S TEP-BY-STEP A.3

1. Switch to the List view by clicking the **View** button and choosing **List**.

2. Move the Control Panel window by clicking on the title bar and holding the left mouse button down. Continue to hold the left mouse button down and drag the Control Panel until it appears to be centered on the screen. Release the mouse button.

3. Point anywhere on the border at the bottom of the Control Panel window. The pointer turns into a vertical two-headed arrow. ↕

4. While the pointer is a two-headed arrow, click the left mouse button and drag the bottom border of the window down to enlarge the window.

5. Point to the border on the right side of the Control Panel window. The pointer turns into a horizontal two-headed arrow.

6. While the pointer is a two-headed arrow, click and drag the border of the window to the right to enlarge the window. ↔

STEP-BY-STEP A.3 Continued

7. Point to the lower-right corner of the window border, and place your pointer on the sizing handle. The pointer becomes a two-headed arrow pointing diagonally.

8. Drag the border upward and to the left to resize both sides at the same time until the window is about the same size as the one shown in Figure A-4. Leave the window on the screen for the next Task.

FIGURE A-4
Scroll bars, arrows, and boxes

Scroll Bars

A *scroll bar* appears on the edge of a window any time there is more to be displayed than a window can show at its current size (see Figure A-4). A scroll bar can appear along the bottom edge (horizontal) and/or along the right side (vertical) of a window. A scroll bar appeared in the last step of the preceding exercise because the window was too small to show all the icons at once.

Scroll bars are a convenient way to bring another part of the window's contents into view. On the scroll bar is a sliding box called the *scroll box*. The scroll box indicates your position within the window. When the scroll box reaches the bottom of the scroll bar, you have reached the end of the window's contents. *Scroll arrows* are located at the ends of the scroll bar. Clicking on a scroll arrow moves the window in that direction one line at a time.

S TEP-BY-STEP A.4

1. On the horizontal scroll bar, click the scroll arrow that points to the right. The contents of the window shift to the left.

2. Press and hold the mouse button on the same scroll arrow. The contents of the window scroll quickly across the window. Notice that the scroll box moves to the right end of the scroll bar.

STEP-BY-STEP A.4 Continued

3. You can also scroll by dragging the scroll box. Drag the scroll box on the horizontal scroll bar to the left.

4. Drag the scroll box on the vertical scroll bar to the middle of the scroll bar.

5. The final way to scroll is to click on the scroll bar. Click the horizontal scroll bar to the right of the scroll box. The contents scroll left.

6. Click the horizontal scroll bar to the left of the scroll box. The contents scroll right.

7. Resize the Control Panel until the scroll bar disappears. Leave the window open for the next Task.

Other Window Controls

Three other important window controls, located on the right side of the title bar, are the *Maximize button*, the *Minimize button*, and the *Close button* (see Figure A-5). The Maximize button enlarges a window to the full size of the screen. The Minimize button shrinks a window to a button on the taskbar. The button on the taskbar is labeled, and you can click it any time to redisplay the window. The Close button is used to close a window.

When a window is maximized, the Maximize button is replaced by the Restore Down button (see Figure A-6). The *Restore Down button* returns the window to the size it was before the Maximize button was clicked.

FIGURE A-5
Maximize, Minimize, and Close buttons

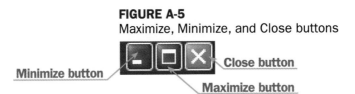

Minimize button   Close button   Maximize button

FIGURE A-6
Restore Down button

STEP-BY-STEP A.5

1. Click the **Maximize** button. The window enlarges to fill the screen.

2. Click the **Restore Down** button on the Control Panel window.

3. Click the **Minimize** button on the Control Panel window. The window is reduced to a button on the taskbar.

4. Click the **Control Panel** button on the taskbar to open the window again.

5. Click the **Close** button to close the window.

Menus and Dialog Boxes

To find out what a restaurant has to offer, you look at the menu. You can also look at a menu on the computer's screen to find out what a computer program has to offer. *Menus* in computer programs contain options for executing certain actions or tasks.

When you click the Start button, as you did earlier in this appendix, a menu is displayed with a list of options. If you choose a menu option with an arrow beside it, a submenu opens that lists additional options. A menu item followed by an ellipsis (...) indicates that a dialog box will appear when that item is chosen. A *dialog box*, like the Turn off computer dialog box shown in Figure A-7, appears when more information is required before the command can be performed. You may have to key information, choose from a list of options, or simply confirm that you want the command to be performed. To back out of a dialog box without performing an action, press Esc, click the Close button, or choose Cancel (or No).

FIGURE A-7
Turn off computer dialog box

S TEP-BY-STEP A.6

1. Click the **Start** button. A menu appears.

2. If you are using *Windows 2000*, click **Shut Down**. The Shut Down Windows dialog box appears. If you are using *Windows XP*, the button on the Start menu and the title on the dialog box is *Turn Off Computer*, as shown in Figure A-7.

3. Click **Cancel** to back out of the dialog box without shutting down.

In a Windows application, menus are accessed from a menu bar (see Figure A-8). A menu bar appears beneath the title bar in each Windows program and consists of a row of menu names such as File and Edit. Each name in the menu bar represents a separate *drop-down menu*, containing related options. Drop-down menus are convenient to use because the commands are in front of you on the screen, as shown in Figure A-8. Like a menu in a restaurant, you can view a list of choices and pick the one you want.

FIGURE A-8
Drop-down menu

You can give commands from drop-down menus using either the keyboard or the mouse. Each menu on the menu bar and each option on a menu is characterized by an underlined letter called a *mnemonic*. To open a menu on the menu bar using the keyboard, press Alt plus the mnemonic letter shown on the menu name. To display a menu using the mouse, simply place the pointer on the menu name and click the left button.

Just as with the Start menu, drop-down menus also have items with right-pointing arrows that open submenus, and ellipses that open dialog boxes. Choosing an item without an ellipsis or a right-pointing arrow executes the command. To close a menu without choosing a command, press Esc or click anywhere outside of the menu.

S TEP-BY-STEP A.7

1. If you are using *Windows 2000*, open the Notepad accessory application by clicking **Start**, **Programs**, **Accessories**, and then **Notepad**. (See Figure A-9.) If using *Windows XP*, open the Notepad accessory application by clicking **Start**, **All Programs**, **Accessories**, and then **Notepad**.

FIGURE A-9
Opening menus in an application

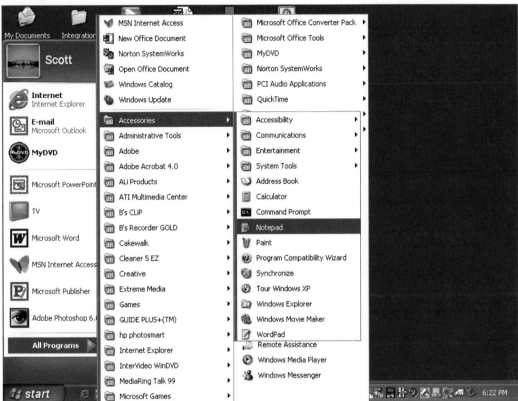

2. Click **Edit** on the menu bar. The Edit menu appears.

3. Click **Time/Date** to display the current time and date.

STEP-BY-STEP A.7 Continued

4. Click **File** on the menu bar. The File menu appears. Point to **Exit**. The Exit option is selected (see Figure A-10).

FIGURE A-10
Exit command on the File menu

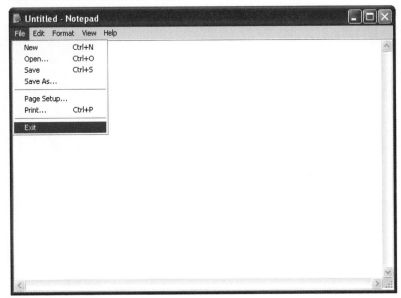

5. Click **Exit**. A save prompt dialog box appears.

6. Click **No**. The Notepad window closes (without saving your document) and you return to the desktop.

Windows Help

This appendix has covered only a few of the many features of Windows. For additional information, Windows has an easy-to-use Help system. Use Help as a quick reference when you are unsure about a function. Windows Help is accessed through the Help option on the Start menu. Then, from the Windows Help dialog box, you can choose to see a table of contents displaying general topics and subtopics, or you can choose to search the Help system using the Index or Search options. If you are working in a Windows program, you can get more specific help about topics relating to that program by accessing help from the Help menu on the menu bar.

Many topics in the Help program are linked. A *link* is represented by colored, underlined text. By clicking a link, the user "jumps" to a linked document that contains additional information.

Using the buttons on the toolbar controls the display of information. In Windows 2000, the Hide button removes the left frame of the Help window from view and the Show button will restore it. In both Windows 2000 and Windows XP, Back and Forward buttons allow you to move back and forth between previously displayed Help entries. The Options button offers navigational choices, as well as options to customize, refresh, and print Help topics.

The Contents tab (or Locate in Contents button in Windows XP) is useful if you want to browse through the topics by category. Click a book icon to see additional Help topics. Click a question mark to display detailed Help information in the right frame of the Help window.

S TEP-BY-STEP A.8

1. If you are using *Windows 2000*, open the Windows Help program by clicking the **Start** button, and then **Help**. If you are using *Windows XP*, click **Start** and then **Help and Support**.

2. If you're using *Windows 2000*, click the **Hide** button on the toolbar to remove the left frame, if necessary. If you are using *Windows XP*, skip to step 5.

3. Click the **Show** button to display the left frame again, if necessary.

4. Click the **Contents** tab if it is not already selected.

5. *Windows 2000* users: Click **Introducing Windows 2000 Professional** and then click **How to Use Help**.

   Windows XP users: Click **What's new in Windows XP**.

6. *Windows 2000* users: Click **Find a Help Topic**.

   Windows XP users: Click **What's new topics** in the left pane and then **What's new for Help and Support** in the right pane.

7. Read the Help window and leave it open for the next Task.

When you want to search for help on a particular topic, use the Index tab (or button) and key in a word. Windows will search alphabetically through the list of Help topics to try to find an appropriate match. Double-click a topic to see it explained in the right frame of the help window. Sometimes a Topics Found dialog box will appear that displays subtopics related to the item. Find a subtopic that you'd like to learn more about and double-click it.

S TEP-BY-STEP A.9

1. *Windows 2000* users: Click the **Index** tab.

   Windows XP users: Click the **Index** button.

2. *Windows 2000* users: Begin keying **printing** until *printing* is highlighted in the list of index entries.

   Windows XP users: Begin keying **help** until *help and support for Windows XP* is highlighted in the list of index entries.

3. *Windows 2000* users: Click **printing Help topics** and then **from a Server** to display information in the right frame.

   Windows XP users: Double-click the **copying and printing Help topics**, then double-click **To print a Help topic or page**.

STEP-BY-STEP A.9 Continued

4. *Windows 2000* users: Read the Help window, and then print the information by following the instructions you read.

   Windows XP users: Read the Help window, and then print the information by clicking the **Print** button on the toolbar.

5. *Windows 2000* users: Click the **Back** button to return to the previous Help screen.

   Windows XP users: Click the **Back arrow** button to return to the previous Help screen.

6. *Windows 2000* users: Click the **Forward** button to advance to the next Help screen.

   Windows XP users: Click the **Forward arrow** button to advance to the next Help screen.

7. Close the Help program by clicking the **Close** button.

The Search function is similar to the Index function, but will perform a more thorough search of the words or phrases that you key. By using the Search option, you can display every occurrence of a particular word or phrase throughout the Windows Help system. Double-click on the topic most similar to what you are looking for and information is displayed in the Help window.

If you need assistance using the Windows Help program in Windows 2000, choose *Introducing Windows, How to Use Help* from the Contents tab; or, if you are using Windows XP, choose *What's new in Windows XP* from the Home page and then *What's new topics*.

If you are using an Microsoft Office application, you can also get help by using the Office Assistant feature.

Other Features

One of Windows' primary features is its file management capabilities. Windows comes with two file management utilities: My Computer and Windows Explorer. The Recycle Bin utility also helps you manage files. When open, these utilities display a standard toolbar similar to the one shown in Figure A-11. Your toolbar may look different from Figure A-11 depending on if it has been customized. To customize your toolbar, choose Toolbars on the View menu, and Customize on the submenu.

FIGURE A-11
Windows XP Standard toolbar

The Back and Forward buttons let you move back and forth between folder contents previously displayed in the window. The Up button moves you up one level in the hierarchy of folders. You can use the Cut, Copy, and Paste buttons to cut or copy an object and then paste it in another location. The Undo button allows you to reverse your most recent action. The Delete button sends the selected object to the Recycle Bin. The View button lists options for displaying the contents of the window.

My Computer

As you learned earlier, there is an icon on your desktop labeled My Computer. Double-clicking this icon opens the My Computer window, which looks similar to the one shown in Figure A-12. The My Computer program is helpful because it allows you to see what is on your computer. Double-click the icon for the drive you want to view. That drive's name appears in the title bar and the window displays all the folders and files on that drive.

FIGURE A-12
Windows XP My Computer window

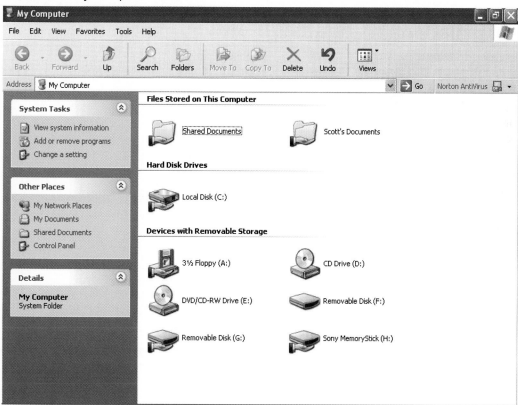

Because computer disks have such a large capacity, it is not unusual for a floppy disk to contain dozens of files, or for a hard disk to contain hundreds or thousands of files. To organize files, a disk can be divided into folders. A *folder* is a place where files and other folders are stored. They help keep documents organized on a disk just the way folders would in a file cabinet. Folders group files that have something in common. You can also have folders within a folder. For example, you could create a folder to group all of the files you are working on in computer class. Within that folder, you could have several other folders that group files for each tool or each chapter.

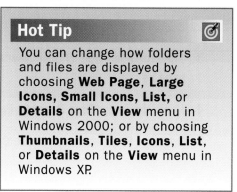

Hot Tip

You can change how folders and files are displayed by choosing **Web Page, Large Icons, Small Icons, List,** or **Details** on the **View** menu in Windows 2000; or by choosing **Thumbnails, Tiles, Icons, List,** or **Details** on the **View** menu in Windows XP.

When you double-click a folder in My Computer, the contents of that folder are displayed—including program files and data files. Double-clicking a program file icon will open that program. Double-clicking a data file icon opens that document in the program that created it.

To create a new folder, double-click a drive or folder in the My Computer window. Choose New on the File menu and then choose Folder on the submenu. A folder titled *New Folder* appears, as shown in Figure A-13. You can rename the folder by keying the name you want. Once you have created a folder, you can save or move files into it.

FIGURE A-13
New folder (Tiles view)

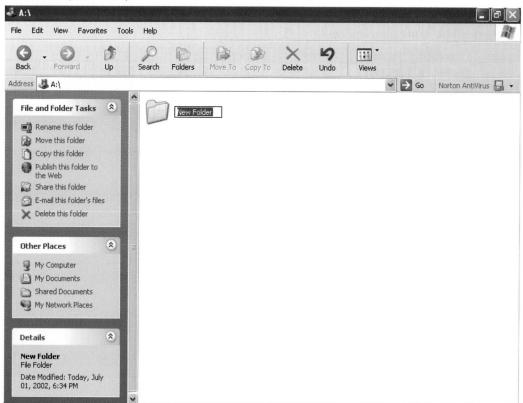

S TEP-BY-STEP A.10

1. Double-click the **My Computer** icon on your desktop.

2. Double-click the drive where you want to create a new folder.

3. Open the **File** menu, choose **New** and then choose **Folder** on the submenu. A folder titled *New Folder* appears.

4. Name the folder **Time Records**. Press **Enter**.

5. Open the **File** menu and choose **Close** to close the window.

Windows Explorer

Another way to view the folders and files on a disk is to use the Windows Explorer program. To open it, click Start, Program (or All Programs), Accessories, and then click Windows Explorer. The Explorer window is split into two panes. The left pane shows a hierarchical or "tree" view of how the folders are organized on a disk; the right side, or Contents pane, shows the files and folders located in the folder that is currently selected in the tree pane. Explorer is a useful tool for organizing and managing the contents of a disk because you can create folders, rename them, and easily delete, move, and copy files.

S TEP-BY-STEP A.11

1. *Windows 2000* users: Open Windows Explorer by clicking **Start**, **Programs**, **Accessories**, and then **Windows Explorer**.

Windows XP users: Open Windows Explorer by clicking **Start**, **All Programs**, **Accessories**, and then **Windows Explorer**.

2. In the tree pane, click the drive where the *Time Records* folder you just created is located.

3. Select the **Time Records** folder in the Contents pane of the Explorer window.

4. Open the **File** menu and choose **Rename**.

5. Key **Finance**. Press **Enter**.

6. Leave Windows Explorer open for the next Task.

Recycle Bin

Another icon on the desktop that you learned about earlier is the Recycle Bin. It looks like a wastebasket and is a place to get rid of files and folders that you no longer need. Items that have been "thrown away" will remain in the Recycle Bin, from which they can be retrieved until you empty the Recycle Bin.

S TEP-BY-STEP A.12

1. Windows Explorer should still be open from the previous Task.

2. Right-click the **Finance** folder.

3. Choose **Delete** on the shortcut menu. The Confirm Folder Delete dialog box appears.

4. Click **Yes**. The folder is removed.

5. Open the **File** menu and choose **Close** to close Windows Explorer.

SUMMARY

In this appendix, you learned:

- The desktop organizes your work. Clicking the Start button displays options for opening programs and documents and shutting down the computer.

- You can connect to the Internet using the Internet Explorer browser, and you can use the Active Desktop and channels to incorporate Web content into your work.

- Windows can be moved, resized, opened, and closed. If all the contents of a window cannot be displayed in the window as it is currently sized, scroll bars appear to allow you to move to the part of the window that you want to view. Windows can be maximized to fill the screen or minimized to a button on the taskbar.

- Menus allow you to choose commands to perform different actions. Menus are accessed from the Start button or from a program's menu bar near the top of the window. When you choose a menu command with an ellipsis (…), a dialog box appears that requires more information before performing the command. Choosing a menu option with an arrow opens a submenu.

- The Windows Help program provides additional information about the many features of Windows. You can access the Help program from the Start button and use the Contents, Index, or Search tabs to get information. You can also get help from the Help menu within Windows programs.

- Folders group files that have something in common. To organize a disk, it can be divided into folders where files and other folders are stored. Other useful features of Windows include My Computer and Windows Explorer, which let you see what is on your computer and help you organize and manage your files; as well as the Recycle Bin for deleting unneeded files or folders.

APPENDIX B

COMPUTER CONCEPTS

What Is a Computer?

A computer is a mechanical device that is used to store, retrieve, and manipulate information (called data) electronically. You enter the data into the computer through a variety of input devices, such as a keyboard, mouse, or joystick; the computer processes it, and then it can be output in a number of ways: such as with a monitor, projector, or printer. Computer software programs run the computer and let you manipulate the data.

Hardware

The physical components, or parts, of the computer are called hardware. The main parts are the central processing unit (CPU), the monitor, the keyboard, and the mouse. Peripherals are additional components, such as printers and scanners.

Input Devices. You enter information into a computer by keying on a keyboard or by using a mouse—a hand-held device—to move a pointer on the computer screen. Tablet PCs allow you to input data by writing directly on the computer screen. They use a technology called handwriting recognition to convert your writing to text. A joystick is an input device similar to the control stick of an airplane that moves a pointer, or character, on the screen. A modem is another input device; it receives information via a telephone line. Other input devices include scanners, track-balls, and digital tracking devices. You can use scanners to "read" text or graphics into a computer from a printed page, or to read bar codes (coded labels) to keep track of merchandise or other inventory in a store. Similar to a mouse, a trackball has a roller ball that turns to control a pointer on the screen. Digital tracking devices are an alternative to the trackball or mouse; situated on the keyboard of a laptop, they allow you to simply press a finger on a small electronic pad to control the pointer on the screen. See Figure B-1.

FIGURE B-1
Keyboard, controller, and mouse

Processing Devices. The central processing unit (CPU) is a silicon chip that processes data and carries out instructions given to the computer. The data bus includes the wiring and pathways by which the CPU communicates with the peripherals and components of the computer.

FIGURE B-2
Motherboard

Storage Devices. The hard drive is a device that reads and writes data to and from a round magnetic platter, or disk. The data is encoded on the disk much the same as sounds are encoded on magnetic tape. The hard drive is called hard because the disk it reads is rigid; unlike a floppy disk drive, which reads and writes data to and from a removable non-rigid disk, similar to a round disk of magnetic tape. The floppy disk is encased in a plastic sleeve to protect its data. The floppy disk's main advantage is portability. You can store data on a floppy disk and transport it for use on another computer. A floppy disk will hold up to 1.4 megabytes (MB) of information. A Zip disk is similar to a floppy disk. A Zip disk is also a portable disk contained in a plastic sleeve, but it will hold 100MB or 250MB of information. A special disk drive called a Zip drive is required to use a Zip disk.

At one time, the largest hard drive was 10MB, or 10,000,000 bytes, of data. A byte stands for a single character of data. At the current time, typical hard drives range from 40 gigabytes (GB) to 120 gigabytes.

Another storage device is the CD, or compact disc, which is a form of optical storage. Compact discs can store 650MB. Information is encoded on the disk by a laser and read by a CD-ROM drive in the computer. These discs have a great advantage over floppies because they can hold vast quantities of information—the entire contents of a small library, for instance. However, most computers cannot write (or save) information to these discs; CD-ROMs are Read-Only Memory (ROM) devices. Drives are now available that write to CDs. Although these drives used to be very expensive and therefore were not used widely, they are becoming more affordable. The great advantage of CDs is their ability to hold graphic information—including moving pictures with the highest quality stereo sound.

Similar to a CD, the digital video disc drive (DVD) can read high-quality cinema-type discs. A DVD is a 5-inch optical disc, and it looks like an audio CD. It is a high-capacity storage device that can contain 4.7GB of data, which is a seven-fold increase over the current CD-ROMs. There are two variations of DVDs that offer even more storage—a 2-layer version with 9.4GB capacity, and double-sided discs with 17GB. These highest-capacity discs are designed to eventually replace the CD-ROM to store large databases. A DVD holds 133 minutes of data on each side, which means that two two-hour movies can be stored on one disc.

Another storage medium is magnetic tape. This medium is most commonly used for backing up a computer system, which means making a copy of files from a hard drive. Although it is relatively rare for a hard drive to crash (that is, for the data or pointers to the data to be partially or totally destroyed), it can and does happen. Therefore, most businesses and some individuals routinely back up files on tape. If you have a small hard drive, you can use floppy disks or CD-ROMs to back up your system.

FIGURE B-3
Hard drive

Output Devices. The monitor on which you view your work is an output device. It provides a visual representation of the information stored in or produced by your computer. The typical monitor for today's system is the SVGA (super video graphics array), which uses a Cathode-ray tube (CRT) similar to a television. It provides a very sharp picture because of the large number of tiny dots, called pixels, which make up the display as well as its ability to present the full spectrum of colors. Most laptop computers use a liquid crystal display (LCD) screen that is not as clear a display because it depends on the arrangement of tiny bits of crystal to present an image. However, the latest laptops use new technology that gives quality near or equal to that of a standard monitor.

Printers are another type of output device. They let you produce a paper printout of information contained in the computer. Today, most printers are of the laser type, using a technology similar to a photocopier to produce high-quality print. Like a copy machine, the laser printer uses heat to fuse a powdery substance called toner to the page. Ink-jet printers use a spray of ink to print. Laser printers give the sharpest image. Ink-jet printers provide nearly as sharp an image, but the wet printouts can smear when they first are printed. Most color printers, however, are ink jet. These printers let you print information in its full array of colors just as you see it on your SVGA monitor. Laser color printers are available, but are significantly more costly.

Modems are another type of output device, as well as an input device. They allow computers to communicate with each other by telephone lines. Modems convert information in bytes to sound media in order to send data and then convert it back to bytes after receiving data. Modems operate at various rates or speeds; typically a computer will have a modem that operates at 33.6 Kbps (Kilobytes per second) to 56 Kbps baud (a variable unit of data transmission) or better.

Local telephone companies currently offer residential ISDN services that provide connection speeds up to 128 Kbps and digital subscriber line technologies (DSL), which can provide speeds beyond 1.5 Mbps (Megabytes per second). Other alternatives include fast downstream data connections from direct broadcast satellite (DBS), fixed wireless providers, and high-speed cable.

FIGURE B-4
Monitor

Laptops and Docking Stations. A laptop computer is a small folding computer that literally fits in a person's lap. Within the fold-up case is the CPU, data bus, monitor (built into the lid), hard drive (sometimes removable), a 3.5-inch floppy drive, a CD-ROM drive, and a trackball or digital tracking device. The advantage of the laptop is its portability—you can work anywhere because you can use power either from an outlet or from the computer's internal, rechargeable batteries. The drawbacks are the smaller keyboard, liquid crystal monitor, smaller capacity, and higher price, though newer laptops offer full-sized keyboards and higher quality monitors. As technology allows, storage capacity on smaller devices is making it possible to offer laptops with as much power and storage as a full-sized computer. A docking station is a device into which you slide a closed laptop so that it becomes a desktop computer. Then you can plug in a full-sized monitor, keyboard, mouse, printer, and so on. Such a setup lets you use the laptop like a desktop computer while at your home or office. See Figure B-5.

FIGURE B-5
Laptop and docking station

Personal Digital Assistants (PDA). A Personal Digital Assistant is a pocket-sized electronic organizer that helps you to manage addresses, appointments, expenses, tasks, and memos. This information can be shared with a Windows-based or Macintosh computer through a process called synchronization. By placing your PDA in a cradle that is attached to your computer, you can transfer the data from your PDA's calendar, address, or memo program into your computer's information manager program, such as Outlook. The information is updated on both sides, making your PDA a portable extension of your computer.

FIGURE B-6
Personal Digital Assistant

Functioning

All of the input, processing, storage, and output devices function together to make the manipulation, storage, and distribution of data and information possible.

Data and Information Management. Data is information entered into and manipulated within a computer. Manipulation includes computation, such as adding, subtracting, multiplying, and dividing; analysis planning, such as sorting data; and reporting, such as presenting data for others in a chart. Data and information management is what runs the software on the computer hardware.

Memory. There are two kinds of memory in a computer—RAM and ROM. RAM, or Random Access Memory, consists of a number of silicon chips inside a computer that hold information as long as the computer is turned on. RAM is what keeps the software programs up and running and keeps the visuals on your screen. RAM is where you work with data until you save it to another media such as a hard or floppy disk. Early computers had simple programs and did little with data, so they had very little RAM—possibly 4 or fewer megabytes. Today's computers run very complicated programs that stay resident (remain available to the user at the same time as other programs) and contain graphics. Both of these tasks take a lot of memory; therefore, today's computers have at least 128 or more megabytes of RAM. ROM, or read-only memory, is the small bit of memory that stays in the computer when it is turned off. It is ROM that lets the computer boot up, or get started. ROM holds the instructions that tell the computer how to begin to load its operating system software programs. Figure B-7 shows random access memory.

FIGURE B-7
Random Access Memory

Speed. The speed of a computer is measured by how fast the drives turn to reach information to be retrieved or to save data. The measurement is in megahertz (MHz). Hard drives on early personal computers worked at 4.77 to 10 megahertz; today, machines run at 1000 MHz (or 1GHz) or more. Another factor that affects the speed of a computer is how much RAM is available. Since RAM makes up the work area for all programs and holds all the information that you input until you save, the more RAM available, the quicker the machine will be able to operate.

One other area of speed must be considered, and that is how quickly the modem can send and receive information. As mentioned earlier, modem speed is measured in baud. The usual modem runs at 33,600 or 56,000 baud per second or more; whereas cable modems, DSL lines, ISDN lines, and DSB offer much faster transfers of information.

Communications. Computers have opened up the world of communications, first within offices via LANs (local area networks that link computers within a facility) and, later, via the Internet. Using the Internet, people can communicate across the world instantly with e-mail and attach files that were once sent by mailing a floppy disk. Also, anyone with a modem and an access service can download information from or post information to thousands of bulletin boards. Figure B-8 shows a network diagram.

FIGURE B-8
Diagram of a network

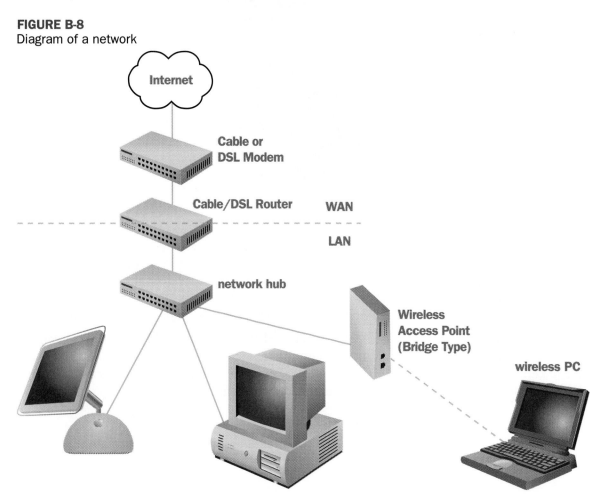

Software

A program is a set of mathematical instructions to the computer. Software is the collection of programs and other data input that tells the computer how to operate its machinery, how to manipulate, store, and output information, and how to accept the input you give it. Software fits into two basic categories: systems software and applications software. A third category, network software, is really a type of application.

Systems Software. Systems software refers to the operating system (OS) of the computer. The OS is a group of programs that is automatically copied in RAM every couple of seconds from the time the computer is turned on until the computer is turned off. Operating systems serve two functions: they control data flow among computer parts, and they provide the platform on which application and network software work—in effect, they allow the "space" for software and translate its commands to the computer. The most popular operating systems in use today are the

Macintosh operating system, and a version of Microsoft Windows, such as Windows 98, Windows NT, Windows 2000, or Windows XP.

Macintosh has its own operating system that has evolved over the years since its introduction. Macintosh has used a graphical user interface (GUI) operating system since its introduction in the mid-1970s. The OS is designed so users "click" with a mouse on pictures, called icons, or on text to give commands to the system. Data is available to you in WYSIWYG (what-you-see-is-what-you-get) form; that is, you can see on-screen what a document will look like when it is printed. Graphics and other kinds of data, such as spreadsheets, can be placed into text documents. However, GUIs take a great deal of RAM to keep all of the graphics and programs operating.

The OS for IBM and IBM-compatible computers (machines made by other companies that operate similarly) originally was DOS (disk operating system). It did not have a graphical interface. The GUI system, Windows™, was developed to make using the IBM/IBM-compatible computer more "friendly." Windows 3.1, however, was a translating system that operated on top of DOS—not on its own. It allowed you to point and click on graphics and words that then translated to DOS commands for the computer. Data was available to you in WYSIWYG form. Graphics and other kinds of data, such as spreadsheets, could be placed into text documents by Object Linking and Embedding (OLE). However, Windows 3.1, because it was still using DOS as its base, was not really a stay-resident program. In other words, it did not keep more than one operation going at a time; it merely switched between operations quickly. Using several high-level programs at the same time, however, could cause problems such as memory failure. Therefore, improvements were necessary and inevitable.

The improvements came with the release of Windows 95 and then Windows 98. These versions of Windows had their own operating system, unlike the original Windows 3.1. Windows 95/98 has DOS built in but does not operate on top of it—if you go to a DOS prompt from Windows, you will still be operating inside a Windows system, not in traditional DOS. Today's Windows applications are the logical evolution of GUI for IBM and IBM-compatible machines. Windows is a stay-resident, point-and-click system that automatically configures hardware to work together. You should note, however, that with all of its ability comes the need for more RAM, or a system running Windows will operate slowly.

Windows 95 and 98 were designed for the consumer. They are easy to use, compatible with most peripheral products, and have features that you would most likely use for personal applications. Windows NT and Windows 2000 were designed for businesses, and include enhanced features for reliability and security. Windows XP brought these two divergent operating systems back together into one product for all users. It combines the versatility of Windows 98 with the stability and security of Windows 2000. Newer versions of Windows continue to be released.

Applications Software. When you use a computer program to perform a data manipulation or processing task, you are using applications software. Word processors, databases, spreadsheets, desktop publishers, fax systems, and online access systems are all applications software.

Network Software. Novell™ and Windows NT are two kinds of network software. A traditional network is a group of computers that are hardwired (hooked together with cables) to communicate and operate together. Today, some computer networks use RF (radio frequency) technology to communicate with each other. This is called a wireless network, because you do not need to hook the network together with cables. In a typical network, one computer acts as the server, which controls the flow of data among the other computers, called nodes, on the network. Network software manages this flow of information. Networks have certain advantages over stand-alone computers: they allow communication among the computers; they allow smaller capacity nodes to access the larger capacity of the server; they allow several computers to share peripherals, such as one printer; and they can make it possible for all computers on the network to have access to the Internet.

History of the Computer

Though various types of calculating machines were developed in the nineteenth century, the history of the modern computer begins about the middle of the last century. The strides made in developing today's personal computer have been truly astounding.

Early Development

The ENIAC, or Electronic Numerical Integrator and Computer, was designed for military use in calculating ballistic trajectories and was the first electronic, digital computer to be developed in the United States. For its day, 1946, it was quite a marvel because it was able to accomplish a task in 20 seconds that took a human three days to do. However, it was an enormous machine that weighed more than 20 tons and contained thousands of vacuum tubes, which often failed. The tasks that it could accomplish were limited, as well.

FIGURE B-9
ENIAC

From this awkward beginning, however, the seeds of an information revolution grew. Significant dates in the history of computer development are listed in Table B-1.

TABLE B-1
History or computer development

YEAR	DEVELOPMENT
1948	First electronically stored program
1951	First junction transistor
1953	Replacement of tubes with magnetic cores
1957	First high-level computer language
1961	First integrated circuit
1965	First minicomputer
1971	Invention of the microprocessor (the silicon chip) and floppy disk
1974	First personal computer (made possible by the microprocessor)

These last two inventions launched the fast-paced information revolution in which we now all live and participate.

The Personal Computer

The PC, or personal computer, was mass marketed by Apple beginning in 1977, and by IBM in 1981. It is this desktop device with which people are so familiar and which, today, contains much more power and ability than did the original computer that took up an entire room. The PC is a small computer (desktop size or less) that uses a microprocessor to manipulate data. PCs may stand alone, be linked together in a network, or be attached to a large mainframe computer.

FIGURE B-10
Early IBM

Computer Utilities and System Maintenance

Computer operating systems let you run certain utilities and perform system maintenance. When you add hardware or software, you might need to make changes in the way the system operates. Beginning with the Windows 95 version, most configuration changes are done automatically; however, other operating systems might not perform these tasks automatically, or you might want to customize the way the new software or hardware will interface (coordinate) with your system. Additionally, you can make alterations such as the speed at which your mouse clicks, how quickly or slowly keys repeat on the keyboard, and what color or pattern appears on the desktop or in GUI programs.

You need to perform certain maintenance regularly on computers. You should scan all new disks and any incoming information from online sources for viruses (a small program that is loaded onto your computer without your knowledge and runs against your wishes). Some systems do this automatically; others require you to install software to do it. From time to time, you should run a program that scans or checks the hard drive to see that there are not bad sectors (areas) and look for corrupted files. Optimizing or defragmenting the hard disk is another way to keep your computer running at its best. You can also check a floppy disk if it is not working properly. Programs for scanning a large hard drive could take up to half an hour to run; checking programs run on a small hard drive or disk might take only seconds or minutes. Scanning and checking programs often offer the option of "fixing" the bad areas or problems, although you should be aware that this could result in data loss.

Society and Computers

The Electronic Information Era has probably impacted society as much or more than the Agricultural and Industrial Eras affected the lives of our ancestors. With the changes of this era have come many new questions and responsibilities. There are issues of ethics, security, safety, and privacy.

Ethics Using Computers

When you access information—whether online, in the workplace, or via purchased software—you have a responsibility to respect the rights of the creator of that information. Treat electronic information in a copyrighted form—the intellectual property of the author—the same way as you would a book, article or patented invention. For instance, you must give credit when you access information from a CD-ROM encyclopedia or a download from an online database. Also, information you transmit must be accurate and fair.

When you use equipment that belongs to your school, a company for which you work, or others, you must not:

1. Damage computer hardware and add or remove equipment without permission.

2. Use an access code or equipment without permission.

3. Read others' electronic mail.

4. Alter data belonging to someone else without permission.

5. Use the computer for play during work hours or use it for personal profit.

6. Access the Internet for nonbusiness use during work hours.

7. Add to or take away from software programs without permission.

8. Make unauthorized copies of data or software.

9. Copy software programs to use at home or at another site in the company without multisite permission.

10. Copy company files or procedures for personal use.

11. Borrow computer hardware for personal use without asking permission.

Security, Safety, and Privacy

The Internet provides us access to improve our economic productivity and offer life-enhancing features, such as distance learning, remote medical diagnostics, and the ability to work from home more effectively. Businesses throughout the world depend on the Internet every day to get work done. Disruptions in the Internet create havoc for people around the world.

The September 11, 2001, terrorist attack on the World Trade Center and the Pentagon raised the awareness of the entire country about the security of our citizens and our country. In response to this attack, President George W. Bush established the Department of Homeland Security and created a division called the National Cyber Security Division (NCSD) to protect our interest in the Internet.

In order to keep the Internet safe for everyone, the National Cyber Security Division encourages all users to use updated antivirus software and keep your operating systems up to date by adding patches designed to enhance your computer's security. They also request that you "report information concerning suspicious or criminal activity to law enforcement or a DHS watch office."

Because electronic communication is the fastest way for terrorists to communicate, we must all raise our level of security awareness when communicating using computers.

Just as you would not open someone else's mail, you must respect the privacy of e-mail sent to others. When interacting with others online, you must keep confidential information confidential. Do not endanger your privacy, safety, or financial security by giving out personal information to someone you do not know. A common scam (trick) is for someone to pretend to work for the online service you are using and ask for the access code or password that controls your service account. Never give this information out to anyone online. The person can use it and charge a great deal of costly time to your account as well as perhaps access other personal information about you. Also, just as you would not give a stranger your home address, telephone number, or credit card number if you were talking on the street, you should take those same precautions online.

Career Opportunities

In one way or another, all of our careers involve the computer. Whether you are a grocery checker using a scanner to read the prices, a busy executive writing a report on a laptop on an airplane, or a programmer creating new software—almost everyone uses computers in their jobs. And, everyone in a business processes information in some way. There are also specific careers available if you want to work primarily with computers.

Schools offer degrees in computer programming, repair, and design. The most popular jobs are systems analysts, computer operators, and programmers. Analysts figure out ways to make computers work (or work better) for a particular business or type of business. Computer operators use the programs and devices to conduct business with computers. Programmers write the software for applications or new systems.

There are courses of study in using CAD (computer-aided design) and CAM (computer-aided manufacturing). Computer engineering and architectural design degrees are also available. Scientific research is done on computers, and specialties are available in that area as well. There are positions available to instruct others in computer software use within companies and schools. Technical writers and editors must be available to write manuals on using computers and software. Computer-assisted instruction (CAI) is a system of teaching any given subject on the computer. The learner is provided with resources, such as an encyclopedia on CD-ROM, in addition to the specific learning program with which he or she interacts on the computer. Individuals are needed to create these instruction systems. Designing video games is another exciting and ever-growing field of computer work. And these are just a few of the possible career opportunities in an ever-changing work environment.

FIGURE B-11
Person in a computer-related job

What Does the Future Hold?

The possibilities for computer development and application are endless. Things that were dreams or science fiction only 10 or 20 years ago are a reality today. New technologies are emerging. Some are replacing old ways of doing things; others are merging with those older methods and devices. We are learning new ways to work and play because of the computer. It is definitely a device that has become part of our offices, our homes, and our lives.

Emerging Technologies

Today the various technologies and systems are coming together to operate more efficiently. For instance, since their beginnings, Macintosh and Windows-based systems could not exchange information well. Today, you can install compatibility cards in the Power Macintosh and run Windows, DOS, and Mac OS on the same computer and switch between them. Macs (except for early models) can read from and write to MS-DOS and Windows disks. And you can easily network Macintosh computers with other types of computers running other operating systems. In addition, you can buy software for a PC to run the Mac OS and to read Macintosh disks.

Telephone communication is also being combined with computer e-mail so users can set a time to meet online and, with the addition of voice technology, actually speak to each other. This form of communication will certainly evolve into an often-used device that will broaden the use of both the spoken and written word.

Another technology is the CUCME (see you, see me) visual system that allows computer users to use a small camera and microphone wired into the computer so, when they communicate, the receiver can see and hear them. For the hearing impaired, this form of communication can be more effective than writing alone since sign language and facial expression can be added to the interaction. CUCME is a logical next step from the image transfer files now so commonly used to transfer static (nonmoving) pictures.

A great deal of research and planning has gone into combining television and computers. The combined device has a CPU, television-as-monitor, keyboard, joystick, mouse, modem, and CUCME/quick-cam. Something like the multiple communications device that science fiction used to envision, this combined medium allows banking, work, entertainment, and communication to happen all through one piece of machinery—and all in the comfort of your home. Another combined technology is a printer that functions as a copier, fax machine, and scanner.

Trends

There are many trends that drive the computer industry. One trend is for larger and faster hard drives. Forty- and 80-gigabyte hard drives have virtually replaced the 540MB drives, and 200GB drives are becoming common. RAM today is increasing exponentially. The trend is to sell RAM in units of 32 or 64 megabytes to meet the needs of 128, 256, and larger blocks of RAM. All of these size increases are due to the expanding memory requirements of GUIs and new peripherals, such as CUCME devices and interfaces with other devices. Although the capacities are increasing, the actual size of the machine is decreasing. Technology is allowing more powerful components to fit into smaller devices—just as the 3½-inch floppy disk is smaller and holds more data than the obsolete 5¼-inch floppy.

Another trend is the increased use of computers for personal use in homes. This trend is likely to continue in the future—especially as the technologies of the PC and standard home electronics such as the television are combined.

Home Offices. More and more frequently, people are working out of their homes—whether they are employees who are linked to a place of business or individuals running their own businesses. Many companies allow workers to have a computer at home that is linked by modem to the office. Work is done at home and transferred to the office. Communication is by e-mail and telephone. Such an arrangement saves companies workspace and, thus, money. Other employees use laptop computers to work both at home and on the road as they travel. A laptop computer, in combination with a modem, allows an employee to work from virtually anywhere and still keep in constant contact with her or his employer and customers.

With downsizing (the reduction of the workforce by companies), many individuals have found themselves unemployed or underemployed (working less or for less money). These people have, in increasing numbers, begun their own businesses out of their homes. With a computer, modem, fax software, printer, and other peripherals, they can contract with many businesses or sell their own products or services. Many make use of the Internet and World Wide Web to advertise their services.

Home Use. As the economy has tightened, many people are trying to make their lives more time- and cost-efficient. The computer is one help in that quest. Maintaining accounting records, managing household accounts and information, and using electronic banking on a computer saves time. Games and other computer interactions also offer a more reasonable way of spending leisure dollars than some outside entertainment. For instance, it might not be feasible to travel to Paris to see paintings in the Louvre Museum; however, it might be affordable to buy a CD-ROM that lets you take a tour of that famous facility from the comfort of the chair in front of your computer. This can be quite an educational experience for children and a more restful one for those who might tire on a trip of that magnitude but who can easily turn off the computer and come back to it later. Young people can benefit enormously from this kind of education as well as using the computer to complete homework, do word processing, create art and graphics, and, of course, play games that sharpen their hand-to-eye coordination and thinking skills.

Appendix C

Concepts for Microsoft Office Programs

Introduction

Microsoft Office is an integrated software package. An ***integrated software package*** combines several computer programs. Office consists of a word-processing program (Word), a spreadsheet program (Excel), a database program (Access), a presentation program (PowerPoint), a schedule/organization program (Outlook), and a desktop-publishing program (Publisher).

The word-processing program (Word) enables you to create documents such as letters and reports. The spreadsheet program (Excel) lets you work with numbers to prepare items such as budgets or to determine loan payments. The database program (Access) organizes information such as addresses or inventory items. The presentation program (PowerPoint) is used to create slides, outlines, speaker's notes, and audience handouts. The schedule/organization program (Outlook) increases your efficiency by keeping track of e-mail, appointments, tasks, contacts, events, and to-do lists. The desktop publishing program (Publisher) helps you design professional-looking documents.

Because Office is an integrated package, the programs can be used together. For example, numbers from a spreadsheet can be included in a letter created in the word processor or in a presentation.

Read below for more information on each Office program.

Word

Word is the word-processing application of the Office programs. In today's busy world, it is necessary to prepare and send many types of documents. Word processing is the use of a computer and software to produce professional-looking documents, such as memos and letters (see Figure C-1). You can also create documents that are more complex, such as newsletters with graphics, and documents that can be published as Web pages.

FIGURE C-1
Business letter in Word

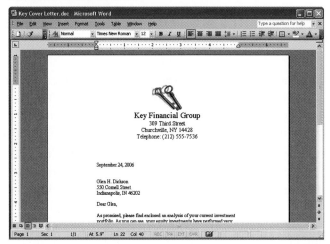

Keying text in Word is easy because it automatically moves, or wraps, text to the next line. After you key your text, you may want to edit it. Use the Spelling and Grammar checker to identify spelling and grammar errors. Correct the errors using the Backspace and Delete keys to delete text, and Overtype to type over text. Cut, Copy, and Paste commands allow you to move and copy data. Word also has an Undo command that reverses your last action.

Word has many automated features that help you create and edit documents. AutoCorrect corrects errors as you enter text; AutoFormat As You Type applies built-in formats as you key; AutoComplete suggests the entire word after you key the first few letters; and AutoText inserts frequently used text.

Word allows you to easily format a document to make it readable and attractive. Formatting includes making decisions about margins, tabs, headings, indents, text alignment, fonts, colors, styles, headers and footers. Word allows you to be creative because you can try new formats and change formats in seconds.

You can also enhance documents by adding graphics or pictures that help illustrate the meaning of the text and make the page more attractive. Word provides pictures called clip art, as well as predefined shapes, diagrams, and charts. Drawing tools permit you to create your own graphics.

Excel

Excel is the spreadsheet application of the Office programs. A *spreadsheet* is a grid of rows and columns containing numbers, text, and formulas. The purpose of a spreadsheet is to solve problems that involve numbers. Without a computer, you might try to solve this type of problem by creating rows and columns on ruled paper and using a calculator to determine results. Computer spreadsheets also contain rows and columns (see Figure C-2), but they perform calculations much faster and more accurately than spreadsheets created with pencil, paper, and calculator.

FIGURE C-2
Spreadsheet in Excel

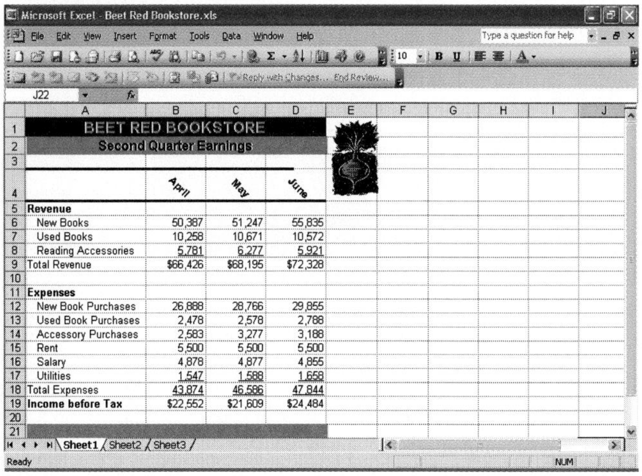

Spreadsheets are used in many ways. For example, a spreadsheet can be used to calculate a grade in a class, to prepare a budget for the next few months, or to determine payments to be made on a loan. The primary advantage of spreadsheets is the ability to complete complex and repetitious calculations accurately, quickly, and easily. For example, you might use a spreadsheet to calculate your monthly income and expenses.

Besides calculating rapidly and accurately, spreadsheets are flexible. Making changes to an existing spreadsheet is usually as easy as pointing and clicking with the mouse. Suppose, for example, you have prepared a budget on a spreadsheet and have overestimated the amount of money you will need to spend on gas and electric and other utilities. You may change a single entry in your spreadsheet and watch the entire spreadsheet recalculate the new budgeted amount. You can imagine the work this change would require if you were calculating the budget with pencil and paper.

Excel uses the term *worksheet* to refer to computerized spreadsheets. Sometimes you may want to use several worksheets that relate to each other. A collection of related worksheets is a *workbook*.

Access

Access is a program known as a *database management system*. A computerized database management system allows you to store, retrieve, analyze, and print information. You do not, however, need a computer to have a database management system. A set of file folders can be a database management system. There are distinct advantages, however, to using a computerized database management system.

A computerized database management system (DBMS) is much faster, more flexible, and more accurate than using file folders. A computerized DBMS is also more efficient and cost-effective. A program such as Access can store thousands of pieces of data in a computer or on a disk. The data can be quickly searched and sorted to save time otherwise spent digging through file folders. For example, a database created in Access could find all the people with a certain ZIP code faster and more accurately than you could by searching through a large list or through folders.

A database is made up of many small sets of data called ***records***. For example, in an Employee database, all the information about an employee is a record (see Figure C-3). Information in a record can include the employee's number, name, social security number, address, birth date, department, and title. In a database, these categories of information are called ***fields***. In Access, data is organized into a ***table***. Tables store data in a format similar to a spreadsheet. In a table, records appear as rows of data and fields appear as columns.

FIGURE C-3
Employee database in Access

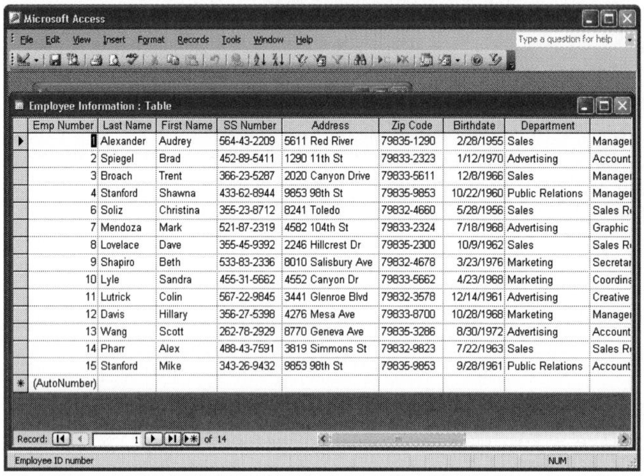

Emp Number	Last Name	First Name	SS Number	Address	Zip Code	Birthdate	Department	
1	Alexander	Audrey	564-43-2209	5611 Red River	79835-1290	2/28/1955	Sales	Manage
2	Spiegel	Brad	452-89-5411	1290 11th St	79833-2323	1/12/1970	Advertising	Account
3	Broach	Trent	366-23-5287	2020 Canyon Drive	79833-5611	12/8/1966	Sales	Manage
4	Stanford	Shawna	433-62-8944	9853 98th St	79835-9853	10/22/1960	Public Relations	Manage
6	Soliz	Christina	355-23-8712	8241 Toledo	79832-4660	5/28/1956	Sales	Sales R
7	Mendoza	Mark	521-87-2319	4582 104th St	79833-2324	7/18/1968	Advertising	Graphic
8	Lovelace	Dave	355-45-9392	2246 Hillcrest Dr	79835-2300	10/9/1962	Sales	Sales R
9	Shapiro	Beth	533-83-2336	8010 Salisbury Ave	79832-4678	3/23/1976	Marketing	Secretar
10	Lyle	Sandra	455-31-5662	4552 Canyon Dr	79833-5662	4/23/1968	Marketing	Coordina
11	Lutrick	Colin	567-22-9845	3441 Glenroe Blvd	79832-3578	12/14/1961	Advertising	Creative
12	Davis	Hillary	356-27-5398	4276 Mesa Ave	79833-8700	10/28/1968	Marketing	Manage
13	Wang	Scott	262-78-2929	8770 Geneva Ave	79835-3286	8/30/1972	Advertising	Account
14	Pharr	Alex	488-43-7591	3819 Simmons St	79832-9823	7/22/1963	Sales	Sales R
15	Stanford	Mike	343-26-9432	9853 98th St	79835-9853	9/28/1961	Public Relations	Account
(AutoNumber)								

PowerPoint

PowerPoint is a program that is helpful in creating presentations in a variety of ways. Presentations can be created using slides, outlines, speaker's notes, and handouts (see Figure C-4). A PowerPoint presentation can include text, clip art, pictures, video, sound, tables, and charts. PowerPoint allows you to apply design templates, customize animations, and insert hyperlinks into a presentation. Slide transitions can be added to further customize a presentation. Other Office programs can be used in conjunction with PowerPoint. Word outlines, charts, and tables can all be incorporated into PowerPoint presentations. Excel charts can be imported into a presentation, and presentations can be saved as Web pages and published on the Web. After you complete a presentation, you can rehearse your timing and delivery using the rehearsal functions. PowerPoint presentations are usually viewed using a projector on a screen, but you can also use a television monitor or an additional monitor connected to your computer.

FIGURE C-4
Presentation in PowerPoint

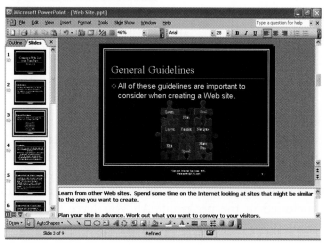

Outlook

Outlook is a desktop information manager that helps you organize information, communicate with people, and manage time. It is easy to use and can quickly summarize your day's activities from Calendar, Tasks, and the Inbox (see Figure C-5). Various features of Outlook allow you to send and receive e-mail messages, schedule events and meetings, record information about business and personal contacts, make to-do lists, record your work, and create reminders. Outlook organizes all this information into categories for viewing and printing. For example, you might group all the information on your important customers into the *Key Customer* category. You can also create a new category for specific groups, such as a *Texas Customers* category, for information on your customers located in Texas.

FIGURE C-5
Outlook Today screen in Outlook

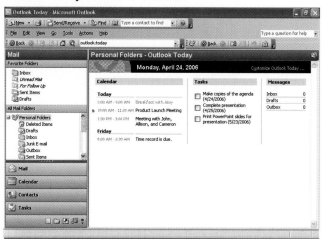

Because Outlook is integrated, you can use it easily with all other Office programs. For example, you can send and receive e-mail messages in Outlook and you can move a name and address from a Word document into your Outlook Contacts List. Outlook has many useful tools and features.

Publisher

Publisher is a desktop publishing program that you can use to create a wide assortment of documents, such as business cards, calendars, personalized stationery, and menus (see Figure C-6). Publisher contains hundreds of predesigned templates you can use as the basis for projects. Personal information sets can be used to store information about your business, organization, or family. Customizations such as logos can be added to an entire series of documents by using the By Design Set option included in the program. All you have to do is add your own custom touches to create professional-looking publications.

FIGURE C-6
Business card in Publisher

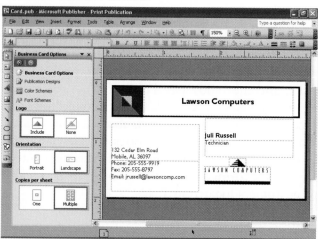

THE MICROSOFT® OFFICE SPECIALIST PROGRAM

What Is Certification?

The logo on the cover of this book indicates that the book is officially certified by Microsoft Corporation at the specialist user skill level for Office 2003 in Word, Excel, Access, and PowerPoint. This certification is part of the Microsoft Office Specialist program that validates your skills in Microsoft Office.

The following grids outline the various skills and where they are covered in this book.

Microsoft Access 2003 Specialist

	SKILL SET AND SKILLS BEING MEASURED	LESSON#	PAGE#(S)	EXERCISE #
AC03S-1	**Structuring Databases**			
AC03S-1-1	Create Access databases	1 1	10	ExtraChallenge (SBS1.4), SBS1.4
AC03S-1-2	Create and modify tables	1	12, 14, 17, 24, 25, 26, 27	Hot Tip (SBS1.5), SBS1.5, SBS1.6, SBS1.8, P1-2, P1-3, P1-4, CT1-1
AC03S-1-3	Define and modify field types	1, 2	14, 39, 43	SBS1.6, SBS2.9, P2-3
AC03S-1-4	Modify field properties	2	39, 42, 43	SBS2.9, P2-1, P2-3
AC03S-1-5	Create and modify one-to-many relationships	4	80	SBS4.10
AC03S-1-6	Enforce referential integrity	4	80	SBS4.10
AC03S-1-7	Create and modify queries	4	70, 72, 89, 90, 91	SBS4.3, SBS4.4, P4-1, P4-4, CT4-3, CT4-4, CT4-5

	SKILL SET AND SKILLS BEING MEASURED	LESSON#	PAGE#(S)	EXERCISE #
AC03S-1-8	Create forms	3	46, 47, 49, 51, 63, 64	SBS3.1, SBS3.2, SBS3.3, SBS3.4, SBS3.5, P3-1, P3-3, CT3-1
AC03S-1-9	Add and modify form controls and properties	3	54, 59, 63	SBS3.7, SBS3.8, P3-2
AC03S-1-10	Create reports	5	94, 95, 99, 97, 98, 101, 112, 113, 114	SBS5.1, SBS5.2, SBS5.3, SBS5.4, SBS5.5, SBS5.6, P5-1, P5-2, CT5-1
AC03S-1-11	Add and modify report control properties	5	103	SBS5.7
AC03S-1-12	Create a data access page	6	126, 134	SBS6.5, P6-4
AC03S-2	**Entering Data**			
AC03S-2-1	Enter, edit, and delete records	1, 2	18, 23, 24, 30, 32, 33, 43, 44	SBS1.9, P1-1, P1-2, P1-4, SBS2.1, SBS2.3, SBS2.4, P2-3, CT2-1
AC03S-2-2	Find and move among fields	1, 2	18, 30	SBS1.9, SBS2.1
AC03S-2-3	Import data to Access	6	116	SBS6.1
AC03S-3	**Organizing Data**			
AC03S-3-1	Create and modify calculated fields and aggregate functions	4	70, 84	SBS4.3, SBS4.13
AC03S-3-2	Modify form layout	3	54, 63	SBS3.7, P3-2
AC03S-3-3	Modify report layout and page setup	5	99, 103	SBS5.5, Hot Tip (SBS5.7), SBS5.7
AC03S-3-4	Format datasheets	2	34, 35, 36, 42, 43	SBS2.5, SBS2.6, SBS2.7, SBS2.8, P2-1, P2-2, P2-3
AC03S-3-5	Sort records	3, 4, 5	59, 63, 70, 82, 84, 90, 76, 77, 89, 97	SBS3.8, P3-3, SBS4.3, SBS4.12, SBS4.13, P4-4, SBS4.6, SBS4.7, SBS4.8, P4-2, SBS5.3
AC03S-3-6	Filter records	4	74, 89	SBS4.5, P4-2, P4-3
AC03S-4	**Managing Databases**			
AC03S-4-1	Identify object dependencies	4	86	Did You Know? (SBS4.13)

	SKILL SET AND SKILLS BEING MEASURED	LESSON#	PAGE#(S)	EXERCISE #
ACO3S-4-2	View objects and object data in other views	1, 3, 5, 6	20, 53, 101, 18, 114, 129	Hot Tip (SBS1.10), Hot Tip (SBS3.6), SBS5.6, SBS1.9, CT5-3, Did You Know? (SBS6.5)
ACO3S-4-3	Print database objects and data	1, 3, 5, 6	21, 53, 101, 126	SBS1.10, SBS3.6, SBS5.6, SBS6.5
ACO3S-4-4	Export data from Access	6	120, 123, 124, 132, 133, 135	SBS6.2, SBS6.3, SBS6.4, P6-1, P6-2, P6-3, CT6-1
ACO3S-4-5	Back up a database	6	118	Hot Tip (SBS6.1)
ACO3S-4-6	Compact and repair databases	2, 3	33, 60	Did You Know? (SBS2.4), SBS3.9

Key: SBS = Step-by-Step   CT = Critical Thinking Activity   P = Project

Microsoft Excel 2003 Specialist

	SKILL SET AND SKILLS BEING MEASURED	LESSON#	PAGE#(S)	EXERCISE #
XL03S-1	**Creating Data and Content**			
XL03S-1-1	Enter and edit cell content	1, 3	9, 11, 18, 19, 47	SBS1.5, SBS1.6, P1-2, P1-3, P1-4, SBS3.3
XL03S-1-2	Navigate to specific cell content	1, 2	13, 19, 36, 8	SBS1.7, P1-4, SBS2.11, SBS1.3
XL03S-1-3	Locate, select, and insert supporting information	6	130	SBS6.10
XL03S-1-4	Insert, position, and size graphics	6	114, 116, 120, 123, 139, 140	SBS6.4, SBS6.5, SBS6.6, SBS6.7, P6-6, CT6-2
XL03S-2	**Analyzing Data**			
XL03S-2-1	Filter lists using AutoFilter	6	113, 137	SBS6.2, P6-3
XL03S-2-2	Sort lists	6	110, 136	SBS6.1, P6-1, P6-2
XL03S-2-3	Insert and modify formulas	4	68, 69, 70, 72, 73, 75, 76, 78, 81, 82, 84, 85	SBS4.1, SBS4.2, SBS4.3, SBS4.4, SBS4.5, SBS4.6, SBS4.7, SBS4.8, P4-2, P4-3, P4-4, P4-5, CT4-1, CT4-2

	SKILL SET AND SKILLS BEING MEASURED	LESSON#	PAGE#(S)	EXERCISE #
XL03S-2-4	Use statistical, date and time, financial, and logical functions	5	90, 92, 94, 97, 99, 102, 103, 105	SBS5.1, SBS5.2, SBS5.3, SBS5.4, SBS5.5, P5-2, P5-3, P5-4, P5-5, P5-6
XL03S-2-5	Create, modify, and position diagrams and charts based on worksheet data	8	161, 164, 165, 166, 168, 169, 173, 174, 176, 177, 178, 180	SBS8.1, SBS8.2, SBS8.3, SBS8.4, SBS8.5, SBS8.6, SBS8.7, SBS8.8, SBS8.9, SBS8.10, P8-1, P8-2, P8-3, P8-4, P8-5, P8-6, P8-8, CT8-1
XL03S-3	**Formatting Data and Content**			
XL03S-3-1	Apply and modify cell formats	2	28, 30, 31, 33, 35, 39, 40, 41	SBS2.6, SBS2.7, SBS2.8, SBS2.9, SBS2.10, P2-2, P2-3, P2-4, P2-5
XL03S-3-2	Apply and modify cell styles	2	33	SBS2.9
XL03S-3-3	Modify row and column formats	2, 3, 6	22, 25, 26, 33, 39, 40, 41, 42, 51, 62, 63, 65, 137, 138, 27, 41	SBS2.1, SBS2.3, SBS2.4, SBS2.9, P2-2, P2-3, P2-5, P2-6, SBS6.3, SBS3.5, P3-2, P3-4, P3-5, P3-7, P6-2, P6-3, P6-4, SBS2.5, P2-4
XL03S-3-4	Format worksheets	7	142, 152, 153, 154	SBS7.1, P7-1, P7-2, P7-3, P 7-4
XL03S-4	**Collaborating**			
XL03S-4-1	Insert, view, and edit comments	6	133, 140	SBS6.11, P6-7
XL03S-5	**Managing Workbooks**			
XL03S-5-1	Create new workbooks from templates	6	126, 138, 140	SBS6.8, P6-5, CT6-1
XL03S-5-2	Insert, delete, and move cells	3	51, 62, 65, 49, 62, 44, 45, 47, 49	SBS3.5, P3-2, P3-5, P3-7, SBS3.4, P3-4, SBS3.1, SBS3.2, SBS3.3, SBS3.4
XL03S-5-3	Create and modify hyperlinks	6	128	SBS6.9
XL03S-5-4	Organize worksheets	7	144, 152, 153, 154	SBS7.2, P7-1, P7-2, P7-3, P7-4
XL03S-5-5	Preview data in other views	3, 6	130, 56, 58	SBS6.10, SBS3.7, SBS3.8

	SKILL SET AND SKILLS BEING MEASURED	LESSON#	PAGE#(S)	EXERCISE #
XL03S-5-6	Customize Window layout	3, 7	53, 62, 144	SBS3.6, P3-3, P3-3, SBS7.2
XL03S-5-7	Set up pages for printing	3, 7	56, 62, 63, 64, 58	SBS3.7, SBS7.4, P3-4, P3-5, P3-6, SBS3.8
XL03S-5-8	Print data	3, 7	58, 148, 152, 153, 154	SBS3.8, SBS7.4, P7-1, P7-2, P7-3, P7-4
XL03S-5-9	Organize workbooks using file folders	1	14	SBS1.8
XL03S-5-10	Save data in appropriate formats for different uses	6	130	SBS6.10

Key: SBS = Step-by-Step   CT = Critical Thinking Activity   P = Project

Microsoft PowerPoint 2003 Specialist

	SKILL SET AND SKILLS BEING MEASURED	LESSON#	PAGE#(S)	EXERCISE #
PP03S-1	**Creating Content**			
PP03S-1-1	Create new presentations from templates	2	23	SBS2.1
PP03S-1-2	Insert and edit text-based content	1, 2, 4	9, 35, 42, 45, 101, 105	SBS1.4, SBS2.7, SBS2.12, SBS2.15, SBS4.1, SBS4.4
PP03S-1-3	Insert tables, charts, and diagrams	3	66, 69, 72	SBS3.3, SBS3.5, SBS3.6
PP03S-1-4	Insert pictures, shapes, and graphics	2, 3	49, 74	SBS2.17, SBS3.7
PP03S-1-5	Insert objects	3, 4	94, 108	SBS3.14, SBS4.5
PP03S-2	**Formatting Content**			
PP03S-2-1	Format text-based content	4	116, 118	SBS4.8, SBS4.9
PP03S-2-2	Format pictures, shapes, and graphics	2, 3	33, 49, 52, 76, 81, 84	SBS2.6, SBS2.17, SBS2.18, SBS3.8, SBS3.10, SBS3.11
PP03S-2-3	Format slides	2, 4	26, 29, 45, 47, 112, 132	SBS2.2, SBS2.4, SBS2.15, SBS2.16, SBS4.7, SBS4.19
PP03S-2-4	Apply animation schemes	2	28	SBS2.3

	SKILL SET AND SKILLS BEING MEASURED	LESSON#	PAGE#(S)	EXERCISE #
PP03S-2-5	Apply slide transitions	2	56	SBS2.21
PP03S-2-6	Customize slide templates	4	112	SBS4.7
PP03S-2-7	Work with masters	2, 3, 4	45, 96, 112	SBS2.15, SBS3.15, SBS4.7
PP03S-3	**Collaborating**			
PP03S-3-1	Track, accept, and reject changes in a presentation	4	131	SBS4.18
PP03S-3-2	Add, edit, and delete comments in a presentation	4	131	SBS4.18
PP03S-3-3	Compare and merge presentations	4	131	SBS4.18
PP03S-4	**Managing and Delivering Presentations**			
PP03S-4-1	Organize a presentation	1, 2, 3, 4	9, 12, 14, 35, 37, 44, 54, 93, 96, 118	SBS1.4, SBS1.7, SBS1.8, SBS2.7, SBS2.8, SBS2.13, SBS2.20 SBS3.13, SBS3.15, SBS4.9
PP03S-4-2	Set up slide shows for delivery	4	120, 122	SBS4.10, SBS4.11
PP03S-4-3	Rehearse timing	4	123	SBS4.12
PP03S-4-4	Deliver presentations	1, 4	7, 120	SBS1.2, SBS4.10
PP03S-4-5	Prepare presentations for remote delivery	4	126, 129	SBS4.14, SBS4.16
PP03S-4-6	Save and publish presentations	4	126, 128	SBS4.14, SBS4.15
PP03S-4-7	Print slides, outlines, handouts, and speaker notes	1, 2	15, 37	SBS1.9, SBS2.8
PP03S-4-8	Export a presentation to another Microsoft Office program	2	56	SBS2.22

Key: SBS = Step-by-Step   CT = Critical Thinking Activity   P = Project

Microsoft Word 2003 Specialist

	SKILL SET AND SKILLS BEING MEASURED	LESSON#	PAGE#(S)	EXERCISE #
WW03S-1	**Creating Content**			
WW03S-1-1	Insert and edit text, symbols, and special characters	1, 2, 3	6, 8, 26, 29, 30, 25, 37, 48, 50, 53, 55, 56, 58, 59	SBS1.2, P1-3, SBS2.2, SBS2.4, SBS2.5, Hot Tip (SBS 2.1), P2-1, P2-2, SBS3.5, SBS3.6, SBS3.7, SBS 3.9, Hot Tip (SBS 3.9), P3-1, P3-2, P3-3, P3-4
WW03S-1-2	Insert frequently used and predefined text	3	43, 46, 54, 58, 59	SBS3.1, SBS3.3, SBS3.8, P3-1, P3-2, P3-4
WW03S-1-3	Navigate to specific content	2	32, 33, 37, 38, 39, 33	SBS2.6, SBS2.7, P2-2, P2-3, P2-5, Hot Tip (SBS2.7),
WW03S-1-4	Insert position and size graphics	6	109, 111, 115, 116, 119, 125, 126, 127, 129	SBS6.3, SBS6.4, SBS6.7, SBS6.8, SBS6.10, P6-1, P6-2, P6-3, P6-4, P6-5
WW03S-1-5	Create and modify diagrams and charts	6	120, 122, 123, 127	SBS6.11, SBS6.12, SBS6.13, P6-4
WW03S-1-6	Locate and insert supporting information	7	139, 150	SBS7.5, P7-1
WW03S-2-1	Insert and modify tables	7	142, 143, 145, 147, 150, 151	SBS7.7, SBS7.8, SBS 7.9, SBS7.10, SBS7.11, P7-2, P7-3, P7-4
WW03S-2-2	Create bulleted lists, numbered lists, and outlines	5	88, 90, 91, 92, 93, 96, 98, 100	SBS5.7, SBS5.8, SBS5.9, SBS5.10, SBS5.11, P5-1, P5-4, P5-6
WW03S-2-3	Insert and modify hyperlinks	8	172, 174, 175, 179	SBS8.14, SBS8.16, Hot Tip (SBS8.16), P8-5
WW03S-3	**Formatting Content**			
WW03S-3-1	Format text	4	64, 65, 66, 68, 69, 71, 74, 75	SBS4.1, SBS4.2, SBS4.3, SBS4.4, SBS4.5, SBS4.7, P4-1, P4-2, P4-3, P4-4, P4-5

	SKILL SET AND SKILLS BEING MEASURED	LESSON#	PAGE#(S)	EXERCISE #
WW03S-3-2	Format paragraphs	5, 6	80, 82, 83, 86, 96, 98, 107, 125	SBS5.2, SBS5.3, SBS5.4, SBS5.6, P5-1, P5-2, P5-4, P5-5, SBS6.2, P6-1
WW03S-3-3	Apply and format columns	6	105, 125	SBS6.1, P6-1
WW03S-3-4	Insert and modify content in headersand footers	7	134, 150	SBS7.2, P7-1
WW03S-3-5	Modify document layout and page setup	1, 5, 7	14, 19, 20, 78, 80, 86, 133, 150	SBS1.7, P1-2, P1-4, SBS5.1, P5-2, P5-6, SBS7.1, P7-1
WW03S-4	**Collaborating**			
WW03S-4-1	Circulate documents for review	8	166	SBS8.8, Hot Tip (SBS8.8)
WW03S-4-2	Compare and merge document versions	8	171	SBS8.13
WW03S-4-3	Insert, view, and edit comments	8	167, 168, 178	SBS8.9, SBS8.10, P8-3
WW03S-4-4	Track, accept, and reject proposed changes	8	169, 170 179	SBS8.11, SBS8.12, P8-4
WW03S-5	**Formatting and Managing Documents**			
WW03S-5-1	Create new documents using templates	8	155, 157, 177	SBS8.1, SBS8.2, SBS8.3, P8-1
WW03S-5-2	Review and modify document properties	2, 7	34, 38, 141	SBS2.8, P2-3, SBS7.6
WW03S-5-3	Organize documents using file folders	1	9	SBS1.4
WW03S-5-4	Save documents in appropriate formats for different uses	8	156, 174, 179	Hot Tip (SBS8.2), SBS8.15, P8-5
WW03S-5-5	Print documents, envelopes, and labels	1, 8	15, 19, 164, 165 178	SBS1.8, P1-2, SBS8.6, SBS8.7, P8-2
WW03S-5-6	Preview documents and Web pages	1, 8	14, 19, 20, 174, 179	SBS1.7, P1-2, P1-4, SBS8.15, P8-5
WW03S-5-7	Change and organize document views and windows	1, 2, 7	6, 11, 19, 20, 25, 136	SBS1.2, SBS1.6, P1-3, P1-4, P1-5, SBS2.1, SBS7.3

Key: SBS = Step-by-Step   CT = Critical Thinking Activity   P = Project

APPENDIX E

KEYBOARDING TOUCH SYSTEM IMPROVEMENT

Introduction

Your Goal – Improve your keyboarding skill using the touch system.

Why Improve Your Keyboarding Skills?

■ To key faster and more accurately every time you use the computer for the rest of your life.

■ To increase your enjoyment while using the computer.

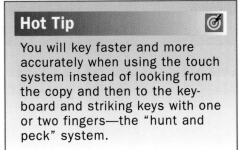

Hot Tip

You will key faster and more accurately when using the touch system instead of looking from the copy and then to the keyboard and striking keys with one or two fingers—the "hunt and peck" system.

Getting Ready to Build Skills

Get ready by:

1. a. Clearing your desk of everything except your book and a pencil or pen.

   b. Positioning your keyboard and book so that you are comfortable and able to move your hands and fingers freely.

   c. Keeping your feet flat on the floor, sitting with your back erect.

2. Taking a two-minute timed writing, page 14, now according to your teacher's directions.

3. Calculating your Words A Minute (WAM) and Errors A Minute (EAM) using the instructions on the timed writing progress chart, page 15. This will be your base score to compare to future timed writings.

4. On the Base Score line (page 15), recording the Date, WAM, and EAM.

5. Repeating the timed writing as many times as you can.

6. Recording each attempt on the Introduction line of the chart.

Skill Builder 1

Your Goal – Use the touch system to key j u y h n m spacebar.

What To Do

1. Place your fingers on the home row as shown in Figure E-1.

FIGURE E-1
Place your fingers on the home row

2. Look at Figure E-2. Notice how later (in step 3) you will strike the letters j u y h n m in a counterclockwise (↺) direction. You will strike the spacebar with your right thumb.

FIGURE E-2
Strike all of these keys with your right index finger—the home finger j

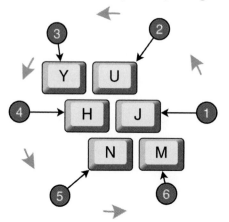

3. Look at your keyboard. Softly say the letters as you strike each key three times (3X), counterclockwise from 1 to 6 with a blank space in between. After striking each letter in the circle, strike j, called the home key, 3X as shown. Don't worry about errors. Start keying:

   jjj uuu jjj yyy jjj hhh jjj nnn jjj mmm

   jjj uuu jjj yyy jjj hhh jjj nnn jjj mmm jjj

4. Repeat the same drill as many times as it takes to reach your comfort level.

   jjj uuu jjj yyy jjj hhh jjj nnn jjj mmm

   jjj uuu jjj yyy jjj hhh jjj nnn jjj mmm jjj

5. Close your eyes and visualize each key under each finger as you repeat the drill in step 4.

6. Look at the following two lines and key:

   jjj jjj jjj juj juj juj jyj jyj jyj jhj jhj jhj jnj jnj jnj jmj jmj jmj

   jjj jjj jjj juj juj juj jyj jyj jyj jhj jhj jhj jnj jnj jnj jmj jmj jmj

7. Repeat step 4, this time concentrating on a rhythmic, bouncy stroking of the keys.

8. Close your eyes and visualize the keys under your fingers as you key the drill in step 4 from memory.

9. Look at the following two lines and key these groups of letters:

   j ju juj j jy jyj j jh jhj j jn jnj j jm jmj j ju juj j jy jyj j jh jhj j jn jnj j jm jmj

   jjj ju jhj jn jm ju jm jh jnj jm ju jmj jy ju jh j u ju juj jy jh jnj ju jm jmj jy

10. You may want to repeat Skill Builder 1, striving to improve keying letters that are most difficult for you.

Skill Builder 2

Your Goal - Use the touch system to key f r t g b v .

What To Do

1. Place your fingers on the home row as you did in Skill Builder 1, Figure E-1.

2. Look at Figure E-3. Notice how (later in step 3) you will strike the letters f r t g b v in a clockwise (↻) direction. Strike the spacebar with your right thumb.

FIGURE E-3
Strike all of these keys with your left index finger—the home finger f

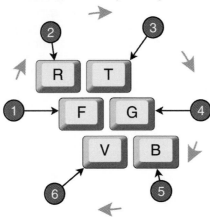

3. Look at your keyboard. Softly say the letters as you strike the keys 3X each, clockwise from 1 to 6, with a blank space in between. After striking each letter in the circle, strike the home key f 3X as shown. Don't worry about errors. Ignore them.

   fff rrr fff ttt fff ggg fff bbb fff vvv

   fff rrr fff ttt fff ggg fff bbb fff vvv fff

4. Repeat the same drill two more times using a quicker, sharper stroke.

   fff rrr fff ttt fff ggg fff bbb fff vvv

   fff rrr fff ttt fff ggg fff bbb fff vvv fff

5. Close your eyes and visualize each key under each finger as you repeat the drill in step 4.

6. Look at the following two lines and key these groups of letters:

   fff fff fff frf frf frf ftf ftf ftf fgf fgf fgf fbf fbf fbf fvf fvf fvf

   fff fff fff frf frf frf ftf ftf ftf fgf fgf fgf fbf fbf fbf fvf fvf fvf

7. Repeat step 6, this time concentrating on a rhythmic, "bouncy" stroking of the keys.

8. Close your eyes and visualize the keys under your fingers as you key the drill in step 4 from memory.

9. Look at the following two lines and key these groups of letters:

   fr frf ft ftf fg fgf fb fbf fv fvf

   ft fgf fv frf ft fbf fv frf ft fgf

10. You are about to key your first words. Look at the following lines and key these groups of letters:

    jjj juj jug jug jug rrr rur rug rug rug

    ttt tut tug tug tug rrr rur rub rub rub

    ggg gug gum gum gum mmm mum

    mug mug mug hhh huh hum hum hum

11. Complete the Keyboarding Technique Checklist, page 16.

Skill Builder 3

Your Goal – Use the touch system to key k i , d e c.

Keys k i ,

What To Do

> ### Teamwork
>
> ■ Ask your classmate to call out the letters in random order as you key them with your eyes closed. For example: k i , d e c. Do the same for your classmate.
> ■ Ask your classmate or your teacher to complete the Keyboarding Technique Checklist.

1. Place your fingers on the home row, as shown in Figure E-4.

FIGURE E-4
Striking keys k i , d e c

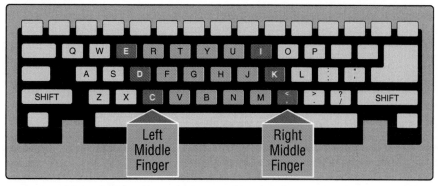

2. Look at your keyboard and locate these keys: k i ,

3. Look at your keyboard as much as you need to. Softly say the letters as you strike each key 3X as shown, with a space between each set of letters.

    kkk iii kkk ,,, kkk iii kkk ,,, kkk iii kkk ,,, kkk iii kkk ,,, kkk iii kkk ,,, kkk

4. Look at the line in step 3 and repeat the drill two more times using a quicker, sharper stroke.

5. Close your eyes and repeat the drill in step 3 as you visualize each key under each finger.

6. Repeat step 5, concentrating on a rhythmic, bouncy stroking of the keys.

Keys d e c

1. Place your fingers on the home row.

2. Look at your keyboard and locate these keys: d e c

3. Look at your keyboard. Softly say the letters as you strike each key 3X as shown, with a space between each set of letters.

    ddd eee ddd ccc ddd eee ddd ccc ddd eee ddd ccc ddd eee ddd ccc ddd

4. Look at the line in step 3 and repeat the drill two more times using a quicker, sharper stroke.

5. Close your eyes and repeat the drill in step 3 as you visualize each key under each finger.

6. Repeat step 5, concentrating on a rhythmic, bouncy stroking of the keys.

7. Look at the following lines and key these groups of letters and words:

    fff fuf fun fun fun ddd ded den den den

    ccc cuc cub cub cub vvv vev vet

    fff fuf fun fun fun ddd ded den den den

    ccc cuc cub cub cub vvv vev vet

8. Complete the Keyboarding Technique Checklist, page 16.

Skill Builder 4

Your Goal – Use the touch system to key l o . s w x and the left Shift key.

Keys l o .

What To Do

1. Place your fingers on the home row as shown in Figure E-5.

FIGURE E-5
Striking keys l o . s w x

2. Look at your keyboard and locate the following keys: l o . (period key)

3. Look at your keyboard. Softly say the letters as you strike each key 3X with a space between each set of letters.

    lll ooo lll ... lll ooo lll ... lll ooo lll ... lll ooo lll ... lll ooo lll ... lll ooo lll ... lll

4. Look at the line in step 3 and repeat the drill two more times using a quicker, sharper stroke.

5. Close your eyes and repeat the drill in step 3 as you visualize each key under each finger.

6. Repeat step 5, concentrating on a rhythmic, bouncy stroking of the keys.

Keys s w x

1. Place your fingers on the home row.

2. Look at your keyboard and locate the following keys: s w x

3. Look at your keyboard. Softly say the letters as you strike each key 3X with a space between each set of letters.

    sss www sss xxx sss www sss xxx sss www sss xxx sss www sss xxx sss

4. Look at the line in step 3 and repeat the same drill two more times using a quicker, sharper stroke.

5. Close your eyes and repeat the drill in step 3 as you visualize each key under each finger.

6. Repeat step 5, concentrating on a rhythmic, bouncy stroking of the keys.

Left Shift Key

1. Look at the following two lines and key the line, and then the sentence. Hold down the left Shift key with the little finger of your left hand to make capitals of letters struck by your right hand.

   jjj JJJ jjj JJJ yyy YYY yyy YYY nnn NNN nnn NNN mmm MMM

   Just look in the book. You can key well.

2. Complete the Keyboarding Technique Checklist, page 16.

Skill Builder 5

Your Goal - Use the touch system to key ; p / a q z and the right Shift key.

Keys ; p /

What To Do

1. Place your fingers on the home row as shown in Figure E-6.

FIGURE E-6
Striking keys ; p / a q z

2. Look at your keyboard and locate the following keys: ; p /

3. Look at your keyboard. Softly say the following letters as you strike each key 3X with a space in between:

   ;;; ppp ;;; /// ;;; ppp ;;; /// ;;; ppp ;;; ///

   ;;; ppp ;;; /// ;;; ppp ;;; /// ;;; ppp ;;; /// ;;;

4. Look at the lines in step 3 and repeat the drill two more times using a quicker, sharper stroke.

5. Close your eyes and repeat the drill in step 3 as you visualize each key under each finger.

6. Repeat step 5, concentrating on a rhythmic, bouncy stroking of the keys.

Keys a q z

1. Place your fingers on the home row.

2. Look at your keyboard and locate the following keys: a q z

3. Look at your keyboard. Softly say the following letters as you strike each key 3X with a space in between:

aaa qqq aaa zzz aaa qqq aaa zzz aaa qqq aaa zzz aaa qqq aaa zzz aaa

4. Look at the line in step 3 and repeat the same drill two more times using a quicker, sharper stroke.

5. Close your eyes and repeat the drill in step 3 as you visualize each key under each finger.

6. Repeat step 5, concentrating on a rhythmic, bouncy stroking of the keys.

Right Shift Key

1. Look at the following lines and key them. Hold down the right Shift key with the little finger of your right hand to make capitals of letters struck by your left hand.

   sss SSS rrr RRR

   Strike the key quickly. Relax when you key.

2. Complete the Keyboarding Technique Checklist, page 16.

Skill Builder 6

Your Goal - Use the touch system to key all letters of the alphabet.

What To Do

1. Close your eyes. Do not look at the keyboard and key all letters of the alphabet as shown:

   aaa bbb ccc ddd eee fff ggg hhh iii jjj

   kkk lll mmm nnn ooo ppp qqq rrr sss

   ttt uuu vvv www xxx yyy zzz

 Hot Tip

You will probably have to key slowly. Strive for accuracy, not speed.

2. Repeat step 1, striking keys with a rhythmic, bouncy touch.

3. Repeat step 1, but faster than you did for step 2.

4. Key the following:

   aa bb cc dd ee ff gg hh ii jj kk ll mm nn oo pp qq rr ss tt uu vv ww xx yy zz

   a b c d e f g h i j k l m n o p q r s t u v w x y z

5. Keep your eyes on the following copy. Do not look at the keyboard and key all letters of the alphabet three times each backwards:

   zzz yyy xxx www vvv uuu ttt sss rrr

   qqq ppp ooo nnn mmm lll kkk jjj iii

   hhh ggg fff eee ddd ccc bbb aaa

6. Repeat step 5, but faster than the last time.

7. Key each letter of the alphabet once backwards:

   z y x w v u t s r q p o n m l k j i h g f e d c b a

8. Think about the letters that took you the most amount of time to locate. Go back to the Skill Builder for those letters, and repeat those drills until you are confident about their locations. For example, if you have difficulty with the c key, practice Skill Builder 3 again.

Timed Writing

Prepare to take the timed writing, page 14, according to your teacher's directions.

1. Get ready by:

   a. Clearing your desk of everything except your book and a pencil or pen.

   b. Positioning your keyboard and book so that you are comfortable and able to move your hands and fingers freely.

   c. Keeping your feet flat on the floor, sitting with your back erect.

2. Take a two-minute timed writing, page 14, now according to your teacher's directions.

3. Calculate your Words A Minute (WAM) and Errors A Minute (EAM) scores using the instructions on the timed writing progress chart, page 15.

4. Record the date, WAM, and EAM on the Skill Builder 6 line.

5. Repeat the timed writing as many times as you can and record each attempt.

Skill Builder 7

Your Goal – Improve your keying techniques—which is the secret for improving your speed and accuracy.

What To Do

1. Rate yourself for each item on the Keyboarding Technique Checklist, page 16.

2. Do not time yourself as you concentrate on a single technique you marked with a "0." Key only the first paragraph of the timed writing.

   Teamwork

   You may want to ask a classmate or your teacher to record your scores.

3. Repeat step 2 as many times as possible for each of the items marked with an "0" that need improvement.

4. Take a two-minute timed writing. Record your WAM and EAM on the timed writing progress chart as 1st Attempt on the Skill Builder 7 line. Compare this score with your base score.

5. Look only at the book and using your best techniques, key the following technique sentence for one minute:

.   2   .   4   .   6   .   8   .   10   .   2   .   14   .   16

Now is the time for all loyal men and women to come to the aid of their country.

6. Record your WAM and EAM on the 7 Technique Sentence line.

7. Repeat steps 5 and 6 as many times as you can and record your scores.

Skill Builder 8

Your Goal – Increase your words a minute.

What To Do

1. Take a two-minute timed writing.

2. Record your WAM and EAM scores as the 1st Attempt on page 16.

3. Key only the first paragraph only one time as fast as you can. Ignore errors.

4. Key only the first and second paragraphs only one time as fast as you can. Ignore errors.

5. Take a two-minute timed writing again. Ignore errors.

6. Record only your WAM score as the 2nd Attempt on page 15. Compare only this WAM with your 1st Attempt WAM and your base score WAM.

> **Hot Tip**
>
> You can now key letters in the speed line very well and with confidence. Practicing all of the other letters of the alphabet will further increase your skill and confidence in keyboarding.

Get Your Best WAM

1. To get your best WAM on easy text for 15 seconds, key the following speed line as fast as you can, as many times as you can. Ignore errors.

.   2   .   4   .   6   .   8   .   10

Now is the time, now is the time, now is the time,

2. Multiply the number of words keyed by four to get your WAM (15 seconds × 4 = 1 minute). For example, if you keyed 12 words for 15 seconds, 12 × 4 = 48 WAM.

3. Record only your WAM in the 8 Speed Line box.

4. Repeat steps 1-3 as many times as you can to get your very best WAM. Ignore errors.

5. Record only your WAM for each attempt.

Skill Builder 9

Your Goal – Decrease errors a minute.

What To Do

1. Take a two-minute timed writing.

2. Record your WAM and EAM as the 1st Attempt on page 15.

3. Key only the first paragraph only one time at a controlled rate of speed so you reduce errors. Ignore speed.

> **Hot Tip**
>
> How much you improve depends upon how much you want to improve.

4. Key only the first and second paragraphs only one time at a controlled rate of speed so you reduce errors. Ignore speed.

5. Take a two-minute timed writing again. Ignore speed.

6. Record only your EAM score as the 2nd Attempt on page 15. Compare only the EAM with your 1st Attempt EAM and your base score EAM.

Get Your Best EAM

1. To get your best EAM, key the following accuracy sentence (same as the technique sentence) for one minute. Ignore speed.

   Now is the time for all loyal men and women to come to the aid of their country.

2. Record only your EAM score on the Accuracy Sentence 9 line.

3. Repeat step 1 as many times as you can to get your best EAM. Ignore speed.

4. Record only your EAM score for each attempt.

Skill Builder 10

Your Goal – Use the touch system and your best techniques to key faster and more accurately than you have ever keyed before.

What To Do

1. Take a one-minute timed writing.

2. Record your WAM and EAM as the 1st Attempt on the Skill Builder 10 line.

3. Repeat the timed writing for two minutes as many times as necessary to get your best ever WAM with no more than one EAM. Record your scores as 2nd, 3rd, and 4th Attempts.

> **Hot Tip**
>
> You may want to get advice regarding which techniques you need to improve from a classmate or your teacher.

Assessing Your Improvement

1. Circle your best timed writing for Skill Builders 6-10 on the timed writing progress chart.

2. Record your best score and your base score. Compare the two scores. Did you improve?

	WAM	EAM
Best Score	___	___
Base Score	___	___

3. Use the Keyboarding Technique Checklist on page 16 to identify techniques you still need to improve. You may want to practice these techniques now to increase your WAM or decrease your EAM.

Timed Writing

Every five strokes in a timed writing is a word, including punctuation marks and spaces. Use the scale above each line to tell you how many words you keyed.

```
        .      2    .      4    .      6    .
If you learn how to key well now, it
   8    .     10    .     12    .     14    .     16
is a skill that will help you for the rest
     .     18    .     20    .     22    .     24    .
of your life.  How you sit will help you key
  26    .     28    .     30    .     32    .     34    .
with more speed and less errors.  Sit with your
  36    .     38    .     40    .     42    .     44
feet flat on the floor and your back erect.
     .     46    .     48    .     50    .     52
To key fast by touch, try to keep your
     .     54    .     56    .     58    .     60
eyes on the copy and not on your hands or
     .     62    .     64    .     66    .     68    .     70
the screen.  Curve your fingers and make sharp,
     .     72    .
quick strokes.
     74    .     76    .     78    .     80    .
Work for speed first. If you make more
     82    .     84    .     86    .     88    .     90
than two errors a minute, you are keying too
     92    .     94    .     96    .     98    .    100
fast. Slow down to get fewer errors. If you
     .    102    .    104    .    106    .    108
get fewer than two errors a minute, go for
     .    110
speed.
```

Timed Writing Progress Chart

Last Name: _____   *First Name:* _____

Instructions

Calculate your scores as shown in the following sample and footnotes (a) and (b). Repeat timed writings as many times as you can and record your scores for each attempt.

Base Score: Date ____   WAM ____   EAM ____   Time ____

Skill Builder	Date	1st Attempt (a) WAM	1st Attempt (b) EAM	2nd Attempt WAM	2nd Attempt EAM	3rd Attempt WAM	3rd Attempt EAM	4th Attempt WAM	4th Attempt EAM
Sample	9/2	22	3.5	23	2.0	25	1.0	29	2.0
Introduction									
6									
7									
8					-----				
9				-----					
10									
7 Technique Sentence									
8 Speed Line			-----		-----		-----		-----
9 Accuracy Sentence		-----		-----		-----		-----	

(a) Divide words keyed (44) by 2 (minutes) to get WAM (22)

(b) Divide errors (7) by 2 (minutes) to get EAM (3.5)

Keyboarding Technique Checklist

Last Name: _____   *First Name:* _____

Instructions

1. Write the Skill Builder number, the date, and the initials of the evaluator in the proper spaces.

2. Place a check mark (✓) after a technique that is performed satisfactorily. Place a large zero (0) after a technique that needs improvement.

Technique	Sample										
Skill Builder Number:	Sample										
Date:	9/1										
Evaluator:	SL										
Attitude											
1. Enthusiastic about learning	✓										
2. Optimistic about improving	✓										
3. Alert but relaxed	✓										
4. Sticks to the task; not distracted	✓										
Getting Ready	✓										
1. Desk uncluttered											
2. Properly positions keyboard and book	✓										
3. Feet flat on the floor	✓										
4. Body erect, but relaxed	0										
Keyboarding											
1. Curves fingers	0										
2. Keeps eyes on the book	✓										
3. Taps the keys lightly; does not "pound" them	0										
4. Makes quick, "bouncy," strokes	0										
5. Smooth rhythm	0										
6. Minimum pauses between strokes	✓										

GLOSSARY

A

Absolute cell reference Worksheet cell reference that does not adjust to the new cell location when copied or moved.

Active cell Highlighted worksheet cell ready for data entry.

Active sheet Worksheet that appears on the screen.

Argument In Excel, value, cell reference, range, or text that acts as an operand in a function formula.

Arranging Lets you view more than one workbook on the screen at the same time.

Ascending order Ordered from the beginning of the alphabet, the lowest number, or the earliest date.

Ascending sort Sort that arranges records from A to Z or smallest to largest.

Auditing To check the results of information to be certain that it is correct.

AutoFilter Displays a subset of the data in a worksheet that meet certain criteria.

AutoFilter arrows Appear at the lower right corner of the worksheet's column headings. By clicking the arrow, a drop down list will appear that allows you to display a specific row, the top ten items in the column, a customized search, or restore all the data in the worksheet.

AutoFormat Collection of font, patterns, and alignments that can be applied to a range of data.

Axis Line that identifies the values in a chart; most charts have a horizontal (or X axis) and a vertical (or Y axis).

C

Case sensitive Indicates that upper and lowercase letters are different. If a password contains capital letters, you will need to enter the password using the same capital letters.

Cell Intersection of a row and column in a worksheet or table.

Cell reference Identifies a worksheet cell by the column letter and row number (for example, A1, B2, C4).

Channels Means of customizing the information delivered from the Internet to your computer.

Chart A graphical representation of data.

Chart sheet Area separate from the Excel worksheet in which a chart is created and stored; the chart sheet is identified by a tab near the bottom of the screen.

Chart Wizard Four-step, on-screen guide that aids in preparing a chart from an Excel worksheet.

Clipboard A temporary storage place in the computer's memory.

Close Removing a document or window from the screen.

Close button "X" on the right side of the title bar that you click to close a window.

Column chart Chart that uses rectangles of varying heights to illustrate values in a worksheet.

Columns Appear vertically in a worksheet and are identified by letters at the top of the worksheet window.

Command   Performs an action.

Comment   Message that provides information concerning data in a cell.

Conditional Formatting   Applies a font, border, or pattern to a worksheet cell when certain conditions exist in that cell.

Consolidating data   A method for bringing data from several worksheets into one worksheet. The consolidated data may be summed, averaged, counted, and so on.

Copy   A copy of the selected text is placed on the clipboard while the original text remains in the document.

Copy to range   Area you create in a worksheet where Excel will copy the records meeting the criteria specified in the Criteria Range.

Correlation   An Excel function that allows you to determine if certain variables have a strong relationship with one another.

Count   A function which counts the number of items. You may then add the Count function to any column in a list.

Criteria   In Excel, information for which you are searching in a list.

Criteria range   Area you create in a worksheet where you indicate what information Excel is to locate for you within the list.

Custom filter   In Excel, a filter in which you indicate specific criteria for which you want to search.

Cut   Removes selected text from the document and places it on the Clipboard.

D

Data labels   Values depicted by the chart objects (such as columns or data points) that are printed directly on the chart.

Data series   Group of related information in a column or row of a worksheet that is plotted on a worksheet chart.

Data Table   Contains the worksheet data displayed in a table. The data table appears with the chart itself.

Data Validation   To indicate that something is acceptable or approved after having checked it first.

DAVERAGE   In Excel, a function that averages the numbers in a column located in a list or database that match the conditions you specify. Average refers to taking the sum of a range of numbers and then dividing this total by the number of items in the range.

Default   Setting used unless another option is chosen.

Dependent   In auditing, a cell containing data on which formulas within the worksheet depend for the calculation of the formula.

Descending order   Ordered from the end of the alphabet, the highest number, or the latest date.

Descending sort   Sort that arranges records from Z to A or largest to smallest.

Desktop   Space where you access and work with programs and files.

Dialog box   A message box that "asks" for further instructions before a command can be performed.

Discussion server   A Web server that accommodates discussion of an Office file on the Internet.

Drag and Drop   A quick method for copying and moving text a short distance.

Drawing tools   Tools to use to insert lines and objects that help make a document or worksheet more informative.

Drop-down menu   A list of commands that appears below each menu name on the menu bar.

DSUM   In Excel, a function that adds the numbers in a column located in a list or database that matches the conditions you specify.

E

Embed   Information becomes part of the current file, but is a separate object that can be edited using the application that created it.

Embedded chart   Chart created within a worksheet; an embedded chart may be viewed on the same screen as the data from which it is created.

Export Refers to taking information from Excel and using it in another program.

Extensible Markup Language See *XML*.

F

Field Category of information (displayed in a column), such as a person's name.

Filling Copies data into the cell(s) adjacent to the original.

Filter A method of screening out all database records except those that match your selection criteria. In Excel, you can filter a list so that only the rows that meet specific criteria will be displayed. Rows of data that do not meet the criteria will not be displayed.

Financial functions Functions such as future value, present value, and payment which are used in worksheets to analyze loans and investments.

Folder A place where files and other folders are stored on a disk.

Font size Determined by measuring the height of characters in units called points.

Font style Formatting feature that changes the appearance of text such as bold, italic, and underline.

Fonts Designs of type.

Formula Equation that calculates a new value from values currently on a worksheet.

Formula bar Appears directly below the toolbar in the worksheet; displays a formula when the cell of a worksheet contains a calculated value.

Freezing Keeps row or column titles on the screen no matter where you scroll in the worksheet.

Function formula Special formulas that do not use operators to calculate a result.

G

Graphics Pictures that help illustrate the meaning of the text or that make the page more attractive.

Graphs See **Charts**.

Grid settings Sets the spacing between the intersections of the gridlines.

Gridlines Lines displayed through a worksheet chart that relate the objects (such as columns or data points) in a chart to the axes.

Group An Excel feature that lets you select items, such as rows or columns, and then group the data together for easier viewing.

H

Handles Small boxes that appear around an object when it is selected. You can drag the handles to resize the object.

Hiding Temporarily removes a worksheet row or column from the screen.

Highlight Entry point of a worksheet; a highlighted cell is indicated by a dark border; to shade text with color to emphasize important text or graphics.

Home page First page that appears when you start your Web browser.

HTML (HyperText Markup Language) File format used to create a Web page.

Hyperlink Allows you to jump to another location.

I

Icon Small pictures that represent an item or object.

Image handles See **Handles**.

Import To bring data/information from another compatible program into Excel.

Indent The space placed between text and a document's margins.

Integrated software package Computer program that combines common tools into one package.

Interactive Relates to two-way computer communication that involves a user's responses or orders.

Internet Vast network of computers linked to one another.

Internet Explorer Office XP's browser for navigating the Web.

Intranet A company's private network.

L

Line chart   Chart that is similar to a column chart except columns are replaced by points connected by a line.

Link   See **Hyperlink**.

List   You can think of a list as a database table. Lists are used to organize, manage, and retrieve information.

Logical function   Function used to display text or values if certain conditions exist.

M

Macro   Sequence of frequently performed tasks that you record. Excel plays the macro back and performs the action.

Margins   Blank spaces around the top, bottom, and sides of a page.

Mathematical function   Function that manipulates quantitative data in the worksheet using operators such as logarithms, factorials, and absolute values.

Maximize button   Button at the right side of the title bar that you click to enlarge a window to fill the screen.

Menu   List of options from which to choose.

Menu bar   A bar normally at the top of the screen that lists the names of menus, each of which contains a set of commands.

Merge   The merging process combines changes from the copied files into a main workbook. To merge workbooks, simply select Compare and Merge Workbooks from the Tools menu.

Minimize button   Button at the right side of the title bar that you click to reduce a window to a button on the taskbar.

Mixed cell reference   Cell reference containing both relative and absolute references.

Mnemonic   An underlined letter that is pressed in combination with the Alt key to access items on the menu bar, pull-down menus, and dialog boxes.

Mouse   A device that rolls on a flat surface and has one or more buttons on it. It allows you to communicate with the computer by pointing to and manipulating graphics and text on the screen.

My Computer   Program to help you organize and manage your files.

N

Name box   Area on the left side of the worksheet formula bar that identifies the cell reference of the active cell.

Named range   Assigning names to specified ranges. This is another method for identifying and organizing data. Range names are especially useful in formulas and when consolidating data.

O

Open   Process of loading a file from a disk onto the screen.

Operand   Numbers or cell references used in calculations in the formulas of worksheets.

Operator   Tells Excel what to do with operands in a formula.

Order of evaluation   The sequence used to calculate the value of a formula.

Outline   A feature which lets you temporarily remove detailed data from display. You can then focus on the totals.

P

Paste   Text is copied from the Clipboard to the location of the insertion point in the document.

Paste Special   Command that allows you to link data among files created in different Office programs.

Password   Refers to a sequence of characters, known only by you, that is required for access to the file. Passwords are case sensitive.

Pie chart   Chart that shows the relationship of a part to a whole.

PivotChart   Refers to a visual representation of table or query data. A PivotChart allows you to interactively rearrange the fields in a chart.

PivotTable   An interactive table that lets you view and calculate data from a table or query. It's called a PivotTable because you can rotate the column, row, and page headings.

Point-and-click method Constructs a cell formula in Excel by clicking on the cell you want to reference rather than keying the reference.

Pointer An arrow on the screen which indicates the position of the mouse.

Precedent In auditing, a cell containing the formula that uses the data (dependents) from other areas in the worksheet.

Protection A feature that enables you to protect a single cell of data from being changed or deleted. You can protect all the data on a worksheet, or you can protect the entire workbook

R

Range Selected group of cells on a worksheet identified by the cell in the upper left corner and the cell in the lower right corner, separated by a colon (for example, A3:C5).

Record A group of related fields in a data source; complete set of database fields.

Recycle Bin Place to get rid of files or folders that are no longer needed.

Regression Typically a function that can be used with two or more correlated variables. An Excel function that produces an equation $Y = mX + b$ from which predictions can be made.

Relative cell reference Worksheet cell reference that adjusts to a new location when copied or moved.

Research tool An Office feature that allows access to information typically found in a dictionary, thesaurus, or encyclopedia. In an Excel, the Research tool can provide numerical data typically used in a worksheet such as statistics or corporate financial data.

Restore Down button Button at the right side of the title bar that you click to resize a maximized window to its previous size.

Rotated text Displays text at an angle within a cell of a worksheet.

Rows Appear horizontally in a worksheet and are identified by numbers on the left side of the worksheet window.

S

Save Process of storing a file on disk.

Scatter chart Chart that shows the relationship of two categories of data.

Scenario Refers to various possible outcomes.

Scroll arrows Drag to move the window in the corresponding direction one line at a time.

Scroll bar Appears at the bottom and/or right side of a window to allow user to view another part of the window's contents.

Scroll box Box in the scroll bar that indicates your position within the contents of the window.

Sheet tabs Label that identifies a worksheet in a workbook.

Sizing handles See **Handles**.

Sorting Arranges a list of words or numbers in ascending order (A to Z; smallest to largest) or in descending order (Z to A; largest to smallest).

Splitting Divides an Excel screen into two or four parts. Splitting is particularly useful when you want to copy data from one area to another in a large worksheet.

Spreadsheet Grid of rows and columns containing numbers, text, and formulas; the purpose of a spreadsheet is to solve problems that involve numbers.

Standard toolbar Toolbar that is normally near the top of the screen and which contains buttons used to perform common tasks.

Start Button on the taskbar that you click to display menus with a variety of options.

Statistical function Function used to describe large quantities of data such as the average, standard deviation, or variance of a range of data.

Status bar Bar normally at the bottom of a screen that contains information summarizing the actions of the commands that you choose.

Structured data   Typically indicates information that's entered into an Excel worksheet in a data list format. This can be copied, for example, into Word as a table.

Style   A predefined set of formatting options that have been named and saved.

T

Task pane   Separate window on the right hand side of the opening screen that contains commonly used commands.

Taskbar   Bar normally at the bottom of a screen that displays the Start button and the names of all open programs.

Template   A file that contains page and paragraph formatting and text that you can customize to create a new document similar to but slightly different from the original. A template normally contains titles, subtitles, formats, and formulas but no specific data values.

Three dimensional cell reference   Formula references that incorporate data from worksheets in an active worksheet.

Toggling   Clicking a toolbar button to turn a feature on or off.

Toolbar   Bar at the top or bottom of the screen that displays buttons you can click to quickly choose a command.

Track Changes   Keeps a record of changes made in a document by one or more reviewers. The Track changes option maintains a history of changes made to the shared file based on the number of days selected. This option needs to be selected in order to merge changes from multiple copies of the same workbook.

Transpose   To switch the order of something. For example, switching the order of data that appears in columns into the same data appearing in rows.

Trendlines   Let you graphically display tendencies in data and therefore to predict future values. A trendline can display a trend in data with such functions as FORECAST and GROWTH.

Trigonometric function   Function that manipulates quantitative data in the worksheet using operators such as sines, cosines, and tangents.

U

Uniform Resource Locators (URLs)   Internet addresses that identify hypertext documents.

V

Validation   Ensures that data is entered as accurately as possible by checking the data against preset criteria.

Value   Refers to a number or data.

Visual Basic   Programming language of macros and functions. You can add a new function to Excel by using this programming language.

W

Web browser   Software used to display Web pages on your computer monitor.

Web discussion   A forum that permits several worksheet users to view and comment on an Excel worksheet that has been posted on the Internet.

Web site   A collection of related Web pages connected with hyperlinks.

Workbook   Collection of related worksheets in Excel.

Worksheet   Computerized spreadsheet in Excel; a grid of rows and columns containing numbers, text, and formulas.

World Wide Web   System of computers that share information by means of hypertext links.

Wrapped text   Begins a new line within the cell of a worksheet when the data exceeds the width of a column.

X

XML (Extensible Markup Language)   Places structured data (such as data lists) in a format that can be read in a variety of applications. It is considered a universal format for data on the Web.

INDEX